Presented to Purchase College
by
Gary Waller, PhD Cambridge

State University of New York
Distinguished Professor

Professor
of Literature & Cultural
Studies, and Theatre &
Performance, 1995-2019
Provost 1995-2004

THE ELIZABETHAN RENAISSANCE

The Life of the Society

Books by A. L. Rowse

THE ELIZABETHAN AGE

The England of Elizabeth
The Expansion of Elizabethan England
The Elizabethan Renaissance: The Life of the Society
The Elizabethan Renaissance:
The Cultural Achievement (*in preparation*)

William Shakespeare: A Biography
Shakespeare's Sonnets
(*A modern text, and prose versions, introduction and notes*)
Christopher Marlowe: A Biography
Shakespeare's Southampton: Patron of Virginia

The Elizabethans and America
Ralegh and the Throckmortons
Sir Richard Grenville of the *Revenge*
Tudor Cornwall
The Cornish in America

A Cornish Anthology
Cornish Stories
A Cornish Childhood
A Cornishman at Oxford

The Early Churchills
The Later Churchills
The Churchills
The English Spirit (*revised edition*)
Times, Persons, Places (The English Past)

THE ELIZABETHAN RENAISSANCE

THE LIFE OF THE SOCIETY

A. L. ROWSE

*

'*To Generalize is to be an Idiot. To Particularize is the Alone Distinction of Merit*' —WILLIAM BLAKE

MACMILLAN

First published *1971* by
MACMILLAN LONDON LTD
London and Basingstoke
Associated companies in New York Toronto
Dublin Melbourne Johannesburg and Madras

SBN 333 12534 7

Printed in Great Britain by
R. & R. CLARK LTD
Edinburgh

I wish to inscribe upon these pages the names of
JAKOB BURCKHARDT
J. H. HUIZINGA

CONTENTS

List of Illustrations   viii

Preface   ix

   I Renaissance Impulse   3

  II The Court   30

 III The Rhythm of Town and Country: The Rôle
     of the Gentry   61

 IV Class and Social Life   90

  V Food and Sanitation   124

 VI Sex   142

VII Parish and Sport   166

VIII Custom   200

 IX Mentality and Belief: Witchcraft and Astrology   227

    Notes   273

    Index   286

LIST OF ILLUSTRATIONS

between pages 150 and 151

1   Sir John Harington

2   Mary Fitton   *photo Royal Academy of Arts*

3   Bess of Hardwick   *photo Courtauld Institute*

4   Sir Henry Lee, by Antony Mor

5   Dr. Dee's letter to Queen Elizabeth on the Defeat of the Spanish Armada   *Harleian MS.* 6986, *f.* 45

6   Merchants' Houses, Exeter

7   The Marriage Fête at Horsleydown, by Hoefnagel
photo Courtauld Institute

8   A Game of Primero   *photo Manchester City Art Gallery*

9   Queen Elizabeth at a Picnic. An engraving from Turberville's *The Noble Art of Venery*

10   The Honours of the Chase. From *The Noble Art of Venery*

11   The Great Staircase at Hardwick Hall

12   The Grammar School at Stratford-upon-Avon

13   The Cross Keys Inn, Oxford. By Buckler

14   The Swan, Minster Lovell   *photo C. Stringer*

15   Witches hanged at Chelmsford, 1589

16   A Fortune-Teller

ACKNOWLEDGEMENTS

The illustrations are reproduced by courtesy of the following: Bodleian Library, 14; Trustees of the British Museum, 5; Earl of Derby, 8; Mary Evans Picture Library, 16; Exeter City Library, 6; A. F. Kersting, 12; Lambeth Palace Library, 15; National Monuments Record, 11, 13; National Portrait Gallery, 1, 4; National Trust, 3; Mr. Fitzroy Newdegate, 2; Radio Times Hulton Picture Library, 9, 10; Marquess of Salisbury, K.G., 7.

PREFACE

IT is now over twenty years since I published the first volume of what was conceived as a portrait of the Elizabethan Age. Perhaps I may, at the end of this long endeavour, explain the scheme of the work. The first volume, *The England of Elizabeth* (1950), described the structure of the society, its government and institutions, the integuments holding it together. The second, *The Expansion of Elizabethan England* (1955), was devoted to its extension, the outward thrust of its energies, both within the British Isles—into the backward areas of the North and among the Celtic peoples of Wales, Cornwall, Ireland—and across the oceans, the voyages of discovery and trade, the first English settlements in America, from which so much was to flow, decisive in history: the British Commonwealth and Empire, the United States of America, greatest of modern nations. It all had its beginnings with our forebears, a backward, but vigorous, people of only some five millions.

The third volume is intended to display the life of the society, as it flowered from its structure and governance, and the expansion in the realm of the mind—its artistic and intellectual achievements, no less remarkable than those in the material sphere. Again, we must never forget, they are those of a small people on the periphery of Europe, engaged in catching up hand over fist, with the wind of Renaissance and Reform filling their sails. Thus this book is a venture into cultural history—what interests me most in the human story, the life of the mind, the values and creative achievements that redeem the record. In my work my aim is above all to recover and re-create the life of the past, from all its evidences. There is no point in writing a dead book—so many are.

Thus this third section of what I conceived as a trilogy has bifurcated into two volumes. The present depicts the social life. The sequel, *The Cultural Achievement*, will deal with its expression in the arts, in drama, literature, music, architecture, painting, in medicine, science and thought—not, I hope, disparately, but exfoliating as diverse though related expressions of the society, with their cross-rhythms and interconnections. Naturally such a picture can never be complete, but my hope is that it is representative and convincing, true to its spirit—with which I find myself in more sympathy than that of today. Today we are at the end of so much of which we see the inspiring beginnings in that heroic age—in the life of the mind as much as in action.

In the course of years I have accumulated many particular obligations, which are acknowledged in the footnotes. But, in general, I am grateful above all to All Souls College, without whose support this book could hardly have been written, and to the Huntington Library in California where much of the special reading for the sequel was done, in most agreeable conditions. I owe debts of gratitude to Professor Jack Simmons, who has helped me at many turns, and directed my attention to material; and to Mr. John Buxton, who has always been ready to discuss questions of Elizabethan literature with me and to share generously his knowledge of the age. I take the opportunity to express my admiration for the imaginative perception of the work of Professor W. G. Hoskins, both concrete and visual—the true nature of history—as against dubious theories and theses. In this volume I have made considerable, but by no means exhaustive, use of the Hardwick papers, which the late Evelyn, Duchess of Devonshire, had brought over from Chatsworth for me to work at, during several summers at Hardwick where she most kindly entertained me. I am also grateful to Miss N. McN. O'Farrell, who has helped me with material from the Public Record Office, the British Museum, and Somerset House; and to Mr. G. A. Webb, assistant librarian at All Souls, who has been constantly helpful over many years in the Codrington Library.

A. L. ROWSE

BOOK I

THE LIFE OF THE SOCIETY

CHAPTER I

RENAISSANCE IMPULSE

'To the discovery of the outward world the Renaissance added a still greater achievement, by first discovering and bringing to light the full, whole nature of man.[1]' Thus Burckhardt, the philosophic historian inspired by art who has best delineated the experience that lies at the threshold of modern history, formative of modern man. In the first volume of this trilogy I treated the structure of Elizabethan society, of England in the age of the Renaissance; in the second, its 'discovery of the outward world', its expansion within the islands and across seas and oceans. With this volume, I come to its expansion in the realm of culture and the spirit – a more difficult matter for it deals at once with the outer and inner world, things visible and invisible. One can only explore and illustrate, for in the nature of things a book cannot contain man's spirit, can only catch glimpses of it on the wing.

Too much has been written about the Renaissance – latterly, to considerable confusion of counsel. Burckhardt is best. There has been a tendency to elide the differences that marked it off from the medieval world, to an absurd degree with such an historian as Lynn Thorndike, antiquarian of medieval science, with whom it was always 'the so-called Renaissance'. Actually Renaissance people undergoing the experience – such representative figures as Alberti, Aldus, Valla, Politian, Leonardo da Vinci, Castiglione, Erasmus – had no doubt that they were engaged in something new, a rebirth of culture: they looked with some contempt on what had gone before, the 'barbarous' period out of which they had emerged, and regarded themselves as indubitably improving upon it.

In what did the change consist? What were the improvements they at least regarded themselves as making? It is time for us to define.

A contemporary guide tells us that 'the Italian humanists were undoubtedly conscious of living in the midst of a great cultural revival, but their awareness of what was new in their age was

3

limited to classical literature and learning and the fine arts.'[2] This directs us to the first essential aspect of the experience; but the second was the inspiration that the rediscovery of the ancient world gave to their own work. We may well consider, from the point of view of aesthetic values, the second to be more important. The point can be brought home visually: however, much we appreciate the architecture of ancient Rome – and the treatise of Vitruvius was accorded reverential authority during the Renaissance – yet the works of Brunelleschi, Bramante, Michelangelo, Sansovino, Palladio – are more inspired: the wind of the spirit blows through them.

Apart from the exciting rediscovery of classical learning and scholarship – relics and evidences of a more sophisticated culture – we must appreciate even more the ends which this served, a new flowering. Erasmus summed it up: *renascuntur bonae literae*. Take for a single example of the difference it made, where it made so many – the new historiography. The Italian humanists nearly all wrote works with a new conception of history, superior in organisation and style, in accuracy and critical acumen, to medieval chronicle. The Italian, Polydore Vergil of Urbino, who spent half a century in England, provided an important example of the new historiography applied to English history, the *Historia Anglica*. (It was not much appreciated by the backward, medievally minded, nationalistic English). But, further than this, the Italian humanists abandoned 'the medieval habit of seeking supernatural causes for historical events'.[3] It was not until the reaction of the Reformation that all that came surging back again.

However, things could never be the same: the cocoon of medieval faith had been breached, the chrysalis liberated. Henceforth man was face to face with his own nature, to explore it, inspired or dismayed by what he found. This is what Burckhardt means when he says, 'the human spirit had taken a mighty step towards the consciousness of its own secret life.'[4] We can *see* the difference in the sculpture of Michelangelo or the tragedies of Shakespeare: they are explorations of the human spirit, man exploring himself. It has been well said of Michelangelo that 'by changing and twisting the forms of antique sculpture, he created an instrument through which the spiritual turmoil of the sixteenth century could be made visible.'[5] So with the tragedies of Shakespeare. Both are filled with the spirit of the Renaissance.

In the Middle Ages France enjoyed an immense cultural ascendancy – the French cathedrals, among the grandest of the

works of man, still stand up to attest it. The Renaissance was
Italian in origin, essence and largely in its effusion over the rest of
Europe. Italians were everywhere in the sixteenth century, germ-
carriers of the new ideas, new modes and manners, the new
inspiration. Naturally enough it was an Italian, Vasari, who
created the conception of Renaissance art itself, at the time, 'as an
organic whole, developing by clearly marked stages.'[6] The
rediscovery of classical, especially Latin, civilisation was much
nearer and more natural to Italians; they had always been
conscious of their Roman past, one had only to reach out a hand to
bring up relics of it.[7] The Apollo Belvedere and the Laocoon were
brought up from the ground at the moment when lost classical
texts were being brought to light in remote or forgotten monastic
libraries. One is reminded of Poussin in the next century putting
out a hand and picking up a handful of marble and mosaic
fragments: 'C'est la poussière de Rome.'

There was a patriotic element in the new writing of history,
radically different from the universalism of the Middle Ages, its
scope moreover emphasising national and secular interests. The
intense self-awareness that is so beautifully illustrated in the
development of portraiture[8] is paralleled by the new achievements
of biography as a literary form. Here also Vasari was a pioneer,
though Burckhardt reminds us of the earlier pen-portraits in the
despatches of the Venetian envoys that are a chief source of the
depiction of the English Court before Holbein. Here, too, modern
diplomacy and diplomatic practice were a creation of the Italian
Renaissance – the internal equilibrium of the states within the
peninsula providing a microcosm of the states-system of Europe.[9]

In fiction 'the Italians were the story-tellers *par excellence* for all
of Europe.'[10] They provided hundreds of plots for the dramatists,
later on, of Spain, France and England – witness the plots
Shakespeare drew on from Italian sources. And not only from
Italian novelists, Boccaccio, Bandello, Cinthio, but from the
exciting events of Italian life – such stories as those of the Cenci,
of the Duchess of Malfi, of Gesualdo the composer, of Borgias,
Sforzas, della Roveres, or the sensational family tragedy of
Trissino, critic and theorist of poetry.[11] In literature they provided
the new form of the Petrarchan sonnet, which raged – though after
a long interval – through French and English poetry; that of the
romantic epic, with Ariosto, or the epic *pur sang* with Tasso; the
pastoral, with Sannazzaro at the beginning of the century,
followed by Sidney with his *Arcadia* towards the end. Or in music

there is the invention of the madrigal before mid-century, the rest of Europe following in its wake. The English madrigal school was at its height at the turn of the century; but where its works are to be counted in hundreds the Italian are to be counted in thousands. Similarly with printing; similarly with almost everything – especially in the realm of art. Art was above all what Italy had to teach the rest of Europe, in particular, form and style.[12] It is not too much to say that Italians began almost everything that was new in the period of the Renaissance: the rest of Europe had to go to school to them again, either in Italy or at home.

It is impossible to account wholly for movements of the spirit, but at least we can decipher signs and symptoms, tell the difference between one thing and another. The Italians of this period were possessed with a passion for physical beauty, whether in women or men – think of the portraits of Botticelli, or the thrilled response of the nerves in Raphael or Leonardo. Of course the dominant Platonism of Ficino or Pico emphasised physical beauty as a mirror of the soul, and this justified to Michelangelo's mind his passionate response – which needs no explanation to anyone with the least psychological perception – to 'the naked beauty of young men'.[13] Spenser puts the philosophic point concisely: 'Soul is form and doth the body make'.

There was, too, the freedom accorded to women that so much struck outside observers – at the top of society, something like equality. Indeed at the Italian Courts there was a cult of women, as reflected in the mirror of Castiglione, with all that that meant in the refinement of sensibility, the challenge and response of the sexes, in sophistication and the dangers run. For, with the Italian temperament and code of 'honour', there were many more sex-murders than in colder climes – and that again made for more stories. There was, in any case, the vivacity and spontaneity of the Italian nature, and now the self-awareness and candour, deviating into cynicism, from disillusionment, with Machiavelli and Guicciardini. Nevertheless, there was always enjoyment, the popular enjoyment of feasts and festivals, into which Lorenzo il Magnifico threw himself with such zest and genius, though not without an element of calculation.

All this, in such a dawn, gave the earlier Italians enjoying such an invigorating experience a feeling of superiority towards the barbarians outside. Even Castiglione expresses it in regard to the French nobility, if we may quote it in the youthful awkwardness of the Elizabethan translation. 'Beside goodness the true and prin-

cipal ornament of the mind in every man, I believe, are letters –
although the Frenchmen know only the nobleness of arms, and
pass for [i.e. set store by] nothing beside. So that they do not only
set by letters, but they rather abhor them, and all learned men
they do count very rascals, and they think it a great villainy when
anyone of them is called clerk.'[14] Castiglione found this regrettable
in a governing class remaining over from the debased medievalism
of Louis XI. But the Italian already foresaw the change that
would come about with the Renaissance impulse to which Francis
I would open the French Court. 'If M. d'Angoulême have so good
luck that he may, as men hope, succeed in the crown, the glory of
arms in France doth not so flourish nor is had in such estimation
as letters will be, I believe.'

Castiglione, who knew the Court of Henry VII at first hand,
went on to make the same forecast for that of his son and successor.
'And to the crown of England and Lord Henry, Prince of Wales,
who presently groweth under his most noble father in all kind
of virtue, like a tender imp under the shadow of an excellent tree
and laden with fruit to renew him much more beautiful and plen-
teous when the time shall come.'[15] Such too were the prospects
discerned, when the young king came to the throne, by the
Venetian Giustiniani and by Erasmus. And they were fulfilled.
Public attention has been so concentrated upon Henry VIII's
matrimonial troubles that it has omitted to notice that, save only
for Charles I, he was the greatest patron of the arts of all English
monarchs.

In the Middle Ages the English had done not badly, for a small
people, in a provincial way, with their poetry, their Gothic
architecture and sculpture, their schools of manuscript illumina-
tion, their alabasters and *opus anglicanum*. With Chaucer they had
produced a poet of European importance – though nobody could
be expected to read his barbarous language. In the sixteenth
century no-one, except the English, was expected to speak English,
and even the English, in diplomacy, were called upon to speak
Latin.[16] We have seen what cultivated Italians thought of the
French: what must they have thought of the English? Text-books
have a depressing phrase, 'the cultural lag'; perhaps we can put it
better by saying that all, or nearly all, was to learn again. It took
the best part of a century to catch up.

The rhythms observable in the process were complex; there
were ebbs and flows, tides and recessions, contacts were varied and
variable, though they were continuous. Even by Polydore Vergil's

time, the first half of the sixteenth century, he observed that as the result of the wars, initiated by Charles VIII's fateful invasion of Italy in 1494, good letters were pouring across the Alps to France and Germany, England and even to Scotland.[17] The Victorians were apt to think of the Renaissance impulse as having exhausted itself in Italy by mid-century, as they certainly exaggerated the degree of scepticism, irreligion and unbelief. The leading English historian of the subject, John Addington Symonds, closed his story too early: he virtually omitted Tasso, seems to have overlooked the great Venetian painters – Titian, Tintoretto, Veronese – and not to have considered Galileo. What was happening was not so much the exhaustion of Italy, which continued to be creative, if not so intensely, as that other peoples were catching up and closing the gap.

It is a theme of this book to depict the process so far as England is concerned, to observe the cross-fertilisation with other, native factors and forces, to portray the fusion, the upshot, the achievement.

English historians, viewing the sixteenth century from too nationalist a standpoint, have seldom seen it in the light of the European Renaissance. They have seen it rather in the glow of the Reformation, 'the establishment of the Church of England, the birth of British sea power, and England's first great economic expansion.'[18] Mr. Ferguson continues by pointing to 'the vigorous vernacular literature that was the chief glory of the English Renaissance.' But when he adds that art was here 'no complicating factor' for 'England had little or none', we are surprised at so summary a judgment. It completely neglects the achievements of English music from one end of the century to another, from the genius of Taverner to the greater genius of William Byrd. While the story of art and architecture, the decorative arts and crafts, has been unravelled in recent decades so that we can see the picture as never before; Elizabethan painting, for example, is now being completely revalued. (It is a sad loss that few historians have any aesthetic sensibility).

We are in search of the *differentiae* that enable us to trace the Renaissance impulse. It is not very significant that there were English students studying in Italy in the fifteenth century or that there were a couple of Italian teachers at Oxford and Cambridge in the 1460's and 1470's.[19] There always had been such contacts in the Middle Ages. The chief channel of communication was the Church, and this remained so right up to the breach with Rome.[20] After the religious breach the secular contacts became stronger and more numerous than ever before. These already existed, but no-one could have foreseen the extension they would receive. This is what is new and significant from our point of view.

The Renaissance in Italy flowered in the cultivated circles of the Courts there, and these formed the effective points of contact, the channels of fertilisation, in place of the modes and means of the Church hitherto dominant. Henry VII and Henry VIII, up to the breach, had their representation at the Court of Rome; Henry VIII maintained his cousin, Reginald Pole's household at Padua for years, hopefully as a nursing ground for young servants of the state. When Pole turned on the king and denounced him before the public opinion of Europe for the divorce and the breach with the Church, some of Pole's companions, notably Starkey, returned to the service of their country for which they had always been intended.[21]

We must look for what is significant. Nothing could be more so than that the greatest servant of the new emerging state, Thomas Cromwell, should have had the kind of Italian background he had. In his youth he was a soldier of fortune, a *condottiere*, in the wars, serving with the French at the battle on the Garigliano. He told Archbishop Cranmer – his confidant rather than his confessor – 'what a ruffian he was in his younger days.'[22] From this he became a merchant, and then attached himself to a Venetian as an accountant; he gathered acquaintance in commercial circles with such firms as the Frescobaldi – later intimate with one of the family in London. After some experience of the marts in Antwerp, he returned to Italy to help a friend to obtain some Lenten indulgences for Boston. Cromwell thought up a characteristic dodge: he waylaid Julius II, returning tired from hunting, with some choice sweetmeats and jellies – and got the indulgences on the spot. Popes had no terrors for him.

In the days of his power he was able to satisfy his love of Italian luxuries – in that like his former master, Wolsey. It had been noted by the Venetians that a way to the Cardinal's favour was to present him with rich carpets, of which he collected scores for Hampton Court and Whitehall. Cromwell, however, knew the language and read Italian books. It is ironical to find Bonner – the later burner of Protestants under Mary – writing to Cromwell in 1530 to lend him Petrarch's *Trionfe* and Castiglione's *Cortegiano*, and reminding him of his promise to make him a good Italian.[23] Another encounter had a sharper edge to it. The scholar Pole was dilating one day at Wolsey's house on how to serve a prince with honour, when Cromwell interrupted him to say that he would do better to leave the theoretical learning of the schools for the practical experience enshrined in a recent Italian book – which Pole subsequently found was Machiavelli's *The Prince*.

Courts were closely concerned with scholarship and the arts, indeed were becoming – in place of the Church – prime patrons of both. Henry VII's education was largely French and he did his serious reading of books in that language; but his secretary was an Italian, the court-poet Carmeliano, and Polydore Vergil was a notable recruit to his Court. It is popular knowledge that the tempestuous Torrigiano – to whom the young Michelangelo owed his broken nose – designed Henry's tomb in Westminster Abbey, though not many may have penetrated into the recesses of the Public Record Office to behold the Renaissance tomb he also made for Dr. Young, formerly in the Rolls Chapel.

The indebtedness of the famous group of Oxford scholars – Colet, Grocyn, Linacre – to Italy, especially for their Greek, has long been appreciated.[24] The inspiration for Colet's epoch-making lectures on St. Paul – cutting out the accretions of scholastic interpretation to go straight to the meaning of the text – came from the new biblical criticism in Italy. In this realm the Renaissance meant the search for a simpler religion, shorn of adiaphora (things inessential), a return to the Bible in the spirit of free inquiry. At the same time Colet's foundation of a new model for schools, St. Paul's, owed something to the educational ideals of Vittorino da Feltre, which had formed the mind of Federico de Montefeltro, creator of the Court of Urbino.

One must make no mistake about the outstanding importance of Linacre, honoured in England as the founder of the Royal College of Physicians. Where others spent a few years or months in Italy, Linacre spent twelve years, 1487–99, several of them in the house of Aldus at Venice, greatest of publishers, who was engaged in the prodigious task of publishing the whole classics of the ancient world, Greek and Roman. Linacre studied under Politian and learned his Greek from Chalcondylas. He is celebrated as 'the first Englishman to publish a work of the new classical scholarship . . . the first Englishman who gained a European reputation as a humanist.'[25] In time he translated the basic texts of Galen, cardinal figure in the revival of classical medicine, into Latin. These translations were frequently reprinted on the Continent but, with the exception of one reprint, not again in England during the whole century.[26] This in itself speaks volumes for the backward medievalism of outlook that still held in English medicine. It affords also an example of the by no means simple or straight-forward rhythms in the operation of the Renaissance impulse, reception and retrocession.

Castiglione himself came to England at the end of 1506 to represent the Duke of Urbino and be proxy for his installation as Knight of the Garter.[27] He brought with him as a present the little painting, by the young Raphael of Urbino, of St. George and the dragon now in the Louvre. He was received at Court by the bishop of Worcester, Silvestro Gigli, whom the king kept there to order its ceremonies. Castiglione found the astute monarch very well informed about the personalities and affairs of the Italian states. On his departure Henry sped him on his way with a present of horses and dogs, and a gold collar of Lancastrian SS links – and himself paid the expenses of the installation. On this visit Castiglione would have met the young heir to the throne to whom he paid tribute in the *Cortegiano*.

We know now that many more foreign artists were at work in England in Henry VIII's reign than had hitherto been realised.[28] The majority were from the Netherlands, with one German of genius: Holbein. We are concerned for the moment with the Italians, and here it may be that Wolsey took the lead in patronage. Certainly we find Giovanni da Maiano making and painting the Renaissance roundels in terracotta at Hampton Court; Toto del Nunziata followed to paint religious pictures and execute decorative work there. The king took them over into his service along with Wolsey's palaces on his fall, and Toto became Serjeant Painter, 1544–54. The Neapolitan, Vincent Volpe, had arrived in 1512, and was employed here for the rest of his life, in painting heraldic work for the navy, decorations for revels and maskings and other miscellaneous work, such as they all did. Nicholas da Modena arrived in 1537 from working at Fontainebleau, where a grander team was employed with grander results – there is no Renaissance work in England to equal the great gallery there. Yet Holbein himself is a Renaissance painter, mediating the clarity of Italy, like Dürer, via the South German school from which they sprang.

Nevertheless the Italian influence made progress against

heavier competition from the nearer Netherlands; and no Court has ever received more powerful and convincing depiction than Henry VIII's from the genius of Holbein. The chronicler Hall notes the first introduction of masking at Court in 1512: 'on the day of Epiphany at night the King, with eleven others, were disguised after the manner of Italy called a Mask, a thing not seen before in England.'[29] Painters such as Volpe and Ellys Carmyan were there to decorate these spectacles; there was already a corps of Italian musicians among the King's Music. Others such as Girolamo da Treviso, killed at Boulogne, served Henry as technicians in his wars.

Here, too, is an aspect of the subject that is only just receiving attention. Mr. Shelby tells us that 'the new style in fortification was developed in Italy during the early part of the century' – no doubt along with the new style in war that is such an inspiration to the natural man.[30] The result here, too, was the rapid diffusion of the new style throughout Europe, with Italian military engineers called in at significant points to advance it. In Italy architecture was already becoming more professionalised, in a sense: with the growing desire to imitate classical building forms, 'architecture became more and more a learned subject – bookish, antiquarian, and archaeological.'[31] At the same time the architect was often a painter or sculptor who turned to architecture later – Michelangelo, for instance. This made for a separation between architecture and engineering.

Mr. Shelby observes an interesting disparity of rhythm here between Italy and England, 'where engineering was emerging as a specialised profession before architecture had achieved the kind of professionalism already known in Italy.'[32] Mr. Shelby puts this down to the expenditure and energy Henry VIII put into fortifying his country all round the southern coasts. He tells us that Henry in his later years displayed a passion for military architecture – as also for naval ship-building, we may add. These may be considered as yet further aspects of his patronage of the arts. We may also reflect that the old emphasis connecting the Reformation with the reinforcement of English nationalism, seen in Victorian times in religious terms, is justified in ours in the more concrete terms of technology. There was a certain propriety in the foremost military scientist of the age, Tartaglia – who in the end gave up his work on account of the threat to human life constituted by its advance – dedicating his masterpiece on gunnery and ballistics to Henry VIII.

Italy's revolution in architecture in time swept away the building forms of the Middle Ages – but they were an unconscionable time in dying in England. It was not until three quarters of a century had passed that there emerged a complete Renaissance architect, and then in an Italianate Welshman, Inigo Jones. Mr. Shelby indicates further consequences: 'this interruption had its impact not only upon architectural style but also upon techniques of architectural drafting, as well as upon the use of architectural drawings in building construction.'[33] In this process, 'the measured drawing came into being, as well as more varied kinds of drawings – plans, elevations, sections, and perspective views of those ancient monuments which had survived.'

In the actual architecture of this preparatory period one sees the new spirit at work only very hesitantly, primitively; and Sir John Summerson tells us that its 'interest converges emphatically on one point – the Court.'[34] When Henry VIII took over from Wolsey he began his career of palace-building; the dissolution of the monasteries gave him the resources with which to display his appetites as an art-patron. It was Henry's additions to Wolsey's buildings at Hampton Court and Whitehall that were really important and made palaces of them. The last phase of English medieval Gothic, in the simplification of its line and mass, in the shallowness, almost obliteration, of mouldings, may be said to be ready for classicism. One sees the contrast in such a dull building as Trinity College chapel at Cambridge, compared with its neighbour, King's, the last splendid flowering of the Middle Ages. (Even so, the superb choir-screen, the gift of Henry VIII, 1533–35, is entirely Renaissance work.) When one looks at such plain late structures as Trinity chapel or the parish church of Saffron Walden, one sees English architecture at pause for a new inspiration.

This is observable at first in bits and pieces, in decorative detail. As one goes about the old country, the eye lights up as one recognises the evidences of the new spirit: a couple of sophisticated Renaissance capitals in Sir Thomas More's church at Chelsea (mercifully saved from the bombs of the barbarians in 1941); the detail, *putti* and floriation, under the last wide bay, going down St. Aldate's, of Wolsey's college at Oxford; the decorative terra-cottas applied to the plain façade of Sutton Place near Guildford; the fine series of Renaissance tombs in Framlingham church in Suffolk, particularly the sarcophagus of Henry's son, the Duke of Richmond, with its pilasters and large assertive shields-of-arms.

In fact, in spite of popular mythology on the subject, the main structures were built by Englishmen; it was the new decoration that was executed by foreigners.

Henry's last Queen, Catherine Parr – an intelligent and kindly woman who brought harmony to his domestic interior, for which the old tyrant was grateful – made herself the centre of a cultivated circle extending patronage in the arts. John Bettes, one of the earliest of English painters – and a good, if modest, one – executed miniatures for her.[35] She read Italian; Princess Elizabeth, already a precocious linguist, was learning Italian from the age of ten and came to speak it fluently; Princess Mary spoke Spanish not Italian – therein lay a difference, not the only one, between the generations. The Queen encouraged the princesses to translate – Mary from Erasmus, Elizabeth from the Reforming Margaret of Navarre. The exalted fashion spread to Henry's young prisoner in the Tower, Edward Courtenay, of Yorkist royal blood, who translated a work of Italian Protestant devotion, the *Beneficio di Giesu Christo crocifisso*. Henry Parker, Lord Morley, devoted years to a career of persistent, if somewhat rough and ready, translation: he rendered several works of Petrarch both from the Latin and directly from Italian, as also Paolo Giovio's Commentaries on the Turks.[36] Several of these he presented to Henry, recommending himself thus to favour. To Cromwell he sent Machiavelli's *Florentine History* and *The Prince* – as if this were necessary; but he improved the occasion by marking the passages reflecting unfavourably upon the Papacy. A devout Catholic, he fathered a Recusant son who went into exile under Elizabeth. One sees how mixed-up people are by the pressures of history.

Before Henry's reign was out, however, the new impulse had made a more decided conquest in literature than in any other sphere, and had set models that were not to be equalled for some forty years. Not, indeed, until the final flowering of the 1580's – in the interval there was a marked recession, a long hiatus. Everyone knows that Wyatt and Surrey introduced the new manner of writing verse that is recognisably modern. The Gothic irregularities of Skelton are still medieval, all the more archaic in that the inflexions in the language had largely broken down since Chaucer and reduced prosody to anarchy. A linguistic revolution had taken place: there is more of a gulf between the language of 1500 and that of 1400 than there is between 1500 and our own, nearly five centuries later. Wyatt and Surrey began the new, modern poetry. Even so we perceive a difference between Wyatt, of an older generation at Henry's Court, and young Surrey who should have lived to be an Elizabethan. The point is brought home by a comparison between their respective renderings of Petrarch's

> Amor, che nel penser mio vive e regna . . .[37]

between Wyatt's:

> The long love, that in my thought doth harbour
> And in my heart doth keep his residence,
> Into my face presseth with bold pretence
> And therein campeth, spreading his banner . . .

and Surrey's:

> Love that doth reign and live within my thought
> And build his seat within my captive breast,
> Clad in the arms wherein with me he fought,
> Oft in my face he doth his banner rest . . .

Mr. Buxton comments, 'the difference is not between a good poet and a bad one, but between a poet who has understood Petrarch's art and one who has merely understood the meaning of his words.' If this is a little too strong, yet we can see that Surrey is already a modern poet.

When Surrey came to have his portrait painted – a memorable, symptomatic picture – though it is in fact by a Fleming, Guillim Stretes, it is in the full-blown manner of Italian classicism, pose, broken columns, *putto* in background, and all. But this reminds us that the Netherlands, like France, formed another conductor of the Renaissance impulse to England. As to that we have a constant reminder in the greatest single influence of them all: Erasmus.

With the death of the old autocrat, who had kept a firm control upon events, and the accession of a boy-king, Edward VI, the floodgates were open, in more senses than one. Henry's last and grandest palace, Nonsuch in Surrey, was not quite complete at his death. Once more the structure was in essence English, but it was embellished all over with Renaissance decoration; and 'in the decorative finishing, the furnishings and fountains, there is no question at all that Henry employed foreigners.'[38] The inner court was plastered with 'antick' figures, statues and bassorelievos. A design that remains for the decoration of throne-room or presence-chamber, a fireplace that has survived at Reigate, and

a number of fragments in country-houses nearby, such as Losely –
the palace was ultimately a victim of the odious Civil War – attest
the Renaissance inspiration at work. With the Edwardian circle
this, for a brief space – so long as Edward lived – was given its
head.

The importance of the architectural work done during this
brief interval has come to be recognised only in our time. The two
leading figures in the government – and, as a French envoy noted
at the time, the only two men capable of conducting it – were
Somerset and Northumberland. The house that Somerset built for
himself in the Strand – using the cloister of old St. Paul's as a
quarry, be it noted as an epitome of the Reformation process of
useful secularisation – was 'probably the first deliberate attempt to
build in England a house composed altogether within the classical
discipline.'³⁹ We need not go into details: the coupling of two
windows, framed by columns, under a pediment, the parapet
above each with 'cipher-and-square' that became so characteristic
an Elizabethan motif.

The Duke of Somerset's right-hand man, Sir John Thynne, was
building a similarly advanced house, with these same motifs, at
Longleat. Another member of this group, Sir William Sharington,
in transforming the monastic buildings at nearby Lacock into an
up-to-date mansion for domestic use, introduced a great deal of
classical detail. A fireplace has Doric pilasters and correct entabla-
ture; an Ionic order appears in the unfinished arcade. Anyone
who has seen the splendid stone-tables in the tower-rooms, carved
with fruit and satyrs serving as carytids, will recognise them as not
out of place in a Renaissance palace in Italy or France.

The works of this forward-looking group were cut short by the
misfortune of Mary's accession, as much a reaction in these as in
other matters – witness the reversion to a completely medieval
type of altar-tomb put up to Geoffrey Chaucer in Westminster
Abbey in 1556. We have literary evidence of the intentions of the
Edwardian circle in John Shute's *First and Chief Grounds of Architecture*, the first English book on the subject. A Devonshireman by
origin, Shute was a member of the London Painter-Stainers'
Company. He was a follower of Northumberland who, in 1550,
specially sent him to Italy 'for my further knowledge . . . to confer
with the doings of the skilful masters in architecture, and also to
view such ancient monuments hereof as are yet extant.'⁴⁰ No
doubt if Edward had lived and Northumberland kept his head, we
should have had a Northumberland House to rival old Somerset

House. On Shute's return he took the drawings he had made to Northumberland; he showed them to the young king who was much pleased by them. They contained 'tricks and devices as well of sculpture and painting as also of architecture', though it was in the last that Shute thought his country might be best profited: 'wherein I do follow not only the writings of learned men, but also do ground myself on my own experience and practice, gathered by the sight of the monuments in Italy.'

In his address to his readers Shute says that his intention had been to study both the ancient monuments and the modern buildings of Italy. His book, so far as he carried it – it seems that he intended more – is no other than a detailed exposition of the various orders of classical columns, with their measurements and proportions, and their spacing. Shute was certainly a painter, and among the unattributed paintings and miniatures of the time there must be some of his. Mr. Hind receives him as 'the earliest native English engraver whose name is known', on the assumption that the engravings in his book are his handiwork.[41] The draped figures, functioning as caryatids, are as classical as the columns, rough-hewn as they are; Mr. Hind regards them as displaying 'an architect's sense of dignity in composition, and a rough use of the graver, which gives the appearance of etching rather than line-engraving in quality.'

In fact, though Shute assures us that, in regard to his delineation of the orders, he has used no terms 'which I have not as well seen and measured in Italy . . . and seeing it indeed is more than only bare reading of it,' his attitude is essentially literary and painterly. He is dependent on Vitruvius and Serlio; his book is imitative. He does not have the first-hand acquaintance with the facts of building, such as Philibert de l'Orme had.[42] Though Shute may have intended more than these 'first fruits of my poor attempts', there is a gulf between this and de l'Orme's masterly *Le Premier Tome de l'Architecture* of 1567. One sees how much more rapidly the Renaissance advanced architecturally in France than in England. Mary's reign represented a conservative reaction in every respect; Shute's book did not see the light until 1563, when she and her works were well out of the way, and Elizabeth and Cecil in place to carry on the work of the Edwardian circle.

We can discern more intimately what this was through the mind and work of the Italianate Welshman, William Thomas. He too, became a follower of Northumberland and dedicated his *History of Italy* to him: 'A Book exceeding profitable to be read because it treateth of many and diverse commonwealths, how they have been and now be governed.'[43] He expatiates on the moral uses of reading history and 'also how mutable fortune is' – as he and his patron would have sharp cause to know. Thomas emerges about 1540 on the Welsh border paying their pensions to the late nuns of Herefordshire. A servant of the Catholic Sir Anthony Browne, the young man was of a gambling disposition and in 1545, appropriating some of his master's money, took bills of exchange on Venice and set out for Italy. He thought fit to spend the next four years in the peninsula and evidently fell in love with it.[44]

In 1549 he published his *History of Italy*, which is both history culled from the chronicles and a contemporary guide-book which deserves its description as 'the best account of any foreign nation written before the seventeenth century'.[45] For he was an observer both acute and sympathetic, with the gift for languages that went with his Welsh temperament – of which he had also the defects. But he loved Italy, the wealth and cultivation he observed in the cities, the courtesy and charm, the refinement of manners, the opulence of dress, especially of the ladies. He enjoyed the fine food, especially the diversity of fruit in summer – we fail to realise how inferior Tudor England was from that point of view. He appreciated the honour in which trade was held, with successful merchants regarded as gentlemen. (After all, were not the Medici merchants by origin, proudly displaying the pawnbrokers' sign for coat-of-arms?) Like Goethe centuries later, he was bowled over by Italy: in Rome, the ruins of antiquity; in Venice, the wealth and power of a well-ordered state; in Florence and Genoa, the opulence of the merchants; in Milan and Naples, the productivity of the soil, the wealth of nature. All in all, he saw it as a well-balanced and well-conducted society with admirable maintenance of public order. The festas and public ceremonies helped to keep order in the nursery, as every Italian ruler well understood.

But he was quite able to see the other side of the picture. He disapproved of the code of revenge on account of 'honour' and insults, which led to so many murders – and to so many stories for dramatists. A countryman himself, he was shocked by the exploitation of the peasants by the landowners. A Northerner, he was still more shocked by the sexual laxity of a Mediterranean people, though he considered that a warmer climate had something to do with it. A Protestant, he was put out by 'the pride and abomination' of the Papacy – no emperor or king was anything to it: he has a hostile description of the Farnese Pope Paul III going in state to

St. Peter's on Christmas Day 1547, with hundreds of attendants, the cardinals each with three or four good-looking pages, 'trimmed like young princes, for what purpose I would be loth to tell.'[46] On the other hand, Rome was not wanting in harlots, there were thousands of them; while the painted courtesans of Venice were one of the sights of the city – he had to admit that they were goodly, well set-up women. The men there were mean as well as lecherous; the Genoese were keen travellers, and so addicted to the art of love that they could give Ovid a point or two.

Thomas cites Livy again and again, as did Hoby contemporaneously. But we must attend to the specifically Renaissance characteristics of his observation. There was his enthusiasm for classical antiquities, his lamentation over the ruins of Rome. 'Then did it grieve me to see the only jewel, mirror, mistress and beauty of this world, that never had her like nor (as I think), never shall, lie so desolate and disfigured.'[47] The remains were, of course, witness to her tyrannies and oppressions. He read Vitruvius on the pillars, capitals, obelisks still lying about; he noted particular objects that appealed to him, such as the red porphyry tomb of St. Constantia in her church. His chief enthusiasm was for the Pantheon, no ruin but 'the perfectest of all the antiquities', and he goes into considerable architectural detail about that.

He has also a Renaissance appreciation for architectural regularity. In Ferrara, for example, 'you shall find above a dozen streets so just and evenly set forth that I warrant you there is not so much as the corner of a house to let [i.e. hinder] a man of his full sight from the one end to the other.'[48] Evidently, no medieval irregularity for him. Some streets went for almost a mile 'with the goodly houses and buildings on both sides so fair and uniform that it seemeth all done at one time and by one agreement.' He expressed much enthusiasm for the new building of St. Peter's and the Duomo at Milan, but doubted whether they would ever be finished. In Florence he was impressed by the hospitals and sweetness, i.e. hygiene, of the houses, and by the good order maintained there: though in the past much burdened with sodomy, 'I cannot perceive there is any such thing now.' (Here came in his Protestant prejudice).

He came back to England in 1549, an enthusiastic propagator of Italian culture and well equipped in the language to offer himself for government service. He dedicated a book on *The Vanity of this World* to a lady of the Welsh Border family of the Herberts, in the inner circle round the young king, expounding the many virtuous examples provided by women to provoke men to reform themselves. In Italy he had written a tract to justify Henry VIII in his proceedings, published in 1552 as *Il Pellegrino*.[49] In these two years he shot rapidly up in the world.

We must turn to his second Italian book, of even greater practical utility, the *Principal Rules of the Italian Grammar, with a Dictionary for the better understanding of Boccaccio, Petrarch and Dante* (in that revealing order), published in 1550. In 1548 a young relative of Archbishop Cranmer, John Tamworth, arrived in Venice and, anxious to learn the language, asked Thomas to write down the rules for him. Tamworth lent the book two years later to his brother-in-law, Sir Walter Mildmay, who thought it 'a necessary book' for the public and caused it to be printed. So Thomas explains. Tamworth was also a brother-in-law of Walsingham; these were promising figures in the Edwardian circle, and shortly Thomas became their brother-in-law too, taking Mildmay's sister as his second wife.

His ideas are more interesting. Thomas's were direct, firsthand impressions, not after a medieval stereotype. His considered view was that 'the Italian nation seemeth to flourish in civility most of all other at this day', i.e. it was the most highly developed culturally.[50] As for literature, 'besides the authors of this time, wherof there be many worthy, you shall almost find no part of the sciences, no part of any worthy history, no part of eloquence, not any part of fine poesy, that we have not in the Italian tongue.' He was one of the first in England to have proper appreciation of Machiavelli – who later in the century became a popular bugbear to frighten children with. The first to give an account of the Florentine academy, Thomas based his history of Florence on Machiavelli's and acknowledged his debt to him again and again; in a later paper of advice for Edward he cites the *Discorsi*. He agreed with Machiavelli on the necessity for strong central government; a more Welsh type, he had not the moderation and circumspection of Cecil.

As to language, he was an out-and-out modernist. 'Whereas both the Greek and the Latin require long time and study, the Italian is in short space and easily obtained.'[51] He looked to Italian as becoming the third language in European culture, as for the rest of the century in effect it was. He applied these views to the circumstances of his own country and ardently advocated the use of English in education. As things were, education brought people up to express themselves in Latin who could not express themselves in their native language. Why was it that, among thousands who have studied in Latin, 'it is almost hard to find any good author in our own mother tongue'?[52] Writing in Latin nowadays was simply carrying water to the sea – how original this view was at the time and for long afterwards! – 'whereas the study of Latin should be to draw the worthy things of the same into their own tongues.' This part of the programme was certainly taken up by the Elizabethans, who brought into being a whole literature of translation. Thomas considered that the master should first teach the scholar to understand well in his tongue, then go on to the liberal arts, i.e. school subjects, before tackling Latin. But English authors were lacking to direct schoolmasters into this course of teaching. 'If our nation desire to triumph in civil knowledge as other nations do, the means must be that each man first covet to flourish in his own natural tongue' – without which he was not likely to do very well in any other. Here was the challenge; but Thomas's ideas had little effect, any more than Mulcaster's later: the inhibiting grip of education *by means of* the classics – another thing from education in the classics themselves – remained on right up into the nineteenth century.

For a brief spell Thomas achieved an unique position from which to put his ideas across. He was made a Clerk of the Privy Council, centre of power and influence, where his knowledge of modern languages and affairs was most useful. And, quite privately, he became an adviser to the young king himself, who already showed a serious-minded concern for the problems of government and was equipping himself for his rôle as ruler. Thomas prepared for him papers of advice on the acute economic problems of the time and the country's exposed position in foreign affairs. He vigorously attacked the debasement of the coinage, i.e. devaluation, and favoured the stabilisation of the currency, which was carried out by Elizabeth and Cecil ten years later and provided a firm foundation for the prosperity of her reign. Thomas apologised for stating his case so passionately – evidently he was aware of his Welsh temperament. He wrote an able analysis of the country's dangerous isolation in foreign affairs, its weakness in the dilemma between the Empire and France – and the line he put forward was a sensible one. In another paper he discussed 'whether it be better for a commonwealth that the power be in the nobility or in the commonalty.' He translated Barbaro's account of his travels into Tana (i.e. the Crimea) and Persia as a New Year's Gift for Edward.

Thomas was in a position that might have grown into real power, had the king lived. The rewards in grants of land and moneys were already pretty considerable, though bishop Ridley – later to be burned – successfully resisted the demand of 'this ungodly man' for a prebend of St. Paul's, which the good bishop wanted for a preacher. In 1551 Thomas accompanied Queen Catherine Parr's brother, Northampton, on the important embassy to France to negotiate a French marriage for Edward. A restless man, in 1552 Thomas was writing privately to Secretary Cecil that he would like the embassy to Venice: he longed for Italy, 'I could find it in mine heart to spend a year or two there, if I were sent.' Instead he was sent in 1553 with the ambassadors to Charles V in Flanders.

The unexpected death of Edward and accession of Mary left him, and all the Edwardian circle, exposed. But he could not keep quiet or lie low. He involved himself, with Sir Peter Carew, in the younger Wyatt's widespread conspiracy which nearly overwhelmed Mary early on, in 1554. After Christmas 1553 Thomas spent three weeks with Carew at Mohun's Ottery in Devon waiting for the Earl to come down and raise the county. (Thomas's explanation was that he had 'sold a ceiling' to Sir Peter: something Italianate, one wonders?). When the Earl failed the opposition, and Wyatt's promising rising was defeated, Sir Peter happily escaped abroad to fight another day. Thomas journeyed in disguise across the western counties, still not giving up hope but sending messages to his friends, until he reached his estate at Barnsley in Gloucestershire on his rash way to London. The warrants were out for him. Weary, he rested at Badgington, 'sometime in his chamber, sometime in the hall, sometime in his orchard, reading of the Bible, Sallust, Marcus Aurelius. And most of all, a book of Italian of his own' – this would be the recently published *Il Pellegrino*. It is a touching picture of a politically minded intellectual in mortal danger.

He set out for London disguised in a white frieze coat and jerkin, a felt hat and a pair of medley hose. He stopped at the 'Boar' at Abingdon; on the top of Henley Hill, looking out over the Thames valley for the last time, Thomas's companion left him, beard shaven, carrying pike-staff and dagger. Soon recognised in London, he was taken to the Tower along with Sir Nicholas Throckmorton. Here Thomas was racked, in the hope of extracting information to implicate the Princess Elizabeth, and he attempted suicide by stabbing himself under the paps. He was charged with a device to assassinate Mary – perhaps this was a little too Italianate, though it would have saved a great deal of trouble, and many people's lives, if it had come off. The evidence rested only on the word of Sir Nicholas Arnold, who may have been a double agent. Thomas made 'a godly end' at Tyburn, where he was hanged, drawn and quartered, claiming unrepentantly that he died for his country. When Elizabeth came into her own, she reversed his attainder and restored in blood the only child of the man who had died for her.

A brilliant and symptomatic figure, he would have had an interesting place in her reign, though he did not have the ballast of the prudent and honest Cecil. However, when the unfortunate hiatus of Mary's reign was over, the Henrician and Edwardian course was resumed, the impulse carried forward.

G. B. Parks tells us that, with Thomas's work, 'a great enthusiasm suddenly arose in England for Italian culture.'[53] Certainly the numbers of young Englishmen going to Italy multiplied in Edward's reign, and they were no longer churchmen but members of the secular governing class, sons of nobility and gentry, diplomats to be, young men preparing themselves for service in government or in their localities. Young Thomas Hoby, the translator of Castiglione's *Book of the Courtier*, was a representative member of this class. His family was a new one, based on monastic land, the delectable lands of the abbey of Bisham, near Marlow, on a pleasant reach of the Thames. The mansion house had been the residence of the Yorkist Countess of Salisbury – whom Henry VIII had executed – mother of Cardinal Pole, and in the abbey church were all the Montagu tombs.[54]

In 1547 Thomas Hoby, at the age of seventeen, was sent abroad to learn languages. He went first to the Protestant household of Bucer, the divine, at Strasbourg, where he studied under the famous educationist, Sturm, and the Reformers, Peter Martyr and Fagius. It is hardly surprising that the youth's first task was to translate the boring Bucer's *Gratulation . . . unto the Church of England for the restitution of Christ's religion and his Answer unto the two railing epistles of Stephen Bishop of Winchester* [i.e. Gardiner], *concerning the unmarried state of priests and cloisterers.*'[55] Such were the exchanges of these religious men. However, far more interesting to us, the young man kept a Diary and next year, 1548, was out of Bucer's household on his way to Italy.[56] Before he left, William Thomas arrived there on his way home, and the younger Sir Thomas Wyatt on his way out.

Young Hoby spent a year, from the summer of 1548 to that of 1549, between Padua and Venice learning Italian and improving his Latin, attending lectures in the humanities, civil law and logic. Parks estimates that while there Hoby encountered at least fourteen fellow Englishmen and another thirteen elsewhere in Italy; and that there were some sixteen of student age at Padua alone, during one year of the Marian exile, 1554–5. From Hoby's Diary we learn some of their names, and they are significant; along with the considerable number Hoby had left behind at Strasbourg, we get an idea of the way the new governing circles in England were prepared to go abroad to learn.

Among Hoby's companions we find Henry Killigrew, who became the most professional and constantly called on of all Elizabeth's diplomats, and brother-in-law of Cecil. Edward Stradling, with whom Hoby went searching out antiquities, became a contributor to and patron of Welsh scholarship all his life long from his castle at St. Donat's, where he gathered a fine library; he made a good servant of the state in all that countryside. Peter Whithorne served under Charles V in his African campaign, and while there translated Machiavelli's *Art of War*, which he dedicated to Queen Elizabeth. He also made a rendering of the Greek *Strategicus* from the Italian of Fabio Cotta. Henry Neville became a gentleman of Edward VI's Privy Chamber. While Hoby stayed in the house of the ambassador at Venice, 'I found also Mr. John Young, with whom I lay [i.e. shared a bed], Mr. George Speke, Mr. Thomas Fitzwilliam, Mr. Thomas Strange, and divers other Englishmen.'[57] At Padua there were many more: 'Sir Thomas Wyatt, Mr. John Cotton, Mr. Henry Williams, Mr. Francis Williams, which both died in England the year '51, Mr. John Arundell, Mr. John Hastings, Mr. Christopher Allen, Mr. John Shere, Mr. John Hanford, and divers others.' He travelled to Rome with Henry Parker, Lord Morley's son and heir, a Barker, probably a relative of Sir Christopher, Garter king of arms, and Whithorne. There followed after them thither, Sir Robert Stafford, Frances Peto (of that old Northamptonshire family), Edward Murphin, a Christopherson, and several others. Many of these are recognisable names in the society of the time, some of them to become well known figures in the life of the age.

Hoby's Diary is essentially that of the youth he was, of eighteen to twenty, while he was in Italy, 1548–50 – though he wrote it up a little later. As such, we do not expect the incisive penetration of William Thomas, a somewhat older man anyway.

Nevertheless, Hoby shows himself an intelligent observer, as we should expect from the young man who was going to translate Castiglione. He, too, is interested in antiquities; he too has read his Livy and Cicero; and he is capable of responding to new works, like Montorsoli's fountain in the chief square at Messina. 'For a new work and that not finished at my being there, I saw a fountain of very white marble graven with the story of Actaeon and such other, by one Giovanni d'Agnolo a Florentine, which to my eyes is one of the fairest pieces of work that ever I saw.'[58] Among antiquities what chiefly impressed him there were the heads of 'Scipio and Hannibal when they were young men, in stone.'

In the neighbourhood of Mantua he visited the reputed birthplace of Vergil, and was much impressed by the pleasure gardens of the Duke with the movable orange-trees in tubs. He tells at length the characteristic episode of the murder of the young duke of Ferrandino by a varlet at a mask – all very Italian – and the deadly feud between the della Torres and the Soveragnani in Friuli. While in Venice he witnessed the state-visit of the (Farnese) duchess of Urbino for the *Bucentoro* ceremonies on Ascension Day, the mystic marriage of Venice to the sea. At Florence he was duly impressed by the bronze gates of the Baptistry. He was enthusiastic about Siena, where 'the people are much given to entertain strangers gently' and where the ladies were very well learned and wrote poetry.[59] Here they met with still more young Englishmen, and Hoby became friends with the Marquis of Capistrano, the duke of Amalfi's son, who showed him frequent courtesies. Thence they went on to Rome, and were there for the requiem and burial of Pope Paul III – whose tomb Michelangelo was to make, according to report.

Like Thomas, Hoby was much impressed by the beauty and fertility of the soil around Naples, and he improved upon him by visiting Sicily. On his way up the peninsula the company was handsomely entertained by the old Duchess of Amalfi in their castle, on account of her son's friendship with Hoby. (This was the family in which had taken place, two generations before, the tragedy that provided Webster's *Duchess of Malfi* with its story.) After supper 'every man was brought to his rest: Whithorne and I were had into a chamber hanged with cloth of gold and velvet, wherein were two beds, the one of silver work and the other of velvet. . . . In another chamber hard by lay Stradling and Greenway.'[60] The other two young men were entertained by the captain of the castle at his house in the town. On their way back through

Rome they were in time for the Jubilee of 1550, with all the ceremonies, the opening of the golden gate in St. Peter's, the indulgences to the faithful traipsing round on foot to the seven principal churches. And we are in for Hoby's Protestant reflections: 'with these and like fond traditions is the Papal seat chiefly maintained, to call men out of all places of Christendom to lighten their purses here, at pardons, indulgences, and jubilees to stocks and stones.'[61] (But how else was St. Peter's ever to be finished?) He goes on: 'but such fond foolishness was never better spied out than it is now, nor less observed in all places, though many perforce be kept blind still.' It was time for him to get home to Edwardian England.

Here he entered into the service of the Marquis of Northampton, in whose train he went on the embassy of 1551, along with William Thomas, who was 'secretary to the lords commissioners' for the marriage-treaty. During Mary's reign Hoby kept his head, and accompanied his much older half-brother, Sir Philip, on a long embassy to Germany, and thence on to Italy once more. At Padua in 1554 there was a still larger number of English gentlemen, swollen by important recruits from the Edwardians opposed to Mary: Sir Thomas Wroth, in whose arms Edward had died and who was involved in the Duke of Suffolk's second rising against her impossible régime; Sir John Cheke, the famous Greek scholar, who had been Edward's secretary of state and Cecil's brother-in-law; Sir Henry Neville, gentleman of Edward's Privy Chamber; Roger and Matthew Carew, a Kingsmill, Drury, Cornwallis, Ashley, Wyndham and others.[62] Shortly arrived Sir Anthony Cooke, Edward's tutor, whose four famous daughters were such prodigies of learning; they all knew Greek, and married respectively Cecil, Sir Nicholas Bacon, Henry Killigrew and Thomas Hoby. Besides these Hoby found his special friend, Thomas Fitzwilliam, Cooke's nephew, 'whom in fore time I had left in France, whose study and industry in obtaining of virtuous knowledge hath spread abroad a worthy fame of itself.'

Hoby spent the gloomy, lurid last years of Mary's reign – lit by so many fires – in retirement, like his brother-in-law, Cecil. One whole summer, Mary's last, they spent together at Burghley. No doubt he was going on with his translation of the *Courtier*, for it was published in the happier days of Elizabeth – and the return of the Edwardians to power – in 1561. Knighted in 1566, he was sent as full ambassador to France and there he died, aged only thirty-six. He was brought home to be buried in the chapel at

Bisham, where one sees him alongside his brother on their tomb, in the appropriate splendour of the Renaissance monuments there.

When we come, in the next generation, to Philip Sidney's Italian experience, we notice a difference of inflexion: though only a boy of nineteen he was capable of weighing it up with critical acumen.[63] He had already been put on his guard by his mentor, the eminent Huguenot scholar, Languet, who could not see why an Englishman should want to speak Italian and himself preferred German. The youth had the sense to resist this barbarism. Languet was in any case opposed to the young man going on to Rome, both on account of his personal safety – this was 1573, the year after the Massacre of St. Bartholomew, which Sidney had witnessed in Paris – and the possible danger to his morals. Languet need not have worried, and Sidney afterwards regretted that he had heeded Languet's advice.

Sidney had done his turn in the Protestant humanist school of Sturm at Strasbourg, and then gone on to Vienna. Here the Florentine medallist, Antonio Abondio, made a couple of portraits of him, now lost. Sidney was at this time the heir not only of the Sidneys but, in the absence of (legitimate) children, of his uncles the earls of Warwick and Leicester – the latter thought of on the Continent as a kind of unrecognised prince consort, the leading luminary of Elizabeth's Court. His nephew, therefore, was everywhere received like a young prince – in addition to his own exceptional intelligence, virtue and grace. Sidney had for companion an Anglo-Italian, Ludovic Bryskett, otherwise Lodovico Bruschetti, who later celebrated their travels across Alps and Appenines in verse:

> through many a hill and dale,
> Through pleasant woods and many an unknown way,
> Along the banks of many silver streams . . .

Sidney's travels were financed by letters of credit on the Italian banker in London, Vetturelli: the English were not yet up to such financial refinements.

At Venice Sidney was welcomed by his cousin, Richard Shelley, of that Sussex Recusant family from which the poet sprang, and Thomas Coningsby, who married Sidney's cousin, Philippa Fitzwilliam – of whom there is a splendid portrait in the John Heron Museum at Indianapolis. Shortly another cousin, Robert Corbet, of the Shropshire family, joined them. Another English friend was Edward, Lord Windsor, who died there in

1575, where 'his monument is still to be seen in the church of SS. Giovanni e Paolo.' Windsor was a friend of Cesare Caraffa, a Protestant member of the family of the uncompromising Paul IV. Sidney was acquainted with the Grimani, one of the exclusive families that provided the Republic with its Doges, and received courtesies from the Council of Ten. But he maintained a reserve, and was not impressed by 'all the magnificent magnificences of all these magnificos.' Young as he was, he was not taken in by external appearances and saw that there was a certain superficiality in all the show. 'Although some indeed be excellently learned, yet are they all given to so counterfeit learning as a man shall learn of them more false grounds of things than in any place else that I do know. For, from a tapster upwards, they are all discoursers. In fine, certain qualities – as horsemanship, weapons, vaulting and such like – are better there [Italy, in general] than in those other countries; for others, more sound, they do little excel nearer places.'

In short, the palm was passing to other countries; the inspiration Italy had communicated to Europe was becoming somewhat spent at home. Not, however, in the visual arts: Venice led in painting. When Languet insisted on having a portrait of him, to remind him of his presence, Sidney could hesitate between Tintoretto and Veronese, Titian being thought too old. The portrait was painted by Veronese, and carried by Shelley and Corbet to Languet in France, where it has been lost. For the rest, Sidney occupied himself, as always, profitably: he read books on Italian affairs, studying their politics and diplomacy, with special reference to Venice, to which the English felt a greater affinity, for its contemporary independence of Papal authority. He was also reading in Italian literature: the letters of Bembo, Bernardo Tasso, Lorenzo de' Medici; books of *imprese*, of which he became the most original expositor at Elizabeth's Court. He may have met Torquato Tasso, for whose poetry he had a high admiration – in this original, too, in a literary atmosphere dominated by Ariosto.

The effects of all this we shall see carried forward in Sidney's own work – of prime importance in the full English Renaissance, now about to burst into flower. We shall see others of these themes, here only suggested, taken up and treated more fully in their place.

With the sharpening of the conflict between Reformation and Counter-Reformation, the peninsula was shrinking to English Protestants. They could not go to Rome or the Spanish territories of the South. Thomas Wilson, who had begun his translation of

Demosthenes with Cheke at Padua in 1555 and pronounced the funeral oration over the unlucky Earl of Devon in 1556, was arrested in Rome as a heretic in 1558.[64] Thomas Sackville was imprisoned there in 1564.[65] Hoby had been an acquaintance of Sir Nicholas Throckmorton, who was in the Tower with William Thomas. When Throckmorton's son and heir, Arthur, went abroad in 1580–2 to equip himself for service to the state by learning languages, he could not go on to Rome and eventually had to fly even from Florence. Of course, the Throckmorton name was well known in Italy: Sir Nicholas had been a bosom-friend of Edward VI and, as Elizabeth's ambassador to France, an abettor of the Huguenots against the Catholic Guises; while his brother Michael had been the lifelong servant of Cardinal Pole.

Arthur Throckmorton's Diary gives a more detailed account of the process of a young Englishman's self-education in Italy, his tutors and what he paid them for teaching him Italian, singing and the lute, the books he bought, the company he kept.[66] It has the same significance as Hoby's: only now it is Neville's son, the diplomat to be; Henry Savile, to become so famous as a scholar later; a George Carew, a Spencer, a Ratcliffe, Thomas Leigh, William Ashby and John Pickering, Northamptonshire neighbours. In Florence Throckmorton made the acquaintance of Anthony Standen, Catholic exile and double agent; shortly after this Throckmorton and Pickering had to fly over the Alps: they had evidently been delated.

But with the 1580's we are at the flood-tide of England's own version of the Renaissance – crossed, and in some ways liberated, by the Reformation experience; while Italy was darkened – though by no means so wholly or without alleviation as Symonds and the Victorians thought – by the shadows of the Counter-Reformation.

CHAPTER II

THE COURT

THE Court was the effective point of contact with the Renaissance influences from abroad, diffused mainly through other Courts: these reflected the increasingly secular character of the age, in itself a mark of the Renaissance. But the Court was also the plane upon which the social life of the country was lifted and exposed, where one observes it at its highest concentration: the nerve-centre of society, government and cultural life. It was the world, the power, and the glory: we shall hope to exhibit it in each of these aspects.

We can observe, too, the dichotomy between Court and Country, the contrasts that everyone was aware of – the sophistication and elaboration of the one, the treacheries and duplicity, the flattery, 'Court incense', Court holy water' (such were the terms people thought in), as against the innocence and simplicity, the wholesomeness and naturalness of the other. They were less consciously aware of the fruitful, fertilising rhythms between the two: country nobles and gentry, coming to Court, went back to spread its culture and civilising standards, import something of its amenities and luxuries, into their localities, if also grumbling about its ruinous expense, its worldliness, its slippery ways, et cetera.

Peers had a right of personal access to the sovereign, who addressed them formally as 'cousin', though admission to the Presence naturally depended upon the sovereign's convenience or health, or the good behaviour of the peer in question. There were other privileges, too, attendant upon this status – apart from that of being summoned to Parliament – such as a certain freedom from scrutiny into their religious observances, (providing always that they made no trouble). The gentry had a right of access to the Court and availed themselves of it in numbers. It does not appear that there was such a freedom of entry for middle-class *bourgeois*. At any rate, in a society where people dressed according to their station, and courtiers would often 'carry whole estates upon their backs,' soberly dressed townsmen would be out of place upon the glittering scene. Even Lord Burghley – though he was the third generation of his family at Court – was conspicuous by the sobriety of his dress and demeanour, always carrying Cicero's *Offices* or a Prayer Book in his bosom or pocket.

Naturally the tone of the Court was set, very considerably, by the personality of the monarch. That of Urbino had been set by the scholarly gravity, the martial experience and cultivated interests of Duke Federico – with a further refinement, owing to the invalidism of his successor, Guidobaldo, when the Court was dominated by the latter's highly intellectual wife, Castiglione's Duchess. The Court of Henri III took the tone of his mingled credulity and scepticism, of sexual ambivalence and the treachery of despair; Henri IV's that of gallantry towards the ladies. What of Queen Elizabeth's Court? Since it was dominated by a woman it was one of greater refinement than her contemporaries', much less brutal, observing dignity and decorum, with considerable restraint upon those competitive and flighty temperaments. But there always had been much more ceremoniousness in the English Court than in the French. A French ambassador had been astonished to see the Princess Elizabeth on her knees three times before her father in the course of one audience. When she was Queen, anyone upon whom her eye lighted as she passed along in procession sank to his knees; when she spoke to him, she graciously raised him up. It was unthinkable that a Tudor monarch should go galloping round the streets, like the Valois brothers – according to L'Etoile – pelting the *bourgeois* of Paris with stones and knocking off their caps. It was Louis XIV who introduced a Spanish gravity and decorum into the ceremonial side of the French Court – and then it ceased to be popular.

The Court of the Virgin Queen naturally reflected others of her characteristics. Henri IV said that there were three things that nobody believed and yet were true: that the Archduke Albert was a good general, that he himself was a sincere Catholic, and that the Queen of England was a virgin. And yet this last fact, to anyone with any psychological perception, is an obvious key to her personality and much of her behaviour. She really had a prejudice against marriage – she frequently expressed herself in this vein to her maids-of-honour, though little good it did them.[1] Her objection to a married clergy was notorious: Bishop Cox of Ely received a rating for a second offence; her favourite Almoner, good-looking Bishop Fletcher, was completely cast off for marrying a young wife – and, shortly after, died; it was a constant recommendation to Archbishop Whitgift that he was celibate, her 'little black husband'. Not to be married was one royal road to her favour: Sir Christopher Hatton plodded consistently along it; Sir Walter Ralegh was very well so long as he kept to it; when she heard the news of Leicester's secret marriage to Lady Essex – of the man the Queen loved to the woman she detested – she threatened to send him to the Tower, until even his enemy, the Earl of Sussex, protested that a man should not be imprisoned for a lawful marriage. Widows had in a sense exculpated themselves by that fact; so the Queen was always kind to the Countess of Southampton, after the early demise of her obstreperous husband; the widowed Lady Warwick was the confidant of her last years. But unmarried Blanche Parry was closest to her, from her cradle for most of her life.

So marriage was apt to be troublesome to many of the gallants of the Court – to Leicester, Philip Sidney, Essex, Ralegh, Southampton, Pembroke, one after the other; and for the young ladies, hence many tears and troubles.

Still the Court was no place for Puritans: it talked the language of love and, as Ralegh complained later, the ageing maiden kept it up for far too long. Moreover, nobody was supposed to do anything about it. This imposed a strain. For the Court was not only worldly, but a place of worldly enjoyments, with constant music and dancing, plays, tilts, entertainments, games and cards, feasts, ceremonies – in all of which the Virgin Queen was the centre. It was also cultivated and even intellectual; there was a radiating interest in the arts and crafts, in painting and jewelry, languages and literature. Elizabeth herself was a good classical scholar; here Burghley could keep company with her – his intellectual interests were distinctly donnish, as were hers. The leading figures needed to be not only intelligent but well-read; several of them read Italian, Leicester for one, as also Hatton, Oxford, Sidney and Southampton; Ralegh, Egerton and others were great readers; many of them wrote verse, including the Queen.

Besides all this, and rather unrecognised, she was really a kind woman; there are unnumbered instances of her kindness. When all is said, she behaved far better to such people as Leicester, Ralegh, Essex (until the last move) than they behaved to her. The contrast is visible between her Court and her father's, between the power, the hardness and latent cruelty in the portraits of Henry VIII's circle, and the refinement and sensibility of those of his daughter's. The reserve in the faces painted by Holbein is reserve in the face of omnipresent danger, the reserve of fear. This is not present in Elizabethan Court-portraits: there was no fear for life, but an open-eyed civilised wariness. Behind Henry's one sees the law of the jungle; behind Elizabeth's, the slippery ladder of favour, the competitiveness, the exhibitionism encouraged at the top, a world of flattery, attentive to the ladies – in a Court ruled by a lady. In the end, Elizabeth's Court was – as Courts go – respectable; she had a hard task keeping it so.

With such a Court at such a time there was bound to be a cult of the monarch – such as Victorian historians little appreciated or understood: it must be seen in Renaissance terms against the background of the age. To this there must be added the special circumstances of Elizabeth's reign: as time stretched out, the length of her rule and what contemporaries regarded as its unique success. From the beginning to the end she was ever a courtier of her people, and there can be no doubt that she encouraged, indeed exacted, adulation. All this, the Queen well calculated, was an *instrumentum regni;* but to contemporaries she was unique, the last of her line, no-one of royal blood to share, let alone dispute, the limelight.

It was in the 1570's, in the second decade of her reign – after surmounting its worst crisis, the troubles of 1569–72, after the Papal excommunication and the Queen's recovery from smallpox brought home to people how much depended on her life – that the cult took shape. Her Accession Day, 17 November, began to be celebrated all over the country with bell-ringing and bonfires, feasts and sermons – and this was a spontaneous movement, not brought into being by any government legislation.[2] Indeed, such was its aura, that the day went on being celebrated long after her death, for more than a century. At the Court it came to be signalised by the famous Accession Day Tilts, and was an occasion for popular rejoicing: a secular feast grander than any of 'the Pope's holydays'. All this reached its apogee in the 1580's, along with everything else.

Spenser has been happily described as 'the Virgil of the Elizabethan golden age, and the *Faerie Queene* its great epic poem.'[3] This was its conscious intention, and it was offered as such: 'To the most high, mighty and magnificent Empress, renowned for piety, virtue and all gracious government, Elizabeth, by the grace of God, Queen of England, France, and Ireland, and of Virginia, Defender of the Faith, etc., her most humble servant Edmund Spenser doth, in all humility, dedicate, present, and consecrate these his labours, to live with the eternity of her fame.' He proved

33

to have spoken well: poets are the best prophets. The whole poem is pivoted on the personality of the Queen; not only does she come into it again and again, a *faux-bourdon* helping to draw the wandering spaces together – like the musical *motifs* in Proust – but from the beginning, according to the author's Letter to Ralegh, it was the keystone of the aesthetic intention. 'In that Fairy Queen I mean glory in my general intention, but in my particular I conceive the most excellent and glorious person of our sovereign the Queen, and her kingdom in Fairy land. And yet in some places else, I do otherwise shadow her. For considering she beareth two persons, the one of a most royal Queen or Empress, the other of a most virtuous and beautiful lady, this latter part in some places I do express in Belphoebe, fashioning her name according to your own excellent conceit of Cynthia – Phoebe and Cynthia being both names of Diana.' In other words, there is the ruler and there is the woman. From what Spenser goes on to say we know that the poem was conceived in relation to the Queen's annual feast, though this was to feature in the last book, the twelfth, which he did not live to reach.

As ruler she bears several names, according to which aspect of her personality her followers wish to emphasise. To Ralegh, she is always Cynthia, the chaste goddess, whom he adores – in vain. An aged countryman in Dekker's *Old Fortunatus* says: 'Some call her Pandora, some Gloriana, some Cynthia, some Belphoebe, some Astraea: all by several names to express several loves. Yet all those names make but one celestial body, as all those loves meet to create but one soul.' To which the other old man replies: 'I am of her own country, and we adore her by the name of Eliza.'

To describe her rule the concept of Astraea was much invoked – and this appears in the *Faerie Queen*, along with (almost) everything else. In ancient myth, the reign of Saturn was the golden age; it was succeeded by the age of silver, then of brass, and at last by the iron age (in which we live) when evil forces got out of control, men ravished the earth for metals and laid waste the planet with war. The Virgin goddess, Astraea, left the ruined world. But Virgil saw in the Augustan peace her return to the earth and the renewal of the golden age:

Iam redit et virgo, redeunt Saturnia regna.

This was consciously applied to Elizabeth's good rule, its justice and clemency, from quite early on – in contrast to the gloomy tragedy of Mary's reign. And not only by her own subjects: when

Catherine de Medici called on Ronsard to dedicate his *Élégies, Mascarades et Bergeries* to Elizabeth, he placed at the head a Merlin prophecy:

> Et l'age d'or voirra de toutes pars
> Fleurir le liz entre les Léopars . . .

while as for Elizabeth:

> Elle rendra son pais honoré
> Par la vertu du beau siècle doré
> Qui florira sous sa riche couronne . . .[4]

The Renaissance itself echoed the idea of the rebirth of a golden age, and Astraea was associated with the concept of right rule, of clemency and justice – Spenser's celebration of it appears in his Book V, which treats of Justice. Peele used the myth for a Lord Mayor's pageant in 1591:

> Conduct thy learnèd company to Court,
> Eliza's Court, Astraea's earthly heaven . . .

Harington, in translating the relevant passage in Ariosto, pointedly adapted it to her circumstances. Sir John Davies devoted a whole volume to the theme, *Hymns of Astraea*, in 1599; twenty-six poems in fifteen-lined acrostic verse, in which the first letters of each line, read downwards, read Elizabetha Regina.

> But whereto shall we bend our lays?
> Even up to Heaven, again to raise
> The Maid which, thence descended,
> Hath brought again the golden days
> And all the world amended.

Justice was the key to her rule, and Hymn XXIII is devoted to this theme:

> Exiled Astraea is come again,
> Lo, here she doth all things maintain
> In number, weight, and measure . . .
>
> By Love she rules more than by Law,
> Even her great mercy breedeth awe:
> This is her sword and spectre;
> Herewith she hearts did ever draw,
> And this guard ever kept here.
>
> In her left hand, wherein should be
> Nought but the sword, sits Clemency . . .

Where can one see this vision?

> Empress of flowers, tell where away
> Lies your sweet Court this merry May,
> In Greenwich garden alleys?
> Since there the heavenly powers do play
> And haunt no other valleys.

There were not wanting Puritans, of course, who thought all this rather nonsense, and possibly ungodly; but when did they have either imagination or taste?

The prefatory Sonnets to the *Faerie Queene* offer us a gallery of portraits of the leading figures at Court, just as it stood in the year after the Armada – for its chief luminary, Leicester, had died in the late summer of 1588, to the Queen's inexpressible grief. There they all are, beginning with Hatton as Lord Chancellor:

> that with your counsel sway
> The burden of this kingdom mightily,
> With like delights sometimes may eke delay
> The rugged brow of careful policy . . .

These verses remind us that Hatton was by no means the lightweight he has often been thought to be; he was a middle-of-the-road man, no factious partisan, prudent and loyal – even if he did owe his favour with the Queen originally to his handsome face and fine figure dancing, a young Inner Temple lawyer, in a mask at Court.

Spenser next promises to bring Essex – who had succeeded Leicester as Master of the Horse – into his last books and sing his heroic parts, but of course never got as far. Oxford is celebrated for 'th'antique glory of thine ancestry'. He is followed by Northumberland and Irish Ormonde, whose country 'through long wars left almost waste, With brutish barbarism is overspread.' Lord Grey of Wilton, Lord Deputy there, was 'the pillar of my life, And patron of my Muse's pupillage', and incidentally the Artegal of Book V. Lord Admiral Howard was the Queen's cousin, who chased 'those huge castles of Castilian king . . . like flying doves.' Ralegh's close association with the inception of the *Faerie Queene* and the presentation of its author at Court is well-known: 'Thy sovereign goddess's most dear delight'; until Ralegh will make known his poem to Cynthia, let Spenser sing her praises. Next comes Burghley,

> On whose mighty shoulders most doth rest
> The burden of this kingdom's government.

Then Cumberland, 'the flower of chivalry'; Hunsdon, first cousin to the Queen, and her Lord Chamberlain – as such responsible for the conduct of the Court; Buckhurst, as Sackville best of the earlier poets of the reign, part-author of *Gorboduc*, now a privy councillor and on his way to become Lord Treasurer:

> Whose learnèd Muse hath writ her own record
> In golden verse . . .

There follow Walsingham, Secretary of State, who here is celebrated as 'the great Maecenas of this age'; and Sir John Norris, the famous soldier 'Black John Norris', its 'honour, And Precedent of all that arms ensue'.

Then comes the Countess of Pembroke, sister of Sir Philip Sidney, the figure most missed from all that assembly, recently dead at Zutphen, never forgotten by any of them:

> Remembrance of that most heroic spirit,
>   The heaven's pride, the glory of our days,
>   Which now triumpheth, crowned with lasting bays
> Of heavenly bliss and everlasting praise . . .
> His goodly image, living evermore
>   In the divine resemblance of your face . . .

The gallery concludes with a portrait of Lady Carew, the Queen's intimate attendant. The last Sonnet is dedicated 'To all the gracious and beautiful ladies in the Court.'

There are all these figures summoned up for us, just as they were in 1589, enforcing from the first the poem's symbolic importance, an English work to challenge a place in European literature beside Ariosto, or even fulfilling something of the function of an English *Aeneid*. It received official recognition as such by the award to Spenser of a pension, in February 1591.

The most conspicuous public expression of the cult was the Accession Day Tilts, for which the Court usually returned to Whitehall from the country early in November, the entry accompanied by bell-ringing, formalities, a crowd from the City. At Whitehall was a large tilt-yard that ran down the western side of the highway between the two gateways – the 'Holbein' gate at the northern end and the inner one at the other – where took place the 'annually enacted romance of chivalry of which the Queen was the heroine.'[5] There was plenty of room for the public, though admission cost the relatively high price of 12d, which must have restricted the spectators to the well-to-do classes. The Queen herself looked down on the proceedings from a window in a gallery, with her attendants.

The courtier responsible for organising these annual tournaments and bringing them to their perfection was Sir Henry Lee.[6] He came of a Buckinghamshire family, the Lees of Quarrendon, whose fortunes had been made by Lee's grandfather under Henry VIII, to whom Robert Lee was gentleman-usher of the Chamber. This enabled him to amass estates in his county and add to his wealth by sheep-farming. His son succeeded him at Court and married a sister of Sir Thomas Wyatt the elder. Young Henry was married to a daughter of Lord Paget, a melancholy woman whose children died in infancy: one sees her kneeling with them on her monument in Aylesbury church. It was the custom there to place a crimson flower before them, or in winter a bunch of red berries: a charming fancy. As a young man Lee did the grand tour through Germany to Italy, and in Antwerp had a portrait of himself painted by Antony Mor.

From 1570 he was well-established at Court, a fine figure of a man, 'a strong and valiant person', the best tilter of them all. Made Ranger of the royal park at Woodstock, Lee invented a romantic entertainment for the Queen's visit on her summer progress to Kenilworth in 1575. It was a contest between knights for the love of a lady, with speeches, poems – probably written by another tilting courtier, Sir Edward Dyer – a banquet *al fresco* under the summer foliage. Next Christmas Gascoigne wrote up the tale, the whole thing like the timeless tournaments of Sidney's *Arcadia*.

These tilts became highly organised affairs, with the leading figures at Court taking part in them and enacting a theme, with their attendants dressed to represent it, themselves exhibiting their *imprese* painted on shields. In 1613 Burbage painted the Earl of Rutland's *impresa* in gold and Shakespeare wrote the words; at that tilt some of the imprese were so dark 'that their meaning is not yet understood, unless perchance that were their meaning, not to be understood.'[7] All tended to the glorification of the Virgin Queen; it helped to build up the mythology of the age – people take to myths rather than truths to feed their minds on – it took something of the place of the pageantry the Church had previously provided, and turned it to secular, monarchical uses.

Speeches and music were also part of the entertainment; sometimes books of the show were presented. A book of Lee's devices for the tilts exists, unpublished; we have the designs for his splendid white and gold armour. He himself was appropriately made Master of the Armoury at the Tower, and in 1597 a knight of the Garter. By this time, with advancing years, he had retired from running the Tilts, but became 'a great Garter knight' – the processions of the Order of the Garter forming another contribution, in April, to the secular ceremonial of the age. Of that we have a full-length roll portraying it, by Thomas Lant, the herald who executed the celebrated roll portraying the funeral of Sir Philip Sidney. Sidney, too, had been a figure in these tilts – they had their part in the making of *Arcadia*; at Accession Day, in 1586 after his death, a riderless 'mourning horse' formed part of the pageant in remembrance of him.

Four years later, at the Tilt of 1590, Lee retired, leading his successor, the privateering Earl of Cumberland, to the foot of the stairs to the gallery whence the Queen and her ladies watched. Suddenly music was heard, 'so sweet and secret as everyone thereat greatly marvelled. And hearkening to that excellent melody, the earth as it were opening, there appeared a pavilion made of white taffeta . . . like unto the sacred temple of the Virgins Vestal.'[8] Lights burned within, and Latin verses upon a pillar celebrated the Vestal Virgin's empire extending beyond the Pillars of Hercules to the New World. It was, of course, propaganda, but what a way of making propaganda the Renaissance had! The theme was appropriate for the dedicated sea-rover. The familiar Hilliard portrait depicts him in fantastic tilting-armour, black and gold, full-skirted cassock, holding long lance upright, carrying in his hat the glove which the Queen had dropped and he had captured.

And how did she occupy herself on these occasions?

With politics, of course. We have a revealing close-up of her at the Accession Day Tilt in 1595, from the pen of the Dutch envoy, Noel de Caron.[9] Essex was the principal organiser of the Tilt; Caron was his guest. All the ladies and gentlemen of the Court were present at the spectacle, where at her window the Queen sat with only Lord Admiral Howard and Lord Chamberlain Hunsdon. Inviting the Dutch envoy to sit with her, she took the opportunity to converse with him all the afternoon on affairs of state. She was in good spirits, much pleased by the immense throng that had gathered below in thousands – there had never been so many. She beamed down upon them, smiling and giving them thanks for their good wishes. To the knights who were jousting she occasionally called out encouraging remarks; but in the intervals her mind was directed to the business in hand. She asked if the Dutch towns were well populated. Caron said, better than ever. She wondered if the people there were poor, through continual war and high prices. Caron said not – they were better off than the Spanish Netherlands. The Queen asked, what about the arrival of the Cardinal Archduke? She told Caron that he had left Genoa with a large suite and some 8,000 men, besides treasure. She commented that there was a marked difference between the Cardinal Archduke Albert and Archduke Ernest, whom he had succeeded, on account of their different upbringings: the latter in Germany and therefore more sluggish, the former in Spain, more malign and obstinate. She was afraid that the Archduke Albert would do the Dutch more harm. She inquired, what was the character of the Prince of Orange (i.e. young Philip William, who had been kidnapped and brought up as a Catholic)? The previous evening she had received letters of submission from Tyrone, admitting that he had had communications with the Spaniards – for which she had been unwilling to pardon him; now, on his submission, she might. She asked for information about the Dutch ships arrested by the Spaniards: had they been released? She confessed herself disturbed by the prospects of Henri IV's reconciliation with Rome and its effects: she wondered whether he might turn against the Huguenots.

Essex's device for the Tilt that day was much commended: it was all about love for his sovereign, and led up to the conclusion that he would never forsake his Mistress. At the end of the tiring day, 'the Queen said that if she had thought there had been so much said of her, she would not have been there that night; and so went to bed.'[10] One can see what the woman behind the public image really thought.

Plenty has been written about the organisation of the Household and the Court; here we are concerned not with organisation but the life. It so happens that there is very full documentation for Elizabeth's life, so that we know her intimately, the first of English monarch's of whom this can be said – in that also marking the transition to modern times. We can follow her even into the Privy Chamber, where the most secret transactions took place. Within that was the Bedchamber, where her ladies waited upon her, though even here there was no real privacy for a monarch. Outside this innermost cell of the hive – where the queen-bee lay, but active and watchful – was the Presence Chamber, open to those officials who had the *entrée* or others who were admitted for an audience or with business to transact, suits to present. This last was the pest of her life: she hated 'importunity and expostulation', with everyone for ever trying to get something out of her. (She once referred to the 'insatiable cupidity of men', fairly enough.) Outside the Presence Chamber was a gallery, in which all the Court walked and talked, and transacted *its* business. Something of this order of apartments, with its functional arrangement, not only existed in all the royal palaces, Whitehall, Greenwich, Nonsuch (her favourite), Hampton Court (which she liked least, after falling ill of small pox there), but was reconstituted in the great houses she visited, Theobalds, Burghley, Wanstead, Kenilworth, for the convenience of Court business. Nor was it essentially different from the arrangements of the French Court.*

Here she is at work, in January 1597, when the temporary alliance of Essex, Robert Cecil and Ralegh enabled them to press the Islands Voyage upon her. The Queen was mourning the death of her faithful Blanche Parry – to whom she gave the funeral of a baroness: we see Blanche upon her monument in the remote church of Bacton in Herefordshire, kneeling before her mistress in full regal panoply. Sir John Stanhope reports to Cecil: 'I found her Majesty and the Lords closed up in the Privy Chamber till it was candlelight. Since, she is at rest, attended by my Lady Scrope.'[11] A few days later: 'I left the Queen at six very quiet and, as I guess, will not stir till very late; but I will attend the time and present it [more business], if she do but breathe a little while afore her going to bed.'

That summer she wept with joy to hear that Essex was safe from the storms that raged in the Atlantic – but was less pleased at the return of the expedition, having accomplished nothing for all the money and care spent upon it. In September she was ill, but raised her spirits to hear better news. Hunsdon reported, 'it did nothing content me to find her hands so burning hot, her complaint of distemperature in all parts, with the feeling of a soreness in her body, back, and legs: which I pray God be no beginning to the fit of an ague.'[12] Recovered, we find her laughing at old Burghley's describing himself in a letter of apology for absence as her 'slender servant' – in Elizabethan English that has the double meaning of our word 'slim', and Burghley was slim in

* Nor was the spirit, perhaps we may add; cf. E. Balmas, ed. *Etienne Jodelle: Œuvres Complètes*, I. 23. 'Mais la cour, miroir des grandeurs et des vanités humaines, sollicite également, chez lui qui se propose de la conquérir, des raffinements plus subtils, qui débordent de l'esthétique vers la morale . . . C'est plus qu'une comédie, c'est une vraie discipline que d'apprendre à se glisser dans les bonnes grâces des puissants.'

both senses. Michael Hicks, Cecil's secretary, records for us a charming scene at Theobalds that summer. Francis Bacon and a couple of others had been there with the old man on business from the Court of Wards. 'They be all gone since dinner, and now we be alone: my lord under a tree in the walks with a book in his hand to keep him from sleeping [Burghley allowed himself very little sleep], and we ready to take the bowls into our hands but that the weather is somewhat too warm yet.'[13]

The constant badgering for suits was the occupational disease of a Court – we remember Queen Mab:

> Sometimes she gallops o'er a courtier's nose,
> And then dreams he of smelling out a suit.

How the Queen, and others, reacted we may read at large in the fascinating correspondence of Rowland Whyte, agent at Court for Sir Robert Sidney, Governor of Flushing. One had, above all, to watch one's opportunity, get one of the Queen's attendants, suitably primed with presents, to intercede. Sidney wanted the Wardenship of the Cinque Ports. On a Sunday afternoon in March 1597, 'Lady Scudamore got the Queen to read your letter . . . "Do you not know the contents of it?", said the Queen. "No, madam," said she; when her Majesty said, "Here is much ado about the Cinque Ports." I demanded of my Lady Scudamore what she observed in her Majesty while she was a-reading of it; who said that she read it all over with two or three Poohs.'[14] Robert Sidney did not get the Cinque Ports: she thought him 'too young and, being Governor of Flushing, could not be present to answer every sudden danger of the Ports.'

Meanwhile Sidney was pressing the government for further supplies, munitions and victual for Flushing. Rowland Whyte reports, 'I showed myself upon Monday morning to my Lord Treasurer, who gave me a nod, and commanded me to be with him in the afternoon. When he had dined I was called in.' Burghley said that he had reported the points of Sidney's long letters to the Queen, who commanded that they should be considered by the Council: she was willing to send over gunpowder, but the previous allowances had been too large and exceeded those for Brill and other places. 'My answer was that his lordship might reform it as pleased him. "As please me?", said he; "Nay as please the Queen, I tell thee." "Then," quoth I, "be it as please the Queen and your lordship." '[15]

Then, somewhat inappropriately, Sidney wanted leave to return to England to attend to family affairs. Whyte got the Lord Admiral to speak up on his behalf. ' "Those six weeks you speak of would be six months," said the Queen, "and I will not have him away when the Cardinal [Archduke Albert] comes there".'[16] Nevertheless Whyte went on lobbying on behalf of his master. Lady Huntingdon protested 'no prince could use better words than the Queen of you. But I told her, "While the grass grows the horse starves"; you saw others graced and your desire for leave for one month only refused.' After that, Whyte 'found a fear in her [Lady Huntingdon] to speak for you.' Essex, himself in growing disfavour, and deservedly, could do no good; the Queen thought that, for a soldier, Sidney was too much addicted to the Presence Chamber. Next Lady Warwick was approached, who reported that 'the Queen says that your entertainment in Flushing is so good as you may put all your own in your purse, and that you received for yourself £1500 or £1600 a year.' Then Essex informed Whyte that the Queen had read Sidney's discourse about the needs of Flushing and put it in her pocket; her view was that 'Flushing was not besieged, therefore could not be in so great danger as you made it . . . That you governors were never well but when you drew her to unnecessary charges.' She took the view that the needs of Flushing might be supplied by the Dutch. In the end, in October, when danger was over, Sidney got his leave, though even so there was trouble about the deputy who would take his place. Of the two named, Sir Matthew Morgan and Captain Goring, 'the Queen cannot abide the first, therefore he must not be named to her. For the second he is held a sufficient man.' So back the matter went to her: Robert Cecil's advice was that Sidney should himself write her a letter not above twenty-two lines, and he would deliver it if no-one else would; but it would be better if Sir John Stanhope did it.

Here we see her in action; but in the course of the long campaign we get various personal side-lights. She was extremely sensitive to smell, and an unfortunate French envoy, M. de Reaulx, suffered from halitosis. 'Good God!,' said she, 'what shall I do if this man stay here, for I smell him an hour after he is gone from me.'[17] This unhappily came to the poor man's ears before he left the country: 'it is indeed confirmed here by divers that he had a loathsome breath.' The exchange between her and the famous soldier, Sir Roger Williams, is well known. 'Faugh, Williams, your boots stink,' she said; 'No, madam,' he replied, 'it is my suit that stinks.' But one comes across many instances of her kindness and consideration. She intervened personally to prevent Lady Corn-wallis, a Catholic, from being molested for not attending church: she was to have liberty of conscience.[18] We find her weeping over Burghley's last illness, going to attend him and feed him from her own hands; she was for long inconsolable after his death. Lord Sheffield thought how difficult it was to fit her humour;[19] but good behaviour was one clue, and faithful service was another. She honoured her fighting men, noticeably soldiers, like Norris, Vere and Mountjoy; and she took a matriarchal interest in the well-being of her peers, one aspect of her conservative concern for the social order. She intervened – it is one such instance out of many – with the Dowager Marchioness of Winchester not to leave her estate away from her son and heir: it would 'blemish her own time of government to allow a great house to be overthrown.'[20] She laboured hard to keep that impossible couple, the Earl of Shrewsbury and his termagant wife, Bess of Hardwick, together – setting such a bad example in their prominent station, she con-sidered. In these last years Essex, whom she had spoiled, gave her constant unhappiness. Once, when his cousin presented her with a letter of submission from him, she was 'exceedingly pleased with it'; but when pressed to restore him to favour – (which he would at once abuse) – she 'answered never a word, but sighed and said it was so, and rose and went into the Privy Chamber.'[21] Alas, poor woman!

Then there were the ladies who formed her background, the older ones who were companions and the young maids of honour who were attendants. In her Court the ladies were naturally to the fore: she had fewer males in close attendance than her father or even her sister – women took their place. In earlier days, those of her long flirtatious affair with Leicester, she had taken a foremost hand herself in the game of Court love, 'the ordinary infection of this place', as Rowland Whyte described it. Gilbert Talbot reported to his father in May 1573: 'my Lord Leicester is very much with her Majesty, and she shows the same great good affection to him that she was wont; of late he has endeavoured to please her more than heretofore. There are two sisters now in the Court that are very far in love with him, as they have been long, my Lady Sheffield and Frances Howard.'[22] With the first of these, with whom he cohabited, Leicester entered into some contract which did not apparently amount to marriage, so that his son by her, Sir Robert Dudley, could never establish legitimacy. These two sisters, 'of like striving who shall love him better, are at great wars together, and the Queen thinketh not well of them, and not the better of him. By this means there are spies over him.' But we see how irresistible he was to women.

Trouble arose when people could not keep to the rules of the game, as ordinary flesh and blood often could not: Elizabeth could – but she had had fearful warnings in the deaths of her mother and her cousin, Catherine Howard, and in the lives of her sister and Mary Stuart. In 1573 Elizabeth was taking up the intelligent and attractive young Earl of Oxford: 'the Queen's Majesty delighteth more in his personage, and his dancing, and valiantness, than any other. My Lady Burghley unwisely has declared herself, as it were jealous, which is come to the Queen's ear: whereat she has been not a little offended with her, but now she is reconciled again.' This does not mean that the blue-stocking Lady Burghley was jealous in the modern sense, but simply that she did not approve: after all the Cecils wanted the handsome young Earl for their daughter – and very miserable he made her. 'At all these love matters my Lord Treasurer winketh, and will not meddle any way . . . Even after the old manner [he] dealeth with matters of the state only, and beareth himself very uprightly.'

Leicester's irreparable, if secret, marriage to Lettice Knollys, Lady Essex, when the Queen learned of it, made a break. Elizabeth's feelings for her beautiful and brazen cousin may be imagined when she became Leicester's wife. Essex's mother, she was last received at Court in March 1598, when her son was staggering to his certain end. Involved in her son's disgrace by her incitement of him, she vigorously intrigued for an audience with the Queen, lying in wait with a jewel worth £300 where Elizabeth was expected in her coach at the Tilt End; but 'the Queen found occasion not to come'.[23] At Essex's submission and return to Court his mother was received, 'kissed the Queen's hands and her breast, and did embrace her, and the Queen kissed her.' A week later she departed from Court, but, 'desiring again to kiss the Queen's hands [a mark of favour], was denied.' Lady Leicester was a woman who would not take even Yes for an answer.

Conscious of her innocence, the ageing spinster could act coquettishly with the men. In May 1578 Gilbert Talbot was walking below the gallery whence the Queen usually viewed the Tilt. It was morning and she was looking out of the window: 'my eye was full towards her; she showed to be greatly ashamed thereof, for that she was unready and in her nightstuff. So, when she saw me at after dinner as she went to walk, she gave me a great fillip on the forehead, and told the Lord Chamberlain, who was the next to her, how I had seen her that morning, and how much ashamed thereof she was.'[24] Indeed, she described herself as 'no morning woman' – for the transaction of business, etc.[25] Simpler souls found her exciting. In 1600, when she was sixty-seven, a mad sailor wrote her a passionate love-letter and drew out his dagger in the Presence Chamber; he proved incredibly strong and broke all the manacles they put on him in Bedlam.[26] Dr. Forman, the astrologer, with whom the unconscious was very active and excitable, had erotic dreams about the Queen. Truly, the cult of love had its limitations.

An unpublished volume in the British Museum brings us very close to her charms in describing the dresses she wore, their making and her domestic interior.[27] In the 1570's she was not so flamboyant as she later became with age and fame: she seems to have fancied black velvet turned out with white satin, with splashes of colour. 'Walter Fish, our tailor' – the Norman Hartnell of the day – alters 'a Flanders gown of black velvet faced with blue taffeta, with black taffeta'; he enlarges 'a forepart of black velvet with a guard embroidered with black and white silk . . . and a Spanish sleeve for a gown of black velvet, the sleeve lined with white taffeta.' A Flanders gown of black velvet was embroidered all over with black satin, the vents (i.e. openings) and sleeves were of lawn striped with purple silk and gold – we recognise this kind of dress in the pictures of the time. A black velvet gown of the 'Polony' fashion was lengthened; a 'pair of bodice' of changeable (i.e. shot) taffeta and a veil of white striped lawn made. A French gown of black velvet has 'a guard embroidered with gold and silver, the gown lined with crimson sarcenet, the pleats lined about with buckram [to keep them stiff] and the vents with frieze, with vents of fustian in the bodice and a roll of cotton.' Double bodices were of the Italian fashion; a pair went with a French gown 'lined with three broad guards of white satin and three broad laces of gold and silver laid upon the guards and six narrow laces by the edges, the gown cut between the guards and turned in, all the bodice cut and lined underneath with narrow gold sarcenet, the gown lined with orange-coloured sarcenet, the pleats lined with buckram, vents of fustian and frise in the ruffs.' This combination of colours must have been attractive with her hair still red-gold then; later she wore a wig.

The embellishments were more brilliant: foreparts of 'tissue with a wreath of satin and two gold laces lined with white sarcenet;

petticoats of cloth of silver bordered with gold, the bodices of
crimson satin lined with crimson sarcenet – the material for the
petticoats coming out of the store in Blanche Parry's charge, the
rest from the Great Wardrobe. The kirtle was the flowing outer
garment open in front to reveal the gown. All the ten kirtles made
in this six-monthly period were French: black cypress lined with
murrey (i.e. mulberry) taffeta, sleeves drawn out with murrey
sarcenet and black lawn striped with silver, ruffs lined with frieze.
Farthingales were a Spanish fashion coming in: John Bate,
'verthingale maker', translates a 'verthingale of white and crimson
taffeta laced with bent ropes to it at two several times', and makes
another of 'black buckram with kersey and bent ropes'. They
grew upon her and achieved a fantastic peacock-spread in course
of time. Adam Bland, 'our skinner', furred a russet satin French
gown with four 'luzarne' (i.e. lynx) skins, mended a pair of sables,
but was mainly employed upon mending gowns and collars with
the same. The Queen's cloak-bag was of black velvet striped all
over with lace and lined with black satin. Her Parliament robes
were kept at the Tower; payments are made for mending coronation and Parliament robes 'with two timber of powdered ermines';
six lb of powder – one lb per month – were employed on these
robes, with 'one load of coals to air our apparel within our Tower
of London.'

Henry Herne, the hosier, made seven pair of cloth hose and
four pair of double linen hose in the period – the former would be
stockings, the latter drawers; evidently Italian silk stockings had
not yet come in. Garrett Johnston, 'our shoemaker', made 'eighteen
pairs of velvet shoes, stitched with silk, lined with satin and in the
soles with scarlet; six pair of velvet pantofles [slippers] lined with
Spanish leather; three pairs of velvet slippers lined with scarlet.'
He translated eight pairs of 'shoes with velvet to perform them in
the heels, and one pair of buskins [long boots reaching to calf or
knee for riding] with velvet and satin.' Such was the rate of
production of clothes and shoes from six months to six months: it
looks as if the Queen wore a new pair of shoes every week, they
then went to the ladies in waiting. The Accounts of the Chamber
were made up every six months: sometimes the consumption of
shoes was slightly larger, or we find two pairs of buskins or two
pairs of Spanish leather shoes called for for outdoor wear.

The Queen's great bearing sword – that was borne before her
on formal occasions and in procession – was regularly burnished
and garnished with silver, once it is given a new scabbard. Over

fifty ells each of holland and white canvas were for sheets, with coarse canvas for bags to carry them, for after a couple of months the Court moved on its round from Whitehall to Richmond, Greenwich, Oatlands, Nonsuch, Hampton Court or Windsor. The wheelwright is paid for 'mending our close car'. There is a 'large counterpoint [counterpane] of tapestry or verdure', and curtain rings, evidently for the Queen's bed. In 1569 the coffer-maker makes a screen covered with green velvet and taffeta, fringed with silk and ribbons, and 'four small coffers covered with leather . . . with locks, joints and handles to them: to put in certain letters in the custody of Sir William Cecil, knight, our principal secretary.' Shortly after two great coffers with locks are necessary for his papers.

Presents to various people appear: a very rich robe and kirtle sent to 'our most dear brother the Emperor' (Ferdinand), cassocks of silk and gold, and a cushion with gold fringe; in 1568 sixteen yards of black velvet, sixteen yards of black satin, and ten yards of black taffeta, for 'the Queen of Scots'; a robe of purple velvet, in 1579, for 'our dear cousin Duke Casimir'; a gown of Watchet cloth of silver, in 1577, for Mary, Countess of Pembroke – she had been given a gown before as Mary Sidney. There are gowns and kirtles for the maids of honour, for Dorothy Habington, Elizabeth Marbery and Elizabeth Stafford, 'our chamberers', who slept in the Queen's bedchamber; outfits of clothes for Anne Knollys, Elizabeth and Katherine Knyvet. Lady Cobham made the Queen's mufflers and Lady Carew her hoods for years; sometimes we hear of a mantle with long train.

Among the most interesting entries are those for her dwarfs. Dwarfs were an especial accompaniment of royalty, as we are reminded by Velasquez – and the cult seems to have spread from the Spanish Court. During the 1560's and 1570's the Queen had a dwarf, Ippolita the Tartarian, 'our dearly beloved woman', whose cassocks were furred with black coney skins. She was succeeded by Thomasina, very richly dressed all through the 1580's; her sister was named Prudence de Paris. The Queen also had a little blackamoor for whom, in 1574, a gaskin coat was made of white taffeta with gold tinsel, and a pair of gaskin trowsers. This means loose-fitting and wide, as the cleric Harrison reminds us in disapproving of women wearing 'galligaskins to bear out their bums and make their attire to fit plum round (as they term it) about them.'[28] The footman of the Privy Chamber in her later years was an Italian, 'Mr. Ferdinando'; she kept over many years

an Italian jester, named Monarcho, or 'the Monarch', for whom
rich clothes were provided: a gown of red grogram chamlet, with
a hat of blue taffeta, or a gown of blue damask; a gown of rich
stuff, copper gold, or of gold tinsel with yellow velvet laid on with
lace. She had an English fool, too, William Shenton, less gor-
geously clad. Monarcho was known outside at the time; in *Love's
Labour's Lost* – which comes close to the Court through its relation-
ship to the Southampton circle – Boyet describes Armado as

> A phantasm, a Monarcho, and one that makes sport
> To the Prince.

We need not suppose that to pick up that, Shakespeare penetrated
into the Privy Chamber.

Denizens of these private apartments, the innermost cell,
providing a décor for the queen-bee, were the maids of honour.
Theirs was a very privileged position: that much is indicated by
the fact that so many of them – Howards, Hunsdons, Knollys –
were the Queen's relations on the Boleyn side. Some-one referred
to them as 'the tribe of Dan', the favoured, for whom the best
things were reserved. How acutely the privilege was valued is
witnessed by the eager competition there was for a place. In the
Throckmorton Diary one descries the pains young Arthur
Throckmorton took, the lobbying and petitioning, to get his sister
Elizabeth into the position: it was her only fortune, and she
proceeded to make the most of it.[29] She captured the Queen's own
young man, Ralegh – he must have been in love with her, or he
would never have married her. The post gave the maids a conspicuous, possibly a strategic, position in the marriage-market. It was
for this that a hopeful father was prepared to lay out £1300 on his
daughter in the Queen's service, as Lady Denny afterwards said
her father had done; on her husband's death, leaving her poorly
off, the Queen awarded her a pension.[30] It is not true that Elizabeth was miserly, as her grandfather, Henry VII, was – merely
careful and provident.

The Queen was in the position of a foster-mother to these
young ladies: hence her constant scrutiny of their conduct of
themselves. She liked to watch them dancing and herself took part
in it, almost to the end. In June 1600, after attending the marriage
of her maid-of-honour, Anne Russell, the Queen supped at Lord
Cobham's. 'After supper the mask came in, and delicate it was to
see eight ladies so prettily and richly attired. Mistress Fitton led,
and after they had done all their own ceremonies, these eight lady

maskers chose eight ladies more to dance the measures. Mistress Fitton went to the Queen, and wooed her to dance; her Majesty asked what she was. "Affection," she said. "Affection!", said the Queen, "Affection is false." Yet her Majesty rose and danced.'[31] She shared in their music, they played the lute, she performed on the virginals – one of her instruments, elaborately decorated, still remains in the Victoria and Albert Museum. One gets the impression that the young ladies were rather at a loose end, hence their troubles, and the trouble they gave their mistress. They were not expected to outshine the Queen. Her godson, Sir John Harington, has a story of young Lady Mary Howard arraying herself in a velvet dress, powdered with gold and pearls, which everybody envied. 'Nor did it please the Queen, who thought it exceeded her own. One day the Queen did send privately and got the lady's rich vesture, which she put on herself and came forth the Chamber among the ladies. The kirtle and border were far too short for her Majesty's height, and she asked everyone how they liked her new-fancied suit. At length she asked the owner herself if it was not made too short and ill-becoming? Which the poor lady did presently [i.e. immediately] consent to. "Why then, if it become not me as being too short, I am minded it shall never become thee as being too fine: so it fitteth neither well".'[32] When Lady Catherine Howard came to Court in 1599 and was 'sworn of the Privy Chamber' – the girls took an oath of service – the comment was made that this 'greatly strengthens that party.'[33] This aspect of the matter, I suspect, was rather exaggerated: the Queen had a mind of her own; nevertheless her confidants among the older ladies were particularly well placed for forwarding people's suits.

In April 1597 there was a storm in the Chamber. 'The Queen hath of late used the fair Mistress Bridges with words and blows of anger, and she with Mistress Russell were put out of the Coffer Chamber. They lay three nights at my Lady Stafford's, but are now returned again to their wonted waiting. By what I writ to you in my last letter unto you by post, you may conjecture whence these storms rise. The cause of this displeasure said to be their taking of physic, and one day going privately through the Privy Gallery to see the playing at ballon.'[34] There was more in it than that: Essex was playing round with Mistress Bridges. Early next year we learn, 'it is spied out by envy that 1000 [Essex] is again fallen in love with his fairest B. It cannot choose but come to 1500 [the Queen's] ears; then he is undone, and all they that depend upon his favour.' However, the fair Bridges survived Essex's catastrophe, and on James's accession found safe harbour in marrying a Scot, Sir John Kennedy.[35]

Mary Fitton was less lucky; here is her true story – as against all the nonsense that has been written about her. She was the daughter of a Cheshire knight of good family, Sir Edward Fitton – one sees her as a girl upon the family tomb at Gawsworth. Born in 1578 she came to Court to serve the Queen in 1595, at about seventeen.[36] Sir William Knollys was Comptroller of the Household and promised the proud father that he would look after his innocent. 'I will not fail to fulfil your desire in playing the good shepherd and will to my power defend the innocent lamb from the wolvish cruelty and fox-like subtlety of the tame beasts of this place, which, when they seem to take bread at a man's hand, will bite before they bark; all their songs be siren-like, and their kisses after Judas' fashion, but from such beasts deliver me and my friends. I will with my counsel advise your fair daughter, with my true affection love her and with my sword defend her, if need be; her innocency will deserve it and her virtue will challenge it at my hands, and I will be as careful of her well-doing as if I were her true father.'

It next appears that, though Sir William in his fifties was old enough to be her father, his feelings were by no means fatherly. He fell in love with the girl, but was himself tied to an old woman whom he had married for her money, the dowager Lady Chandos – ladies retained their rank and title, if superior, on a second marriage. He took refuge in writing to Mary's sister, in flowery parables about his garden in the leaf being blasted by the hoar frost, by reason of which 'my looking for any fruit of my garden is in vain, unless the old tree be cut down and a new graft of a good kind planted.'[37] Sir William's intentions were honourable; he merely wanted his wife to die. In his next missive Sir William described himself as 'cloyed with too much and yet ready to starve for hunger. My eyes see what I cannot attain to, my ears hear what I do scant believe, and my thoughts are carried with contrary conceipts. My hopes are mixed with despair and my desires starved with expectation; but were my enjoying assured, I could willingly endure purgatory for a season to purchase my heaven at the last.'[38] Next it seems that the young lady is playing up her elderly fool of a lover; he cannot write any more, he is so distempered with tooth-ache and 'your sister's going to bed without bidding me goodnight.' In the next letter Sir William thought that his purgatory might be due to 'my many offences committed against the Highest, the rather because I am more observant and devoted unto His creature than Himself.' If only he might feel the pleasing comfort of a delightful summer, but no sooner are his desires warmed up 'by the heat of the morning sun but they are blasted by an untimely frost,' i.e. old Lady Chandos, who refused to give up the ghost.

Mary's sister, Anne Newdigate, now invited Sir William to the christening of her daughter and to name the child. He was tied to Court and could not go down into the country, 'such is my bondage to this place as I have neither liberty to please myself nor satisfy my good friends' expectation.'[39] But 'imagine what name I love best and that do I nominate . . . and if I might be as happy to be a father as a godfather! . . .' Then Sir William writes in the midst of the Essex troubles to complain that Mary blames him for his melancholy and his little regarding her 'who, when I am myself, is the only comfort of my heart. She is now well and hath not been troubled with the mother [i.e. nerves] of a long time. I would God I might as lawfully make her a mother as you are.' Mary, however, fears that 'while the grass groweth the horse may starve, and she thinketh a bird in the bush worth two in the hand.'

So she went out birding, hoping to catch the young Earl of Pembroke, as Elizabeth Vernon had caught Southampton, and Elizabeth Throckmorton Ralegh. We have a portrait of her at this period in all her Court finery, grey-eyed, brown-haired, long-nosed, a haughty-looking, brazen beauty. She became Pembroke's mistress, and, we learn, 'would put off her head-tire and tuck up her clothes, and take a large white cloak as though she had been a man to meet the said Earl out of the Court.'[40] The next we hear, from Sir Robert Cecil in February 1601, is that 'there is a misfortune befallen Mistress Fitton, for she is proved with child, and the Earl of Pembroke, being examined, confesseth a fact, but utterly renounceth all marriage. I fear they will both dwell in the Tower awhile, for the Queen had vowed to send them thither.'[41]

Neither Sir Edward Fitton nor his son could prevail upon the Earl to marry the young woman; though 'my daughter is confident in her claim before God, and wishes my Lord and she might but meet before indifferent hearers. But for myself I expect no good from him that in all this time has not showed any kindness. I count my daughter as good a gentlewoman as my Lord, though the dignity of honour be greater only in him, which has beguiled her, I fear, except my Lord's honesty be the greater virtue.'[42] This it did not prove to be; the Queen committed him to the Fleet, and Mary Fitton to the care of Lady Hawkins for her confinement, where she was delivered of a boy that died.[43] These events were thought, by interested spectators, to be likely to bring down 'a persecution' upon the fair maids of the Chamber, or at least to prove 'discouraging' to them.

On release from *his* confinement the unregenerate Pembroke was rusticated; whereupon he wrote to Cecil, 'I have not yet been a day in the country, and I am as weary of it as if I had been prisoner there seven year. I see I shall never turn good Justice of the Peace. Therefore I pray, if the Queen determine to continue my banishment and prefer sweet Sir Edward before me, that you will assist me with your best means to go into some other land, that the change of the climate may purge me of melancholy; for else I shall never be fit for any civil society.'[44] Even Wilton was not good enough for a young courtier; later, 'if the Queen continue her displeasure a little longer, undoubtedly I shall turn clown, for Justice of Peace I can by no means frame unto, and one of the two a man that lives in the country must needs be.' Finally he obtained leave to travel abroad, but, after the Queen's death, married the Earl of Shrewsbury's rich, but misshapen, daughter: with whom he lived unhappily and by whom he had no children. Clarendon says that 'he paid much too dear for his wife's fortunes by taking her person into the bargain.'[45]

Good old Sir William was more faithful: 'I must confess the harvest was overlong expected, yet had I left nothing undone in manuring the same but that it might have brought forth both wholesome and pleasing fruit. But the man of sin [i.e. Pembroke], having in the night sowed tares amongst the good corn, both the true husband was beguiled and the good ground abused.'[46] Yet he would refuse no penance to redeem what was lost and 'to bring this soil to her former goodness.' Sir William felt that his love had been undeservedly rejected, and, though he spoke in riddles, 'I may boldly say that Mary did not choose the better part.' Anyway, he still could not offer marriage, old Lady Chandos still remaining above ground; it was not until 1605 that she died and Sir William, now sixty-one, could rush straight into matrimony with a girl of nineteen, Lady Elizabeth Howard.

Mary Fitton became the mistress of Sir Richard Leveson, the naval commander, whose fine bronze figure – all that is left of his tomb – we see in the parish church of Wolverhampton. At the beginning of 1607 she is in disgrace again over another bastard.

Her mother writes, 'I take no joy to hear of your sister nor of that boy. If it had pleased God when I did bear her that she and I had been buried it had saved me from a great deal of sorrow and grief, and her from shame – and such shame as never had Cheshire-woman, worse now than ever. Write no more to me of her.'[47] There is some uncertainty about this son; born before marriage, it seems to have been that of the Cornish sea-captain, William Polwhele, no longer young, into whose arms she fell after Leveson died. At any rate, Polwhele – who had had a good record against the Armada and was captain of the *Lion's Whelp* under Leveson in 1603 – married her.

The explanation seems to be that Leveson handed her on to Polwhele, for Perton in Staffordshire, where they resided, was Leveson's property. The Fittons took a very low view of Polwhele, though the truth is that he came from a family as old as their own. Lady Fitton considered him 'a very knave and taketh the disgrace of his wife and all her friends to make the world think him worthy of her, and that she deserved no better.'[48] Mary's sister, now Lady Newdigate, spoke out against the marriage, and Lady Egerton – to become Countess of Bridgewater – said 'she was the vilest woman under the sun.' The menfolk were altogether more kindly disposed, especially after Captain Polwhele made an honest woman of her. Her great-uncle, Francis Fitton, left his usual riding sword to Polwhele, and also his best horse 'as a remembrance and token of my love to him.' Next year, 1609, the sea-captain died, leaving his wife co-executor with Sir Walter Leveson and Sir Richard Tichborne. It seems that Mary Polwhele remained on friendly terms with her sister, staying sometimes with her at Arbury. In the letters of Francis Beaumont of Bedworth there are occasional messages for Mary: 'when you see my counsellor [in his love-suit], your only sister, commend I pray you unto her mine affectionate love.'[49] After Polwhele's death Mary married a Captain Lougher, of an old Pembrokeshire family, who died in 1636. She had (by him) a daughter, to whom she left the lease of a property in Pembrokeshire: the girl was named for her old mistress, in whose service she had passed those few dazzling, dizzy years – Elizabeth.

If Mary Fitton can hardly be regarded as a paragon of virtue, here – to redress the balance – is a maid of honour who was. Margaret Ratcliffe adhered to her mistress's injunctions in favour of virginity, and topped it by an obsessive devotion to her brother, Sir Alexander. He was killed at the Curlews in Ireland, in 1599:

the news 'by the Queen's command is kept from her, who is determined to break it unto her herself.'[50] When she learned of it she 'pined in such strange manner as voluntarily she hath gone about to starve herself, and by the two days together hath received no sustenance: which, meeting with extreme grief, hath made an end of her maiden modest days at Richmond upon Saturday last, her Majesty being present.'[51] She was buried in St. Margaret's, Westminster, not far from Blanche Parry; Ben Jonson wrote her epitaph in acrostics:

> Marble, weep, for thou dost cover
> A dead beauty underneath thee
> Rich as nature could bequeath thee:
> Grant, then, no rude hand remove her. . . .
> Rare as wonder was her wit,
> And like nectar ever flowing,
> Till time, strong by her bestowing,
> Conquered hath both life and it.
> Life whose grief was out of fashion
> In these times, few so rued
> Fate in a brother. To conclude
> For wit, features, and true passion,
> Earth, thou hast not such another.

So much for the facts of Court-life. The ideal of a courtier was that held up in the mirror of Castiglione's *Il Cortegiano*, and recognised as such all over Europe. The book was the most popular prose-work of the Italian Renaissance, having over a hundred editions in various languages before 1600.[52] In England no less than seventeen versions have been published, beginning with Hoby's endearing translation of 1561. In his prefatory Epistle to Lord Henry Hastings, to become a leading figure as third Earl of Huntingdon – whose family had entertained Castiglione half a century before – Hoby expresses the hope that so shall 'he get him the reputation now here in England which he hath had a good while since beyond the sea, in Italy, Spain and France.'[53] Hoby goes on to advocate enriching the language with translations as against the opinion of learned pedants who wanted to keep learning to themselves, a professional expertise. He wished that every man might 'store the tongue according to his knowledge and delight above other men in some piece of learning, that we alone of the world may not be still counted barbarous in our tongue, as in time out of mind we have been in our manners. And so shall we perchance become as famous in England as the learned men of other nations have been and presently are.' This indeed came about – the Elizabethans brought into being a whole literature of translation; but it is significant that it was chiefly the work, not of academic pedants but of people with a wider culture, such as Sir Thomas North, Sir John Harington, John Florio, Philemon Holland, Geoffrey Fenton, Arthur Golding, William Adlington, Arthur Hall and others.

However cynically we may be inclined to reflect that Castiglione was more honoured in the breach than the observance, it is more remarkable how closely the profession of courtier, even in England, adhered to his specification. The courtier should be born a gentleman and of a good house. He should have a comely shape of person and countenance, be intelligent and have a certain grace. (We have seen how true this was of the men Elizabeth delighted to honour, Leicester, Hatton, Oxford, Ralegh, Essex, Mountjoy). A courtier, above all, should be a man of courage, good at feats of arms and skilled in the use of his weapon, quick to make use of advantage in the quarrels that arise. Here there was an observable difference between Italian and English circumstances, with the Court of a lady, and between the prevailing temperaments. In spite of the quarrels at Court between Philip Sidney and Oxford, Oxford and Ralegh, Grey and Southampton, these were nothing like so deadly as the Italian, pursued to the death, with the growing cult of the duel and the Italian code of 'honour' of which we have seen Englishmen disapprove. The duel did spread, however, with evil results, notably among military men.

The courtier should be a skilled rider, an addict of manly exercises, especially hunting. Here we may notice King James's mania for hunting: he must have spent months every year away from the centre of affairs, leaving administration in the hands of Robert Cecil, up to his death in 1612. Even Cecil, with his poor frame and hunched back, was keen on out-of-door sports like falconry. Tennis is much commended, 'where the disposition of the body, the quickness and nimbleness of every member is much perceived.'[54] Castiglione commends swimming – of which art the chief exponent at Elizabeth's Court was handsome Sir John Packington, whom she dubbed 'Lusty Packington', but forbade the wager he laid with three other courtiers to swim from Westminster to London Bridge.

In Italian circumstances it was natural that Castiglione should expect some knowledge of painting in courtiers. This must have been much less in England, though it increased as the years went on, and the appreciation of Hilliard was widespread. The tilt or tournament was a characteristic exercise for a courtier, and he should have 'proper devices, apt posies, and witty inventions that may draw unto him the eyes of the lookers-on'.[55] The pressure for suits, preferment, promotion, offices, grants, jobs, pensions, we have seen to be one of the busiest occupations of a Court. Castiglione advises the courtiers against scrounging – one would have thought a counsel of perfection: 'let him rather look to have favour and promotion offered him than crave it so openly in the face of the world, as many do that are so greedy of it that a man would ween the not obtaining it grieveth them as much as the loss of life.' Here there was a contrast between the Cecils, who could afford to let their services speak for themselves and for the rest observed their chance with a cloak of humility, as against Essex who was for ever badgering the Queen on behalf of himself or his friends. It was not lost on her that he was building up a party: that was one of the chief causes of her growing distrust of him, that he would not follow in the submissive footsteps of his step-father, Leicester. Castiglione advised that a man ought 'always to humble himself somewhat under his degree, and not receive favour and promotions so easily as they be offered him, but refuse them modestly.' This was Burghley's constant mood; though he refused nothing that was remunerative, he refused an earldom as too great an honour. (Both his sons accepted earldoms, but that was under James under whom there was an inflation in such things.)

Castiglione concluded that 'to purchase favour at great men's hands, there is no better way than to deserve it'; this was true in the Queen's reign, less so under her successor. One should recommend oneself by talking oneself down – this was Burghley's technique, as opposed to Ralegh's, and much more successful. Nor should one hope to rise by the arts of malice, or giving rein to an evil tongue – for which Elizabeth put no confidence in horrid Lord Henry Howard, though he was her cousin, and never awarded him anything (except a spell in the Tower), while James made him a leading minister. A gift for languages was very useful, especially French and Spanish, said Castiglione; in English terms that meant French and Italian, in which several of the courtiers were proficient. All Courts made a profession of the cult of love; Castiglione was humane enough to object to fathers forcing their daughters into marriages, against their wishes, with old men. For the rest, where there was no guilt, the profession of love could afford to be open. It was the proper rôle of a courtier to advise his prince for his good, 'that he may break his mind to him and always inform him frankly of the truth of every matter meet for him to understand, without fear or peril to displease him.'[56] This was what Elizabeth charged William Cecil with when she made him her Principal Secretary at the beginning of her reign, 'and I shall not fail to keep taciturnity therein.' It was the duty of courtiers to provide entertainments for their prince: Wolsey had been particularly good at this with Henry VIII, and all Elizabeth's courtiers laid themselves out to entertain her according to their means, some of them beyond it.

The popular parlance, almost the folklore, about the Court is, then, very understandable. It is expressed, as everything is, by Shakespeare – the 'envious Court':

> Lord, who would live turmoiled in the Court
> And may enjoy such quiet walks as these?

'Those that are good manners at the Court are as ridiculous in the country as the behaviour of the country is most mockable at the Court. You told me you salute not at the Court, but you kiss your hands.' Very well: 'the courtier's hands are perfumed with civet . . . of a baser birth than tar, the very uncleanly flux of a cat.' Queen Mab gallops

> O'er courtiers' knees, that dream on curtsies straight.

The qualifications for a courtier are summed up by Touchstone: 'I have had a measure; I have flattered a lady; I have been politic with my friend, smooth with mine enemy; I have undone three tailors; I have had four quarrels, and like to have fought one.'

Ralegh's bitter words about the Court are well known, though he owed everything to his reception there:

> Say to the Court it glows
> and shines like rotten wood . . .

Much less known is an extraordinary poem that is no less effective, and obviously written by someone very much in the know:

> Chamberlain, Chamberlain,
> He's of her Grace's kin,
> Fool hath he ever been
> With his Joan Silverpin:
> She makes his cockscomb thin
> And quake in every limb;

Quicksilver is in his head
But his wit's dull as lead
    —Lord, for thy pity!

This refers to Lord Chamberlain Hunsdon; the suggestion is that
he is under mercury treatment for venereal disease; I can testify
that his hand was extraordinarily shaky.

Parti-beard was afeared
    When they ran at the herd,
    The Reindeer was embossed,
    The white doe she was lost:
Pembroke struck her down
And took her from the clown
    —Lord, for thy pity!

We can now recognise some of these references – to Mary Fitton,
Pembroke, Knollys (the clown) and the Queen's anger: 'embossed'
refers to a deer foaming at the mouth – the Reindeer would be the
Queen.

Little Cecil trips up and down:
    He rules both Court and crown,
    With his brother Burghley clown
    In his great fox-furred gown,
With the long proclamation
He swore he saved the town
    Is it not likely?

We may leave the last word to Robert Cecil, fourth generation
at Court, who presided over the transition from Elizabeth's to
James's.

In the last year of her life, himself indisposed, we find him
writing to Windebank in attendance on her, a letter that reveals
both his solicitude for his mistress and something of the difficulties
of his office. 'Upon some intelligence received, I have directed a
longer letter to the Queen than is fit for her fair eyes to read. Pray
deliver it, and crave liberty to read it to her; but read it by
yourself first, to be perfect, and then seal it up with my seal, which
I send you. P.S. Do not show the Queen this letter, but tell her
I willed you to desire leave to read mine to her, rather than to
trouble her. If she asks how I do, say my man told you I could go
with a little stick very well, and say no more, nor that but by
accident of her question. Pitch your time to offer it not when she
is disposed to sleep ... If she should say it is not my hand, do not
in any way say but that it is, for when I take leisure I write

legibly.'[57] We see how close her prying scrutiny still was, and also how difficult it was to handle her.

At the symbolic moment of the transition he wrote to Harington, a life-long courtier: 'You know all my former steps: good knight, rest content, and give heed to one that hath sorrowed in the bright lustre of a Court, and gone heavily even on the best-seeming fair ground. 'Tis a great task to prove one's honesty, and yet not spoil one's fortune. You have tasted a little hereof in our blessed Queen's time, who was more than a man and, in troth, sometime less than a woman. I wish I waited now in her Presence-chamber, with ease at my food and rest in my bed. I am pushed from the shore of comfort, and know not where the winds and waves of a Court will bear me . . . My father had much wisdom in directing the state, and I wish I could bear my part so discreetly as he did.'[58]

CHAPTER III

THE RHYTHM OF TOWN AND COUNTRY:
THE RÔLE OF THE GENTRY

ENGLAND in the sixteenth century was overwhelmingly rural –
like nearly all countries, with the partial exception of the
Netherlands and the northern half of Italy, the most civilised
areas of Europe in the precise sense of the term. Within this context foreigners saw England as dominantly a country of woodland
and pasture, parks and chases: they were struck by its greenness –
as Americans still are today, when the countryside is given half a
chance to expose itself beneath industrial conurbations. A Frenchman in 1606 declared that it differed in that there was no country
'which uses so much land for pasture as this.'[1] Those who observed
it with fresh eyes coming from abroad saw it as a grass-growing
country, with pasture, grazing, cattle in the fore-front of the picture. An Italian noticed more butchers in London than in any two
of the chief towns of northern Italy. Observers did *not* comment on
rural poverty – that eternal theme – for the simple reason that it
was so much less than the grinding poverty of European countries.

The country was indeed happily underpopulated, with plenty
of room to expand into all round – in contrast to the hideous over-
population of today, more crowded than almost any other area of
the earth's surface. Forest and woodland were extensive everywhere, except for the bare moorlands of North and West – and
they too offered plenty of room to expand into. Some sense of the
open spaces of the mind may be seen behind the literature of the
time, in such plays as *A Midsummer Night's Dream, As You Like It,* or
A Winter's Tale, with their perspective opening upon forest and
woodland. People proceeded to take advantage of the opportunities inviting upon their threshold. The later sixteenth century saw
an expansion into forest, moor and fen with greater zeal than at
any time since the early medieval colonisation of the land – and
that was on a smaller, more primitive scale. New energies were
released after the critical disturbances and readjustments of mid-
century – largely released by the processes of Dissolution and

61

Reformation, the rough and rapid secularisation of society. 'A rising population in both town and countryside increased the demand for food and the demand for land.'[2] It was a country very much on the upgrade.

Hence the higher standard of living than that enjoyed by the oppressed peasantries of Europe. An Italian observed that England was known as 'the land of comforts'.[3] A Netherlander considered that the English were not as industrious or hard-working as Netherlanders or Frenchmen. Foreigners' impressions of a better standard of living were, by all tests, correct – increasingly in the later sixteenth century, once out of the general hugger-mugger of the Middle Ages.

But text-book accounts scarcely do justice to the variety of the land, its diversities and uses. Anyone brought up in the West Country, the North or Wales, does not recognise the patterns, derived from the Midlands or East Anglian agriculture, imposed as a standard account for the country as a whole – common-fields, nucleated villages, enclosure-movements – as an adequate description. The appreciation in our own time of the fundamental difference between Highland Zone and Lowland, between North and West as against Midlands, South and East, has been far more illuminating for the whole of our history. The Highland Zone is dominantly pastoral and cattle-grazing; there the regular process of expansion has gone on, as one sees it still going on up the hillsides in Devon or Cornwall, or Wales or the Pennines, enclosure a process popular with everyone. In the Lowland Zone it was disturbing to traditional rights of common, disturbing socially, unpopular with the peasantry who got scant justice out of it. Even here there were forest, heath and fen into which to move. Surveyors at the time noted the populousness of forest communities, as in Northamptonshire, and in the Fens, the preponderance of cottagers, the addiction to a life free and 'idle', fostered by large unstinted pastures or unrestricted stretches of swamp. There was always poaching, fish, birds, game. Even in the South there were forests all the way from the New Forest to Savernake in Wiltshire and to the Chilterns, or across much of Surrey and Sussex into Kent, or in the West Midlands from Sherwood into Worcestershire and Staffordshire. A county like Warwickshire (or Leicestershire) was divided between woodland and champion. The unit of East Anglia had three farming regions: arable with common fields, wood and pasture, sands and heaths. Lancashire, too, had three distinct farming regions; so, too, Essex with champion and mixed husbandry, woodland and pasture, marshland. Half of a large parish like Tonbridge in Kent, with the Weald on its doorstep, was waiting to be colonised. The Highland areas possessed minerals to offset their poorer soil and farming: the tin and copper of Cornwall and Devon, lead in Derbyshire and Cumberland, calamine in Somerset, coal on Tyneside, in West Midlands and South Wales. In many areas of so strongly pastoral a country there was cloth-making, from the large herds of sheep in upland or downland.

Sixteenth-century observers noticed the accompaniments of these variations in the differing temperaments of the population. The surveyor Norden thought that woodland people were more stubborn and 'uncivil', lawless and independent. Something of this is reflected in works of imagination, as with Autolycus, no less than in the evidence of a Northamptonshire diary, like Throckmorton's. Nearly all the rebellions came from the Highland areas: those of 1497 and 1549 from the West Country, the Pilgrimage of Grace and the Rising of 1569 from the North. They offered fertile seedbeds for Puritanism and Dissent, along with the towns – partly because both were less under the thumb of squire and parson, the authorities of State and Church, the bonds of an hierarchical social system.

It was a well-knit and well-integrated society, as societies go – more efficient in relation to its resources than any other, except the Netherlands. There was a balanced rhythm between town and country, the main-spring of it all being London. A town of some 70,000 at the beginning of the century, it had a population of 220,000 at its end, the largest in Europe – in itself a striking indication of the increased wealth, power and resources of the little country, the progress achieved by good fortune and good management. London was even more dominant, relatively, then than today: the only town of European importance, already a commercial and financial, as well as political and cultural, metropolis. No other town was in the least degree comparable: in 1543–4 London paid thirty times the amount of subsidy paid by the second town in the kingdom, then Norwich.[4]

We may vary the image profitably to think of the country as a spider's web, with London as its operative centre, the other towns placed functionally at intersections and junctions, the fabric holding together strongly, resisting the strains of the period better than most. Professor W. G. Hoskins puts the towns illuminatingly into three groups. First come those that are the capital cities of their respective regions: York, Norwich, Bristol, Exeter, Salisbury.

Next come those county towns that are either the centres of county government or markets for an exceptionally wide area: such as Leicester with some six hundred households, Derby with five hundred, Manchester with four hundred; to these we may add such towns as Reading, Lincoln, Gloucester, Worcester, Nottingham. Thirdly come towns that were not administrative centres but served as markets for a wider range than average, towns of two to three hundred households, a population from one to two thousand: Stamford in Lincolnshire, Bridgnorth in Shropshire, Maidstone in Kent, Bridgwater or Taunton in Somerset, Barnstaple in Devon, or such a lively little town as Stratford-upon-Avon, busy as a bee. Professor Hoskins comments, 'everything is on a miniature scale: all except the quality of the people.'[5] We note the contrast with today.

The towns were well integrated into the surrounding countryside. Leicester lay surrounded by 2600 acres of arable, pasture and meadow in three large open fields, in which many townspeople had holdings, besides the general right of burgesses to common their beasts. Within their bounds, whether walled or no, the towns had much of a rural character. We recall the hundreds of elms in which Stratford was embowered. 'Elizabethan Leicester kept a country air about it. Orchards, barns, and stables, and large gardens lay among the streets; windmills stood silhouetted as one looked up against the southern skyline; the streets petered out in ten minutes' walk into lanes redolent of cowdung and hay.'[6] Within the town-walls of such an ecclesiastical city as Canterbury or Exeter, the cathedrals had spacious closes and the monasteries large gardens and grounds. With the Dissolution the latter became available for development of various kinds, commercial, administrative, domestic. Medieval London had an exceptionally large number of churches and churchyards, monasteries and monastic precincts: many of these provided scope for the immense increase in urban building that marked the Elizabethan age – Blackfriars, Austin Friars, Greyfriars, St. Bartholomew's precinct at Smithfield, the Minories, Charterhouse, Southwark: we can follow it all in detail in Stow's vivid and veracious *Survey*.

Here we are concerned mainly with the rhythm between town and country. All towns of any size exerted a powerful influence on their regions: as markets, as a convenient location for small industries, for the professions – notably the lawyer, for schools and the dissemination of culture. London, in all these ways and more besides, was in a class by itself. There was the network of its excellent communications with its own hinterland – the corn barges coming down Thames, Colne and Lea; the Great North Road and Watling Street carrying animals and people both north and south – for Watling Street started at Dover; the numerous water-routes linking up round the coasts with the Thames estuary and so to the Continent. Not only this, but there were filaments innumerable that connected it will all other towns strung out along the nationwide web, commercial, administrative, governmental and personal. London was a large recipient and consumer of the energies of the country, and, as we shall see, it returned them a hundredfold. For many country-folk coming to town, it was a fate: witness the Warwickshire-born William Shakespeare, as for thousands of others.

We may now examine how the web of society held together, explore the rhythms and tremors that ran along it, so that even the remotest areas could feel its vibrations, in varying intensity, could communicate and respond. The most obvious and glittering display of the central institution of the state – the monarchy – to the country at large took place when the Queen went on progress in the summer. To some extent government went with her – she was usually accompanied by the leading members of the Council; and wherever she pitched the Court was constituted. Still these exhibitions were irregular, dependent on the whim of the Queen – though of course they served the purposes of government, helped her to keep in touch with her people, whose response was carefully noted. From the first she always made up to them, and was correspondingly popular – unlike her predecessor and her successor. On the whole, we may regard her progresses as an aspect of social life, and adduce them as such later. Nevertheless, they were a part of the complex rhythms helping to keep society together, the centre in touch with the localities, even if irregularly.

The innermost centre of government was more systematically represented in the regions by the Lords Lieutenants, in the counties by their deputy-lieutenants. It is well known that the office of Lord Lieutenant, quasi-military in origin, sprang out of the crisis of Henry's Reformation, with the appointment of Russell in the disturbed West; Harrison described them concisely as noblemen set over shires in time of necessity. Indeed as the crisis of the Armada drew near the whole country was brought into the network of their responsibilities. The key-figures of the government had overriding surveillance of the counties and could transmit the orders of the Council direct. Let us look at them in the critical year 1587.[7] Burghley himself, for all the burden of the state on his shoulders, was responsible for Lincolnshire, Essex and Hertford. Actually, the Queen had originally designated Leicester for Essex and Hertfordshire; his appointment as commander-in-chief of the army made way for Burghley, who had been sore at Leicester's nomination, though he said that he would have been more grieved at being rejected for Northamptonshire where he was 'no new planted or new feathered gentleman', nor did he welcome the claim of the Earl of Lincoln to his (Burghley's) 'native county' of Lincolnshire.[8] In the event Lord Chancellor Hatton got Northamptonshire, Burghley the other three counties. We see how much a matter of prestige, a sign of pre-eminence, this was. Hunsdon was responsible for Norfolk and Sussex; the Earl of Warwick for his county; the Earl of Shrewsbury for Nottingham, Derby and Staffordshire; the Earl of Derby for Lancashire and Cheshire. But consider the burden of government and representation upon Huntingdon and Pembroke: Huntingdon, as President of the Council of the North, was in charge of all the northern counties and, in addition, of Leicestershire and Rutland; Pembroke was not only responsible for all twelve of the Welsh and Border counties, but also of his own Wiltshire and Somerset.

It will be seen that there was something of a two-way traffic: these grandees, the ruling few, transmitted the orders from the centre but they also represented back the responses, and to some extent the interests, of the areas in which they had their estates, usually the basis of their prominence. (Not so Ralegh as Lord Lieutenant of Cornwall: he owed that to the favour of the Queen, in a county where the royal Duchy was the leading landowner; even so, as also Lord Warden of the Stannaries, he was official head of the tin-industry). The military aspect of the Lord Lieutenant's office retained something of its primacy: he was primarily responsible for defence, and hence for the musters and measures protective of order and security. Hence, too, their concern with finance and the supervision of the economy in times of crisis, whether from external or internal danger. They raised the loans from the counties to meet the expenses incurred in 1588. (From these we discern among the richest counties, Kent, Sussex, Essex, Suffolk; among the poorest, Cornwall, Durham, Huntingdon, Rutland.)[9] It fell to the Lord Lieutenants to make provision of corn in times of dearth and issue regulations as to supply and price; and, in the sphere of order, to keep an eye on those troublesome deviationists, Recusants and dissenters, as also to mediate in disputes among prominent people, reconcile quarrels within the governing class itself, among the gentry.

The crucial contribution of this rôle to society may be judged from one or two examples; some of its effects may be seen even today. All through his long active career the persecuting and puritanical Huntingdon – cousin of the persecuting and Catholic Cardinal Pole – pushed forward a radical Protestantism in Leicestershire where his family influence lay, from the Hastings castle at Ashby-de-la-Zouch. In Leicester itself he bought a town-house, Lord's Place, from which to keep a close watch on the well-being of the town.[10] He refounded the grammar-school, he supported Puritan preachers and their sermons, he filled all his livings with indubitable Protestants. The result of his life's-work was to be seen in the Puritan inflexion of the county, its long-term effects in Leicestershire Dissent and Nonconformity dominant up to our own time.[11] Contrast northern and coastal Lancashire. The Elizabethan Earls of Derby did not dare to come out as open Catholics against the central government, of which they were the representatives in Lancashire and Cheshire. But they dragged their feet in the execution of the laws against Recusancy in those areas where the gentry remained Catholic; and so 'north Lancashire remains strongly Catholic and Preston has the largest number of Catholics in proportion to its population of any town in England.'[12] In east Lancashire, however, Huntingdon was able to press his campaign; 'his persistence had its reward, and in the Lancashire towns, particularly in the hundreds of Salford and Rochdale, a radical type of Protestantism flourished.' (The Queen, however, was ungrateful).

Let us look a little further at these glittering summits of society. The policy of the Tudor monarchy was to group them around the apex itself, if somewhat below, to subordinate them to the purposes of the Crown in a well ordered state. The purpose of Henry VIII in pushing Russell into the place of the Courtenay Earls of Devon in the West Country is obvious: the Marquis of Exeter belonged to the conservative opposition and was an enemy of the new deal. Henry had him attainted and his wide lands forfeited to the Crown. John Russell was provided with large monastic estates, his town-house in Exeter the former Blackfriars, while Cowick priory in the suburbs made a convenient country residence for the President of the Council of the West. This policy was carried further as part of Henry's stepping up of defence in the

Channel counties, tightening up secular society as against the effete monasteries. Such was the purpose of his building a bastion for Lord Chancellor Wriothesley, based upon Titchfield and its possessions, with a strategic eye to Southampton. Similarly with the Herberts, based upon Wilton, convenient for Salisbury; and with the Montagus in Sussex from their place at Cowdray.

The first Herbert Earl of Pembroke, Henry's creation, had been a chief beneficiary of the lands of the see of Winchester – a see phenomenally rich, out of all proportion either to its proper place in society or its social utility. (Not even the Reformation sufficiently reduced it, and so the Puritans thought). The second Earl reigned in Wiltshire for thirty years. One observes him in his place watching over the general interests of society and the social order. 'In short, he was representing the Crown to the county, and the county to the Crown ... Authority could thus be transmitted from the Privy Council to the humblest churchwarden in the smallest parish.'[13] The pre-eminence of these magnates is significantly witnessed by their interest in the return of members to Parliament. There is plenty of evidence from a number of them in various parts of the country that they expected their wishes to be regarded in the return of a member for a local seat.

Towards the end of Elizabeth's reign the deputy-lieutenants were becoming important – two or three of them in a shire, sometimes more, having precedence over and more range and scope than the ordinary J.P.s. Thus they were envied by their fellows: Pembroke comments significantly, 'all men cannot be deputy-lieutenants; some must govern, some must obey.'[14] His overriding concern for the governing element in Elizabethan society, the gentry, is clear: 'I would have all gentlemen to have their due reserved unto them: which is, from time to time as Parliaments fall out to be chosen, now some and then some, as they are fit, to the end they may be experimented in the affairs and state of their country.'[15] (One sees how this led on to the Long Parliament, when the gentlemen of England took control.)

An analysis of the Wiltshire representation in the House of Commons[16] – the most significant of central institutions from a social point of view – brings home the increasing preponderance of the country gentry at the expense of the towns. As early as the Reformation Parliament of 1529 'the ousting of townsmen from the borough seats to which they alone were entitled was all but complete.' By 1584 only Salisbury, of the Wiltshire boroughs, returned two residents in accordance with the statute; three other boroughs returned only one each: a total of five out of thirty-four for the whole country. From 1559 onwards Malmesbury only once returned a clothier, all its other members belonged to the gentry; other cloth towns, too, took to returning outside gentlemen instead of their own burgesses. Townsmen in the House of Commons were essentially pre-occupied with the local interests of their particular town; now the interest of the Wiltshire cloth industry was committed to the care of the gentry of the county. They could not only afford better the expenses of sitting but could take a larger view.

There was mounting pressure on the part of the gentry for seats in Parliament in Elizabeth's reign: hence the enfranchisement of boroughs to accommodate them – occasionally of such mere villages as Mitchell and Bosinney in Cornwall, for which people like Sir Walter Ralegh, Francis Bacon, and Sir Frances Drake sat. In 1584 out of the thirty-four Wiltshire M.P.s sixteen were gentlemen of the county; five were middle-class townsmen, but of the rest – government officials, lawyers, professional men – a considerable proportion would belong to the class of gentry. The same holds good for the Commons as a whole; of 460 members, 240 were country gentlemen, 53 townsmen; but of the remainder, courtiers, officials, lawyers, it is probable that at least some were gentlemen. In Wiltshire, as for most counties, by far the largest element was constituted by its own native gentry. Their number increased from some two hundred families at the beginning of Elizabeth's reign to three hundred at the end of James's; of these, eighty-four families returned members to Parliament.

Cornwall offers rather a special case, but revealing. It has been a subject of discussion why so many small insignificant places there were allotted the right to return a couple of members, until the inflated number of forty-four (with the county) was arrived at, and Wiltshire took second place. We can now conclude that, though it may have been a convenience to the Crown to provide seats for a small number of official members, it was far more so for gentlemen from counties outside, who outnumbered both native Cornish gentry and official members. An average number of eleven Cornish gentlemen sat in Elizabeth's Parliaments.[17] Twice as many gentry from other counties found Cornish seats to oblige – noticeably from Devon and Dorset, both Sir Walter and Sir Carew Ralegh, a Courtenay, Drake, Champernowne, Wrey, Rolle, Seymour, Chudleigh, St. Leger, Horsey; but also gentry from further afield, both Peter and Paul Wentworth (no devotees of the Crown), Walter Cope, a Cromwell, Spencer, Harrington, Verney, Savile, Onslow, Leveson, Sampson Leonard from Kent. Among the remaining quarter we find a number of courtiers and officials: Sir William Knollys, John Stanhope, Edward Phelips of Montacute – Walsingham's decipherer, Robert Beale, clerk of the Council, and Burghley's indispensable secretary, Michael Hicks. One or two lawyers, and a tiny sprinkling of merchants – a Mitchell of Truro is singled out – make up the total. The picture we derive speaks for iteself.

In general, we may say that it was only cities of the first importance, York, Norwich, Bristol that could afford the luxury of sending two of their own burgesses and paying their expenses – though perhaps it was no luxury if their affairs were large enough to warrant it. Sometimes a town like Bath or Taunton would send its own burgesses, if matters concerning the cloth industry in which they were interested were coming up. But the usual pattern was for even important towns like Exeter or Winchester to divide its representation, and send one burgess, leaving the other seat free for an outsider, county gentleman from within the county or outside, or official Winchester usually sent its Recorder. Towards the end of the reign Exeter sometimes returned two of its own burgesses, one of them the Recorder – tribute to its increased wealth and importance.[18] Plymouth got along with one local man, and one outsider. There were simple ways of getting round the theoretical limitation of seats to resident burgesses in these cities: to make them a titular burgess was easy, by buying a piece of property, or making the M.P. a member of the Gild Merchant, as Winchester made Recorder Fleming in 1582, or Sir Edward Stafford in 1592 to qualify him for election in 1593.[19] The M.P.s for Barnstaple – an important commercial and marketing centre – follow the same pattern: one citizen, one outsider. In 1593 Barnstaple returns a client of the Lord Lieutenant, the Earl of Bath, who lived at nearby Tawstock, and one outsider, who was made a freeman *ad hoc*. Four years later one member was replaced as 'misliked of the Earl of Bath'.[20]

London was a quasi-independent power, alongside of Westminster, treated as such by the Council with respect and circumspection. It returned its own members, and for most practical purposes was governed by its Lord Mayor and Corporation; to whom the Council sent its orders for them to execute. Alternatively orders went to the Lord Mayor who gave effect to them by his instructions to the City Companies. His position was practically comparable to that of a Lord Lieutenant – there was none for Middlesex in 1587: this was given expression by his title as the only Lord Mayor – titles meant something then.

If towns were at the intersections of the web of society, there is no doubt what constituted the filaments – they were the gentry, with all their affiliations and cross-connections over the borders of their native counties. If the magnates ruled at the centre, in the Privy Council with its offshoots in Wales and the North, it was the gentry who ruled in the country as a whole. The Earl of Derby could hardly have prevailed against the passive resistance of the Catholic gentry in their area of Lancashire, even if he had wished to. We have seen that with regard to representation in Parliament the towns were retreating before the advancing tide of the gentry. All over the country it was the regular thing for the neighbouring gentry to take a hand in the affairs of the local towns, with the exception of only the largest, where they would have to tread carefully. We have noticed the Earl of Huntingdon's close supervision of Leicester; true he was a magnate, and he made no bones about it, 'considering that in such cases I hold my authority somewhat more than any common Justice amongst you.'[21] In the case of a smaller town like Stratford, though it has its own marked identity and institutions, the neighbouring gentry are frequently in and out upon its affairs and those of government.

In town accounts, such as those of Stratford or Plymouth, we note the deference the gentry are accorded along with the expenses of their entertainment: sometimes dinner, often wine or hippocras, sugar-loaves or wafers. They are given the proper respect due to their status in an hierarchical society, and they take the lead in what affects it, particularly with regard to public order, the economy and social betterment. It is noticeable how much to the fore they are in the country in regard to education – though the chief townsmen are very ready to follow their lead. At Wakefield, for instance, George Savile of Haselden Hall takes the lead in founding the grammar school and procuring its charter in 1591.[22] This was happening all over the country; I cite him only because he was the younger son of a younger branch of the Saviles of Thornhill, and so provides an instance of the exfoliation of such families at a time of increasing wealth from the land. Purchasing Haselden in 1584 he embellished it with plaster-ceilings and (of course) his coat of arms.[23] A number of Elizabethan houses all round Wakefield testify to increasing wealth and higher standards of housing: Stanley Hall, Clarke Hall, Chapelthorpe Hall, Flanshaw Hall – all smaller gabled Elizabethan houses of the rising gentry.

Ocular evidence of their expansion is evident all over the country for anyone with eyes to see. It needs no confused theoretical argumentation – it is only commonsense when one reflects on the immense mass of property, or tithes to invest in, made available for new secular owners. Let us take the case of my own native county, Cornwall. At Padstow the Prideaux got the tithe-barn and manor that had belonged to Bodmin priory and built their house there in the year of the Armada – a younger branch of a Devon family, where there had been no gentry before. At St. Germans John Eliot, a Devon merchant, bought the priory demesnes and turned the domestic buildings into a house – Port Eliot, where there had been no gentry before. At Lanhydrock Richard Roberts, a Truro merchant, bought the monastic tithe-barn and rectory, and built his fine house in James's reign – where there had been no gentry before. These families are still there. This is not to mention smaller monastic properties, which also presented their opportunities. The small cell of St. Cadix made a pretty estate for a junior cadet of the Courtenays; the cell of St. Anthony-in-Roseland in time to come made a nest for the maritime Sprys; St. Michael's Mount, from harbouring three or four religious under an arch-priest, provided a perch for the St. Aubyns. Historians who question the rise of the gentry simply do not use their eyes.

The proper method to follow is to watch the process of settlement concretely, county by county – as Miss Youings has done for Devon.[24] Here she observes a first class of old West Country families who took their opportunity to increase their holdings, Fulford, Stucley, St. Leger, Champernowne, Edgcumbe, Grenvilles, Carews – several of these last two. There was a larger class of Devon-born lawyers and merchants who became landed gentry – a notable afforcement of the class. George Rolle of Steventon made his fortune as a legal official in London and invested in land in his native county; early in the next century his heir married the Dennis heiress – another monastic estate – and thus constituted the largest of the kind in Devon. In time it formed the immense estate of a peerage – Rolle, then Clinton. Sir Thomas Dennis, as chancellor to Anne of Cleves, was in a good position to buy, and bought; so also the lawyers John Arscott, John Ridgway, John Slanning, John Southcote, all creators of county families.

Some of these, Dennis, Arscott and Slanning, along with Richard Pollard, were younger sons, 'founders of families which soon outran the senior lines.'[25] Or there were merchants on the way up, like John Northcote of Crediton – from whom the Earls of Iddesleigh descend – or Walter Smythe of Totnes; or newcomers into the county like Anthony Harvey, who married into Devon and built up a nice monastic estate around his wife's quite small holding. William Abbot was a newcomer, serjeant of Henry VIII's cellar, who got delectable Hartland: his representatives have been there ever since, where formerly there had only been monks. One observes cases where the monastic purchases 'make all the difference: to raise Roger Bluett of Holcombe Rogus, for instance, or John Drake of Musbury, into the select circle from which were chosen the commissioners of the peace.' These Drakes were those from whom the Churchills were to descend. Buckland abbey near Plymouth, bought and reconstructed by the Grenvilles, was ultimately purchased by Sir Francis Drake, who thus seated a quite new family among the county gentry where the monks had been. So, too, with beautiful Forde abbey near Chard, then in Devon. The process is visible today.

The largest beneficiary of the Dissolution among Devonshiremen was the Catholic Sir William Petre. Though he got some pickings out of Buckfast abbey and Plympton priory, as a Secretary of State he needed to be nearer London and built up his estates mainly in Essex, round Ingatestone and Thorndon. The son of a Torbryan yeoman, he made a new recruit not merely to the gentry but to the peerage. The Catholic Lord Rich, tormentor of Sir Thomas More, built up an enormous monastic estate in Essex, based on Leighs priory, which he transformed into a great house: another new recruit to the peerage. And so one could peregrinate around the country, county by county: into Wiltshire, where a junior branch of the Catholic Arundells of Lanherne built up a grander estate from the possessions of Shaftesbury abbey; or to Wilton of the Herberts; to Titchfield abbey in Hampshire, of the Catholic Wriothesleys. Or to the estates and houses of Protestant grandees, who also sensibly profited from the Dissolution, the Russells at Woburn, the Cecils at Burghley. East, West or North – into Yorkshire, where Sir Stephen Procter built his beautiful Jacobean Hall out of the stones of Fountains – the conclusions are the same.

The ascendancy is no less visible in the churches: where previously had been the altars and the images of the saints are now the tombs and effigies of the gentry. In many hundreds, possibly thousands, of English churches one can watch this development: history in stone. Sometimes a family built or partly reconstructed a chapel in their parish church for their burial-place, as the Longs did at South Wraxall in Wiltshire in 1566.[26] Sometimes they took over a chantry, as at Macclesfield, where Archbishop Savage of York had built himself a chantry just before the Reformation. The Savages made it their burial-place; the function was the same, the intention different: in place of improving the state of the dead in purgatory, a memorial, a reminder to the living, family pride and tradition: of greater social utility. So one comes upon these mortuary chapels dedicated to the gentry all over the country: of Catholic Arundells of Lanherne in their church at St. Columb major, Arundells of Wardour at Tisbury, Throckmortons at Coughton, Blounts at Mapledurham; Protestant gentry everywhere. Sometimes the crowded monuments offer both a museum and a history of the family: as of the Spencers at Brington, the Manners at Bottesford, Russells at Chenies. Occasionally the exhibition of family pride is outrageous, as in the case of the princely monument to the Earl of Hertford that dominates the whole end of the south choir-aisle in Salisbury cathedral. The Protectoral Seymours were notoriously family-proud.

Family pride blazed forth in such a society as never before: it took many forms and there are a thousand evidences of it. Houses and churches alike were plastered with coats of arms; a line was traced between those who were armigerous and those who were not. No wonder William Shakespeare – better born on his mother's side than his father's – was so keen to equip himself, or rather, his father, with a coat of arms: *Non sans droict!* Sir Anthony Wagner tells us that the pedigree craze was 'well under way before the end of the fifteenth century but reached its zenith under Elizabeth, and was no doubt a natural accompaniment of the emergence of a new aristocracy in a society with a passionate and patriotic attachment to its past and its roots.'[27] I think the process was more complex and needs a subtler explanation. For one thing, the aristocracy was not 'new', though it had received a new reinforcement: Riches, Herberts, Cromwells, Russells, Wriothesleys, Bacons, Cecils. The strenuous shake-up Tudor society experienced in the course of the Reformation, the ups and downs of families, the marked increase in the number of the gentry and aspirants to enter the sacred enclosure, brought this kind of social awareness to the fore: it mattered more whether one was a gentleman or no – and has mattered ever since, up to the social dissolution of our day – more than it had done in the Middle Ages. For another thing, it had something to do with the secularisation of society. Medieval society was dominated by religion – the Elizabethans ran up houses, great and small, not churches. Men have, or had, to worship something: when many significant objects of devotion were taken away, the family came to take the place. Where medieval wills often express a wish to be buried in front of some image, Elizabethan wills define a wish to be buried beside father or mother, husband or wife, or at any rate with the family around one.

The funerals of these people were in keeping. The expenses of those of peers and grandees were often prodigious and more than the estate could afford. The body of the third Earl of Huntingdon lay above ground for four months in 1595–6 while widow, family, and state wrangled as to who was to bear the expense of burying it. Many wills expressly required a simple funeral, for, of course, one was supposed to be buried in accordance with one's station. It was a question of the family's social prestige. Many such grand funerals are described in the diary of Henry Machyn, a London merchant.[28] Sir Philip Sidney's funeral was never forgotten; but then, it was made a state occasion – he was given the funeral of a prince – and it was commemorated in a work of art, which was engraved, Thomas Lant's Roll. Here is an ordinary knight of good family, Sir John Savage, buried at Macclesfield in 1597. A grand procession was formed, headed by a trumpeter 'sounding a doleful note', and two yeomen followed by 'so many poor persons in gowns as he was years of age, which was seventy-four.'[29] Next came his colours, his numerous household servants, then his banners and emblems, 'his great horse covered to the heels with black, with arms thereon.' There followed a numerous company of knights and gentlemen carrying mottoes, and spurs and sword. The mayor headed the local neighbours and townsmen. After the burial the trumpeters were 'to sound up aloud and so return homeward'. This kind of spectacle might have been observed at any time, in country or town, throughout the period.

Sir Anthony Wagner refers to 'the passion for ancestry developed rather suddenly by the new men of the Elizabethan era from Burghley downwards.'[30] But the passion was as marked with men of old family like Sampson Erdeswicke, William Habington, and Thomas Trevelyan as it was with 'new' Burghley. Burghley indeed wrote down that 'gentility was but ancient riches', but that cannot have exhausted his thought on the subject. The family self-consciousness pops out again when Robert Cecil interposed himself upon the scene at Essex's trial to say: 'I am your inferior for nobility for I am not in the rank of the prime nobility, yet noble I am' – as the son of a new peer.[31] Francis Bacon expressed himself with patronising snobbery at a bright economic proposition of Lionel Cranfield's – 'more indeed than I could have looked for from a man of his breeding.'[32] This was a bit much coming from the scion of a very recent family, whose grandfather had kept the sheep and swine accounts for the abbey of Bury St. Edmunds. The seventeenth Earl of Oxford constantly referred to Sir Walter Ralegh as 'the Jack' and 'the Knave', choosing to regard him as an upstart; actually the Raleghs were a very old Devon family, and Sir Walter might well have been the seventeenth in his line. This excruciating concern with status, the anguished selfconsciousness, the necessity to define one's position, was rendered all the more acute by the rise of the gentry.

The rhythm between town and country operated like a kind of systole and diastole to form the pulse of the nation. It was a major factor in the social life of the time – in fact more important then, on account of the higher death-rate in towns, especially London. Every ten years there was a major visitation of the plague; under the surface of filth, stench and insanitariness it smouldered endemically. This affected the towns much more drastically; into the large gaps made in the ranks of the population came sturdier types from the countryside, from near and far. Hence the mercurial changeability of town life as against the stability and continuity, the conservatism, of the country. Urban families came and went in three generations, few even lasted as long in any prominence. The rhythm was – especially for London, the magnet of the national life – from the land to the town and back to the land.

At Exeter, for example, the leading merchants 'had, with few exceptions, come into the city from outside, some from far afield, from Wales, Cheshire, Suffolk and Worcestershire, others from the adjoining counties of Somerset and Dorset, and most from the Devonshire countryside. Of the Devonians who rose to be mayors of Exeter, the Periams, Hursts, Staplehills, Spurways and Peters, among others, were all members of franklin families, with pedigrees and lands going back two or three hundred years; and those who came in from other counties were often similarly descended.'[33] But these families did not last long in town: at Leicester, for example, 'it was rare for any business to last a hundred years. . . . In London and in the provincial towns the merchant class was constantly changing in composition, losing its successful members to the landed class and recruiting from the same class, though possibly from a lower level.' We may comment on this: usually from a lower level, for they came to town to make their fortune; even when these merchants came from the landed gentry, they were almost always younger sons, the eldest stayed at home to run the estate. As for changeability, where today are the Whittingtons and Greshams, the Skevingtons, Suttons, Judds and Smiths? While even in nearby East Anglia there are still Walpoles and Bacons, Bedingfields and Fountains, still Townshends at Raynham and Cokes at Holkham.

The overwhelming preponderance of eastern England against western, visible all through the Middle Ages and into the succeeding centuries – it decided the Civil War as it had done the Wars of the Roses – is being somewhat counteracted by the increasing fluidity of a money economy in the later sixteenth century. We see this at work in the remarkable rise of Bristol and Exeter at this time, and the doubling of its population by Plymouth, still however a town of the third rank for all its bustling maritime activity. Nevertheless fifteen of the twenty-five leading towns 'still lay on the eastern side': there was no doubt where the balance of power lay, and this was clinched by the linch-pin of it all, London.

'London, too, recruited her merchant class to a marked degree from the younger sons of small landed families in the provinces.'[34] It would be possible to trace this process for hundreds of individuals, from all the counties of England and (for many of them) back again. Let us look at an eloquent example from North Wales, the Myddeltons of Denbigh – there are still Myddeltons in Denbigh, if no longer in London.[35] They were an old stock of small Welsh gentry. Richard Myddelton was governor of Denbigh, in Leicester's great lordship; he had sixteen children living – too many to support at home: three or four of them went to London, of whom two won fame and fortune, Sir Thomas and Sir John Myddelton. Some of these went back with their gains to the land they came from. The eldest son remained on the land, to found another landed branch of the family at Wrexham; and of his eleven children three became London merchants, following the lead of their two brilliantly successful uncles.

Aided, rather than impeded, by four business marriages, Thomas Myddelton prospered in sugar and was lucky in his privateering ventures – unlike the aristocratic Earl of Cumberland, who laid out far more than his returns. Myddelton was ambitious, and wealthy, enough to aspire to buy Leicester's Crown lordship of Denbigh on his demise; disappointed of this he purchased Leicester's other lordship of Chirk with its castle. He proceeded to buy up estates in North Wales, particularly in his native county, to invest happily in mortgages, to consolidate the freeholds he bought, especially in the neighbourhood of Chirk. No wonder his descendants are still there today. His activity, and his investments, his purchases of grain and other foodstuffs for expeditions to the Indies and to Ireland, infused new blood into the local economy, while his interchange of cattle between his Welsh and Lincolnshire estates provided a fruitful rhythm.

In this Welsh family one observes even more intensely than with English folk the ties of blood and kin. They intermarried noticeably with their in-laws, to a degree that would hardly have been possible before the Reformation. The brothers helped each other out with cash or combined in loans to third parties. Thomas's ledger is full of cash transactions with brothers Hugh, Charles, Foulk and Peter; nor was William excluded after he married in Ghent, became a Catholic there and a pensioner of Spain, friend of Hugh Owen the traitor. William was still received as a guest in the house in Tower Street, if not in the country mansion at Stansted Mountfitchet. 'Blood was after all thicker than water. . . . Like any good Welshman, Thomas of Galch Hill and Tower Street was in touch with the whole *cenedl*, paying marked deference to the *pencenedl* (head of the clan), his Oxford-educated cousin William of Gwaenynog – poor relation though he was to the wealthy capitalist of the clan.'[36] Brother Hugh, following Thomas to London, became a bigger public figure by his achievement of bringing the New River to the city. The same themes are observable in his career: marriage to a well-to-do widow, intense family feeling, the strong pull back home to the native hills. Hugh Myddelton never lost his interest in Denbigh; when he became successful in London, he used his influence there to obtain a new charter for the borough, making the journey home for its presentation. Like so many others of his type and class, he recognised the social obligation attaching to success and purchased lands for a charitable endowment in his native town. We find him presenting silver cups – still in their possession – to the corporations of Denbigh, Ruthin, and Oswestry, where he had property, and also, by a nice touch, to William Myddelton, head of the old house of Gwaenynog.

The most conspicuous and lasting expression of this movement between town and country is perhaps in the realm of social betterment – what immediate post-Reformation society accomplished towards its own improvement, in the fields of public charity, poor relief, aid to employment, education. All this was largely secular in character, though it invoked the Protestant ideology of the age and was influenced in part by its motives, even more by those of social utility. This subject has only in recent years been thoroughly mastered and depicted in detail.[37] When all allowances are made, the achievement was prodigious, and now that it is better understood it must profoundly affect our view of the age, qualify our opinion of its brutality – all societies exemplify residual violence – its hard acquisitiveness, soften some of the raw edges, enforce a subtler comprehension. English society at the end of Elizabeth's reign was altogether better off, its social needs better provided for, both more efficient and more humane, than at the beginning. The middle decades from 1533 to 1558, about a generation, were a period of upheaval and disturbance amounting to revolution, with grave dissension and losses, both economic and cultural. But once the upheaval settled down, the experience was digested with its gains, it proved an immense increase of wealth and strength to society, on more efficient, secular lines; it provided the groundswell for the astonishing efflorescence of the age. This did not begin to be evident till the first decade of Elizabeth's government, with its lenity and internal peace, of which she was justifiably proud and consciously sought people's approbation.

We can now appreciate the dominant rôle that London's wealth enabled it to play in the expansion, amounting to a transformation, of the country's social institutions. We learn from Professor Jordan that one-third of the philanthropic funds contributed over the whole country during the period 1480–1660 came from 'this one almost prodigally generous city. When we reflect that at no time . . . did London's population amount to much more than 5 per cent of that of the realm, the dominant rôle of the city in founding the necessary institutions of a new age becomes abundantly clear . . . The greatness of London's cultural and historical achievement can be assessed only against that of the realm as a whole: it can be compared sensibly with that of no county, while it was vastly greater than that of all the remaining urban centres of the realm combined. London stood *solus* in England and, for that matter, in the western world.'[38] These are generous, if enthusiastic, words. Two comments may be made.

There is no reason to think the Elizabethan section of Professor Jordan's total period any other than average: if the outpouring of wealth for social betterment was greater in the decades before the Civil War, the outpouring in Elizabeth's reign was larger than that before. A more important point is that, though the money was made in London, it was mostly made by incomers from other parts of England, and most of their philanthropy went to the parts they came from. It reflected the large gains these merchants made in the city, but, as Professor Jordan remarks, they were as generous as they were rich. The money came, in larger proportion, from a small number of the very rich: the consistent attitude they display shows their overriding regard for social responsibility: they recognised that money had its obligations and they acted nobly upon it. We can only say that this stands in some contrast to the Victorian age.

The Elizabethans were engaged in meeting the visible needs of society, as against the invisible. The Reformation ended the useless expenditure of wealth on prayers for the dead – though the policy emanating from London and the progressive South and East had to be imposed on the backward North. Similarly the amount of money spent on church-building dropped to a negligible amount – the country had enough churches already: more resources free to dispose of. Professor Jordan points out that before the Dissolution the monasteries were abnegating social responsibilities, in the withdrawal of alms and shrinking support for the poor – while they went on building, as notably at Glastonbury, we may add. In Yorkshire the monasteries had gone on fulfilling 'an essentially medieval function in an essentially medieval society.'[39] Yorkshire and Lancashire people went on with their prayers for the dead. when the South was already leaving off before the Reformation. The Reformation administered a shock to the North, and in the course of its prolonged opposition to the new course leadership passed to new hands, to men who had staked their fortunes on the new order and were engaging in re-shaping its institutions to operate more efficiently. Yorkshire and Lancashire alike lagged a full generation behind the South. The northern capital, York, received a double blow with the decline of its medieval cloth industry, and the drastic reduction of its ecclesiastical institutions and their wealth. Both Bristol and Norwich overtook it in population. Then came the industrial expansion of Halifax, Leeds and Wakefield, with broadcloth and kerseys, of Sheffield with its cutlery and the numerous small mines opening up. Yorkshire, too, saw a transformation by the end of the reign; not until then did it reach its pre-Reformation level of charity. 'Secularism had at last gained as complete a triumph in Yorkshire as in the rest of the realm.'[40]

Since Professor Jordan has made so detailed an investigation of a large subject, we need here suggest only its main lines and characteristics. All classes were engaged in what was a conscious national effort at social betterment. The nobility were given, as might have been expected, to the more conspicuous form of building almshouses at their gates or in their towns – as we can still see in Burghley's home-town of Stamford, or Bess of Hardwick's at Derby, or Northampton's Trinity Hospital at Greenwich; or Archbishop Whitgift's at Croydon, Abbot's at Guildford. The gentry were more concerned with poor relief. 'It seems evident in scores of wills that the gentry were distressed by what they saw of poverty . . . and that these bequests for outright relief, whether as doles or as endowments for permanent relief, represent the admirable and sympathetic concern of men who perhaps possessed no mature grasp of the problem or the means for its solution.'[41] As one goes about the churches of England one can still come across bread-doles going back to those times, or the cupboards in which they were kept, like that in the church of Coughton, Warwickshire. More remarkable was the determined leadership of the great merchants of London, above all – though followed by other towns – to endow experimental schemes about the country to put the poor and unemployed on work, or to provide a stock to lend out to young apprentices starting a trade, or to give dowries to help girls to get a husband. And this in addition to the more obvious forms of philanthropy – outright bequests of money, the founding of almshouses and schools. The national endeavour in regard to education, the founding and endowing of schools, was on an immense scale, right up to the Civil War which destroyed and arrested so much. The clergy, as we should expect, devoted their charities chiefly to education, in particular the universities. The yeomanry followed on behind, though on nothing like the scale of the dynamic elements in society, the gentry and merchants. All in all, the age witnessed a tremendous effort in bringing society abreast with social needs, after the dislocation, and under the inspiration, of the Reformation.

The extraordinary generosity of the London merchants was written on the face not only of the city itself, but of innumerable towns and villages from which they had come. We learn that the philanthropic effort of ten average counties, considerable as it was, was not to be compared with the immense total contributed by London benefactors: with double the population these counties gave one quarter of what London gave, which means that London gave proportionately eight times as much as ten average counties.[42] Of course, this reflects the fact of London's concentration of wealth; we must also remember that the bulk of these benefactors came from all over England – it is doubtful whether we should regard them as Londoners, unless born and bred in the city.

Within the city the evidences of philanthropy were visible in concentrated form – thank-offerings for success as well as recognition of social obligation. A conspicuous example, which should give pause to summary and ignorant reflections upon the age, is that of Thomas Sutton: for this acquisitive Lincolnshireman became the richest commoner in the land and gave the whole of his fortune to charity. 'The total contribution made by Thomas Sutton to English charitable needs was but little short of £130,000 [multiply by forty or fifty!], a truly immense sum which would probably have impoverished any other private person of his generation, be he merchant or great noble. The benefaction also constituted a challenge to all men of his age, being a kind of model against which humbler but still capacious designs of good works could be measured; for, as a contemporary accurately put it, this was "the greatest gift that ever was given in England, no abbey at the first foundation thereof excepted".'[43] It is significant that Sutton should have purchased the London Charterhouse – centre of what monastic resistance there was to Henry VIII, then the mansion of the unsatisfactory Duke of Norfolk, executed in 1572 – and founded a famous English school. He also founded a hospital alongside of it, for impoverished gentlemen, merchants, soldiers, or royal servants. And there were other charitable bequests besides. It was deplorable of Bacon, who combined nobility of intellect with a touch of the ignoble, that he should have advised James I to set aside so unexampled a will. It is to the credit of Thomas Sutton that he should have resisted the temptation of a peerage to endow James's younger son with the fortune.[44] The founder appropriately rests in the Charterhouse beneath one of the most splendid Renaissance monuments in London, sculpted by Nicholas Stone.

Thomas Sutton was only the most conspicuous of a number of rich men who won fame by their benefactions. Early in the reign Sir Martin Bowes, a Yorkshireman who made his fortune as a goldsmith in London, left a large bequest, one half for poor relief, the other for general charitable purposes. Sir Thomas Rowe, a rich merchant tailor, left a large bequest shortly after, similarly disposed. Sir William Craven, another Yorkshireman, made his fortune as a merchant tailor in London; charitable enough to make donations to Oxford in his lifetime, at his death he left a handsome bequest to found a grammar school at his native Burnsall near Skipton, besides a varied number of charities in London, characteristically to the poor of his parish there. Sir William was one of the patrons of an interesting scheme for turning Ripon Minster into a college, from which there might have developed a Yorkshire university; but this failed to take effect.[45] His son continued his father's generosity, becoming the founder of the Craven scholarships at Oxford and Cambridge, besides leaving money to a number of neighbouring parishes in Yorkshire. Sir James Lancaster, well known for his East Indies voyages, being a bachelor, was able to leave the whole of his fortune to charities. He divided it between London, where most of it went to the charitable purposes of the Skinners' Company, of which he was a member, and his native Basingstoke. There, in addition to poor relief, he left money for a lectureship in the church – he was tinged with Puritanism – besides, more usefully, endowments for trading apprentices and for young maids to marry. His church is one where the ancient bread-dole continues.

When one walks round the City with Stow one is struck by the number of almshouses of recent erection, in addition to those of earlier date: nearly every City Company had its foundations for old and impoverished members, and many parishes had their almshouses besides. Within a few streets in neighbouring Bishopsgate and Broadstreet Wards we find the almshouses of the Parish Clerks, next of the Leathersellers, then those built by Sir Andrew Judd – founder of Tonbridge School – in the parish of St. Helen's. His daughter Alice, widow of Customer Smythe, augmented the foundation; 'she hath also given in her last will and testament in other charitable uses, as to the hospitals and to the poor of other parishes and good preachers, the sum of £300. As also to the poor scholars in the two universities of Oxford and Cambridge £200 . . . according to her godly and charitable mind.'[46] In nearby Broad Street Sir Thomas Gresham had built eight almshouses – in addition to founding Gresham College and building the Royal Exchange for the city, besides the family foundation of Gresham's School, Holt, where they came from. In the same ward the Tailors and Linen-armourers had 'builded about a proper quadrant or squared court seven almshouses' for their decayed members and their wives. Not far in the same ward were the medieval almshouses of St. Anthony's. We see how generous these merchants were within the walls, as well as outside, and can watch them almost vying with each other in good works.

By 1600 Bristol, with a population of 17,000, had moved into the second place after London – though *longo intervallo* – in numbers, wealth and expenditure on social betterment. Professor Jordan tells us that it was led by a merchant class of 'great vitality, boldness and imagination.'[47] Certainly the city made the most of its grand opportunity at the Dissolution, buying the monastic properties constricting its growth in and around for £1790, towards which sum the parishes contributed over £500 from the sale of superfluous church plate. In contrast with London nearly all its merchant class came from the town and its own neighbourhood. When Professor Jordan calculates that one-fifth of Bristol's charitable expenditure came from London, one must remember that most of these donors were Bristol men. A large bequest of £10,000 came from Lady Ramsay in 1601; she was the widow of a London grocer, but she was the daughter of a Bristol clothier.[48] Of sixty-nine London benefactors to Somerset, for example, fifty-one were born in the county, while others had ties with it. Such was the usual interchange, the regular rhythm.

Bristol merchants were dominantly concerned with poor relief and schemes for employment, as befitted a busy industrial town. But educational provision was no less remarkable. The Thorne family, pre-eminent in Bristol, recognised their social responsibilities by founding the grammar school; Robert Thorne left munificent bequests totalling £6775, over £2000 for poor relief in Bristol, £500 for London. The London merchant, Sir John Gresham, left £2000 to be invested for the poor of Bristol – with which he must have had business ties from which he had made money: bequests usually had this element of recognition. The Reformation immensely increased the opportunities of putting provision for the poor on a solider foundation. Henry VIII gave his doctor, George Owen, a parcel of lands of the Order of St. John of Jerusalem, which Owen applied to the support of ten more almsmen in Bristol, with more for education and the clergy. William Chester purchased Black Friars and turned it into an almshouse. The Merchant Venturers established their own for aged seamen: prudently administered, the endowment was worth

£100 a year by 1600. The largest almshouse benefactor was a rich clergyman, Thomas White – but he was the son of a Bristol clothier. This generous man nearly exhausted his estate in his lifetime, some £19,000, most of which went to London. John Willis reduced himself to charity – which he received – by spending all he had on constructing seven miles of causeway round the city. A group of merchants privately financed bringing a water-supply to the town-quay. A public library was founded in 1614, second after Norwich. 'Merchants in the later years of the Elizabethan era almost invariably included in their wills at least modest sums for the older almshouses.'[49]

Somerset was a rich and populous county, with some 120–130,000 people: twice that of the poor county of Cornwall. It produced a large number of charitable donors, with an unusually high proportion of yeomen – in this like Kent. Professor Jordan pays tribute to 'the high sense of public duty borne by quite simple and often wholly untrained men.'[50] In Somerset, as also in London, the proportion of women donors was above average: in the county this may have been chance, in London it probably reflected the higher mortality among business men – as in America today. Between 1512 and 1599 nine almshouses were added across the county. Then began the large foundations: Nicholas Wadham's at Ilton, Sir John Popham's at Wellington, Bishop Still's addition at Wells, the London merchant, Richard Huish's, at Taunton. Thomas Bellott, steward of the royal Household – in addition to helping to rebuild Bath abbey – converted a large house he bought there for the benefit of the poor seeking relief from the waters. Before his death he had got rid of almost the whole of his estate for charity. It was a tiny group of donors that contributed half of all benefactions: in that reflecting the inequality of wealth – but also their proportionate recognition of social obligation. In Somerset few were noblemen; most were gentry and merchants, with the yeomanry playing their modest part. In the upshot Somerset was a favoured county, with 'no less than ninety-two parishes with charitable endowments of over £100; fifty-one of these had funds ranging up to £400; there was a surprisingly large group of twenty-nine parishes, well distributed across the breadth of the county, with endowments for the relief of the poor ranging upwards from £400.'[51]

The wealth of the towns went to irrigate the countryside, that of London irrigated the whole country. But in different proportions. London was relatively less active in East Anglia, though

Norfolk sent out so pre-eminent a family as the Greshams; partly because Norfolk was a rich county – well populated with 170–180,000 people – more self-sufficient than most areas, a microcosm of England. East Anglia had its own university in Cambridge, to which benefactions flowed: Caius was virtually a Norfolk college. As a manufacturing, clothing area Norfolk benefactors showed an advanced interest in new schemes for employment and rehabilitation of the poor, their dominant concern.

London benefactors concerned themselves more with the home counties intimately connected with the capital; secondly with the relatively poor and backward counties of the Western Border – Cheshire, Shropshire, Worcestershire, Gloucestershire. Still more with Wales, a poor country, but a prolific supplier of manpower to England, and of merchants to London. Wales was the gainer by this intercourse; for, of forty-three London benefactors 'only twenty-three were certainly Welsh-born and twelve were certainly English-born.'[52] In this matter London was subsidising Wales, helping to even things out. This was a conscious process with the backward North Country: London benefactors made a determined effort upon Catholic backwardness, notably in fostering schools and Protestant preachings in Lancashire.

Let us look at two areas, by way of contrast, one in the North-West, Lancashire, the other in the South-East, Kent.

Kent was one of the richest and most populous counties, remarkable for the size and spirit of its yeomanry – reflected in the large number of yeoman benefactors.[53] Yet in this county the nobility were also to the fore – in Cornwall there were none – no doubt on account of Kent's proximity to the capital and possession of a royal palace in Greenwich. There Northampton built his Trinity hospital for twelve Greenwich men and eight from his Norfolk birthplace; he also founded almshouses at Castle Rising, Norfolk and at Clun, Shropshire. Lord Cobham rebuilt a suppressed college of canons at Cobham for eighteen poor men, all on a generous scale. William Lambarde the antiquary acted as executor – himself the son of a London draper hailing from Herefordshire, he spent a large part of his estate on another almshouse at Greenwich for twenty poor. Sir John Hawkins built a hospital at Chatham for twelve poor seamen and their wives, leaving funds for the poor of London, Deptford and Plymouth, his native town. A large benefactor was William Lambe, a Kent man by origin, who made a fortune in the London cloth trade: he founded two grammar schools, at Maidstone and his native Sutton Valence, an almshouse at the latter for twelve persons, besides many other benefactions.

The chief burden of responsibility was borne by the gentry and the merchants, with the infiltration of new merchant wealth moving from London into Kentish gentry. The society of Kent – as of other counties immediately bordering on London – was more fluid and flexible than that of counties farther away: the farther away the more conservative, until one encountered the resistance of Yorkshire and Lancashire to the movement of the age. But the ruling elements in society – the gentry in the counties, merchants in the towns – found the new device of the charitable trust an effective instrument in safeguarding their bequests according to their intentions and directing the future shape of society the way they wished. Kent found itself better provided than any other county, with eighty-five parishes rich in charitable funds, just over a hundred adequately provided; a hundred and thirty rural parishes, thinly populated, had funds ranging up to £100. Altogether some two hundred and forty parishes had reasonable provision of their own already – apart from what government or county might do – for distressing poverty. All this had come from private benefactions, to which in well-off Kent even husbandmen – exceptionally – contributed. Social obligations were thus regarded and acted upon by all classes, according to their means.

The rhythm of social change varied from region to region, class to class, and above all between town and country. Lancashire exhibited a very different pattern from Kent. It was a very poor county, for wealth thirty-fifth among English counties: which meant, considering its size, that it was among the lowest, with Cornwall, Cumberland, Durham, or Wales.[54] It was also a very backward one, still living in the Middle Ages: right up to the Reformation and into it, Lancashire people were still giving largely to religious purposes. Even after the Reformation some wills allot money for masses for souls, 'if legal'; but of course the government of Elizabeth was not going to let them thus waste their money. If not legal, 'otherwise to the poor': it went to the poor.[55] Actually a strikingly low proportion went to poor relief in Lancashire – there may have been more private charity: there could not have been more trifling allocations for municipal betterment. Not until 1600 did Lancashire begin to catch up in regard to poor relief, lagging half a century behind the rest of England.

Towards 1600 Lancashire was picking up, with improved

returns from the land increasing the economic well-being of the gentry; still more with manufacture and commerce beginning to move forward in the eastern towns, Manchester, Bolton, Rochdale, Bury, Leigh. These became strongholds of Puritanism: a popular form of philanthropy, if that is the word for it, was the founding of lectureships in the churches – perhaps further evidence of an endemic religiosity. Protestant archbishops, Hutton and Sandys, founded almshouses and schools; the outstanding direction of charity is to be seen in the founding of schools – no less than sixteen from the Reformation to 1600, a still greater number thenceforward up to the destructive Civil War. Indeed more schools were founded than in any other county; they were more needed, so few had existed before the Reformation, and the impulse was largely the Protestant desire to reclaim so backward an area. It was the grander gentry who put up a stubborn resistance to progress – and supported the priests whom Dr. Allen, a Lancashire man, educated abroad to keep the flame going. It is significant that it was the smaller gentry who provided the largest group of benefactors, donating four times more than the upper gentry. These smaller folk were on the upgrade as the result of the Dissolution. The lands of Cartmel priory were bought by yeomen; the immense parish was without gentry, until in 1610 the manor was bought by George Preston, a yeoman of Holker, on his way to becoming a squire. One sees Holker Hall and the Cavendishes looming up in the perspective of time. Nearly all the fifty-five London donors to Lancashire during Jordan's period (1480–1660) were really Lancashire men. Those prominent ecclesiastics, Archbishop Sandys, Bishop Pilkington, Dean Nowell – founders of schools at Hawkshead, Rivington and Middleton – were Lancashire men: Pilkington and Nowell from old gentry. Archbishop Sandys was *not* of humble parentage.[56] He came of yeoman stock at Graithwaite for centuries;[57] his father was receiver-general for Furness abbey, his son entered the peerage with a fat manor of the episcopal see of Worcester for his base: a nice epitome of the rise of the gentry upon the opportunities afforded by the Reformation. By 1600 Lancashire was in large part – dragging the Catholic gentry reluctantly with it – launched upon its modern course, and with a considerable increase of population: about 100,000, still underpopulated for so large an area.

As to the rise of the gentry not merely this chapter, but this whole book, will provide evidence. And in every sphere, not only political and economic, but social and cultural, in art and architecture, the standing witness still of hundreds of houses and monuments for those with eyes to see.

To quote a passage from William Blake, supremely one with eyes to see, cited by an historian with those qualitites of inspiration and imagination: 'To Generalize is to be an Idiot. To Particularize is the Alone Distinction of Merit.'[58] Though this may not be true for philosophy or mathematics, it is profoundly true for history, for it is of the nature of the subject.

CHAPTER IV

CLASS AND SOCIAL LIFE

DIFFICULT as it may be for the denizens of a democratic society to imagine, let alone understand, Elizabethan society, it is less so for anyone who grew up in the country in the early decades of this century. For, until the earthquake of the first world war of 1914–18, society remained recognisable as continuous, at least in rural England, from Elizabethan days. It exemplified an organic structure, which recognised a principle: it was based on hierarchical order, in which social class expressed social functions. People knew their place in it, where they stood and how they were expected to behave – always with a margin of exceptions, the inassimilable, the misfit, the criminal, in a word, the exceptional (a Marlowe, for instance). Here is a principle upon which to thread the immense tapestry of social life, which this book is to portray. Here we can only illustrate how it was organised. Completeness is impossible; even the plays of Shakespeare, the most complete portrait of Elizabethan life, omit one of the most important areas of that society – the religious.

We should begin at the top, the point at which the Court, monarch and magnates, came directly in contact with the country at large and rubbed shoulders with the people.

The Queen's summer progresses were a prime means of making that contact, of showing the monarch to her people and acquainting her with the country: it served a purpose both social and political and – at a profounder level – anthropological. We have had a glimpse of the quasi-hieratic rituals of the Court at the centre; its peregrinations followed a fairly regular round. The Queen was usually back at Whitehall for those ceremonies and jollifications at her Accession Day on 17 November. ('It is a curious fact that the day continued to be observed as a public holiday at the Exchequer, and in the schools of Westminster and Merchant Taylors' up to the middle of the nineteenth century – so long has the impetus of the age continued, in small matters as in great.')[1] Christmas, the holiday season of the year running to

Twelfth Night, was usually spent at Whitehall, with its crowded jollities, dancing, gaming, masks, plays, revels, with its glittering show of New Year Gifts, from her courtiers to the Queen, and from her to them – some ocular evidence of their favour and standing. Plays were resumed at Candlemas and Shrovetide, the Court moving round to Greenwich and Richmond, Oatlands or Nonsuch or Hampton Court. Back at Whitehall for spring and early summer, the ambivalent monarch performed the ceremony of washing the feet of twelve poor men on Maundy Thursday, just as the Pope did – on one occasion, to underline good relations with Spain, observing to the ambassador, 'You see, in essentials, we Catholic monarchs think alike.' St. George's day saw the Garter ceremonies at Windsor, just as today; Elizabeth performed them by deputy, since it was then a purely masculine occasion. But she saw the plays that accompanied them, *The Merry Wives of Windsor*, for example.

High summer was the period for the progresses, which were apt to last for two or three months; so the chief councillors and officials of the Household accompanied her. The places visited were a microcosm of the country and significant of its main activities and concerns. The two chief commercial cities, Norwich and Bristol, were thus favoured; the universities several times received visits, with prolonged festivities and entertainments, plays, speeches, disputations. Cathedral cities and lesser towns were taken in their stride; everywhere the pageant passed, bell-ringing and the citizens turned out in fur and feather. The journeys were made in short stages, mostly from great house to great house, with intermediate stops at one of the royal manors lying in the way, Woodstock, or Havering, or St. Augustine's at Canterbury.

The main problem was how to house all the courtiers and their train, for the *cortège* would number two or three hundred. Burghley stated that he had enlarged Theobalds – it became a palace – for this purpose and at the Queen's insistence. Only the largest magnates could entertain them all – such as Burghley at Theobalds or Burghley, Leicester at Kenilworth or Wansted, Lord Rich at Leighs priory, Hatton at Holdenby – and it cost a fortune. Burghley considered that it had cost him £2–£3000 a time – though this was certainly an over-estimate – and he had the honour twelve times. The Queen got no farther than Bristol – when prayers were offered in church for her preservation on so dangerous a journey – and into Worcestershire and Staffordshire; she never ventured into the rude North or got so far as its capital, York.

Naturally the progresses were most frequent in the first two decades, when the Queen had to show herself to, and acquaint herself with, the country: they were not mere joy-rides, though she derived much pleasure from them, as her successor did not. In 1561, when things were well settled, she made a prolonged tour into Hertfordshire, Essex and Suffolk, taking in such houses as Wansted (not yet Leicester's), Ingatestone (Sir William Petre's, as it is Lord Petre's today), Leigh's (Lord Rich's), St. Osyth's (Lord Darcy's), Helmingham (of the Tollemaches, as it still is); and such towns as Hertford, Ipswich, Harwich, Colchester. Next year, 1562, was occupied with the crisis of the unsuccessful intervention in France: no progress, and 1563 saw only a visit to Eton.

In 1564 and 1566 came the well-known visits to Cambridge and Oxford respectively, each with its week's programme of entertainments and useful encouragement of academic discipline and morale. At Oxford, when the puritanical leader, Dr. Humphreys, kissed her hand the Queen commended his large, loose gown, with 'I wonder your notions should be so narrow.'[2] Wherever she passed the students knelt in the streets. 'And here it may not be amiss to observe that the Queen's countenance and the Earl of Leicester's care [he was Chancellor, as Cecil was of Cambridge] had such an effect upon the diligence of this learned body that, within a few years after, it produced more shining instances of real worth than had ever been sent abroad at the same time in any age whatsoever.' The universities had been through a bad time in the black decades, the religious upheavals of the 1540's and 1550's. This was now a period of recovery, which these state-visits were designed to foster.

Each of these years saw progresses into the home counties; in 1568 into Northamptonshire, in 1569 from her own Oatlands in Surrey to Guildford and Farnham, to Titchfield and Southampton, and back to Lord Treasurer Winchester's vast house at Basing (destroyed in the odious Civil War). In 1572 there was a more extended progress from Theobalds, where the Queen stayed three days, to St. Alban's, Woburn (of the Russells then as today), Kenilworth and Warwick, back by Compton Wynyates and Charlecote (of the Comptons and the Lucys and still in their families), to Reading and Windsor. At Warwick, where the Queen stayed in the castle she had conferred upon Ambrose Dudley (and made him Earl), took place several incidents germane to our theme.

After the 'princely sports' at Kenilworth, the Queen made up her mind to return to Warwick late at night to see 'what cheer my

Lady of Warwick made.'³ She unexpectedly descended upon Thomas Fisher's house, the leading townsman, and found the party at supper there. She sat for a while with them and then 'went to visit the good man of the house, who at that time was grievously vexed with the gout. Who, being brought out into the gallery and would have kneeled or rather fallen down, but her Majesty would not suffer it, but with most gracious words comforted him. So that, forgetting or rather counterfeiting his pain he would, in more haste than good speed, be on horseback the next time of her going abroad.' Next day, Sunday, she remained in the castle resting, 'until it pleased her to have the country people resorting to see their dance in the court of the castle, her Majesty beholding them out of her chamber window: which thing, as it pleased well the country people, so it seemed her Majesty was much delighted and made very merry.' At night there were fireworks and a sham siege of a castle, held by the Earl of Oxford, by a battery brought by Warwick from the Tower. In the course of this a miller's house was set on fire at the end of the bridge. Next morning 'it pleased her Majesty to have the poor old man and woman that had their house brent brought unto her: whom she re-comforted very much. And by her Grace's bounty and other courtiers' there was given towards their losses that had taken hurt £25. 12. 8, which was disposed to them accordingly.'⁴ Enough to build another house – a simple, jolly world! and thus was order kept in the people's nursery.

That the roads were not easy to traverse may be seen from Burghley's report to Shrewsbury next summer, August 1573, that 'the Queen had a hard beginning of her progress in the Weald of Kent and namely in some part of Sussex, where surely were more dangerous rocks and valleys, and much worse ground, than was in the Peak.'⁵ They were making for Rye and afterwards Dover, 'where they should have amends.' Burghley wrote 'from the Court, at Mr. Guilford's house', i.e. Hemsted in Benenden, the Court being wherever the Queen was. She had spent a week with Archbishop Parker at Croydon, thence to Orpington, fat old Sir Percival Hart's place, to whom her father had given it: Hart rewarded her with a magnificent entertainment, nymphs and a sea-conflict on the water. Her next stop was at Knole, then her own house, not yet granted away to the Sackvilles. And so to Sissinghurst, where she knighted the owner, Boughton Malherbe (Thomas Wotton's), Hothfield, her own manor of Westenhanger, where she was received by Lord Buckhurst, and Dover. Before the progress, the Archbishop sent Burghley Lambarde's *Perambulation of Kent*, still in manuscript, with a tract on Dover, 'that the Queen, who would be inquisitive concerning the places where she journeyed, might have the more satisfaction given her by her said Treasurer, whom she looked upon as a man of special learning and knowledge of the history and antiquities of her kingdom.'[6]

The Court returned via Canterbury, where the Archbishop was hard put to it to put her up: 'his house was of an ill air, hanging upon the church, having no prospect to look on the people.'[7] In the event she stayed in St. Augustine's, which Henry VIII had transformed from abbey to his own use. This enabled the Archbishop to billet the courtiers in the canons' houses, while he fed the whole Court handsomely in his hall. The Queen attended evensong in the cathedral in state, processing under a canopy 'borne by four of her temporal knights' – the Virgin Queen where not so long before the Virgin Mary would have been borne in state under her canopy: a measure of secularisation, not without its hieratic over-tones.

The Queen's progress to Bristol in 1574 – for her reception there Thomas Churchyard wrote the verse orations – was signalised by the signing of the Convention of Bristol, by which the breach with Spain arising from the events at sea in 1569 was terminated.[8] The Court returned via Wilton, where the Herberts gave her a grand reception, with ordnance shot off in the park. Thence to Salisbury for most of the week, 'during all which time her Majesty was both merry and pleasant.'[9] On the Saturday a hunt in Clarendon park was interrupted by heavy rain, so that the banquet prepared for her out of doors in a house prettily constructed of boughs and arras, which did not keep out the wet, had to serve for the lords while she dined within the lodge.

Next year, 1575, took place the most magnificent of the entertainments on progress, the Queen's three-week stay at Kenilworth – the inner significance of which seems to be that it was Leicester's last bid for her hand. There certainly was some strain between them there; however, we are not concerned with their relations, but with those with her people. The water-pageants that took place on the lake that then existed on the south side of the castle were the chief feature of the shows, though there were a big bear-baiting with dogs in the courtyard, fireworks, ordnance shot off, an Italian tumbler, verses 'not easily read by torchlight', Most interesting to us are the Coventry men who came and sought permission to perform their accustomed history-play, which had been suppressed by the zeal of officious preachers in the city. They petitioned that they 'might have their plays up again';

the Queen, the reverse of a kill-joy, much pleased them by commanding them to perform before her and rewarding them. On a day of grace set aside she dubbed five knights, including the Catholic Sir Thomas Tresham, and charismatically touched nine poor persons for the King's Evil. The entertainments were described at length in a pamphlet by Robert Laneham, in a modified version of Hart's reformed spelling.[10] The 'Princely Pleasures of Kenilworth' were written by the poet Gascoigne, who also wrote an entertainment for Woodstock; as Lyly wrote entertainments for Sudeley, Elvetham and Quarrendon, and Nashe wrote 'Summer's Last Will and Testament' for Archbishop Whitgift at Croydon. We see that these entertainments have their affiliations with literature and music, as well as the visual arts.

One last illustration of a theme, from the prolonged progress of 1578 into Suffolk, Cambridge and Norfolk. The Court stayed three or four days with Burghley at Theobalds, which he was turning into a palace, galleries, gardens, canals. He invited the Scottish ambassador, though he said, with his usual deprecation, that he would find 'nothing worth his desire, considering his foreign travels', adding 'although percase you may see as much to content you as in Muscovia. With no other will I offer any comparison.'[11] (Burghley was well acquainted with the palaces being built abroad: he had a plan of Philip's Escorial in course of construction in his possession).[12] Building was Burghley's only immodesty. And so to Audley End, which became twice the size of the house we see today, with two whole courts. At Cambridge the Latin entertainment was written by Gabriel Harvey.

Norwich sported a utilitarian theme among the pageants: a stage with eight small girls spinning worsted yarn at one end, and at the other eight more knitting worsted hose, the rest of the stage occupied by woollen workers at their work. 'This show pleased her Majesty so greatly as she particularly viewed the knitting and spinning of the children, perused the looms, and noted the several works and commodities.'[13] The minister of the Dutch congregation that had introduced the new draperies made a Latin oration, which she was well qualified to follow and reply to. Thomas Churchyard wrote the entertainments, with their moral:

> Fear not, O Queen, thou art belovèd so
> As subjects true will truly thee defend . . .

At night there were masks, with gods and goddesses, at one of which the mayor was made much of: she took him by the hand in

thanking him, and 'used secret conference, but what I know not.'
On leaving the city, she knighted him, with 'I have laid up in my
breast such good will as I shall never forget Norwich.' Proceeding
onward, she 'did shake her riding-rod and said, "Farewell Norwich," with the water standing in her eyes.' It is unlikely that
Norwich forgot her, or that the city gave her government any
trouble thereafter.

With the political crises of the 1580's, the progresses became
more restricted: the posture of affairs, the war with Spain,
demanded her presence continuously at the centre: it was not
possible to go far. After the Armada pressure was relaxed, and in
the 1590's they were resumed with all their old gaiety, even more
fanciful and literary than before. Elvetham in 1591 – where the
Earl of Hertford had reason to make a special effort to regain
favour (and an expensive entertainment was a recognised way of
doing so) – reached a peak in this period as Kenilworth had in the
earlier. Even in the last two years of her life, in 1601 from Sir
William Cornwallis's at Highgate and in 1602 with Sir Richard
Buckley at Lewisham, the Queen was willing to go a-Maying –
with its folklore significance not lost on the hostile Puritans.

In our time a good deal of information has come to light about
the conduct of the great households: we are particularly concerned here with their function in society, their outgoing side. Let
us take Burghley's own household. His chaplain tells us that he
kept two full-time establishments, one at Cecil House in the
Strand and his country palace of Theobalds in Hertfordshire.[14] In
addition he maintained Burghley, or partly, for his mother lived
there, blind, to an advanced age; besides his establishment at
Court. At Cecil House there were over eighty persons in the
household, besides his Court attendants, officers, secretaries and
their servants. The London house took £1560 a year to maintain
all the year round, whether Burghley was there or not; when he
was, the charges increased by £10 or £12 a week, or more. At
Theobalds the regular household consisted of some twenty-six
or thirty persons; the weekly charge £12. Twenty or thirty poor
people were relieved daily at the gate there, even in his absence,
while his chaplain distributed 20s. a week in money.

This kind of distribution was quite regular from all large
households. For some twenty years each Christmas he gave £35 or
£40 in beef, bread and money to his parishes, in London and in the
country; suits of apparel yearly to twenty poor men lodging in the

Savoy; in his latter years, £40 or £50 a term for releasing prisoners, and towards his end he was distributing 45s. a week to poor prisoners and poor parishes. So that his regular alms amounted to some £500 a year. At Stamford, his home-town, he built and endowed an almshouse for thirteen poor men, and gave an endowment of £30 a year to St. John's, his college at Cambridge. His wife, Mildred, who was something of a blue-stocking, also contributed to educational foundations for scholarships. It would be fair to say that Burghley's foundations were by no means on a generous scale, unlike some other people's; after all, he was founding two grand families, the two branches of his house, and no doubt considered that he was doing enough to set a good example.

That other people thought so is witnessed by the competition there was to get young nobles and sprigs of leading families brought up in his household. This was a feature of the age: boys of good families were often recommended to a noble house for their training and upbringing, for better educational opportunities, company and manners. When the fourth Duke of Norfolk was brought to the block by Cecil (or rather by his own folly), he recommended his children to Cecil's care and protection. His household was recognised as a school of virtue and prudence – though little good in that regard it seems to have done the young Earls of Oxford, Southampton and Rutland who were brought up in it. These young colts were all spoiled, in a way, by their blood and position. On the other hand, Burghley saw to it that they were well educated: more than that he could hardly do – except try to marry them into his family.

Our informant tells us that a number of the principal gentlemen in England sought to prefer their sons and heirs to his service: 'insomuch as I have numbered in his house, attending on the table, twenty gentlemen of his retainers, of a thousand pounds per annum a piece. And of his ordinary men as many.' Burghley, like other nobles and great gentlemen, kept open table in his hall for those of his class resorting to him. 'His steward kept a standing table for gentlemen, besides two other long tables, many times twice set: one for the clerk of the kitchen, the other for yeomen.' For a visual impression of it one has only to think of meals in hall at an Oxford or Cambridge college today – many of them go back to that period and continue some of the usages. The charges of the stable for such a large establishment was not less than £600 a year. Besides which regular charge, 'he bought great quantities of corn in times of dearth, to furnish markets about his house at under prices, to pull down the price to relieve the poor.' Altogether, it is not surprising that his household expenses at his two principal residences amounted to some £2700 a year, even when he was mainly at Court.

'All which great charges and expense do prove he was neither covetous nor miserable.' Even so, he was able to build, on a vast scale, at Burghley and Theobalds – though he had forty years to do it in – and build up a second accumulation of estates for his son Robert and the junior branch of the Cecils. Yet we may accept the conclusion of his dependant, knowing what was to come in the next reign: 'nay I dare undertake, if some had his office, place and credit but seven years, they would gain more in that time than he did in forty years' painful service.'

Burghley was one of the wisest of men, and he saw to it that such an establishment – it was certainly not the largest – was run by faithful, dependable officers. Though coming from ancient Welsh stock, he was a new nobleman. For a more intimate picture of how badly things could go wrong with a great estate, we may look into the mind of one of the old nobility, the ninth Earl of Northumberland, the 'Wizard Earl', He was no fool, but grew – in the Tower – to be a remarkable man. His father, a Catholic, out of sympathy with the trends of the age, had killed himself there at the outbreak of the war with Spain. He had done his best for his son under the new deal by having him instructed by a Protestant clergyman, with the result that the boy grew up believing not very much and became an intellectual associate of such free-wheeling minds as Ralegh and Hariot.

But Northumberland's father had left him without instruction in the secrets of his estates and in the hands of officers and servants who took advantage of his youth and ignorance, and encouraged his wilful extravagance. To these two facts Northumberland attributed the immense losses he inflicted upon his estates when young. 'Want of experience made me negligent in picking them [officers and servants] out fittest for my profit; though wise enough to choose them answerable to my humour, which was to be young, handsome, brave, swaggering, debauched, wild, abetting all my young desires; and all these had their shares with me in my little fortune. Some out of the wasteful expenses that they nourished in the house, others out of the gain of clothes, out of my credit in mercers' and silkmen's shops; others by defalking part of debts from the true owners, using delays of payments to the creditors, too common in the world amongst servants of careless masters; others out of false disbursements in extraordinary expenses, being favourites of the chiefer officers. Then were my felicities, because I knew not better, hawks, hounds, horses, dice, cards, apparel, mistresses: all other riot of expense that follow them were so far afoot and in excess as I knew not where I was, or what I did. Till, out of my means of £3000 yearly, I had made shift in one year and a half to be £1700 in debt.'[15]

What to do in these circumstances? 'Well, woods were concluded the next means of relief, so as the axe was put to the tree; and officers, being forward to clear themselves of their bonds lest an untimely death might give them future troubles, made so speedy sales as within a few years was sold the value of £20,000 well worth £50,000, jewellers and silkmen making their nests in the branches.' And the result? 'In preserving of woods that might easily have been raised, the memory of good trees in rotten roots doth appear above ground at this day: being forced now for the fuel relief of your house at Petworth to sow acorns, whereas I might have had plenty, if either they had had care or I knowledge.'[16]

At this juncture Northumberland took a grip of his own affairs, conning the books of his estates, surveys, plots of manors, records, accounts. 'The fault will be your own, if you understand them not better than any servant you have' – he advises his son and heir.[17] 'They are not difficult now they are done; they are easy and yet cost me much time and much expense to reduce them into order.' As for the servants, 'I must confess I was forced to discard to the very kitchen boys before things could be settled as I wished. For you shall ever find it that servants will strive what they can to uphold any liberty winked at before, if anyone of a former corrupt family [i.e. household] be left.' The Earl had learned the way of hard experience to discard corrupt instruments and 'to hug in mine arms faithful servants, jewels too too precious.'

In spite of these bad beginnings, the Earl was able to turn his estate right round, and hand on a profitable patrimony to his successors. It shows what could be done with a great estate, if proper care was taken of it and the owner looked into his affairs for himself. Conspicuous examples of loss and waste are cited in the case of the third Earl of Huntingdon, who sold most of his estates, and the seventeenth Earl of Oxford, who wasted all his. But precisely: Huntingdon inherited a heavily encumbered estate and neglected his own affairs to rule the North as Lord

President away at York for many years; while Oxford, a gifted aesthete, was of a psychotic instability incapable of managing anything. These exceptions support the rule – and enable us to cast a cold eye on theses and theories about the 'crisis' of aristocracy in our period.

For extreme competence in the management of a great household, and a more intimate glimpse into how it was done, we may turn to the papers of the famous Bess of Hardwick.[18] Moreover, her astonishing career showed what could be achieved, by a combination of good looks, determination and sheer business ability, by a mere woman in that age. She was only the third daughter of a small Derbyshire squire, but she was lucky enough to nurse a neighbouring young gentleman who was much better off; he married her and promptly died, leaving her everything. This enabled her later to buy out her brother from the family home, Hardwick, and to make a potent marriage to Sir William Cavendish, by whom she had her able sons. She persuaded him to sell the monastic lands he had garnered for service to Henry VIII and buy Chatsworth from her sister's husband's family. On Cavendish's death she married a soft-hearted soldier, Sir William St Loe, who was so besotted on her that he left everything away from his own family to her and hers. On his death, now a very rich widow, she was willing to marry the grandest peer in the kingdom, the sixth Earl of Shrewsbury, and to arrange a double dynastic marriage between their children, Talbots and Cavendishes. They ultimately quarrelled – and a resounding row it made; the Queen twice stepped in to bring them together, but in vain, and the public scission split the families, some taking one side, some the other.

However, she had accomplished her work: her splendid houses with coroneted E S everywhere attested her pride and wealth. She was the real founder of the three dukedoms that grew out of her acquisitions – Devonshire, Newcastle and Portland. Her ambition grew with success: when Darnley's brother, young Lennox, was passing through Derbyshire he was captured for a daughter of hers. The upshot of this effort was the little Arabella Stuart, her grand-daughter, who was next in succession to the throne after James I. Not bad going for a small squire's daughter!

A study of her accounts shows how much these great houses were the hub of their localities, dominating the agricultural and economic life of the neighbourhood, with large transactions over cattle and pasture, sales of wool, the provisioning of such a household, the employment of labour, the marginal support of the poor

– the whole thing towering over the neighbourhood as the turrets upon the roofline of Hardwick tower over the landscape all round. Such a house and household were equivalent to a village or small country town. One observes, too, the localism, the basic self-sufficiency of it – the stone, timber, sand, coals on the spot for building and fuel, the draught oxen, cattle and horses, the making of wains, wheels, yokes, shovels, axletrees, so many things on the place; the brewing and baking, candle- and soap-making; butchering, tailoring and carpentering.

The special characteristic of Bess's activities is her money-lending and land-grabbing: in her sphere she was an empire-builder. In all this her chief minister and confidant was her able second son, William Cavendish. She entrusts to him large sums for all kinds of business: her buildings, the annuities she granted her sons, gifts to other members of the family, moneys for New Year's Gifts to the Queen, for law-charges in London, for taxation (an inconsiderable item compared with her immense wealth), the multifarious small change of a vast estate. Bess performed the functions of a banker in her area: the mortgages and lands fell in to the Cavendishes. On the threshold of her Chatsworth lay Edensor: the privateering Earl of Cumberland, no business man, mortgaged it to her, and she got it. She similarly purchased lands outright from impecunious or extravagant local families, a Savage, Lodge, Shakerley, Fuljambe, Markham;[19] other lands fell in to her from mortgages, from a Byron, or Molineux, a Stanhope or Sacheverell – all this over a fairly short priod. Her industrial concerns were a minor affair, though she had an interest in lead-mining and ironworks – she was in at but the beginnings of the subsequent industrial expansion of the northern Midlands.

Compared with the immense receipts and outcomings of such an estate, taxation was derisory: it was this that enabled the Elizabethans to build palaces and fill them with objects of art and beauty, in contrast with the waste of a welfare state on consumption without significance, without beauty or taste, or any lasting value. On 6 December 1591 she made her first payment on the second subsidy granted by Parliament two years before, £44.8; though this gives little idea of her total tax payments, for a number of Crown grants of lands and rectories (on the rectory of Kirkby she paid 32s at the same time), nevertheless it is obvious that taxation was no impediment to building a fortune. She paid far more on wages: an average of £300 a year. One observes, with envy, the impression of stability her household gives: practically the same wages to the same people in her service for years. It is a tribute to a well-ordered and stable society, but also to her excellence as a manager.

Her gifts were immensely larger than any taxes, even those to the poor – for the Countess, though intensely acquisitive, was by no means ungenerous. As with Burghley, the regular rate of payments to the poor where each of her houses lay – Chatsworth, Hardwick, Chelsea – was 20s weekly. But this was merely the minimum; everywhere there were extras. In May, 'to my Lady at her going from Hardwick to Wingfield to be given to the poor' – this meant along the route – £20, 'of which Mr. William Cavendish to give the poor of Derby £5.' In August, 'for the relief of Derby till next sessions' – William had evidently attended sessions earlier – '£7, in addition to giving £5 before.' Whenever she journeys her steward gives her a sum in cash, £10 or £20, to distribute on the way. At Chelsea in 1591 the poor at her gate receive, in addition to the regular weekly 20s, 'for Christmas and Twelve days more, 13s.' St. Thomas's Hospital, 'at the feast of St. Martin in winter last,' received the large sum of £17. 15. 7. While around Chatsworth that winter twenty poor men and women received £6. 13. 4 to buy them coals, twenty poor children £4 for the same; 5s to the poor who turned up one Monday morning at the gate.

It would be a fair conclusion that those parishes were lucky that had a great house in their midst, others were helped by having a manor-house of any size or resources, for they were integrated into society and, *ceteris paribus*, fulfilled an essential function. The really grinding poverty, with little hope of relief in time of dearth, fell upon more 'democratic' communities (to use an anachronism), in the North, where there were fewer such houses.

Towards her latter end, like other rich folk, Bess bethought herself of her duty to perpetuate her memory in an almshouse. The arrangements were left to son Will, who laid out £108. 18. 7 for building, though there was a subsequent bill of £6. 7. 1 for woodwork. Then came the furnishing: scores of yards of woollen for blankets, linen for sheets and harden (coarse canvas); twelve pair each of shovels, tongs, iron candlesticks, skellets; cups, spoons, saucers, cans, pots, pans, pewter dishes, pot-hooks and brandreths (iron tripods) for the fire; yards of bolstering and blue cloth for liveries. One October day Will rode over to Derby to instal the poor: a large dinner for them, to the ringers 2s., and, no doubt for himself, wine and sugar 18d.: altogether the bill was £5. 11. 5.

Evidently Bess's bedesmen were going to be considerably more comfortable than the poor outside.

In November 1591 she travelled up from Hardwick to Chelsea for the winter, to do her duty at Court and spend immense sums for equipping the splendid new house at Hardwick – in addition to the old one she had enlarged into a mansion – with plate, silver, tapestries and other luxuries. The journey, by short stages on the short days and bad roads of November, took eight days; usually in summer it took four days, with only three nights on the road. Accompanied by a considerable part of her household, a large party, travelling in state, she spent her first night at Nottingham: where the kitchen charges were £7. 11. 6, stable charges and gears for horses, £5. 18. 11; to the poor 40s., to the waits 5s. The charges were much the same at each stage. At Leicester 20s. were contributed towards repairing Belgrave bridge; at Market Harborough the ringers received 8s. 4d. at two sundry times, evidently for ringing her in and ringing her out. Next stages were Northampton, Stony Stratford, Dunstable, Barnet, London – the latter part of her journey along Watling Street. At each of these places she was greeted by church-bells and the town-waits. The whole journey cost £96. 13. 9 (how many times must one now multiply by, for contemporary comparison? Fifty? With us monetary values have lost all stability). Meanwhile there were being driven along the roads up to Chelsea a couple of fat oxen and forty sheep. There would be plenty of mutton for *her* household that winter!

Many were her miscellaneous gifts, though usually to some good purpose. A Mr. Hatfield of Alton was given £5 towards maintaining his son to school; Mr. Broadbent received £20 towards maintaining his brother at the university – but then he was a useful Crown official in Derbyshire. The bishop of London got out of her the large sum of £100 'towards purchasing certain lands at Paul's Cross towards maintaining certain learned men or the universities to preach at Paul's Cross.' The bishop of Bristol's three sons were given, 20s to the eldest, 10s each to the others. Bess paid for the bread and wine for the communion at Edensor, and rewarded the parson of Chelsea with 10s for the communions of 'my lady Arbella and Mr. Cavendish.' The numerous footmen and messengers of great personages are always rewarded: the bishop of London's man that brings a bible, so too the Queen's gardener whenever the Countess takes the air in the garden, or Mrs. Markham's man when he brings flowers and plants to set in Bess's own garden. There is a whole page of New Year's gifts this winter: to William Cavendish and his wife £26. 13. 4, Henry Cavendish and Lady Grace (Shrewsbury's daughter) £20, Sir Charles Cavendish and his wife £20 – we note the preference for Will. These gifts were fairly regular each year. The Queen's footman received 20s when he brought her New Year's gift. For her Majesty the Countess had had made a garment for which she paid her tailor £59. 14, and to the embroiderer £50 for embroidering the gown – no mention of what the materials had cost.

Large as were these disbursements they were little compared with the sums the Countess was prepared to pay out to her family, for dynastic ambition was the driving force of her later life. The little 'Arbella', as she is always called, with her residual right to the throne, was the apple of Bess's eye. Nothing was too much for her; no care too great. At Hardwick she slept in a little chamber within her formidable grandmother's state bedroom: no-one could get at her. In May 1594, 'by my Lady's command to my Lady Arbella, £200. To my Lady Arbella the same day £350, to be repaid when my Lady shall demand it.' In June the girl is given forty marks towards Mr. Thomas Hood's wages, presumably her tutor. Another time Arbella is given no less than £500 towards a purchase of lands in Lincolnshire. When, in July 1598 the Countess hands over £700 to Mr. John Manners with the marriage of his son George to Grace Pierrepont, one realises that the old lady is contributing handsomely to a grand-daughter's dower; it is followed by a gift of £100 to the lucky young man to buy plate against setting up house. Even so he gets a tip of £5 at Christmas. One of Bess's ladies in waiting, a Digby, is given £60 for her marriage – the Countess was no skinflint. As for her sons, they cost her a mint of money: each had out of her a basic annuity of £400; but on top of this there were constant presents, especially of course to the favourite Will, but even to Henry, the eldest, with whom she quarrelled. (She had married him to the Earl's daughter, Grace, who was barren, in order that the family succession should pass through the abler William – and so it came to pass.) Her total receipts from Michaelmas 1593 to Michaelmas 1594 were £7568. 1. 5, so there was plenty to go round, even with her building at Hardwick and Oldcotes (the new house at Chatsworth had been finished some years before).*

---

* One must observe that, in this total, capital receipts are included along with income: there is no knowing what her true income was. On this subject I am in agreement with Mr. Alan Simpson's expressed scepticism as to 'the possibilities of statistical sampling', in his *The Wealth of the Gentry, 1540–1660*, 20.

Her visit to London in the winter of 1591–2 was partly for the purpose of equipping Hardwick, and in the week ending 4 December she paid out the large sum of £425. 4. 5; while a fortnight later Will Cavendish drew £366.5 to discharge her debts. Most of this may be regarded as capital expenditure, however, not a consumption of resources on trivial objects. Prescott or Nicholas Duett or Hunt, goldsmiths, would come by boat up the Thames to Chelsea: of them she bought several gold chains, one of pillars, another with one link wreathed, the other square; plain gold bracelets, another pair set with diamonds, pearls and rubies; a boiling pot with cover of silver. For the new Hardwick nothing was too good: gilt candlesticks, tankards, salts, livery pots, bowls. From Prescott alone she bought livery pots, silver plates, a dozen silver bowls with covers, a nest of graven bowls, a pear cup, a double cup, a sugar-box, tankard, a double salt, a little flagon, three casting bottles, a perfuming pan, cruets, a basin and ewer a great porringer, mouncer (mazer?) bowls, a spot pot for wine, three dozen gold rings. We may fairly comment that she was providing employment for the luxury trades in London.

Then, too, there are the quantities of rich stuffs she bought: 30 yards of velvet at 22s. the yard; 20 yards of satin at 12s. 2d., and 20 more at 11s.; 16 more yards of velvet, and 50 yards of damask at 9s. 4d.; scores of ells of linen for linings; silver thread and '1 lb of satin silk for my Lady Arbella.' At this time a litter was made for the Countess, which must have rivalled the Queen's it was such a grand affair: the hangings of tawny velvet and tuft taffeta, with deep gold fringe and fringes of tawny silk, silver and gold. At one swoop she bought the late Lord Chancellor Hatton's tapestries – 17 pieces of arras, 1005½ ells, with the Story of Gideon, for which she paid a small fortune, £326. 15. 9. But she was allowed £5 to replace Hatton's arms with her own.

Thus the Derbyshire squire's daughter – uneducated as she was, for there are no purchases of books among her prodigious payments – graduated to a Renaissance taste. Those tapestries, faded now to the colour of shadows, are still there in the shimmering, many-windowed palace she built. For she was touched by the spirit of her age in her love of magnificence and precious things. On her way home that summer of 1592 she stopped to look at Holdenby, Sir Christopher Hatton's Northamptonshire palace, and Wollaton, Sir Francis Willoughby's in the outskirts of Nottingham, for comparison with and inspiration for what she would achieve at Hardwick – for herself and for posterity.

It was generally recognised that the prime function of nobility was leadership in action. In his book *The Complete Gentleman* Peacham expresses this for England as Castiglione had earlier for Europe: it is defined as the honour conferred upon a line for some notable action performed beneficial to the commonwealth.[20] It continues in the lineage of a family, naturally, in conformity with the laws of descent customary in the society. That is, in England it followed the rule of primogeniture, as succession to the land generally did. This had consequences fundamental to the society, and on the whole extremely beneficial to both incentive and social flexibility. Keeping the title together with the land helped to keep a firm social framework; while, as Professor Tawney once described it, throwing all the kittens into the water to swim or sink, encouraged initiative and movement. Some kept up, others went down. It was a contrast to the more rigid class-system on the Continent, where, if you were born into the nobility you remained a noble and, however poor, were too good to go into trade or work for your living. In England, the younger sons of even dukes were commoners – like Sir Winston Churchill's father, Lord Randolph, on the threshold of our time.

Peacham has an interesting comment on noble bastards, who, he says, often received social recognition for good service on the field, though not recognised by law. We recognise the nobility inherent in Shakespeare's portrait of Faulconbridge. Leicester's natural son Sir Robert Dudley – who spent a life-time asserting in vain his legitimacy – exhibited all, and rather more than all, his father's gifts. The last Lord Dudley of the old line lived with a concubine, Elizabeth Tomlinson, by whom he had the famous Dud Dudley, the metallurgist, much the ablest of that line. Bastards often kept the family name: the excellent poet and translator of Tasso, Edward Fairfax, kept his. Further north, on the uproarious Borders, the Foster family hardly recognised the inhibiting restrictions of matrimony and cheerfully made little difference among their progeny. Bastardy, too, had some social utility: it was apt to be improving to looks and upgrading to stocks.

Peacham tells us that education was particularly important for a nobleman, and that many bewailed their loss of opportunity in youth. This was a new emphasis in Elizabethan society, by contrast with earlier in the century, and Burghley consistently urged it forward. As noblemen were given pre-eminence in action, Peacham says, so they were not to be given up to contemplation or stoical retiredness. Nor would the Queen excuse them without cause from the duties, often burdensome, laid upon them by their station. In 1600 Lord Zouche had but recently returned from an embassy to Denmark – envoys were always left out of pocket by their service – when he was called upon to undertake some military charge. He was refractory and was denied the Queen's presence: he took it 'grievously that her Majesty will not permit him access unto her to deliver his reasons of his unfitness to be employed in this service . . . and until such time as he could make trial of your [Robert Cecil's] favour therein, he was willing to submit himself to any punishment rather than to prepare himself towards that journey before he have yielded his reasons to her Majesty.'[21]

There were indeed some disadvantages in being too exalted. Before his death Norfolk recalled the misfortunes attending the name of duke under the Tudors, hoped that it would end with him and wished that he himself had been of a lower degree.[22] With his execution in 1572 there were no more dukes in England until James I's sentimental elevation of young Villiers. In the backward North, however, feudal sentiment lingered towards Percies, Nevilles, Dacres, Stanleys. The Earl of Derby lived in princely state, with a household that went up to 145 members – far larger than Burghley's.[23] He had his own council, like a prince, headed by a steward, a comptroller, and a receiver-general, each with his own three servants. Eight gentlemen were in attendance, four of them taking turns daily. When the Earl wrote to a gentleman as important as Sir Piers Legh of Lyme, a large landowner with estates in three counties, he always subscribed himself 'you assured loving Master' and directed his missives to 'my right trusty and well beloved Servant.'[24] There was no disgrace attaching to the name of servant – the proper function of service was recognised at every level. When Sir Piers came to die, his will was 'that my poor house might ever continue and remain to the house of my Lord and his posterity for ever . . . and in case my posterity should not appertain and retain to their honours and their posterity, as I and my precedessors ever heretofore have done, if a dead man might have knowledge thereof and receive and take grief thereat, there could not be any greater grief unto me than that in all this world.'

We see in such a society less envy than in ours, precisely because people knew their place in it and recognised its obligations, unlike an egalitarian disorder which naturally encourages envy because they fail to do so. But along the margins and in the rifts human motives break out in class-conscious assertiveness. The Dowager Lady Russell in 1597 was outraged that such a base fellow as a draper should, for an old debt 'sue me to an *exigent* [i.e. a writ of outlawry], being not lawful to outlaw any baron, my husband being known to be more than a baron.'[25] (He had been heir to the earldom of Bedford.) She had recourse, as usual, to her nephew Cecil: 'I trust it may be your case and every one's of the nobility as it is mine now . . . I pray commend me humbly and heartily to my lady of Warwick, and wish her to look to the like, for it may to her what doth to me.' Letter after letter came from the querulous old lady, who paid up, but was not going to put up with indignities offered to the widow of any earl. 'As long as I can crawl I will marry some one that shall want four of his five wits rather than I will receive any indignity or disgrace by such base fellows for not being a wife to an earl or a baron.' The old widow was one of the blue-stocking (but not blue-blooded) daughters of Sir Anthony Cooke, which no doubt made her the more conscious of her rank.

So, too, perhaps with Bess of Harwick's daughter, married to Gilbert Talbot, who became seventh Earl of Shrewsbury. There was a feud between Cavendishes and Stanhopes, and the lady instructed two of her men to tell Sir Thomas Stanhope before witnesses that 'though you be more wretched, vile, and miserable than any creature living; and for your wickedness become more ugly than the vilest toad in the world; and one to whom none of reputation would vouchsafe to send any message; yet she hath thought good to send thus much to you – that she be contented you should live . . . but to this end, that all the plagues and miseries that may befall any man may light upon such a caitiff as you are; and that you should live to have all your friends forsake you; and without your great repentance, which she looketh not for, because your life hath been so bad, you will be damned perpetually in hell-fire.'[26] The more opprobrious insults the merely male messengers omitted out of mildness. What Sir Thomas can have done to call this formal curse down upon him is not known to me – perhaps he had blemished the lady's reputation. Such a message between men of standing would have resulted in a duel, but of course ladies were privileged.

Even the Lord Treasurer Burghley got as good as he gave for a dressing down he had directed against Sir John Holles, in his absence, in Star Chamber for encroachments upon his tenantry. Holles could put up with being described as 'a most miserable wretch, a covetous cormorant, an unworthy and noisome member to the commonwealth.'[27] But 'when your lordship then digged into my ancestor's grave and, pulling him from his three-score and ten years' rest, pronounced him an abominable usurer, a merchant of broken paper, so hateful and contemptible a creature that the players acted him before the king with great applause: these hateful imputations and disgraceful histories I must needs answer . . Touching my ancestors, I am not so unnatural as not to acknowledge them, nor so foolish proud as not to confess them as they were. I will hold myself to their name and, if I cannot prove them gentle, I will not take myself to another man's pedigree nor usurp others' arms.' This was intended as a hit at Burghley, for few knew of the Cecils' descent from the old, if impoverished, house, of Alltyrynis. Anyway, even if Holles's grandfather were a merchant of the basest kind – which he was not – 'I am certain in your lordship's reading you find many from vile and base traders, as potters, colliers, shepherds, swineherds, etc, have risen to be great emperors and princes, and many others from innkeepers, butchers, and other mechanical occupations to be sole governors of great commonwealths.' These were palpable hits all round, for Burghley's ancestor was generally thought to have been an inn-keeper at Stamford; the Bacons to have been descended from a swineherd of Bury St. Edmund's abbey – actually a receiver; the Spencers from graziers; and so on. Sir John scored with his con-clusion, from Iphicrates: 'Let them who are noble from the beginning reprove others' unnobleness.'

Family pride merges with class feeling in a hot-blooded letter from Sir William Herbert of St. Julian's in Monmouthshire, whose daughter and heiress was bound by him to marry another of the name of Herbert, so she was married to Lord Herbert of Cherbury. A young Morgan of the same county had delivered a challenge to a man of Sir William's, 'on the behalf of a gentleman as good as myself. Who he was he named not, neither do I know.'[28] So Sir William wrote to the young Morgan's father: 'if he be as good as myself, it must either be for virtue, for birth, for ability, or for calling and dignity. For virtue, I think he meant not, for it is a matter that exceeds his judgment. If for birth, he must be the heir male of an earl, the heir in blood of ten earls (for in testimony thereof I bear their several coats); besides he must be of the blood royal, for by my grandmother Devereux I am lineally and legiti-mately descended out of the body of Edward IV.' (It was his Devereux descent that made Essex regard himself as being as good as Elizabeth I.) Sir William proceeded to give Morgan's son the lie, in form, and to offer him a challenge in any place 'where I stand not sworn to observe the peace', i.e. in the county where he was a J.P. Within his own jurisdiction, he would chastise the young man for his malapert misdemeanour and bind him over. 'And so I thought fit to advertise you hereof, and leave you to God.'

The reader may think all this very childish; but it is characteristic: all humans in all places and at all times are children.

The theory was, according to Peachman, that mechanics or those who laboured for their livelihood cannot be regarded as gentlemen. We are not concerned, however, with theory but with actualities, and even theory said nothing against social advancement. A discourse on *The Institution of a Gentleman*, of 1568, allowed that 'ascent from "a low house" or "a poor stock" to high office and honour as "an ungentle gentle", or first generation gentleman, was proper enough provided that a man was of good moral character and personality, and that his starting-point, his original family status, was above that of "goodman", ascribed to handicraftsmen. If he became a "well beloved and high esteemed man, a post or stay of the commonwealth", and rich, it was possible to drag a line of relatives up with him. The same author is bitter on the subject of handicraftsmen's sons who, without education but simply through laying hold of land since the dissolution of the monasteries, by suspect means, have risen to be knights or esquires. Presumably he was not averse to their ascent through professional education, as in divinity or law.'[29] This was the recognised way, according to Sir Thomas Smith. Miss Thrupp sagely concludes, 'one would surmise that the criteria of tolerance in practice varied a good deal from one generation to another, with the extent of new economic or educational opportunity and also with the conditions of downward mobility.'

Well, there was plenty of downward mobility – blessed concept: plenty of kittens went to the bottom, and some of these even came up again. On the threshold of the Tudor period one of the noble Berkeleys 'more bowed towards a country life, befitting a younger brother's younger son, than for the Court or greatness, as the sequel of his life declared . . . He, for the most part of his elder brother's life . . . was a perfect Cotswold shepherd, living a kind of grazier's life, having his flocks of sheep summering in one place and wintering in other places as he observed the fields and pastures to be found and could bargain best cheap. And the better to be his own auditor, he kept a book of his own handwriting of all his receipts and payments, gains and losses touching those flocks: during which time he sold his wool usually for 12s 8d the tod.'[30]

Evidently keeping accounts was as unusual for a nobleman's son as pasturing flocks on Cotswold; but it stood him in good stead when he unexpectedly succeeded to the barony and was able to keep his own accounts.

It is observable that Elizabeth I was socially more conservative – this was observed by Naunton – as befitted a lady, than her father, who unleashed a revolution.

The rule that a rich gentleman kept in his household naturally followed, on a smaller scale, that of a magnate. Of the many examples we might cite let us take the interesting one of John Harington, a cadet of the house of Exton, father of Sir John, court-wit and poet, godson of the Queen. Harington *père* was a servant of Lord Admiral Seymour and, having his way to make, spied out a (financially) lucky match.[31] John Malte was Henry VIII's tailor, who rewarded him with several fat manors of Bath abbey in Somerset, principally Kelston and charming St. Catherine's Court. Malte had an illegitimate daughter, Ethelreda, whom he proposed to marry to an illegitimate son of Sir Richard Southwell. But Harington got her, and with her all her fat manors; in time he proceeded to build one of the grandest houses in Somerset at Kelston, to which the poet succeeded and where he entertained the Queen on her visit to Bath in 1592. Hence the Somerset Haringtons; but they were not descended from Ethelreda who had brought them their luck. She had died childless, but she left her estates happily to her husband, who was now free to make a love-match.

Sir John Markham, Lieutenant of the Tower, had a daughter, Isabella. Harington was something of a poet, like his son after him, and wrote romantically of the girl, one of the Princess Elizabeth's waiting women, 'when I first thought her fair as she stood at the Princess's window in goodly attire and talked to divers in the courtyard.' As Queen, Elizabeth – more generous than posterity has recognised – was extremely kind to the Haringtons and rewarded their service with constant gifts, including the monastic manor of Lenton in Nottinghamshire. So John was enabled to build the fine house, for which he wrote the rules following grander models. 'Item, that none toy with the maids, on pain of 4d. Item, that none swear any oath, upon pain for every oath 1d.' In summer time the men were to be in bed by ten at night, and out of bed by six; from Michaelmas to Ladyday, September to March, in bed by nine, out by seven in the morning. There was no hardship: ten hours' sleep in autumn and winter, eight hours in spring and summer. 'Item, that no man make water within either of the courts, upon pain of, every time it shall be proved, 1d. Item, that no man teach any of the children any unhonest speech, or bawdy word, or oath, on pain of 4d. Item, that meat be ready at eleven or before at dinner, and six or before at supper, on pain of 6d.' Such were the usual times of the principal meals.

John Harington was able to embody his household adjurations to his wife in verse:

> Our house both sweet and cleanly see,
> Order our fare, thy maids keep short;
> Thy mirth with mean well mixèd be,
> Thy courteous parts in chaste-wise sort.
>
> In sober weeds thee cleanly dress . . .
> Small sleep and early prayer intend,
> The idle life as poison hate;
> No credit light nor much speed spend,
> In open place no cause debate.

The Elizabethans were nothing if not sententious and didactic – after all they had a whole society to educate and bring out of medievalism. There is nothing to show that John and Isabella did not enjoy an entirely happy life together.

For a less well ordered household of new gentry, in some contrast, let us turn to that of Sir William Holles, second son of that mercer upon whom Lord Burghley had cast his aspersions in Star Chamber. Both the Harington and the Holles fortunes were made in London; the first from Court-service, the other from trade. Sir William's descendant was the Cavalier antiquary, Gervase Holles, who consoled himself in exile after the ruinous Civil War in writing the story of his family for the benefit of his progeny: here they might 'behold both the features and dispositions of their deceased ancestors and retrieve, as it were, a conversation and intercourse with those who death hath silenced.'[32] The Mercer Lord Mayor made such a large fortune that he was able to settle additional estates in Nottinghamshire upon his second son, another Sir William, and to procure for him a marriage to a Cornish heiress, Anne Denzil – the name, now extinct, comes from a little farm near Newquay, with Denzil downs above it. (Hence the name of Denzil Holles, one of the Five Members whom Charles I failed to arrest).

So young William, after his father's death, set up his roof-tree at Haughton: 'a seat both pleasant and commodious, lying between the forest and the clay, and partaking both of the sweet and wholesome air of the one and, in a reasonable manner, of the fertility of the other, having the river Idle running through it by several cuts in several places.'[33] The celebrated Earl of Cumberland fell in love with Holles's handsome daughter and asked to marry her. Sir William utterly refused the honour as unsuitable to his station. 'When his friends did most passionately persuade him to it, telling him what an honour it would be to his family and what an advancement to his daughter to have her matched to a person so highly noble, he answered: "Sake of God" (that was his usual word of asseveration). "I do not like to stand with my cap in hand to my son-in-law: I will see her married to an honest gentleman with whom I may have friendship and conversation".' So he married her to a man of her own class, which Gervase Holles thought much to his credit. However, the children of that marriage either went to the bad or were unfortunate; while the Earl married an earl's daughter, the puritanical Margaret Russell, with whom he lived unhappily all his life. I draw no moral – it was all the luck of the pot.

At Haughton Sir William kept open house, not dining till after one o'clock in case some neighbour was travelling from a distance to dine with him. 'He always began his Christmas at All Hallowtide [Nov. 1] and continued it until Candlemas [Feb. 2], during which time any man was permitted freely to stay three days without being asked from whence he came or what he was. . . . I have heard that his proportion, which he allowed during the twelve days of Christmas, was a fat ox every day with sheep and other provision answerable . . . This liberal hospitality of his caused the first Earl of Clare to let fall once an unbecoming word, that his grandfather sent all his revenues down the privy house.'[34] Nevertheless, in spite of his prodigality, Sir William became ancestor of the earls of Clare and a second line of dukes of Newcastle.

Gervase Holles tells us that he kept his own company of stage-players, 'which presented him masks and plays at festival times and upon days of solemnity.' Nothing of this in Bess of Hardwick's household! It is no wonder that he added nothing to his patrimony except what he got with his Cornish wife. Gervase Holles says of his own grandfather, who was seated very comfortably in the Grey Friars at Grimsby, that he was 'as well furnished with learning as, in his own opinion, befitted a gentleman. For I have heard him say that he would have a gentleman to have some knowledge in all the arts, but that it did not become him to be excellent in any of them.'[35] This, again, was in keeping with received theory coming down from the classics. However, 'he was no stranger to the softer muses': like the Haringtons he wrote verses, 'which discovered no vulgar but a very sprightly fancy, such an one as might have marched with the foremost in these days.' Yet elsewhere Holles expressed no very high opinion of early Elizabethan poetry – an elegy upon an ancestress is described as 'but mean poetry, such as the beginning of Queen Elizabeth's reign usually afforded.'

This Grimsby grandfather went with Essex on the Islands Voyage of 1597 and was a tough old customer who lived, exceptionally for those days, to see his great-grandsons. 'He had also two illegitimate children which he begot after his wife's decease: a son called Peregrine, who died before him, whom he got upon one Mistress Holden, and a daughter, (by a woman called Peg with the White Hand), who, as I remember, was married in London.' Once, when this gallant fellow was down in Cornwall among his kindred, he heard 'much talk of one Mr. Coryton, then called "Mad Coryton" as my grandfather was usually called "Wild Holles". And, entertaining a strong emulation at the description made of him, he was very desirous to see him.' At meeting the Cornish gentleman politely saluted the gentleman from Lincolnshire and desired his better acquaintance. 'My grandfather told him he scorned his acquaintance, for he was a thief. The other demanding a reason of that uncivil return, he replied, "Thou has stolen a fool's head and set it upon thy own shoulders." This caused a quarrel, and that a combat, and it a very hearty friendship ever after.'

So much for the humour of those times.

Housing is a prime ocular demonstration of the character of a society – as we can see today with the pickling of the great houses of the past for the benefit of the people, the decline and ruin of hundreds of country mansions, the emptying of their contents upon the market, with all that they represented of continuity of culture and of historic significance in the nation's heritage: in the interests of the tenement-houses of cities and suburbia, the housing estates eating up the landscape, sanitary, heated and lighted, but utterly without any significant contribution to make towards any higher culture.

The period between Elizabeth's accession and the tragic Civil

War was that of the 'Great Rebuilding', during which almost the whole of society, in all but the backward areas of Wales and the North, was rehoused. That is to say, notably in all classes of society except the poorest – though there was a good deal of new cottage-building in many different areas where waste land was being colonised or squatted on: it reflected not only the increase of population but gave elbow-room, even provided something of a safety-valve, along the margins of an ordered, somewhat repressive (if necessarily so) society. We see this last consideration at play in forest-areas, into which poor people crowded because they were freer there to fleet the time carelessly. Professor Hoskins tells us that there was new cottage-building, for example, 'on the moors and heaths of mid- and east-Devon, and we find some in the Lancashire forest of Rossendale, which was being opened up rapidly after the middle of the sixteenth century . . . Here in Rossendale we should have found a few Elizabethan farm-houses built upon the waste; but mostly we should have seen the smaller and more primitive buildings of squatters. In addition, there was a considerable amount of cottage building in the lowlands generally.'[36] Instances are reported such as the manor of Epworth in Lincolnshire and three or four villages around, where no less than a hundred cottages had been built during 1590–1630. In 1596 it was said that thirty new cottages had been built at Misterton in the past forty years, and that the households at Crowle had increased by some forty, great and small, between 1536 and 1576. This was in and around the rich soil of the Isle of Axholme. But in the forest neighbourhood of Brigstock in Northamptonshire forty new houses were built between 1600 and 1637, besides those that were modernised or converted from barns and stables into dwellings. Carew notes the marked improvement in the living conditions of cottagers that had been made in a remote, poor county such as Cornwall by 1600. We can conceive how much more so in the richer southern counties, the Midlands and, wealthiest of all, East Anglia. Altogether. 'almost all the rural population, except the poorest, enjoyed a higher level of domestic comfort, in the way of furniture, fittings, and household equipment on the eve of the Civil War than their grandparents had done seventy years earlier.'

As for the gentry, Dr. Simpson sums up crisply, 'a man no sooner succeeded in the sixteenth century than he built himself a new home – and more than one if he could afford it.'[37] No sooner had the Catholic Sir Thomas Cornwallis been retired from the delights (and profits) of Queen Mary's Court, than he embarked upon building himself Brome Hall in Suffolk. 'But Sir Thomas no sooner had a country house to his liking than he began to plan a town-house in Norwich.' This involved transforming the dissolved Chapel in the Fields. Building went on here and at Brome, with some intervals, over the rest of his life. After a brief lull, 1579–1582, 'building began again in 1583 and continued in some form or another until 1596 – a new wing at Norwich; towers, courtyards, a park, a mill, a granary and a costly gallery at Brome; a tomb inside the church and almshouses outside . . . All in all, the building activities of this retired courtier must have consumed close to £3000.'

This was little compared with the activities of the successful lawyer, Sir Nicholas Bacon, who had so much longer in office to do it in, as Elizabeth's Lord Keeper for twenty years. In three of the counties in which he had amassed estates there arose 'one of those monuments which were the passion and sometimes the ruin of the Tudor gentry – a new-built mansion. First had come Redgrave Hall, where the monks of Bury St. Edmunds had kept a hunting lodge; then Gorhambury, where the monks of St. Alban's had owned a group of farms; then Stiffkey, which a son had just begun to build out of his father's money and under his vigilant eye.'[38] This was by no means all: there was the Library at Gray's Inn, the family inn-of-court; Cursitors' Inn in Chancery Lane; a grammar school at Botesdale; a town house for son Edward.

For Lord Keeper Bacon's building, and his building up of estates, were directly geared to his dynastic ambition of establishing his sons among the gentry of East Anglia. He never acquired a peerage, unlike his brother-in-law Burghley, and he did not build two palaces. Over the porch of his moderate-sized house at Redgrave he inscribed *Mediocria Firma*. This was a sufficient reply to the Queen, who thought Gorhambury rather small too. He replied, 'Madam, my house is well, but it is you that have made me too great for my house.'[39] His eldest son, another Sir Nicholas, succeeded him at Redgrave with a block of estates and a wife who brought him the Butts and half the Bure estates besides. The Lord Keeper settled his son, Nathaniel, at Stiffkey – who, on marrying a wealthy widow for his second wife, built himself a second mansion at Irmingland. The third son by the first marriage, Edward, founded another Bacon family at delightful Shrubland near Ipswich. The two brilliant sons by the second marriage, to one of the famous Cooke blue-stockings, Anthony and Francis Bacon, were genetically disappointing: neither had offspring – probably both were homosexuals.

Nevertheless the Lord Keeper's successor more than made up for it by carrying the dynastic process further. The second Sir Nicholas's eldest son, Edmund, succeeded to Redgrave; Robert got an estate at Riborough in Norfolk, Butts at Mildenhall, Nicholas at Gillingham, Nathaniel at Culford. Nothing remains at Redgrave now, whence all this Elizabethan activity exfoliated: the house destroyed in our time, only the tombs in the church remain, the archives – upon which this account rests – whisked away to Chicago.

Dr. Hoskins tells us that the evidence for this immense rehousing of a considerable part of the population is 'more abundant in the rural districts than in the towns, where there has necessarily been more replacement of buildings during the past three hundred years. It is probable, however, that the Great Rebuilding was originally as noticeable in the towns as in the country, if we may judge by those English towns (such as Shrewsbury and Totnes) which retain much of their old character.'[40] To this we may add our own observation, if we are visually alert. As one walks about the older streets of a town like Oxford – Holywell, Grove Street, Merton Street, Ship Street, or even parts of the High or the Broad – in addition to the obvious gabled Elizabethan houses one recognises at once, one can often tell that a Georgian façade conceals a Tudor house. Just as in the country a Queen Anne front at Trevissick, across the fields from my home, has been added to a Jacobean hall-house at the back; similarly with a Caroline front at Erisey near the Lizard, or a William and Mary front at Roscarrock near Padstow, each with the Tudor house behind.

Actually, for various reasons, Elizabethan evidences are not so frequent in Cornwall; in the Devon countryside, which has had a more static history, with altogether less mining and upheaval, they are ubiquitous. Dr. Hoskins says that 'a personal inspection of the 430 or so medieval parishes of Devon brings to light overwhelming evidence of the rebuilding or substantial reconstruction of farmhouses, large and small, all over the county.'[41] My own forays into Devon corroborate this, and the Great Rebuilding is very evident also throughout Somerset and most of Dorset. Less so in Hampshire, one would say, much of which was forest or downland in those days. But it visibly extends across England along the oolite belt that makes such beautiful building stone and the dry walling so familiar to us in Cotswold towns and villages, all the way from eastern Somerset, through Gloucestershire, northern Oxfordshire (think of Deddington or Adderbury) and Northamptonshire, into Rutland and Lincolnshire.

The clay lands of the Eastern Midlands have seen a great deal of rebuilding in brick from the nineteenth century onwards, but 'the evidence of household inventories is conclusive about the enlargement of farmhouses and to a lesser extent of cottages at this time.'[42] So too in East Anglia. In the wooded county of Essex half-timbered houses were at their peak in the Tudor period – one sees them still in such towns as Thaxted or Finchingfield, or in the farmhouses of the prosperous yeomanry, often pargeted and dated. 'The number of houses required to meet the demand markedly reduced the available supply of good oak, which there-after became dearer, while brick chimneys added appreciably to the cost.'[43] Building costs went up, but that did not deter the demand: farmers were better off with increased returns from the land. It was this fundamentally that enabled people to eat better, reduced infant mortality and led to an increase in population.

In Suffolk, at Monewden along the Otley road, one sees 'three adjacent farmhouses . . . all excellent examples of Elizabethan yeoman houses. One is dated 1592, another 1593; the third is undated but is undoubtedly of the same years.'[44] Along the Severn counties and the Welsh Border the 'characteristic black-and-white timber-framed houses are very largely the product of the same building period.' While even the smaller houses of Monmouth-shire reveal 'the fundamental change in character and mode of construction that took place about 1560.' Even in the Yorkshire dales 'we can still see the sturdy dwellings built at the end of the sixteenth and in the early part of the seventeenth centuries, with the initials of their proud owners and the date of erection carved on the ornate lintel above the door. Many were merely transforma-tions into stone of the earlier timber and wattle structures.' So too in the better parts of Lancashire where 'new "halls" were erected and old farmsteads were reconstructed.' 'The "halls" were the houses of lesser gentry . . . but the yeomen show the same tendency to rebuild in stone and on a larger scale than their old houses.' The farther North one goes the later the rebuilding, though there are exceptions with the more cultivated gentry building more sophisti-cated houses, like Levens Hall in Westmorland with its topiary garden.

Nor was the remote Lake District exempt from the currents of the times. There too the gentry were reinforced by the younger sons of old families. Sir Henry Curwen, for instance, set up his son in style at Thornthwaite in 1576, bought the manor of Rottington, St. Bees, in 1579, added the estate of Sella Park in 1594, and extended Workington Hall in 1597.[45] A younger son of the Porters of Allerby founded another branch at Weary Hall, Bolton. Levens Hall was built by James Bellingham, a younger son of a Northumbrian family who came into the county and gathered a clutch of manors around his Hall. The Braithwaites of Ambleside offer an example of yeoman stock achieving gentility: by 1591 three families of them were armigerous. The Bindloss family and two families of Patrickson were similarly of yeoman stock; more conspicuously the Fletchers, who flowered from trade at Cockermouth into gentility.

New standards of comfort reached right down through society to all but the lowest ranks – though even here, with labourers in the richer open-fields of the Midlands, there was improvement. Here we are concerned mainly with their housing – not only the framework of their lives but the outward expression of their material condition. Recent studies on housing, in country and town alike, have brought home to us the immense amount of alteration and reconstruction in rebuilding. Perhaps the most general improvement was the insertion of a ceiling in the hall hitherto open to the rafters: this provided a chamber, or a couple of lofts above, useful for storage among other purposes, apart from the diminution of draughts.[46] Access to the loft in simpler houses was by ladder; there was not the space for stairs. Nor, in the lowest class of house, was there always room for a fireplace: it was more usual to add on a little pent-house outside.

In the houses of more prosperous husbandmen, farmers and especially yeomen, fireplaces were coming in with attendant chimneys. This is what Harrison is referring to when he is so much impressed by 'the multitude of chimneys' going up in his time – the larger the house the more of them. A hardly less important increase of comfort was provided by the ubiquitous glazing of windows. Hitherto occupation for glaziers had been provided almost wholly by churches; at the Reformation, demand fell off disastrously for a couple of decades. With the Elizabethan renewal of society on a more secular basis the demand for glass windows for houses multiplied enormously. It provides a perfect illustration of what happened in society at large. Further structural comforts were provided by the multiplication of ceilings in general, with the opportunities they provided for decorative plasterwork – whole schools of such decorators sprang up, as we shall see later. Then, too, in superior houses there was wainscotting and panelling, frescoed or painted walls, besides the hangings that were frequent in houses from yeoman rank upwards. All these things usually – though not invariably – reflected wealth, class, status. We see every one of them exemplified in the improvements being made simultaneously in the halls of city companies and gilds, whether in London or provincial cities and towns. Their records are quite eloquent on the subject – sometimes members paid their fine by glazing a window – and tell their own tale.

In his description of classes Harrison notices the frequent interchange, or inter-mixture, between town tradesmen and gentry – as we have seen, a number of gentry had their townhouses, like Sir Thomas Cornwallis in Norwich, or even nobles, as the Earl of Bedford had in Exeter or the Earl of Huntingdon in Leicester. 'Citizens and burgesses have next place to gentlemen, who be those that are free within the cities and are of some likely substance to bear office in the same . . . In this place also are our merchants to be installed as amongst the citizens, although they often change estate with gentlemen, as gentlemen do with them, by a mutual conversion of the one into the other, whose number is so increased in these our days.[47] . . . The point is borne out in the housing of so characteristic a town as Exeter, which ranked about fifth in the country, after Norwich, Bristol, York, Coventry. The really splendid timber-framed houses of Exeter High Street began to be built after the middle of the century. They may be compared for status and wealth with those of the gentry, though they show a contrast in character, vertical instead of horizontal, running back laterally instead of being planned around a roomy quadrangle, jettied out at each stage to gain light and air, planned as much for storage as for accommodation.

For other classes, 'those at the bottom of the social scale . . . could usually afford only a mean, one-roomed dwelling where the whole family cooked, ate, slept, and stored any goods it might possess; though in some cases an extra room would be contrived by sub-division or partial lofting over. The class of small craftsmen and tradesmen above these was most likely to occupy a house of two storeys, like that of a baker of Trinity parish who died in 1564. Behind his shop on the ground floor lay the kitchen and bakehouse, and above these were his hall and chamber. The more substantial members of this group might add a cockloft, but when the house was raised to three storeys it was likely to shelter the lesser merchants and manufacturers, and the professional men. These would have further chambers at the top of the building, and they might introduce a parlour or a buttery on one of the lower floors. There would sometimes be a cellar as well, and there was always the possibility of another room or two across the courtyard – a kitchen or a brewhouse or a workplace. However, it was in the houses of four and five storeys, those containing from ten to sometimes nearly twenty rooms and often extending to a second block across the courtyard, that the greatest diversity occurred. These were inhabited by the wealthy merchants and manufacturers who comprised the civic *élite* and in whose hands the government of Exeter largely rested.'[48]

We are familiar with the old-time praise of 'the yeomen of England' – that class to which Shakespeare's maternal grandparents belonged, the Ardens of Wilmcote, with their roomy house and the arras hangings on the wall. Bacon praised them, Thomas Fuller regarded them as 'an estate of people almost peculiar to England', others spoke of them as the backbone of the country.[49] Harrison describes them: 'they commonly live wealthily, keep good houses and travail to get riches.' This last consideration may have inclined others to regard them as capitalist farmers – in farming for business not, like most husbandmen, for subsistence. It is an admirable Devon antiquarian, John Hooker, who describes for us the yeoman in his social aspect: 'his fine being once paid [i.e. in entering upon his lease], he liveth as merrily as doth his landlord and giveth himself for the most part to such virtue, conditions and quality as doth the gentleman.' Hooker was a townsman, chamberlain of Exeter, but Robert Furse, who was a yeoman-gentleman, describes the type more closely in his predecessor, John Furse: 'he always maintained a good house, a good plough, good geldings, good tillage, good rearing and was a good husband [i.e. farmer]. Indeed he would never be without three couple of good hounds, he would surely keep company with the best sort.'[50]

All this increase of prosperity attests the internal expansion of society cognate with that into the borderlands and across the seas described in a previous volume.*

Harrison defines 'the fourth and last sort of people in England' as 'day-labourers, poor husbandmen, and some retailers, which

* Cf. my *The Expansion of Elizabethan England*.

have no free land, copyholders and all artificers, as tailors, shoe-makers, carpenters, brickmakers, masons, etc.'[51] With his usual patriotic optimism, he says, 'as for slaves and bondmen, we have none. Nay, such is the privilege of our country . . . that if any come hither from other realms, as soon as they set foot on land they become so free of condition as their masters.' This may have been so in the case of slaves, defining them as mere chattels. But there were still bondmen in England, in the sense of being tied to the soil: I have come across them in Duchy manors in Cornwall and on the large Crown manor of Eye in Suffolk. And they existed elsewhere, in Lancashire for example; for in the Derby household at Lathom they were not to sit in the hall but in place appointed for them.[52] It would seem that they existed mainly on Crown or Duchy manors: in 1575–6 Sir Henry Lee was granted the privilege of enfranchising 300 bondmen and women for reasonable fines. The fact that one's legal status was that of a bondman did not prevent one from having money. Even so, manumissions went on into the reign of James I. People of the name of Bond carry into today a memento of their status when the family got its name.

'The fourth and last sort of people therefore have neither voice nor authority in the commonwealth, but are to be ruled and not to rule others. Yet they are not altogether neglected, for in cities and corporate towns, for default of yeomen, they are fain to make up their inquests of such manner of people. And in villages they are commonly made churchwardens, sidesmen, aleconners, now and then constables, and many times enjoy the name of headboroughs.' This was quite as much as they were capable of: they had their part.

But whence the expansion, the prosperity? – In the increasing returns from the land and from trade, from the discovery and more efficient exploitation of real resources, mineral and manufacturing, as shown in my first volume.* This led to a marked increase of population. It has been remarked on in Lincolnshire, while in Leicestershire, at Wigston Magna 'there were about 70 families in 1523, 80 in 1563, and between 120 and 130 in 1603: at the most conservative estimate a rise of fifty per cent in the forty years 1563–1603. A good deal of this can be shown to arise from immigration into the parish, but well over a half of it is a natural increase.'[53] Of course, this is favourable agricultural land; not all areas could do so well. 'In the towns, the increases are even more striking. The population of Plymouth more than doubled in the last quarter of the century; Bideford more than doubled in the fifty years 1560–

* Cf. my *The England of Elizabeth*, chaps. III, IV.

1610; Tiverton more than doubled between 1560 and 1620. At Birmingham there were about forty baptisms a year in the 1560's, and seventy in the decade 1600–10.' There are particular reasons for this more than average increase in each of these cases: in Plymouth and Bideford the marked expansion of the port and of trade; in Tiverton that of woollens and in Birmingham of hardware and every kind of smithery. Nevertheless the fact of expansion remains.

As to population, Professor Hoskins suggests that the fertility-rate may have risen towards 1600; 'it is likely that the infant mortality-rate (and perhaps maternal mortality also) fell sharply below the level of the medieval and sub-medieval period at the same time. Whatever the dominant factor, it seems probable that the better and more varied food consumed by the mass of the population after the middle of the century, and the simultaneous increase in house-room, in comfort, and in living conditions generally, must have had a cumulative effect in raising the vitality and resistance of the population of the country, especially in the rural districts, and were major factors in the increase of population in these years.'[54] Better living meant that people could marry earlier, as Carew noticed; anyhow the rather superior stocks represented by the clergy were free now to reproduce themselves, and their quivers were full of arrows. In one Exeter parish at least, the infant mortality-rate was lower in the later sixteenth century than in the later seventeenth or the eighteenth. Increasing congestion accounts for this; it is likely that in the Elizabethan period, 'the infant mortality-rate, in the rural and semi-rural areas at any rate, was reduced to a figure not achieved again until well on into the nineteenth century.'

However that may be, the population – like the gentry – rose. Nevertheless, as in all earlier societies, the expectation of life among poorer people was much less than among the well-to-do. Only 10 per cent of the population lived to reach forty – in general the fittest survived.[55] Among poor people females had a shorter expectancy of life than males; whereas they had a longer expectancy than males among the upper classes. In this we see the greater hazards, the burden of their station, among the governing elements.

CHAPTER V

FOOD AND SANITATION

WITH this framework and these forms in mind, we may turn to the life lived within, sometimes outside, them. And, first, for the physical necessities of food, sex and shortly, exercise. Food and feeding markedly conformed to the manners and differences of class. So also, to a lesser extent, did sport – some sports were specifically reserved to the upper class, deer-hunting for example, while bowling was for the middle class and upwards. The elemental fact of sex can hardly be close-cribbed and confined in itself, but even here the manners and modes of experience were supposed to observe the society's rules as to class and decorum. The rules, however, were often more honoured in the breach than the observance, and nothing is more revealing than the breach of rules or deviations from them.

All foreigners were struck by what good trenchermen the English were and especially by the amount of meat they consumed. Harrison defended his countrymen on this score on account of the northerly climate: this necessitated ampler nourishment than hotter regions – we recall that English visitors to Italy were struck by the variety of fruits consumed there. Also 'the heat of our stomachs [is] of somewhat greater force' – this in accordance with the medical theory of humours that prevailed.[1]

Harrison, as befits a poor clergyman, comments on the extraordinary extravagance of grand households in regard to food and, as a patriot, deplores the tendency of the grandees to employ as their cooks 'musical-headed Frenchmen and strangers.' What he says about extravagant expenditure is borne out by all the household accounts that survive, though we must remember that it was owing to the size of the households and to the open house they all kept, the hospitality they dispensed. We should hardly know how to interpret the long lists of dishes served, the immense variety of the meats offered, if it were not for Harrison's account of how the meal was served. One did not taste of every dish that stood upon the table, 'which few use to do, but each one feedeth upon that meat him best liketh for the time. The beginning of every dish notwithstanding being reserved unto the greatest personage that sitteth at the table: to whom it is drawn up still by the waiters as order requireth, and from whom it descendeth again even to the lower end, whereby each one may taste thereof.'

This solves the mystery for us of the immense amounts of varied viands that appeared together as one 'course', contrary to modern usage. The 'course' was first placed on the table for the grandees at the dais end of the hall. 'When they have taken what it pleaseth them, the rest is reserved, and afterwards sent down to their serving men and waiters, who feed thereon in like sort with convenient moderation, their reversion also being bestowed upon the poor which lie ready at their gates in great numbers to receive the same.' This was the order for high table, where the family and their guests sat. Besides this, 'they have a certain ordinary allowance daily appointed for their halls, where the chief officers and household servants – for all are not permitted by custom to wait upon their master – and with them such inferior guests do feed as are not of calling to associate the nobleman himself. So that, besides those which are called to the principal table, there are commonly forty or three score persons fed in those halls, to the great relief of such poor suitors and strangers also as oft be partakers thereof and otherwise like[ly] to dine hardly.' This is in keeping with what we have already seen of these households.

After dilating upon the show of plate on the tables – food served 'in silver vessels, if they be of the degree of barons, bishops, and upwards' – pots, goblets, bowls of silver, earthenware garnished with silver, the new Venice glass coming in as fine as crystal, pewter for the lesser folk, Harrison continues with the next class. 'The gentlemen and merchants keep much about one rate, and each of them contenteth himself with four, five, or six dishes when they have but small resort; or peradventure with one, two, or three at the most, when they have no strangers to accompany them at their tables.'[2] Again, as in great houses, the servants have a regular allowance of food, 'besides such as is left at their master's boards and not appointed to be brought thither the second time'; sometimes the master would prefer cold meats, or they might be reserved for supper. Harrison let himself go in a gorgous account of merchants' feasts, the special occasions on which they would vie with the nobility. There would be 'jellies of all colours, mixed with a variety in the representation of sundry flowers, herbs, trees, forms of beasts, fish, fowls, and fruits, and thereunto marchpane [marzipan] wrought with no small curiosity; tarts of divers hues and sundry denominations, conserves of old fruits, foreign and home-bred, suckets [conserves], codinacs [quince-jellies], marmalades, march-pane, gingerbread, florentines; wild fowls, venison of all sorts, and sundry outlandish confections altogether seasoned with sugar' . . .

Evidently Harrison had been present at a feast of a city company, in London or elsewhere; at this point the sober fustian of an Elizabethan clergyman takes on a Renaissance richness. He tells us that the quarterly feasts of companies, tradesmen and artificers, were hardly inferior to the nobility. Their ordinary fare, however, consisted principally in bread, beef and ale, butcher's meats such as mutton, veal, lamb, pork, brawn, bacon, fowls, eggs, etc. Even husbandmen, ordinary peasant-farmers, 'do exceed after their manner, especially at bridals, purifications of women and such odd meetings, where it is incredible what meat is consumed and spent, each one bringing such a dish, or so many with him, as his wife and he do consult upon.'[3] In fact Harrison considered that every class exceeded in its feasts, and some in their ordinary diet. No doubt this was not true of the lowest class that lived chiefly on 'white meats, i.e. milk, butter, and cheese, which were never so dear as in my time, and wont to be accounted of as one of the chief stays throughout the island.' This diet, supplemented by eggs, bacon, fowl, a limited range of vegetables, fruits and berries, along with wholemeal bread, a modern dietetic expert considers 'must have been in most ways a good diet', though it depended naturally on the amount available.[4] 'The large amount of wholemeal bread eaten by all classes must have given ample protection against most of the disorders of health' associated with a deficiency of vitamin B. On such a diet people's teeth must have suffered much less from caries. The Queen, who was served with specially refined white bread and moreover had an addiction to sweetmeats, exhibited bad black teeth and suffered recurrent toothache.

Some mitigation of this heavy meat diet on the part of the upper classes was afforded by fast-days and fish-days. Friday, by universal custom, had long been a fast-day of the Church, when meat was not supposed to be eaten; so, too, during the forty days of Lent. But licences, strictly regulated by statute, could be obtained to eat flesh during restricted periods, from the bishop of the diocese or parson of the parish – bringing in useful supplementary fees to those persons – and from higher up for larger dispensations. To the Friday fast-day, when fish took the place of meat, the government added a second fish-day, Wednesday.[5] This had the double motive of encouraging fishing and thereby the Navy, and preserving cattle. A Proclamation of 1595 enforced the reasons for it, and claimed that 135,000 head of beef 'might be spared in a year in the city of London by one day's abstinence in a week.'[6] This rule was fairly widely adhered to and enforced: many were the prosecutions and fines for offences against it. One sees, in a matter like this, that government in those days thought in the long-term interests of the country.

Bread was, of course, the staple of diet – 'Give us this day our daily bread' the most frequent of petitions – and was 'made of such grain as the soil yieldeth.'[7] Harrison tells us that the gentry provided wheaten bread for their own tables, while their households and poorer folk in most shires ate barley bread or bread made from rye. The poorest folk in times of dearth were reduced to make their bread of beans, peas, oats, or acorns. Sir Hugh Plat, that ingenious man, provides a recipe for boiling the mess two or three times over, to suck out their rankness, then dry out the flour to make bread of them. We need hardly repeat that this was a subsistence economy; when there was dearth poor people went short – at all times some people were undernourished. And again at times, especially in winter, some people, especially children left to fend for themselves, died of starvation.

Dietetic opinion was dominated by the theory of the humours. The four elements of the universe had each its characteristic quality: earth was dry, water moist, fire hot, air cold. Combinations of qualities produced complexions or humours: sanguine was hot and moist, phlegmatic cold and moist, choleric hot and dry, melancholic cold and dry. The qualities and effects of foodstuffs were related. 'Lamb, for example, was very moist and phlegmatic: therefore . . . unsuitable for old men, whose stomachs were supposed to have already too much phlegm.'[8] Children also were supposed to be phlegmatic, therefore to be nourished 'with meats and drinks which are moderately hot and moist' – there introducing a qualification. As they grew older they tended to become more sanguine or choleric. Youths, therefore, were to eat 'meats more gross of substance, colder and moister; also salads of cold herbs, and to drink seldom wine, unless it be allayed with water.' In old age, when the body was losing heat, hot and moist meats were again the thing. We remember Falstaff's 'I love not the humour of bread and cheese, and there's the humour of it.'

Until about 1500 little beer was brewed – medieval Englishmen drank ale; the introduction and rapid spread of the use of hops acted as a strong preservative. Hence Harrison: 'the beer that is used at noblemen's tables . . . is commonly a year old, or peradventure of two years' tunning or more; but this is not general. It is also brewed in March, and therefore called March beer; but, for the household, it is usually not under a month's age, each one coveting to have the same stale as he may, so that it be not sour, and his bread new as is possible, so that it be not hot.'[9] As a middle-class man, and as a patriot, Harrison deplored the excessive importation of wine, for not only rich men's consumption either: 'neither anywhere more store of all sorts than in England, although we have none growing with us, but yearly to the proportion of 20,000 or 30,000 tun and upwards.' Nevertheless the staple drink was ale and beer, and Harrison gives us a practical disquisition on brewing, how to turn barley into malt, how to treat it, the importance of the quality of the water (Thames water is best, he says; but what about Trent – hence the fame of Burton-on-Trent?). We recall the store of malt that William Shakespeare held in his house in 1598, after the dearth of the previous years; his close friends held even larger quantities – but then Stratford was very much a malting town.[10]

Let us look in more detail into a few concrete illustrations of these themes. A fine series of household account books enables us to observe the food consumed at Gilling Castle in Yorkshire during the years 1571–82.[11] Dinner and supper were served in three sections. There was the table for the Master, Sir William Fairfax, and his guests; secondly there was the 'board's end' – presumably these meals were served in Sir William's grand new dining-room, with its carved panelling and frescoed wapentakes. Thirdly there was the hall for the gentlemen attendants of the guests and 'yeomen throughout'. When the Earl of Rutland paid a visit, 14 May 1579, the first course served at the Master's table consisted of boiled meats, boiled beef, roast veal, rabbits, and pigeons, pigeon pie.[12] The second course: roast lamb, rabbits, chickens, kid, and moorcocks, baked chickens, moorcock pie, lamb pie, soused pig, tarts. Plenty of choice, so far as meats were concerned, but no vegetables mentioned. At the board's end the first course was much the same, slightly smaller; the second course varied more: mutton in pottage, chickens boiled, stewed rabbits, boiled pigeon and calves' feet, sliced beef (i.e. probably cold, as usually for supper), roast mutton and veal, baked calves' feet, roast capon and dulcets, i.e. sweet dishes. In the hall there was less choice: for the first course ten messes, i.e. usually for four, of boiled beef; for the second: mutton in pottage, boiled pigeon, stewed rabbits, sliced beef, roast mutton and veal, pigeon pie, and dulcets. Supper was much in accordance with dinner. One can imagine what a kitchen staff this entailed – though this was a guest night with Lord Rutland, Mr. Manners, Sir Robert Constable, Sir William Bellasis, Mr. Henry Bellasis and his wife, and many others.

We must cite a fast-day at Gilling. Archbishop Sandys of York, Sir William Bellasis, Mr. Vavasour and his wife were present with many others for supper on a summer evening, Friday 24 July 1579.[13] At Sir William's table the principal guests were offered, three salads, butter, green pottage, boiled chickens, eggs in broth, turbot broth, salt ling, white herrings, keling (cod), turbot pie, fresh salmon, roast capon, baked venison, and dulcets – sixteen dishes in all. Perhaps the chickens, capon and venison were for those who had a dispensation to eat meat on Friday. The second course consisted of salmon chine, roasted rabbit and conger and chickens, salmon trout, roast kid, brite (a kind of fish), fresh ling, conger in souse, roast moorpoults (moorfowl), roast tench, florentine (a custard, or sweet pie), tench in jelly, tarts – fourteen dishes. Supper at the board's end was much the same, but with less choice for the second course – only ten dishes. In hall, there was noticeably less choice – ten messes of green pottage, turbot broth, butter, salt ling, keling, custard, with a 'reward', which means a second course, of conger, fresh ling, tarts.

For Christmas Day 1572 enormous amounts of food were consumed, for there were many guests, Sir William and Lady Bellasis, Robert and Edward Fairfax with their wives, John Vavasour and wife, Mistress Stapleton, William Harington and wife, *cum multis aliis*.[14] All sorts of dainties appear on the board: frumenty – hulled wheat boiled in milk, seasoned with sugar; there were many recipes for it in different parts of the country – the dish continued in country places in Dorset to Hardy's time, for it appears in his novels; numble pies, made of the entrails of a deer; turkey, swan, teal, mallard, crane, capon. It reminds one of nothing so much as the Mallard Song still sung on Gaudy nights at All Souls:

> The griffin, bustard, turkey, capon,
> Let other hungry mortals gape on,
> And on their bones with stomach fall hard,
> But let All Souls men have their Mallard . . .
>
> Then let us drink and dance a galliard
> In the remembrance of the Mallard,

And as the Mallard doth in pool
Let's dabble, dive, and duck in bowl.

These doggerel verses may well go back to that time, or at least to
the time when people still danced galliards.

Little account is made of breakfast, but occasionally we find
that the Master is served brawn and mustard, beef and brewis,
i.e. a North Country dish of slices of bread with fat broth poured
over them; the yeomen in the hall had two messes of beef and
brewis. Lady Fairfax had a more ladylike breakfast of butter and
eggs; while the work-folks had three messes of beef, and three of
brewis. These accounts cover only the meats. Bread was dealt with
in the pantry, and drink in the buttery, as in an Oxford college
today. For one week in 1572 the pantry took in 14 dozen manchet,
i.e. best white bread, 30 dozen household bread, the buttery 14
hogsheads of beer. Then there were the spices and niceties, of which
we have an account for the year 1580, complete with prices:
pepper, cloves, mace (the outer covering of nutmeg), sugar,
cinnamon, ginger, nutmegs, currants, raisins, prunes, almonds,
dates, liquorice, anniseed, biscuits and carroways, isinglass,
sandal-wood, probably to burn for perfuming.[15]

It is not surprising that the expense of these household provisions for this year 1580 amounted to £440. 0. 2½d.; even so we
must allow a considerable sum for provisions produced on the
estate. What we must chiefly remark is the immense amount of
hospitality, the trains of guests; there is a vast difference between
the ordinary rate of such a household and the guest-days and
nights. Sir William Fairfax belonged to the greater gentry, almost
coming up to a peer. When we arrive at the household of the grandest of peers the Earl of Derby, the expense for the year 1561, quite
early in the reign, reached the enormous total of £2895. 0. 6.[16]

It may interest the reader to know the regimen maintained by
that careful woman, the Queen, in her own private apartments,
and the food consumed there – she signed her household books
regularly, just as any other great lady did.[17] Breakfast makes much
more of an appearance in her books (1576): manchet and cheat,
i.e. the next best sort of fine white bread, ale, beer and wine –
Elizabeth drank either small beer or light wine. Then there were
various meats and bones for pottage, so there was a variety of
soups and broths, with butter. Dinner and supper followed much
the same order as we have seen, with two courses specified. But

there is this difference, that there are no guests eating with the Queen in private: when she entertains some visiting foreign potentate or makes a feast for an ambassador, it will be a public feast in the hall of her palace. These accounts evidently cover the food provided for her immediate attendants, the ladies in waiting. And one notices a feminine taste in the lighter diet: many more birds, cocks or godwits, larks, partridges, plovers, pheasants, snites (snipe); and more sweet dishes, as we should expect: custard, fritter, tarts, dulcets, friants (dainties).

Naturally the Queen's household rigorously observed the rules about fish-days and flesh-days. One finds separate services for the lords coming to her to transact business. In this same month of November 1576 the following services are provided: two services of meat served to the Lords (i.e. of the Privy Council), one to the Lord Chamberlain (the Earl of Sussex), one to Secretary Walsingham, one each to the Treasurer and Comptroller of the Household. There were six services for a flesh-day and six for a fish-day. Then there were two services for the ladies in presence, and one for the first of the ladies – both fish and flesh: six services altogether. There follows a separate service for the Master of the Horse, both fish and flesh; a separate service for the Secretary; eleven services – two for Treasurer and Comptroller, two for the gentlewomen of the Privy Chamber, one for the Cofferer, two for the Clerk of the Green Cloth (who dealt with the Household below-stairs, as the Lord Chamberlain above-stairs), two to the Clerks Comptrollers, one to the chief Clerk of the Kitchen, and one to the Master of the Jewel House: all these for both flesh and fish. Next follow separate diets for the Secretary and Master of the Horse, winding up with an immense number of services for all the officials of the Household: five services for ladies sitting in the Queen's chamber, four for knights, squires, gentlemen ushers, chaplains, physicians, clerks, serjeants, grooms, master cooks, porters, lastly the numerous servants of the officials and ladies in waiting. A number of household officials and ladies had their separate chambers, and hence tables. So there must have been numerous services of meals all through the palace, in addition to the great hall: one visualises the hurrying and scurrying – a perfect rabbit-warren.

Elizabethan statistics can hardly ever be relied on, but they sometimes give one an indication, or serve for comparison. 'According to her Majesty's book . . . the whole charge of the diet with the breakfasts for one whole year: £15,616, 10. 2. According as they are served by the year, £21,639, 3, 5¼. So increased,

£6022. 13. 3¼.' For all the Queen's efforts she could never keep pace with the rising expenditure.

After this it may be instructive to observe the diet of a single gentleman coming up to London, with apparently two or three men in attendance – this is the almost legendary 'Wild Darrell' of Littlecote in Wiltshire, of whom the sinister story is told: of the new-born illegitimate baby thrown upon the fire, the midwife brought blindfold to the house at night, and the upshot. Apparently the diets, 16 April to 14 July 1589, cover Darrell and his two men.[18] 'At my coming up, Wednesday dinner April 16. A piece of beef, 18d; a leg of mutton, 20d; 2 chickens and bacon, 20d; 2 chickens and 2 pigeons roasted, 18d; for dressing all, 7d; for parsley, cloves, and sauce for the mutton, 6d; bread and beer, 16d. Total 8s 9d. Supper *eodem:* shoulder of mutton, 20d; 3 pigeons, 8d; for roasting the mutton, pigeons, 2 chickens and 2 rabbits, for sauce, sops and parsley, 5d; bread and beer, 14d. Total 4s 10d.' This seems to have been the regular proportion maintained, dinner usually costing rather more than supper. Fish-days were much cheaper: for Friday dinner, April 25, there was 'a piece of ling, 8d; butter, 2d; mackerel, 6d. Supper *eodem:* fish, butter, and cheese, 14d. Friday dinner, May 2, was much more expensive: 'a side of haberdine [salted cod] and another of green fish, 14d; 4 plaices, 12d; 2 whitings, 8d; conger, 8d; butter, 4d; lettuce for salad, 2d; a pint of white wine and another of claret, 6d; sugar, 2d; a pound of butter, 5d; for dressing the fish, 8d; oil and sugar for salad, 2d; more for butter, 2d; a pound of candles, 4d. Total, 7s 3d.' There was no supper that evening.

When Wild Darrell went out to dinner at an inn, expenses varied. On Whitsunday dinner for five at Ratcliffe cost 4s., and Alden's 4d.; at the Queen's Head in Paternoster Row, 5s. 1d., with Alden's and Anthony's dinners, 10d.; at the King's Head in New Fish Street, 16s., Alden's 4d. As summer wore on one frequently finds a quart or a pint of strawberries, or oranges and lemons. With his fruit Darrell sometimes drank a pint of charnico, a sweet wine from near Lisbon. One Friday towards the end of June, in addition to beef, mutton, veal, rabbits, one finds '2 pecks of peascods, 8d, a quart of cream, 6d, 3 quarts of strawberries, 16d, 2 lb of cherries 20d, ½ lb of musk comfits 10d, ½ lb of violet comfits 11d, oranges 3d, 2 lemons 6d', with bread and beer. This was a fish-day, but it was evidently not observed.

One finds much the same kind of régime followed by Arthur Throckmorton, when a young man footloose in London, in the Throckmorton Diary.[19]

After the pleasures of food, exoneration. I know of no more intimate account of the systematic purgings to which Elizabethan gentlemen were apt to subject themselves, in spring or autumn, sometimes both, than Throckmorton's. Though he may have been something of a hypochondriac, there is no need to suppose that he was abnormal, except in his dedication to the subject and the interested expression he gave to it. It was a regular thing for gentlemen of the upper classes to give as an excuse for not answering a summons, to the Privy Council or such, that they had taken physic and were not available for a few days. When one reads Throckmorton's Diary, one sees how it worked. In the autumn of 1609 he was in the care of Dr. Chenell of Oxford, to whom he frequently sent over his footman, Timothy, for physic.[20] He was not content with a mere eight stools in a day, so he takes a potion that gives him twelve. 'Brought from Oxford an electuary to take before I sweat, 2s.; three purging potions, 7s. 6d.; bottles of small and strong diet drink, 7s. for each lot, four purgations, 12s. . . . I drank of the strong diet drink at four and when I went to bed, and once at supper of the small.' Next, 'I was very ill in my stomach at night,' so he took another potion which gave him twelve stools. And even this was not his record.

In 1596 there came out a book that made a great stink in its time, Sir John Harington's *The Metamorphosis of Ajax*. This was but a prelude to Harington's pamphlet, with illustrations, on his invention of the water-closet, a literary fantastication of the theme by a witty and clever writer. It is, in fact, a comic masterpiece, one of the few pieces of Elizabethan humour, outside the drama, that remains funny. With its unashamed gusto, its delight in life, in jokes and jakes – not to say japes – it reminds one of the best comic invention in the literature of our time: Evelyn Waugh's 'Connolly's Patent Thunder-box'. I cannot think that those who cite Harington's invention in their dull textbook fashion can have read his book. The Elizabethans were much less repressed about physical functions, were more open in their expression of them, before the Puritans conquered the country twice over – once in the seventeenth century with the Civil War and again in the Victorian age. What got Harington into trouble was not what he said about privies, but because he laughed at the sacred bull, Leicester, eight years after his death – an indication of the Queen's loyalty and devotion.

But Harington laughed at everything and everybody. A cultivated man, he was not only well read in Ariosto but also in

Rabelais, who had not yet been translated. He has a passage on Rabelais' celebrated disquisition on the use of the goose-feather, then improves on it by suggesting tearing a leaf out of Holinshed's Chronicles! – anyone who knows the enormous volume in the original will appreciate the joke. There are shameless puns in Latin and English, about the Popes on their Apostolic Seat; he quotes the unsuitable apothegms written by the sainted Sir Thomas More when young, the bawdy epigrams of Heywood. He laughed at poor old Bishop Cooper of the big Latin Dictionary, as Martin Marprelate had done – the bishop was everybody's target, since everybody knew that he was cuckolded by his wife and put up with it. Harington laughed at the laughable old dowager Lady Russell, a comic character to anyone who knows her; he laughed at other pomposities and – most shocking of all – he laughed at the Puritans.

He laughed at the Ladies of the Privy Chamber, with whom, as Elizabeth's godson, he was very familiar; and when he was sent home from Court, threatened with Star Chamber and what not for his misdemeanour, he indited them a sonnet: 'To the Ladies of the Queen's Privy Chamber, at the making of their perfumed privy at Richmond.' With a straight face he asked them to commend his new device:

> Sith here you see, feel, smell that his conveyance
> Hath freed this noisome place from all annoyance.
> Now judge you that the work mock, envy, taunt,
> Whose service in this place may make most vaunt:
> If us, or you, to praise it were most meet,
> You that made sour, or us that make it sweet.

Harington knew quite well what was what in the Privy Chamber, and shamelessly spelled it out: 'I think I might also lay pride to their charge, for I have seen them [close-stools] in sugared cases of satin and velvet – which is flat against the Statute of Apparel – but for sweetness or cleanliness I never knew yet any of them guilty of it; but that if they had but waited on a lady in her chamber a day or a night, they would have made a man, at his next entrance into the chamber, have said "So, good speed ye".' (i.e. take his departure).[21] The smells of these great houses, especially the palaces with their enormous households, must have been appalling – if not quite so bad as eighteenth-century Versailles, which everybody said could be smelt three miles off. No wonder Elizabethan grandees – particularly the Queen and Leicester – were addicted to perfuming everything, or had such an acute sense of smell, like Shakespeare.

Harington had a remedy to propound: in short, the modern water-closet, cistern, lavatory-pan and seat, stop-tap, sluice, sewage-tank, all the works. He teased the ingenious, and slightly ridiculous, inventor Plat, who was interested in the uses of manure, with the proposal of a monopoly: it should bring in so much money, that 'if I had such a grant, he that were my *heres ex asse* would be the richest squire in England.'[22] With a not quite straight face Harington put himself forward as a public benefactor: 'and so we might one day be put in the Chronicles as good members of our country: more worthily than the great bear that carried eight dogs on him when Monsieur [the Duke of Anjou] was here.' (Anyone with any sense of language should spot the puns at every point.)

Harington considered that the cost of his invention was inconsiderable compared with the convenience, for, with the rapid increase of population in London, people were more and more incommoded. Lincoln's Inn had installed upstairs privies with their own chimney-vents, but the draughts did not always operate upwards. His own device was much preferable, and the more necessary the larger the household. He mockingly appraised its worth in his own house at £100, 'in yours £300, in Wollaton £500, in Theobalds, Burghley and Holdenby £1000, in Greenwich, Richmond and Hampton Court £10,000.'[23]

A few people installed it, but why not more widely? One argument was that 'in the Prince's houses, where so many mouths be fed, a close-vault [i.e. sewage-tank] will fill quickly. And that objection did my Lord of Leicester make to Sir John Young, at his last being at Bristol, who commended to my Lord that fashion and showed him his own of a worse fashion, and told him that at a friend's house of his at Peter Hill in London there was a very sweet privy of that making.'[24] The general answer would seem to be that the installation of the miles of pipes that would have been necessary, quite apart from water-supply and cisterns, was beyond the technical resources of the Elizabethans – in that like the Rev. William Lee's stocking-knitting frame. They both had to wait for the Industrial Revolution.

Harington's rustication from Court was more a matter of form with the Queen than any disgrace; as a matter of fact, that sensible woman rather approved of the book. A couple of years and his cousin was writing :'your book is almost forgiven, and I may say forgotten – but not for its lack of wit or satire . . . And though her Highness signified displeasure in outward sort, yet did she like the marrow of your book.'[25] She was minded to take him back into favour, provided he did not write epigrams on her and her all too vulnerable ladies.

The book had been produced in 1596 by Richard Field, Shakespeare's school-fellow at Stratford, who, two or three years before, had printed *Venus and Adonis* and *Lucrece*. Both authors may well have been in and out of Field's establishment in Blackfriars – where Lady Russell lived and made her presence felt – correcting proofs. More important is the sympathy of outlook between Harington and the rising dramatist. Harington refers to the pirated edition of *The Taming of a Shrew*, which had appeared but a couple of years before. He recommended the book for reading, 'which hath made a number of us so perfect that now everyone can rule a shrew in our country, save he that hath her. But indeed there are but two good rules. One is, let them never have their wills; the other differs but a letter, let them ever have their wills. The first is the wiser, but the second is more in request and therefore I make choice of it.'[26] It is pleasant that this old joke came up again as recently as President Johnson's reception of the Princess Margaret and her husband at the White House in the 1960's.

But anyone well up in Elizabethan usage will recognise the *double-entendre* in the word 'will', so beloved and frequently used by Shakespeare.[27] Harington has a reference to the nuisance of dogs in people's houses, which reminds one of the marvellously realistic passage – straight out of the life of a great house – written not long before in *The Two Gentlemen of Verona*. Launce's lower-class dog, Crab, 'thrusts me himself into the company of three or four gentlemen-like dogs, under the Duke's table. He had not been there (bless the mark!) a pissing-while, but all the chamber smelt him . . . "Out with the dog!", says one. "What cur is that?", says another. "Whip him out", says the third. "Hang him up!", says the Duke. I, having been acquainted with the smell before, knew it was Crab; and goes me to the fellow that whips the dogs. "Friend," quoth I, "you mean to whip the dog?" "Ay, marry, do I," quoth he. "You do him the more wrong," quoth I, " 'twas I did the thing you wot of." He makes me no more ado, but whips me out of the chamber. How many masters would do this for his servant?' Harington realised that cats behaved themselves better than dogs, and set an example even to humans.

When, a couple of years later, Shakespeare came to write *As*

You Like It and invented the character of the melancholy Jacques (pronounced Jakes), one wonders whether he was not influenced, consciously or unconsciously, by Harington's notorious and amusing book with its pun on the word running all through it. It were a pity if Harington never met Shakespeare, but it is clear that he had read or seen his plays.

Towns and manor-courts, and therefore villages, had some sanitary arrangements, though they varied very much. Principally private enterprise prevailed: people were supposed to keep their bit of street or lane in front of their own houses clean, as in the more backward parts of Europe today, where one can see it operating, smells and all. People were not supposed to leave their household refuse in the street, though it was not always possible to avoid doing so. In 1552 John Shakespeare was fined at the manor court leet for making a muckheap in Henley Street; others fined were Adrian Quiney and the deputy steward of the manor himself.[28] It was a very common offence. More important was to keep waters, streams and wells clean – especially where the water was used for drinking or brewing. One finds continual regulations against people washing clothes in or near waters used for drink, or against washing the entrails of beasts after slaughter. Naturally regulations were stricter in towns; it is evident from innumerable documents how frequently they were broken.

In Exeter in 1568 the city council decided that 'there shall be three common jakes or widraughts made within this city, viz. one in Friernhay, and one at the town wall in St. Paul's parish, and the third about the Watergate.'[29] Dr. Portman tells us that Bedford House, the residence of the Earls – though they were hardly ever there – had six privies about the premises for gentlefolk and servants alike. From inventories it emerges that only a minority of citizens possessed chamber-pots, usually of tin, or close-stools; very few had both. The position of the close-stool is, it seems, 'a reliable guide to the habits of the Exeter manufacturing and trading classes. They were not squeamish . . . Occasionally the close-stool would be put in the cockloft, at the head of the stairs or in the gallery, but it was commonly to be found in a chamber on one of the middle floors, and the inventory usually records a bed in the same room . . . The apothecary who in 1596 had a screen to shield the close-stool from the bed in his parlour was an exceptional individual.' Dr. Portman concludes that 'the great majority of Exeter people had to fend for themselves or in the nearest open spaces.'[30]

This was where the scavengers came in. Most towns of any size had some system of scavenging. In London every ward had a number, varying from four, to (more usually) six or seven, though Faringdon Within had as many as eighteen. Bishopsgate, where Shakespeare lived for some years up to 1599, had seven scavengers; Cripplegate where he was living in Silver Street in 1600, had four; the borough of Southwark, where he lived in the following years, had six.[31] They made little impression on this sensitive man, with his superior tastes: they are not mentioned in his plays. In his native Stratford there were no regular scavengers; the job was left to the townsfolk themselves, except for a few special assignments which were nobody's job. In 1576, when Shakespeare was a boy of twelve, Mother Margaret was paid 3d. for 'making clean afore the Chapel': she must have been a familiar figure to him, for 'old Margaret' goes on sweeping the street before or around the Chapel for years – it is next door to the grammar school and just across the street from Shakespeare's fine house, New Place.[32] In 1592, when the former schoolboy was beginning to write the Sonnets, the 'woman that sweepeth before the Chapel' was regularly paid 16d. a year for her services – they must have been occasional. As with the woman who is paid 2d. for cleaning the gaol in High Street. A larger expense was entailed for cleaning the bridge – a necessary expense, Stratford's connection with the South, London and Oxford.[33] Richard Meakins, the Town Whipper, was paid more generously, 5s. a quarter, to drive beggars and vagabonds out of the town and whip persons appointed to be whipped.[34]

The City of Oxford was better provided: we find that from 1541 a common scavenger was appointed 'to carry all sweepings of men's houses and the dirt that cometh of the sweepings of the streets' – when horses were the chief means of transport.[35] Every householder was to pay 1d a quarter 'for the carriage of the same, and they that have horses to pay for their dung-carriage as the scavenger and they can agree.' So that was how it was managed. By 1578 there was more than one scavenger, and two persons in each parish were to find out what every household would pay quarterly and collect the money. In 1582 the city authorities laid down a lengthy sanitary code, enforcing special care, in that city surrounded by rivers, that the waters should not be polluted by dumping dung or rubbish in them. Privies and hogsties set over or near streams leading to any brewhouse were to be removed; hogs were not to be kept within the city, but only inside people's 'several backsides', i.e. separate back-premises. No butchers were to keep slaughter-houses within the walls, nor chandlers keep melting-houses or melt any tallow (the smell and the nuisance were both bad). Chimneys were to be swept once a quarter. From all this we can imagine how things in fact were; nevertheless the regulations show the trend of opinion.

Other towns, of any size, similarly. At Leicester from 1557 none was to cast any weeds or filth into the Soar or 'wash any immets [inmeats, i.e. entrails] or such like in the same water near to any place where any burn [brewing water] is taken up.'[36] In 1579 washing clothes at the common wells was prohibited. From an order of 1582 we learn that inhabitants owning empty houses were nevertheless responsible for cleaning the streets in front of them, and garbage was to be carried away weekly. Urgent and special measures were everywhere taken at plague-time, fires burning in the streets, wooden houses erected for resort outside the town, the infected confined to their houses, etc: this recurred roughly every decade. We shall deal with it when we come to medical matters.

The greatest possible amenity to towns of any size was the bringing of water-supplies into them. There was already a number of medieval conduits in London, but Stow enables us to see how many the Elizabethans added, in some cases piping water into the houses. Near London Bridge a Dutchman brought his expertise to work in 1582 by installing 'a most artificial [i.e. skilfully made] forcier [gusher]' which piped Thames water into houses on the east side of the city.[37] Another forcier to serve the western section was installed by the ingenious Bevis Bulmer in 1594, while a number of ordinary conduits were set up, often beside the parish churches. The prime example of bringing water to a town was the famous achievement of Sir Francis Drake in bringing a supply to Plymouth from the River Meavy, completed in 1591. From ten miles away up on the moor, the open channel cut was about eighteen miles, to allow a gentle incline. The water served several purposes, not only to supply the town, but to water ships and scour the inner harbour, then becoming one of the first naval ports in the country. Along the course mills were set up, from which Drake drew profits. It was a tremendous effort, worth setting beside Drake's other exploits, like the 'Singeing of the King of Spain's Beard' and the raids on the West Indies: this one is still celebrated every year by a water-feast high up on the Meavy. Drake's effort for Plymouth formed the model for the even larger one of the

Welshman, Sir Hugh Myddelton, in bringing the New River to London a decade or so later.[38]

Plymouth town documents are full of references to the scheme and its consequences in these years. They also serve to introduce us to a no less characteristic subject: since Plymouth was a naval port the 'carting' of strumpets was much in evidence. In Armada year there were so many that 'when the Irish woman was carted' the cart had to be 'amended'.[39] Next year six 'hoares' were whipped, and 'Bellamy and his fellows were paid 1s 'for whipping of women about the town'. In 1596 when Mistress Pricket was carted – from her name she would seem a familiar figure – six men attended her, by the mayor's command. Only once do we find a note of charity: 'given to a poor woman which had been carted, 6d'; even then, 'paid for carrying her away, 4d.' The puritanical authorities of towns were far removed from the tolerance of Shakespeare:

> Thou rascal beadle, hold thy bloody hand.
> Why dost thou lash that whore? Strip thy own back:
> Thou hotly lusts to use her in that kind
> For which thou whip'st her.

The Middle Ages had been more tolerant too, or more primitive. Up to Henry VIII's Reformation a famous row of licensed brothels had stood on the South Bank, next Winchester House, on land owned by the bishopric. Stow gives us the constitution of Henry II's Parliament regulating these 'Stews': any single woman to go and come freely when she chose; 'no single woman to take money to lie with any man but she lie with him all night till the morrow'; 'no stewholder to receive any woman of religion [i.e. a nun], or any man's wife'; 'no stewholder to keep any woman that hath the perilous infirmity of burning'; 'the constables, bailiff, and others every week to search every stewhouse.'[40] Here lay the justification of the authorities: it was in their province to safeguard public health. In the last year of moral king Henry VIII's reign the stews were put down by proclamation, to the sound of the trumpet. But long were they remembered, if not regretted; and the remembrance went on in the popular phrase, 'Winchester goose', which meant a venereal sore in the groin. As Pandarus says in the Epilogue to *Troilus and Cressida*:

> 'Brethren and sisters of the hold-door trade,
> Some two months hence my will shall here be made.

It should be now, but that my fear is this,
Some gallèd goose of Winchester would hiss.'

It is not to be supposed that the closing of the stews was the destruction of the trade. Shakespeare's plays are sufficient evidence of that, with the brothel-scene in *Pericles*, the realistic happenings at the Boar's Head in East Cheap, the characters of Mistress Quickly – with the suggestiveness of the name – Doll Tearsheet, Mistress Overdone, poor Kate Keepdown, Pandarus and the goings-on in *Troilus and Cressida*. And this apart from all the other dramatists. Shakespeare, however, is the sexiest writer in the language – more thoroughly so than the Restoration dramatists – to anyone who knows the Elizabethan idiom well enough to recognise the constant barrage of innuendo, double meanings, lascivious puns, in addition to the frank bawdy, the open appeal to sensuality. This is one reason, no doubt, why he was the most popular dramatist of the age, and it is a salty element in his preservation that he goes straight to the source of life.

CHAPTER VI

SEX

O NE cannot do justice here to the sex-life of the Elizabethans: it would need, and merit, a whole volume – one of far greater significance than most works of historical research. After all, it was the necessary condition of the life of the age. Here one can only suggest a few pointers.

The paradoxical thing is that, at the apex, society was given an example of chaste virginity. No-one has explored the anthropological significance of that, though there are many evidences of the ways – conscious and overt, in literature and art, as well as half-conscious and surreptitious, in rumour and dream – in which it penetrated into men's minds. It was an extraordinary thing in itself, an unique phenomenon, which entered in the subtlest as well as the most obvious fashion into the myth of the age. The Queen herself was not averse to calling attention to it, in the most public way, when badgered by Parliament to marry and assure the succession. She prayed God 'to continue me still in this mind to live out of the state of marriage . . . And in the end, this shall be for me sufficient, that a marble stone shall declare that a Queen, having reigned such a time, lived and died a virgin.'[1]

Ordinary mortals, especially at the beginning, could not understand it; they grew to accept it, and in the end to find inspiration in it. Some people, then and since, have thought that there was something wrong with her. Those in the best position to know – Burghley, for example – did not think so. Common sense was a sufficient warning as to the dangers of child-bearing at the time, and there were the fearful examples of her sister and her mother to bring it home to her. It is fairly clear to a perceptive eye that she did not intend to marry. The Scotch ambassador, Melville, saw well enough that her deepest passion was to rule and that she would never give herself a master – as any sixteenth-century woman did by marrying. Leicester told the French ambassador at the time of the Anjou marriage-negotiations – which were all politics, of course – that over the past twenty years she had always said, 'I will never marry.'[2]

Though she was fond of her women companions, especially in later years, of Lady Warwick, there was nothing Lesbian about her. There is indeed no evidence of that interesting phenomenon in the Elizabethan age; for that we have to wait until the Court of the Restoration, with its understandable reaction from the rule of the saints.[3] In fact, she combined a cold, exhibitionist temperament with a politic head, and this enabled her to offset her emotional preferences by rational judgment – a necessary quality in a ruler, in complete contrast to both Mary Tudor and Mary Stuart.

We have already noticed her dislike to matrimony for her ladies, and her attempts to persuade them against it. She detested clerical marriage. Poor Archbishop Parker, who had the misfortune to be married, was quite early on treated to a severe rating on the subject. He told Cecil, 'I was in an horror to hear such words to come from her mild nature and Christianly learned conscience as she spoke concerning God's holy ordinance and institution of matrimony.'[4] Parker thought that it was in keeping with God's word and that clerical marriage was better than 'counterfeited chastity.' She returned with 'a repentance that we were thus appointed in office, wishing it had been otherwise.' She would undoubtedly have preferred a Catholic episcopate, but that was not practical politics: she reluctantly accepted the inevitable. Her jealousy of the hot-blooded young men and women of the Court having the fun she couldn't have, which she could control in herself when they couldn't, is sufficiently obvious. It all adds up to the recognisable characteristics of the unsatisfied, jealous spinster.

Of course, in the country and abroad, people talked about her relations with Leicester. Ordinary persons could scarcely conceive the complexity and necessary abortiveness of their relations. Here is one such, as late as 1581: one Henry Hawkins said that 'my Lord Robert hath had five children by the Queen, and she never goeth in progress but to be delivered.'[5] Other such references occur in the State Papers. There is something deeply anthropological in the popular hatred and jealousy of Leicester for being too close to the Virgin Queen. When his first wife, who was already dying of cancer, fell down the stairs dead at Cumnor Place, everybody believed that he had had her murdered. There was nothing whatever in it – though it is still popularly believed today.[6] This was the kind of thing Leicester had to put up with, for his privileged position, all his life.

In fact, Elizabeth thoroughly mixed up his sex-life by preventing him from marrying. For some years the Lady Douglas Sheffield was his mistress and was infatuated with him: there is a wonderfully revealing, exculpatory letter from him when he wanted to taper their relations off.[7] For he was now in love with, and living with, Elizabeth's cousin, Lettice Knollys, Lady Essex; but not until her third pregnancy did he incur the risk of marrying her. In the event Leicester's hope of founding a family was nullified. Amy Robsart, an invalid, had no children; Lady Sheffield's son by him, Sir Robert Dudley, was illegitimate; the Countess Lettice's little boy died. Ambrose, Leicester's brother, had no children. Both the Dudley peerages died with them. Of all Northumberland's fine brood of five sons, there was no legitimate progeny: some indication of the demographic risks attaching to high station in Tudor society.

A unique insight into the stimulating effect of the Virgin Queen upon the susceptible imagination of menfolk occurs in the diary of Simon Forman, the astrologer and empiric – one might describe him as a forerunner of the modern psychiatrist. It is true that Forman was very suggestible; his dreaming of her is all the more revealing. At Lambeth, 23 January 1597, about 3 a.m., 'I dreamt that I was with the Queen, and that she was a little elderly woman in a coarse white petticoat all unready; and she and I walked up and down through lanes and closes, talking and reasoning of many matters. At last we came over a great close where were many people, and there were two men at hard words. One of them was a weaver, a tall man with a reddish beard, distract of his wits. She talked to him and he spake very merrily unto her, and at last did take her and kiss her. So I took her by the arm and put her away; and told her the fellow was frantic. And so we went from him and I led her by the arm still, and then we went through a dirty lane. She had a long white smock, very clean and fair, and it trailed in the dirt and her coat behind. I took her coat and did carry it up a good way, and then it hung too low before. I told her she should do me a favour to let me wait on her, and she said I should. Then said I, "I mean to wait *upon* you and not under you, that I might make this belly a little bigger to carry up this smock and coats out of the dirt." And so we talked merrily and then she began to lean upon me, when we were past the dirt and to be very familiar with me, and methought she began to love me. And when we were alone, out of sight, methought she would have kissed me.'[8] But that desired consummation awoke him.

A month later, 21 February, Forman dreamed of her again coming to him all in black, with a French hood. It needs no very deep knowledge of psychology to spot the Freudian symbolism of this, the Virgin Queen all in white, then trailing in the dirt, and finally appearing in black; nor the obvious sex-rivalry with the 'tall man with the reddish beard', who may be a dream-image of Essex. One may compare this revelation of the unconscious life of the mind with the public celebration of her by the poets. Simon Forman's case-books enable us to pry into the innermost crevices of Elizabethan sex-life, including his own, to lay our fingers on the pulses of these long-dead folk, learn their secrets and the pathos of their lives, as so rarely. He had a wide following of all classes, from the Earl of Hertford and that wicked young woman, Frances Howard, Countess of Essex, downwards. Vice-Admiral Sir William Monson, Sir Barrington Mullins, and Sir Thomas Shirley were regular clients, and we find some unexpected names, Henry Wotton for one, Sir George Carew, Lady Howard, Lady Norris, and Sir Henry Killigrew's daughter, Dorothy. Most constant, in their applications were Dean Blague of Rochester and his wife. But along with these one finds a cross-section of the low-life of London, sailors and their wives, servants and loose women. Forman had a pretty following from Ratcliffe among the sea-faring folk, with their anxiety to know how they or their men would fare on their voyages, or coming to him up the Thames to his house in Lambeth to inquire (astrologically) if their missing ones would ever return.

Here, in 1598, is Joan, Mr. Borace's servant of Ratcliffe, aged forty-seven, with pains in her stomach, belly and legs; it seems 'from putrefaction of some dead conception in her womb. She hath taken grist and it seems she is *gravida* [pregnant] by her Master, and he hath given her some ill medicine and gone to somebody to bewitch her that she should die.'⁹ Mary Beckingham Cockeron alias Garnet, of sixteen years, 'is an enemy to herself', not sick, but fearful, with pain in stomach, back, head and heart. 'She supposeth herself with child, but it is not so: full of scabs and itch, and it will be the pox for her blood is infected.' A few weeks later: 'she is *gravida* by one Lodwick, a merchant beyond Aldgate. Her husband was not with her since before Christmas.'

Let us move somewhat further up in society. Sylvanus Scory, forty-seven: 'the humour abounding is that of melancholy, which breeds a stone. He hath had it long and can never be cured thereof . . . weakness in his genitals *quod non potest coire* and grieveth much, and it comes through much lechery. He is unfortunate by accident and will not be ruled.' Who was Sylvanus Scory? John Aubrey comes to our aid here, and corroborates Forman. He was the son and heir of the bishop of Hereford, 'who loved him so dearly that he fleeced the church of Hereford to leave him a good estate . . . He was a very handsome gentleman and had an excellent wit, and his father gave him the best education, both at home and beyond the seas, that that age would afford.'[10] He enjoyed a prebend at Hereford when young, but preferred to go and fight in the Netherlands. An accomplished person, he was a favourite with the Duke of Anjou on his visit to England – in itself no recommendation of his morals. He reduced the considerable estate his father scraped together for him to nothing, 'allowing himself the liberty to enjoy all the pleasures of this world.' However, he lived on until 1617, in the rather disreputable neighbourhood of Shoreditch, here the theatre folk lived.

In May 1600 Forman is writing notes about Jean Sandys, aged twenty-seven.[11] This is his spelling for Jane Sondes, one of the younger daughters of Sir Michael Sondes of Throwley Park near Faversham.[12] She had married one Flud, or Floyd, six years ago; this is correct: she had married Edward Flud, esquire, of Bearsted. But three or four years ago she was with Sir Calisthenes Brooke, who wrote her letters which she placed under her head at night and wished to sleep with him at Throwley Park, 'and no-one with her but Susan Rigden her maid.' Sir Calisthenes Brooke, of the Cobham family, was a soldier of fortune. 'Since, she hath loved Henry Wotton and Sir Thomas Gates and others.' Gates was another Netherlands soldier of fortune, who later became a stern governor of Virginia, the wreck of whose flagship, the *Sea Venture*, on Bermuda sparked off *The Tempest*. Wotton was, of course, to become the famous diplomat and connoisseur, who so much enjoyed life in Venice. Wotton and Gates became friends – had they not both enjoyed the favours of Mistress Flud? 'And now,' adds Forman, 'Sir Thomas Walsingham': he was the cousin of Sir Francis, remembered now only as Marlowe's patron. 'And loved one Cofield, a priest of Throwley, and Sir Robert Rivingston. And Robin Jones, her father's man, a clerk.' We find that one Robert Copell was rector of Throwley from 1597 to 1605.[13]

Forman continues: 'Also, Wilmar, Sir Thomas Flud's man, and he is dead. She wears willow for his sake, and a bramble for Sir Calisthenes Brooke, and thyme for Sir Thomas Gates. Also she loved my Lady Vane's son of Kent, and he took her garter from her leg to wear for her sake. And now there is one Vincent Randall that she supposeth and hopeth will have her.' Forman sounds rather disapproving, though he was no better an example himself; however, censoriousness about other people's sins is a regular human pleasure. Nor was the agreable lady impeded from making a successful second marriage, to Sir Thomas May of Mayfield in Sussex. All these people may be identified. Sir Thomas Flud had been treasurer-at-war in the Low Countries. They are all a Kent clutch together: Forman's notes on them are more revealing of life than whole volumes on the age.

The estimable Henry Wotton, a Kent man himself, consulted Forman from time to time – nothing of this is known to his biographers or to histories of literature. On 16 June 1600 Wotton, then thirty-two, consulted Forman about 'a rheumatic humour in his stomach and head'; his complexion was saltish.[14] Next month he was back with heat in his stomach and his 'body rheumatick – in danger of an imposthume' (an abscess or ulcer). There follows an astrological diagnosis, concluding with 'the blood goeth upward.' Whether the prognosis was favourable or not, Wotton lived out lengthy days. These consultations took place during the unquiet interval between Wotton's hurried return from Ireland with Essex, and his discreet retirement abroad at the end of 1600.[15] Whether as the result of his experience with Mrs. Flud or not, Wotton never married and was thus able to write his 'Character of a Happy Life':

> How happy is he born and taught
> That serveth not another's will . . .

(Remember the double meaning of will.)

> Who God doth late and early pray
> More of his grace than gifts to lend,
> And entertains the harmless day
> With a religious book, or friend.

We come to that precious ecclesiastical couple, Thomas Blague, a chaplain to the Queen, Dean of Rochester, and his wife. During the brief period covered by Forman's surviving case-books, 1598–1600, the Blagues were his most assiduous clients. A Cambridge man, of Queen's College, Blague had been a well-beneficed clergyman ever since writing a book in his youth. Since 1591 he had been Dean of Rochester; now, in March 1598, the bishopric of Salisbury was vacant and he gets Forman to cast his horoscope and find out whether he would obtain the favour of Archbishop Whitgift or no.[16] 'This day he went forth to the Court by my counsel and direction and moved the matter to the Archbishop: he granted him his good will and furtherance and all went well with him this day.'[17] In April the Dean wrote from Rochester asking again for the question to be cast whether he would be bishop of Salisbury, and whether the Archbishop had moved the matter to the Queen, or Sir Walter Ralegh. In May the Dean asked for the question to be cast whether good or ill was toward him.

In January 1599 Blague, then fifty-six, was found to have gout 'in the hands of Onim'. His wife, with whom Forman had had intercourse some six years before, sent several times for her son, who was not well, and to know what should ensue between her and one Scot. On 14 March she wanted to know what would happen to David Wood, a friend's son, who was going as far as Wales with Essex on the journey to Ireland, and whether he would return. In July she wished to learn whether good or evil were towards her 'because of the crickets' she had evidently heard, and whether it were best for the Dean to go to Rochester. She paid several more visits in the next week, full of her fears and jealousies. We learn more about the source of these when, in February 1600, she wants 'to know whether Dean Wood will continue his faithful love to her only, or no, and what will become of him'; in March she sends the names of Dean Wood's lovers, with the questions to be put, what would come of them and of him, and between him and her – this in Latin.[18] She gave Forman 26s. 8d., 'and she will pay me £5 more when he is a full friend to her.'

In April Dr. Blague wants the question put for his wife, 'whether she be enchanted by Dean Wood or no.' In May they were both ill, she with 'much pain in the pit of her stomach,' and their inquiries were merely medical: they were both to purge. In June she inquired, for her husband, 'whether he will die within two years or whether he will be near his time, as Mary Havers saith.' In fact, he died in the same year as friend Forman, 1611.

But who was the enchanting Dean Wood? It seems that he was the Richard Wood who was both prebendary of St. Paul's, 1585 to 1609, and prebendary of Westminster, 1587 to 1609, when he died.[19] Forman, as usual, had some information about him: 'Mary, Dean Wood's woman, told me that she saw Dean Wood occupy Wem's wife in her own house in the garret. Mary Shaker-ley, his wench, confessed that her Mr. Dean Wood did occupy her against the bedside, her mistress being abed at Tottenham.' It was only four years before, in 1595, that Dean Wood had made a good marriage for himself. The invaluable Roland Whyte, Robert Sidney's agent in London, had reported to him: 'my noble and worthy cousin, Mr. Dean Wood, the Queen's chaplain, is married to rich Ballet's widow of Cheapside. He hath by her £300 a year jointure, and she is besides worth £4000.'[20] It is hardly surprising that the Queen should set little store by the spiritual ministrations of her married chaplains, when one looks into their lives.

In November Dr. Blague wants to know the future about some law-suit against the church of Rochester, while Mrs. Blague wants to know what will happen to the beloved Dean Wood, because the Archbishop of Canterbury has sent for him. In January 1599 Mrs. Blague is asking for her mother, without her consent, whether she will live or die – she was fifty-eight; this evidently had financial implications, for the next inquiry is whether Owen Wood will make restitution of that good he hath had from her.'[21] The answer came, 'No: she must go to law for it.' With these family names, David and Owen, it would seem that the deleterious Woods were Welsh.

Forman tells us, of the Blagues' daughter, Frances, born at Lambeth 1586: 'this was a very untoward thing in her youth: when she was born, she was all hairy and much long hair on her shoulders. She was married in 1600 at fourteen to one John Dove, D.D., then nearing forty, 'a very Judas and cursed villainous and treacherous unkind priest.'[22] Actually he was rector of St. Mary, Aldermary, 1596–1618, and the author of a religious *Confutation of Atheism* and other uplifting books.[23] The poor young wife 'had but one child and died 1604', i.e. aged eighteen. Her mother has a fuller character sketch. She too had been married young, at fifteen, to Blague who was already a widower at thirty or so – women had a far higher death-rate, from the chances of maternity. So there must have been a shortage of women in Elizabethan society, making them all the more sought after by the men and married off young.

Alice Blague was of good family, the daughter of Sigismond Brock and Anne Jerningham, born 9 May 1560 in Essex. Her husband had been born at Gloucester, evidently in 1542–3.[24] They had six children. 'She had wit at will [i.e. intelligence at her command], but was somewhat proud and wavering, given to lust and to diversity of loves and men, and would many times overshoot herself, was an enemy to herself, and stood much on her own conceit. And did in lewd banqueting, gifts and apparel, consume her husband's wealth, to satisfy her own lust and pleasure, and on idle company. And was always in love with one or another. She loved one Cox, on whom she spent much; after that she loved Dean Wood, a Welshman, who cozened her of much. She consumed her husband for love of that man; she did much over-rule her husband. She was long visage, wide mouth, reddish hair, of good and comely stature; but would never garter her hose and would go much slipshod. She had four boys, a maid, and a shift [a miscarriage]. She loved dancing, singing, and good cheer. She kept company with base fellows and such as she was herself, of lewd conversation, and yet would seem as holy as a horse. And she was never without one bawd, or cunning woman or other, to keep her company to her great shame, to paint her, etc.'

What a wonderful psychologist Simon Forman was! His profession made him exceptionally observant of every quirk of personality, every detail of appearance. What a writer he would have made! He has hitherto been treated as a quack. But, as we see, almost everybody believed in astrology; and Forman's own neurotic personality gave him exceptional psychological insight into others, accounts for his telepathic experiences and indubitable gifts of divination. That it was all mixed up with occultism and quackery is very Elizabethan: he was exploring the darker margins of experience like John Dee, or William Lilly later. All this was so much more stimulating to the imagination (as Yeats found in our time), and is but part of what came to flower in the drama. It is an extraordinary chance that Forman's writings have been so neglected by scholars.

At this time Simon was looking for a wife to satisfy, or partially so, his very active sexual desires. He was after Sarah Archdell, a girl of twenty, himself a man of forty-six in 1599. He several times cast a horoscope to know whether she would marry him, if he put the question.[25] An addict of the theatre, 'the 19th April I was at "The Curtain"; there she came, her uncle and friends, and sat before me. After the play we went into the fields together and so I had some play with her, but nothing of anything touching the matter. She seemed very kind and courteous, and I held her by the hand all the way almost.' . . . Three days later he cast the question whether her uncle would be against him or assist him in his suit. 'This day he and I met at "The Curtain" again, and after walked in the fields, but I never moved the matter to him.'

SIR JOHN HARINGTON

MARY FITTON

BESS OF HARDWICK

SIR HENRY LEE

Most Gratious Soueraine Lady, The God of heauen and earth,
Who hath mightilie, and evidently, given vnto your most excellent
Royall Maiestie, this wunderfull Triumphant victorie, against
your mortall enemies) be allwaies, thanked, praysed, and glorified:
And the same God Almightie, euermore direct and defend your
most Royall Highnes from all evill and encumbrance: and finish
and confirme in your most excellent Maiestie Royall, the blessings,
long since, both decreed and offred: yea, euen into your most
gratious Royall bosom, and Lap. Happy are they, that can
perceyue, and so obey the pleasant call, of the mightie Ladie,
OPPORTVNITIE. And, Therfore, finding our duetie concurrent
with a most Secret beck., of the said Gratious Princess. Ladie
OPPORTVNITIE, NOW to embrace, and enioye, your
most excellent Royall Maiesties high favor, and gratious great
Clemencie, of CALLING me, Mr Kelley, and our families,
hoame, into your Brytish Earthly Paradise, and Monarchie
incomparable: (and, that, abowt an yere since: by Master
Customer Yong, his letters,) J. and myne, (by God his fauor
and help, and after the most convenient manner, we can)
Will, from hencefurth, endeuour our selues, faithfully, loyally,
carefully, warily, and diligently, to ryd and vntangle our
selues from hence: And, so, very devowtely, and Sowndlie,
at your Sacred Maiesties feet, to offer our selues, and all,
Wherein, we are, or may be hable, to serve God, and your most
Excellent Royall Maiestie. The Lord of Hoasts, be our
help, and Gwyde, therein: and graunt vnto your most excellent
Royall Maiestie, the Incomparablest Triumphant Raigne, and Monarchie,
that euer was, since Mans Creation. Amen.

Trebon. in the kingdome of Boemia,
the 10th of Nouebre: A. Dm: 1588: Stylo.

Your Sacred and most excellent
Royall Maiesties
most humble and dutifull
Subiect, and Servant:
8 John D

DR. DEE'S LETTER TO QUEEN ELIZABETH ON THE DEFEAT
OF THE SPANISH ARMADA

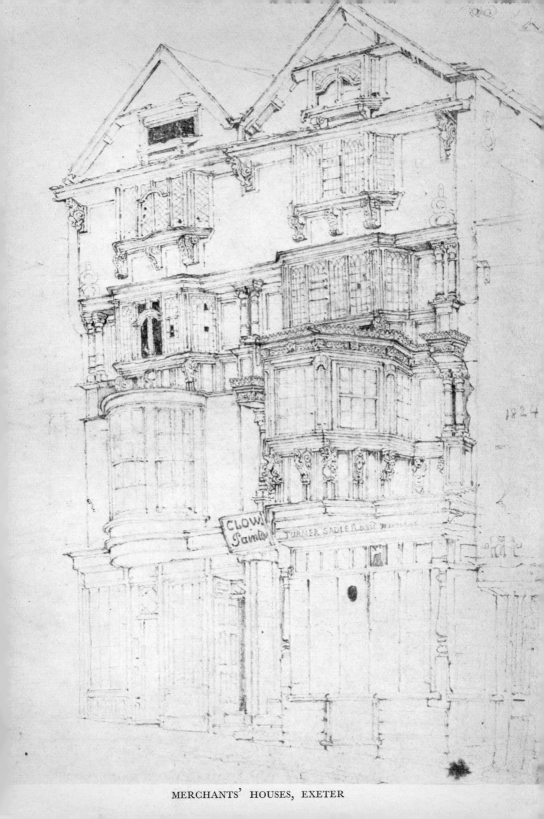

1824

CLOWN
Painter

TURNER SADLER

MERCHANTS' HOUSES, EXETER

THE MARRIAGE FÊTE AT HORSLEYDOWN, BY HOEFNAGEL

A GAME OF PRIMERO

QUEEN ELIZABETH AT A
PICNIC. AN ENGRAVING
FROM TURBERVILLE'S
'THE NOBLE ART OF
VENERY'

THE HONOURS OF THE
HASE, FROM 'THE NOBLE
ART OF VENERY'

THE GREAT STAIRCASE AT HARDWICK HALL

THE GRAMMAR SCHOOL AT STRATFORD-UPON-AVON

THE CROSS KEYS INN, OXFORD

THE SWAN, MINSTER LOVELL

¶ The Apprehenſion and confeſſion
of three notorious Witches.
Arreigned and by Iuſtice condemned and
executed at Chelmſ-forde, in the Countye of
Eſſex, the 5. day of Iulye, laſt paſt.
1 5 8 9.
¶ With the manner of their diuelish practices and keeping of their
ſpirits, whoſe fourmes are heerein truelye
proportioned.

WITCHES HANGED AT CHELMSFORD, 1589

A FORTUNE-TELLER

Another day while supping with friends, he looked out of the window and saw Sarah passing by with her uncle. He overtook them in the fields beyond Moorgate, but could not say his mind for two companions.

Nothing came of the affair, and Simon married Ann Baker at Lambeth on Sunday, 22 July 1599 at 7 a.m.: she was a niece of Sir Edward Munnings of Kent. It seemed that he was becoming increasingly respectable: he was prospering reasonably in physic and two parish offices were laid on him, as sidesman and gatherer for the poor. His descriptions of his sexual experiences are even more intimate than Boswell's in his *London Journal*. So we will leave them in the decent obscurity of his dog-Latin, noting however that 'halek', whatever its origin, was his code-word for intercourse. '7 September at 9 p.m. I did halek cum uxore mea et eo tempore fuit illa valde cupida de halek et matrix se fugit virgam.' He then cast the question whether she conceived at that time. That summer Bess Parker, who had left his service and been married off two months before she was delivered of a daughter, 'sent to know my mind.' There followed various payments to Bess's nurse and to her brother for keeping her, several pounds altogether. But in a subsequent note on Fenenna Parker, Bess's child, born 9 June 1599, Forman calculated that '22 August 1598 Bess was sent to Mary Fardell that lay in child-bed, and Nicholas Fardell did occupy her before she came away. And 5 June following made nine months, and so it seemeth to be Nicholas Fardell's child.'[26]

Marriage did not quench his ardour. On 15 March 1600 he had an assignation with Ann Sedgwick alias Catlyn, right against the 'Cock' in Aldersgate, whom he had seen at the play of *Sir John Oldcastle*.[27] This was the play put together by Drayton, Hathway, Mundy and Wilson, for Henslowe at the 'Rose' to cash in on the success of Shakespeare's *I Henry IV*, with the rival, Lord Chamberlain's Company.[28] Eleven days before, 4 March, Forman wrote down notes of the significant happenings in the play, *Cox of Cullompton* by Day and Haughton, which he had seen at the 'Rose'. Assignations made with women at a play formed one of the Puritan complaints against the theatres: here one sees one made under our eyes.

Great ladies were no better than their lower class sisters. Here is Frances Howard, daughter of the first Viscount Howard of Bindon, and grand-daughter of Elizabeth I's Duke of Norfolk. We must distinguish her from the wicked Lady Frances Howard,

Suffolk's daughter, who was a later client of Forman's, and used his love-potions to enchant James I's boy-friend, Somerset, and poisoned Sir Thomas Overbury in the Tower. Forman's surviving books inform us that the first Frances Howard was born 27 July 1578, at 9.30 p.m. at Lytchett in Dorset, in a fortunate conjunction.[29] Nevertheless, her mother died when she was a year old, her father when she was two. (These facts are correct: it was obviously important for astrological purposes that they should be. But one is struck by the way Forman is corroborated, wherever one can check him.)[30] In 1597 she was nineteen; her horoscope: 'she shall change her estate three times. She hath a woman enemy, tall, long visage, and ruddy. She is melancholic.'

Frances Howard was first married to Henry Pranell. As such she comes, 19 June 1597, to put the question for Katherine Howard, alias Neville, wife of Thomas Howard, for Henry Wriothesley, Earl of Southampton. On 4 August Mrs. Pranell sent her urine, supposing herself with child. On 10 January she asks the question whether Southampton will love her better or not, and what will happen to her; and next month, 'whether he doth bear her any good will, or did tell of the letter, and whether she shall speed in the country.' The answer came: 'he bears her little good will and she will do ill in the country – be robbed and in peril.' Forman noted that at the end of that year Southampton married Elizabeth Vernon. His client did change her estate three times, according to her horoscope. In 1600 she married the Earl of Hertford, as we have seen – both of them unhappily. 'I cannot understand,' he wrote, 'how my wife's estate is to be pitied, unless she does not discern her own happiness or acknowledge from whom, next under God, it came. Whatever she hath been to me, I resolve to deal honourably with her.'[31] After his death she joined the royal family as the third wife of Lewis Stuart, Duke of Lennox and of Richmond, and lies with him under a grand tomb in Henry VII's Chapel in Westminster Abbey.

Her horoscope turned out right. Was that due to her attractions? We need not think so. Each time a woman was widowed, she enjoyed one-third of her husband's estate for life. The more husbands the more attractive: the marriage of widows was a profitable market.

As at all times plenty of people were happily married – the Haringtons, for example, in both generations blissfully so. Even Southampton, in spite of the perturbations, the ambivalence of his earlier years, was recognised to be exceptionally happy in his family life. Most jogged along well enough, especially since they had to accept the fact that there was no loosening the bond. Some could not stand the burden, or their partner, and were very unhappy or broke apart. Yet others were divagatory. There was such a thing as married love, after all; but divagations leave more interesting evidence in the documents.

The Canon Law of the medieval Church did not recognise divorce in itself (*a vinculo*), merely separation (*a mensa et thoro*) for carefully restricted reasons, mainly for adultery. In England the Reformation did not change the situation: the Canon Law of the English Church remained what it had been. But many of the forbidden, and complicated, degrees of consanguinity, including even godparents, were sensibly abrogated: they had, of course, made nullity easier for privileged persons, a backdoor way of divorce. Archbishop Cranmer – that eminent, if imperfect, exemplar of the Middle Way – was in favour of clerical marriage, but was strongly opposed to divorce or any relaxation of the rule of marriage.[32] In Elizabeth's reign Protestant divines made some progress with opinion favouring divorce on the ground of adultery, but the legal position remained the same, and marriage, being a sacrament, was governed by the law of the Church. In practice, the Church did not allow the re-marriage of divorced persons.

The social life of the age resounded with the difficulties and trials this situation made for conspicuous persons – plenty of evidence as to their unhappiness: Southampton's mother and father, the Earl and Countess of Worcester (whom the Queen ordered to come together), the Earl of Cumberland and his wife, the 'Wizard' Earl of Northumberland and his, Bess of Hardwick and her Earl, the Oxfords and the Windsors, the horrid second Viscount Howard of Bindon who was a wife-beater (but he was hardly sane). These come readily to mind; the list could be extended indefinitely. Let us content ourselves with one example, from a more modest station.

Sir John Stawell was a Somerset gentleman of considerable estate in and around the Poldens, who married Mary, daughter of Sir William Portman in 1556. But he could not command her affections, which were humiliatingly conferred upon his servant, John Stalling. For the next five or six years the lady and her man were frequently seen about together; and 'there were strong presumptions that they had committed or would shortly commit adultery and fornication together' – the language is translated

from the law-Latin of the divorce-suit – 'as by using him too
familiarly, talking sweetly together, putting her arms around his
neck in a meretricious manner [*meretrix* means harlot], and
visiting his couch early and late, and walking and sitting alone
with him in places and at times thought out as if with care given
thereto, and fit and suitable for shameless minds and lawless
loves'. . . .[33]

Sir John seems to have been very longsuffering, but he
remonstrated once and again: 'Wife, if you will not leave these
light toys with my men, you shall not find me to be your husband.'
At Cothelstone, where they lived, one of the tenants, an honest
matron, spoke far more strongly to the mistress. The servants, as
usual, were well aware of the goings-on and that their lady had
'soiled her marriage-bed with marks of shame and had carnal
knowledge with him, and often, and on repeated occasions lived
in fornicatory and adulterine embraces . . . and slept with the same
John on one and the same bed often.' John Stalling had had to
buy off those of the servants who had seen them at it – Elizabeth
Goore with a pair of black satin sleeves, ruffs, gloves, pins and a
cloak; Arthur Guntrey, a pair of fine black hose lined with sarse-
net, and three shillings at another time. At last the lady and her
lover were surprised in bed at his house at Cothelstone – from this
it would seem that Stalling was a superior servant, perhaps a
steward.

In her own house the lady would often arise from her husband's bed early in the morning to cross over to John Stalling's
chamber – the husband seems to have been complaisant up to a
point. He was also very unobservant, in the usual masculine
manner: he was unaware of his wife's pregnancy, incurred in his
absence, or that about the feast of Pentecost, 1561, she brought
about an abortion by the use of drugs. Sir John must have been
even more innocent than most men. But when his wife, not content with the superior Stalling, went on to relations with the men-
servants – this was too much.

Stawell's diocesan, the bishop of Bath and Wells, was sympathetic to his plea and wrote to Archbishop Parker commending
his suit 'that he might marry notwithstanding that she that was
his former wife is yet living.'[34] For Stawell had found a Somerset
lady with whom he could be happy, sister of Sir Edward Dyer,
the courtier and poet, and whom he wished to make his wife. But
to disentangle himself from his first marriage took years. First,
suit was brought in the bishop's consistory court at Wells, where

it was opposed by the wife and her friends. Thence suit was made to the Archbishop's Court of Delegates, which pronounced divorce from bed and board, i.e. merely a judicial separation, not divorce *a vinculo*, i.e. from the bond of marriage. By 1572 Stawell was becoming impatient. His bishop wrote to Archbishop Parker that Stawell had no son and heir, only a daughter by Mary Portman whom he doubted to be his. In April the Archbishop granted Stawell a licence to marry; but in November Mary Portman sued Stawell in the Court of Arches for restitution, and simultaneously he was charged in the Archbishop's Court of Audience for 'the public offence given by him to the country where he dwelleth for cohabiting with a gentlewoman as his wife, his former wife being alive.'[35]

Now, Parker reported to Burghley, 'I perceive the matter is very hotly taken, and Stawell careth not what to spend so as he may have his fair lady; for, as one informed me overnight, he is offered £100, and another of my house £200, to mollify me in this case.'[36] So far from the respectable Archbishop being mollified by an attempted bribe, when Stawell refused to answer whether he had remarried or not, for fear of prejudicing his case, Parker popped him into prison. Now the greater laity stepped in to untie the knot the clerical estate could not: both Burghley and Leicester wrote in protest to Parker, who replied peaceably, 'for my part I am right sorry, for that he seemeth to be a Protestant, that we should be compelled in him to restrain this foul disordered thing, to avoid further example.' It was a good thing to have a friend at Court, for evidently Sir Edward Dyer had intervened on his new brother-in-law's behalf. In the course of the month Dyer entered into a double covenant, with Mary Portman's brother and with Stawell, against any suit being undertaken in the ecclesiastical courts. The consideration was £600 that passed: a re-insurance against Stawell's marriage to Frances Dyer being challenged. We may regard it, more crudely, as a bribe.

So John Stawell and his second wife lived together for the rest of their lives unchallenged; they produced a son and heir: the family would continue.[37] Mary Portman kept quiet. But when the son and heir died in 1604, less than a year after his father, leaving a child of three in the custody of the Court of Wards, old Mary Portman popped up with a petition for the recognition of her marriage and her right to dower. She obtained both. But her former husband had taken steps to protect the succession to the estates – in case of any charge of illegitimacy against his progeny –

by resettling them, so that his successor took them as by purchase and not by descent.[38]

One sees the difficulties attaching to any process of divorce, other than directly by act of Parliament for grandees.

In the circumstances we have depicted there was, naturally, a great deal of bastardy, particularly in the higher and lower ranks; the middle classes were rather more respectable. There is an immense amount of evidence on the subject at every level: among the nobility and greater gentry since they lived conspicuous lives and were apt to be written about; among the poorer classes, because maintenance was a social problem. A subsistence-society as it was, on these lower levels, it did not leave its bastards to starve: the parish made an effort to discover the father and make him contribute to the maintenance of the child. If he could not be discovered, and the woman was unable to support the child, the charge fell on the parish. Hence the vigour, and the rigour, of the parish authorities in discouraging such things and punishing offenders: their simple means could not afford much expense. However, human nature will out, and parish records are full of the consequences. If the case were not provided for at this level, it came up to Quarter-Sessions, where the J.P.s made bastardy-orders. So Quarter-Sessions records also are full of the subject.

Here we can give only a few illustrations as to how things worked. Let us take Staffordshire – not that this county differ from any other in this respect, but it happens to have a finer set of Sessions Rolls surviving for our period.

It was usual in such cases for the midwife to put the question who was the father at the moment of the child's birth, in the anguish of labour – a piece of crude, but usually effective, psychology. Here is one instance out of many, about 1600. 'Jane Shepherd of Elford, found in the cow-house of Alice Smith, widow, made known to Isabel Baillie, midwife, that John Draper, a fiddler, born deaf and dumb, was the father of her child.'[39] There follow the names of the other women present, as witnesses. Here is someone laid by the heels by these means. At the labour of a Walsall woman, Alice Godwin, the midwife got out of her that John Sabin was the father of her child. 'Therefore he is to pay 10d weekly [i.e. a good day's wage] towards its maintenance for two years, and then to take charge of the child, receiving 1d weekly from the said Alice, until it shall be able to get its own living. Further, the said John Sabin shall sit by the heels [in the stocks] the next Sunday for the space of three hours, immediately after 1 o'clock in the afternoon, if found in Walsall, or else the next Sunday after his coming there. The like for Alice after her churching,' (i.e. the usual service of purification held necessary after childbirth).[40] Such scenes, and such services, were very frequent.

Sometimes there was doubt in the matter. Robert Spookes of Dunston petitioned, in 1601, that 'Joyce Acton, his servant, gave birth to a bastard-child in his ox-house, from which she was forcibly removed by her father and William Acton, leaving the child on the hands of the petitioner. That Thomas Whitby, another of his servants, upon whom she fathered the child, being but fifteen years, has fled, and that the woman has since confessed that her accusation was false. Therefore, the petitioner and his wife being old people and never acquainted with such like troubles, he asks that some order may be given in the matter by the J.P.s and quorum.'[41]

Often enough the men disclaimed responsibility. In 1589 a J.P. called Margaret Bull and Ralph Lees before him, when Margaret 'charged the said Ralph Lees to his face that he had got her with child, and said she got it in her master's house, being his next neighbour, on the last Sunday after All Saints day last. At which time he had to do with her both in the house and in the chamber [i.e. bed-chamber].'[42] And she cited two more occasions. 'At another time he was in his stable and called her to him, and would have had to do with her, and that she answered, "I fear you have done too much already." "Why," said he, "art then with child?" . . . And then said, "It is time for me now to make provision." And so let her depart and go her way. And the said Ralph Lees, being thus charged before me, denied nothing of all this. But confessed all to be true, saving that he had never any carnal dealing with her.' The fellow sounds a simpleton.

No less simple appears John Cotgreve, of Chester diocese, when brought to book for begetting a child 'upon an honest maid afore, and in good service, and of good fame.' He said that the child was none of his. A witness: 'Yes, by the same token, it was behind the mill-door.' 'Cock's [i.e. for God's] wounds,' quoth John Cotgreve, 'can a man get a child standing? for I never had anything to do with her but standing.'[43]

William Woodward of Wetton was more knowing. A weaver of Wetton gave evidence that Joan Woolley 'came to his house weeping, being then great with child and confessed unto him that

William Woodward was the father of her child, and none but he. And showed him six shillings which Woodward had given her in Wheatlands Field', out of which she paid 14d. she owed the weaver.[44] John Hall, Woodward's servant for over twenty years, deposed that his master practised with him 'to do so much at his request as to bear the name to be the father of the child', and Woodward would pay all the charges for its bringing up. When Hall refused, he was put out of Woodward's service. Woodward had tried a similar trick when previously he had got Alice Carr with child: he practised with William Fool, evidently an addle-pate, to have intercourse with Alice and father the child upon a third man, promising William Fool half a year's board. Others witnessed that Mr. Woodward had been suspiciously familiar with Joan for a matter of seven or eight years together. The day of reckoning seems to have been quite long postponed; but further evidence shows up Joan as no better than she should be.

Such was Elizabethan life – or, indeed, life at all times. We notice, however, an interesting difference between town and country in the much higher proportion of brides that came to marriage pregnant in the country than in towns – in a rural Devon parish 33 per cent, compared with 13 per cent in the city of York.[45] This certainly represented in part the stricter conditions of town life. We can also deduce from the pattern of births that the highest rate of conceptions were in high summer and Christmas holidays. All very natural, like the animals.

It is, perhaps, a duty to include some treatment, if only for completeness' sake, of homosexuality, though the difficulty here is not an *embarras de richesses* but an insufficiency of evidence – and what there is has never been collected. Here, too, the Reformation made a dividing line. Up till then sodomy had been an ecclesiastical offence, naturally enough with all that clerical celibacy. The penitentiaries, it seems, were full of provisions for penance, but Maitland thought that 'the temporal courts had not punished it and that no-one had been put to death for it for a very long time past.'[46]

It was time to put an end to that lax state of affairs, and so it came about with the tightening up effected by the Reformation and the subjugation of the Church. In the very year of the moral Henry's clandestine marriage to Anne Boleyn and of the Submission of the Clergy, 1533, Parliament passed 'An Act for the punishment of the vice of buggery.'[47] The preamble specifically stated, 'forasmuch as there is not yet sufficient and condign punishment appointed and limited by the due course of the laws of this realm for the detestable and abominable vice of buggery committed with mankind or beast', the offence was constituted a felony, i.e. the penalty being death with forfeit of property, without benefit of clergy. J.P.s were to have power and authority to hear and determine such cases. The more humane atmospher of the régime of Protector Somerset qualified this ferocious legislation in one respect: such offenders 'attainted by confession, verdict, or outlawry', might incur the new death-penalty 'without loss of lands, goods or corruption of blood', i.e. property and inheritance were safeguarded – more important than men's lives.

In the first year of Mary's reign her repeal of much of Henry's Reformation legislation repealed this statute along with the rest. For the next ten years the action was not punishable – a situation that could not be allowed to endure. So the Parliament of 1563 revived that of 1533, specifically claiming that since the repeal 'divers evil disposed persons have been the more bold to commit the said most horrible and detestable vice . . . to the high displeasure of Almighty God.'[48] That may be as it may be, but certainly the utmost use had been made, at the time of the Dissolution of the monasteries, of the royal Visitors' findings with regard to the monks. They found some such cases, but Dom David Knowles is of the opinion that most of the far more numerous cases noted in the Northern Province really refer to masturbation, for which presumably there was no term.[49]

Protestants, however, had a strong demographic point in their campaign against clerical celibacy; they constantly enforced this argument, rather than the undoubted good effects on the stock, eventually, from breeding from more intelligent strains rather than less. Victorian prudery has operated to blanket the subject, to omit to give it proper treatment in the legal text-books and, it would seem, to suppress records of convictions and punishments in the courts. I have failed to find any statistics in this field of investigation. The historian of English Criminal Law, Sir James Stephen, considered that the subject had no social interest. But that is precisely the significance it has. One observes its close connection in medieval minds with sorcery; in the Reformation period legislation against it goes along with the cruel legislation against witchcraft, under which so many human beings needlessly suffered. We see that the whole subject is more a matter for anthropology than for ethics.

Of course, sodomy and homosexuality are not interchangeable terms: neither one need imply the other. We may now pass on to consider the second, which may cover almost as wide a spectrum as heterosexuality, from the physical to the platonic and ideal, with its comparable forms of expression in literature and the arts.

A breach within a very aristocratic Catholic group of friends at Court in 1581 suddenly throws a beam of light upon their tastes. The scapegrace young Earl of Oxford, who denied his wife (Burghley's daughter) with the asseveration that, if she had a child, it would be none of his, had returned from Italy with Italianate tastes. He had also been reconciled to the Roman Church; so had his friends, Lord Henry Howard and Charles Arundel. When this fact was extracted from him by the Queen, to exculpate themselves this precious pair made envenomed charges against the Earl. Charles Arundel deposed, 'I will prove him a buggerer, of a boy that is his cook', by Oxford's own confession as well as by witnesses.[50] 'I have seen this boy many a time in his chamber, doors close-locked, together with him, maybe at Whitehall and at his house in Broad Street; and, finding it so, I have gone to the back-door to satisfy myself, at the which the boy hath come out all in a sweat, and I have gone in and found the beast in the same plight. But to make it more apparent my Lord Harry saw more, and the boy confessed it unto Southwell and himself confirmed it unto Mr. William Cornwallis.' All these are Catholic names, but these *croyants* went on to add atheism to Oxford's vices, as well as the intention to murder Leicester and Sir Philip Sidney, leaders of the extreme Protestant Court-faction.

We need hardly go into any further disagreeable details, except that Oxford had often expressed the kind of view that Marlowe was well known to hold, and that 'Englishmen were dolts and nidwits' not to realise that there was better sport than with women.[51] Not to go into detail, we may merely add that in addition to the cook's boy, there was 'Orache' the Italian boy and others of his pages. Now we can at least understand why it was that Oxford turned his back on his wife after his return from Italy, of which such a mystery has neen made. Nor deed we add anything more that the spying Lord Henry Howard saw, who was himself a homosexual; they were clearly birds of a feather in that circle.[52]

That such tastes were not confined to Italianate courtiers but extended to Protestant men of action may be inferred from Professor D. B. Quinn's view of Sir Humphrey Gilbert.[53] Gilbert was certainly an interesting psychological case, with the symptoms of disturbed personality that often go with men of mark, not at all the simple Elizabethan seaman of Froude's Victorian view. He was passionate and impulsive, a nature liable to violence and cruelty – as came out in his savage repression of rebels in Ireland – but also intellectual and visionary, a questing and original mind, with the personal magnetism that went with it. People were apt to be both attracted and repelled by him, to follow his leadership and yet be mistrustful of him. Edward Hayes, who was a partner in Gilbert's last voyage to Newfoundland and wrote the famous account of it in Hakluyt, obviously thought that Gilbert was too fond of William Medley, the alchemist, with whom Gilbert was engaged in mineral speculations in the West Country. Hayes wrote to Burghley, 'I pray your lordship send Sir Humphrey down and let him take some handsome man with him – I named one to him; but he is somewhat too much assotted upon Mr. Medley.'[54] This is not necessarily conclusive: 'handsome' might mean, in the context, competent. When Gilbert and Medley quarrelled in 1572, Medley writes, 'finding by Mr. Gilbert's letter that he looketh to have attendance of me in things that my nature cannot, nor will not, permit.'[55]

The writings of contemporary voyagers are full of references to the deplorable habits of peoples overseas, especially among American Indians, but also in Russia and the countries of the Levant. One has come across a case of an English seaman, in Hakluyt, being strung up for the offence of sodomy. But Spanish writers on the conquest of Mexico, such as Bernal Diaz, deplore its prevalence among the Mexicans – as if it were not endemic in their own Mediterranean countries.

Philip II's famous Secretary of State, Antonio Perez, with his brilliant gifts, was a recognised homosexual; his complex relations with the Princess of Eboli, which have been absurdly romanticised in the European tradition, had nothing to do with love: they were all politics and power.[56] Francis Bacon's tastes are quite well known, and indeed obvious;[57] when Perez came to lodge with him during his exile in England, Lady Bacon wrote severely to the elder brother, Anthony: 'Though I pity your brother, yet so long as he pities not himself but keepeth that bloody Perez, yea as a coach-companion and bed-companion: a proud, profane, costly fellow, whose being about him I verily fear the Lord God doth mislike and doth less bless your brother in credit, and otherwise in his health.'[58] This refers to the brilliant Bacon's failure to get preferment from Elizabeth; his tastes were no impediment to his rapid advancement under James I, nor were Lord Henry Howard's, we may add.

At the time of Bacon's fall some of the more innocent members of the public thought that a charge of sodomy might be preferred against him; but it can hardly be supposed that James I's exotic entourage would allow this to be brought into the open. So, Sir Simonds D'Ewes informs us, 'would he not relinquish the practice of his most horrible and secret sin of sodomy – keeping still one Goderick, a very effeminated youth, to be his catamite and bedfellow . . . Men generally after his fall began to discourse of that his unnatural crime, which he had practised many years, deserting the bed of his lady, which he accounted – as the Italians and Turks do – a poor and mean pleasure in respect of the other.'[59] The fact about Bacon seems to have become widely known by Aubrey's time, who also comments on it. But, since no public notice was taken, D'Ewes continues, 'nor did he ever, that I could hear, forbear his old custom of making his servants his bed-fellows.'

By this time Southampton had settled into happy family life, though earlier his tastes were ambivalent. When James became king, it was thought at first that Southampton might become a favourite. But James had brought James Hay with him, to be succeeded by Robert Carr, and eventually by George Villiers, whose beauty outshone them all. In earlier years Southampton had been very close to the younger Danvers brother, Sir Henry, a man of great charm who never married: Southampton gave up his projected Italian tour when he couldn't have him with him. But, when fighting under Essex in Ireland, he had the consolation of the company of Captain Piers Edmonds, a professional soldier whom Essex made much of. In Ireland Edmonds lay in the Earl's tent, who 'would cull and hug him in his arms, and play wantonly with him.'[60] There was, indeed, an emotional atmosphere in the masculine circle surrounding Essex, though the Earl himself was addicted to women. All the same, it would seem that Shakespeare has an inflexion of Essex and his sullen withdrawal from Court in his depiction of Achilles and Patroclus in *Troilus and Cressida*, the only direct reference to the subject in the plays.

It would not be unfair to say that the outstanding patron of homosexuality in the literature of the age was Marlowe, for he was very much a propagandist of his opinions. At the time his religious heterodoxy was more dangerous, for 'almost into every company he cometh he persuades men to atheism, willing them not to be afeared of bugbears and hobgoblins.'[61] Then there was the famous *mot* people repeated, that 'all they that love not tobacco and boys were fools.' One observes the similarity in point of view with the Earl of Oxford; he and Marlowe were of much the same kidney: literary aesthetes with cultivated foreign tastes, neurotically unstable personalities, both given (it would seem) to drink, both sceptical about people's religious pretensions, preferring Catholicism to Protestantism, both brilliant, attractive to their friends, shocking to the respectable and dull, inclining to Machiavellianism and violence.

One need not labour the point that the subject appears or is touched on in every one of Marlowe's works, from *The Tragedy of Dido* to *Edward II*: he evidently found inspiration in it and made the subject the dominant theme of this last play. But it is not generally realised – people simply are without the imagination – that his famous lyric,

> Come live with me and be my love . . .

would not be addressed to a woman; so that Ralegh's reply to it would have an ironic inflexion – just like Ralegh. Echoing in Marlowe's mind was the Corydon and Alexis theme of Virgil's Eclogue.

The influence of Marlowe's propagating genius is to be discerned in a delightful poem of 1594, Richard Barnfield's 'Complaint of Daphnis for the Love of Ganymede'. In spite of its Victorian editor's tribute to it as 'remarkably free from the coarseness which disfigures so much of the Elizabethan literature', it made a little ripple in its time; for where the theme,

> Sweet love, come ease me of thy burden's pain,
> Or else I die, or else my heart is slain . . .

is regularly, repetitiously directed to women, here it has the interesting irregularity of being directed to a youth.[62]

> Why do thy coral lips disdain to kiss
> And suck that sweet which many have desired? . . .

the poignant dilemma has been well known to many before and since, but Barnfield was one of the few to put it into poetry.

> But I began to rue the unhappy sight
> Of that fair boy that had my heart entangled,
> Cursing the time, the place, the sense, the sin:
> I came, I saw, I viewed, I slippèd in.

But the youth prefers the love of Guendolen, who falls for him and pursues him. Daphnis assures him that his love is truer than that of women, given to pride and disdain:

> I love thee for thy gifts, she for her pleasure,
> I for thy virtue, she for beauty's treasure.

We recognise this as one of the themes of Shakespeare's Sonnets.

Next year, 1595, Barnfield published another volume, *Cynthia*, including his own charming sonnets. In his preface 'to the courteous gentlemen readers', he tells us 'Some there were that did interpret *The Affectionate Shepherd* otherwise than in truth I meant, touching the subject thereof; to wit, the love of a shepherd to a boy: a fault the which I will not excuse because I never made.' He assures us that his poem was but an imitation of Virgil's second Eclogue. However that may be, his sonnets continued the theme. They may be a literary exercise – unlike Shakespeare's, which are so markedly autobiographical. Yet Barnfield assures us,

> Sweet Thames I honour thee, not for thou art
> The chiefest river of the fairest isle,
> Nor for thou dost admirers' eyes beguile,
> But for thou hold'st the keeper of my heart.

He goes on –

> And yet, alas, Apollo loved a boy,
> And Cyparissus was Sylvanus' joy –

to reveal that he was well acquainted with the classical lore of the matter.

Indeed, students at the universities whose education was based on the classics could hardly avoid some acquaintance with the subject, so much more prominent in the literatures of those more sophisticated societies. The satires of Marston – like Barnfield, a Brasenose poet – are clearly inspired by Juvenal, but aspire to reflect on the contemporary scene:

> Had I some snout-fair brats, they should endure
> The new-found Castilian calenture
> Before some pedant tutor in his bed
> Should use my fry like Phrygian Ganymede . . .

He proceeds to direct his insinuations, more patriotically, against the seminaries abroad:

O now, ye male stews, I can give pretence
For your luxurious incontinence.
Hence, hence, ye falsèd seeming patriots
Return not with pretence of salving spots,
When here ye soil us with impurity
And monstrous filth of Douai seminary.
What though Iberia yield you liberty
To snort in sauce of Sodom villainy? . . .

Nevertheless, according to Marston, Clerkenwell and Hoxton –
the lowest haunts of Elizabethan London – were no better, if not
worse, for there worse pleasures were to be found:

At Hoxton now his monstrous love he feasts,
For there he keeps a bawdy-house of beasts . . .

We refrain from quoting any further: Marston really hadn't a
very nice mind, though he ended in the Church – perhaps from
repentance, as much as for a living.

This is the place to state firmly, if briefly, that the Sonnets of
Shakespeare are not homosexual. Any doubt on the subject is
resolved by the very sonnet, No. 20, in which Shakespeare describes
the ambivalent nature of Southampton as a youth:

And for a woman wert thou first created,
Till Nature, as she wrought thee, fell a-doting,
And by addition me of thee defeated,
By adding one thing to my purpose nothing:
But since she pricked thee out for women's pleasure,
Mine be thy love, and thy love's use their treasure.

Nothing could be clearer: Shakespeare is not interested in him
sexually: his love is platonic, idealised. And that is in keeping with
all that is known of Shakespeare – highly sexed, and completely
heterosexual.[63]

But these tastes would receive an immense extension with the
Court of James I.

CHAPTER VII

PARISH AND SPORT

LET us reverse our usual procedure and look at society from the bottom upwards; and first for the parish, since the parish was the prime unit of organised social life – as it has been for centuries over the face of England. (It still is in rural areas, though not of course in the sprawling chaos of suburbia that is most characteristic of contemporary life.) We may perhaps compare parish life, as it appears in the records, in two opposite corners of Southern England, Kent and Devon.

Professor W. K. Jordan asks the question if traditional parish religious activity was seriously impaired by the Reformation.[1] The answer is a complex one, involving the dimension of time. On one level, that of strictly religious activity, it was disrupted, and for the time impaired. The Reformation *was* a revolution, affecting men's intimate beliefs and social rituals, disturbing – most of all – the life of the unconscious, the subliminal and numinous. After the earthquake in this region people gradually settled in their religious habits, many of them remaining unchanged, on a different level, less sacramental, rather more ratiocinative at least – for it is doubtful how far one can ever use the word 'rational' of ordinary humans and the conduct of their lives. *Capax rationis* men may be, but few of them exhibit much of it in their social behaviour – which may, indeed often has, a *rationale*, if it does not display much reason.

On another level – the more conscious, the social – parish life exhibited an essential continuity all through. The forms remained much the same, if with a different inflexion: the Church was no longer dominant. The process of secularisation, which we see practically complete in modern society, had begun. The Elizabethan world was already far more secular than the pre-Reformation, even if it carried on much that was medieval. We are studying society in cross-section, and in that way we can see different levels and types co-existing at the same time. In that world of four hundred years ago we notice a number of enlightened and emanci-

166

pated minds who would be no disgrace to our day – to think only of leading spirits, like Elizabeth and the Cecils; Sidney, Spenser, Shakespeare and Bacon; Ralegh, Hariot, William Gilbert. We think of them as the characteristic Elizabethans, not the benighted and vituperative clerics, whether Protestant, Catholic or Puritan, for ever disputing non-sense questions that could never be settled – for non-sense, metaphysical or theological, is self-proliferating and interminable. Such people, of course, were far more numerous, and perhaps – *mutatis mutandis* – always will be. But since they do not constitute the *difference* in the age, they can hardly give it its name.

On the other hand, medieval or pre-medieval types are always with us at any given time – look at the idiot believers in astrology, or whatever, today. Some types will be prehistoric, or positively regressive in the human scale: one has only to keep one's eyes about one in the streets – some of these might be in trees, others behind bars of one kind or another. The co-existence of such widely differing types at any given time – for, of course, the notion of human equality in any significant sense is visibly untrue – is a hopeful consideration for the attainability of historical knowledge. One is *not* studying the unobservable, the dead and vanished: they are all around one. The subtlety lies in catching the differences of inflexion; the art of the historian – how few achieve it! – in rendering them like an artist.

With these considerations in mind we may turn to Elizabethan Kent, and at once realise that the Reformation changes were more abrupt and harsh there – so near to London and its seismic disturbances – than in remote, conservative Devon. The ocular evidence still corroborates this, for anybody with eyes to see: the churches in the latter are less mauled, many more rood-screens and pre-Reformation arrangements, even stone-images on towers and in less accessible places, remain.

In Kent the Archdeacons' Visitations, sometimes the Archbishop's, enable one to see what the situation was; the parish returns through its accredited representatives, the churchwardens. At Elmstone in East Kent, in 1560, they have neither parson, vicar, nor curate resident; the parson, i.e. rector 'doth receive the fruit and profits, being a temporal man, leaving none to serve the cure.'[2] Actually, the rector, who enjoyed the tithes, was an Edwardian priest who had said only one or two masses in the parish under Mary and spent his life agreeably as a Fellow of Corpus Christi College, Oxford. He did not resign Elmstone until 1580. In 1563 he was not resident, and 'they have no chalice to change [i.e. for a communion-cup], but they have a glass.' At Wye in 1569 'William Nightingale and Henry Wood hath sold a cross of silver and gilt and a chalice of the parish. Also Richard Hawke hath a chalice of the parish and the book where the wardens were wont to engross their accounts, nor will not deliver the same book to the churchwardens.'³ Here are evidences of disruption; probably these were previous churchwardens who may not have approved of the new deal. Nor had the steps to the high altar been taken away, nor the rood-loft thoroughly pulled down 'according to the order prescribed.' At the pulling down of the rood-loft in Throwley church, Richard Goteley, who had been 'an accuser in Queen Mary's time,' protested at the new churchwarden's doings: 'let him take heed that his authority be good before it be pulled down, for we know what we have had, but we know not what we shall have.' That was very much to the point. He added, 'I will see the Queen's broad seal ere I have it down.'⁴

That cultivated woman, the Queen, had objected to the pulling down of rood-lofts, but could not prevail in the matter: the Protestant bishops refused to serve unless she gave way. The result is the destitution of some thousands of churches of goodly works of craftmanship, in some cases of sculptural art which they once enjoyed. Works of men's hands are so much more worthy of respect than the nonsense people think; but the Protestants were able to defend themselves by citing instances of popular silliness, also in the realm of belief, in regard to such roods as that at Ashurst not far away. Lambarde tells us that, before the Reformation, 'it was beaten into the heads of the common people – as what thing was so absurd which the clergy could not then make the world to believe – that the rood or crucifix of this church did, by certain increments, continually wax and grow, as well in the bush of hair which it had on the head, as also in the length and stature of the members and body thereof.'⁵ This wondrous rood brought money into the parish, as had the miraculous rood of Boxley, also in Kent, which rolled its eyes, opened its mouth, etc. for the benefit of the stupid people.

Thus the Protestants were determined to destroy the objects of these observances as the most effective way of destroying the observances. (Popular idiocy – people being what they are – then looked elsewhere: there was a notable increase in credulity about witches and the persecution of poor old crones as such.) It is a pity that so few people could attain the cultivated attitude of the Queen and enjoy the works of art without the penumbra of nonsensical belief that surrounded them. Few people were, or perhaps are, capable of the disjunction: hence iconoclasm, then as today.

The Reformation must have been a terrible time for civilised people to endure. Works of art of all kinds were destroyed: pictures, paintings, sculptures, images; reredoses, alabasters, crucifixes, wooden carvings, canopies, shrines, reliquaries; tapestries, vestments, altar frontals, corporases, embroideries, *opus anglicanum;* illuminated manuscripts, missals, breviaries; painted glass, pyxes, chalices, censers, jewels; monuments, brasses ripped up, bells melted down, splendid towers sent crashing to the ground; bare, ruined choirs. We have a reference from just these years, in Corrozet's *Antiquités de Paris* (1577) of a public sale in Paris in Edward VI's time, of 'plusieurs images, peintures et autres ornements d'église qu'on avait apporté et sauvé des églises d'Angleterre.'[6] Occasionally even today we recover something of the damage that was wrought then: at the parish church of Launceston in Cornwall, there is being uncovered, beneath layers of varnish, the coloured Renaissance designs painted upon a pulpit just before the catastrophe, in all their pristine freshness.*

At Wickhambreux on the pretty banks of the Lesser Stour, in this year 1569, 'Mr. Robert Formell of our parish hath pulled down, by his own private authority, an old chapel called Hooke chapel and kept the chapel churchyard forcibly from the parson, contrary to his ancient right and interest.'[7] At Ashford 'in certain windows of the church are many monuments of idolatry and superstition not defaced. In the revestry are certain copes and vestments for priest, deacon and sub-deacon, with other trumpery.' Plenty of people retained old-fashioned prejudices. At New Romney a tailor, who is described with some disapprobation as 'a common drunkard, a common ribald, a common railer, and a contemner of the minister of God's holy Word', is 'also a slanderer and contemner of the holy matrimony of priests. In so much that on St. James' day last he did both at the ale-house or tavern and also openly in our street call John Forsett, our vicar, knave; and the said John Forsett's wife arrant whore, and said moreover that all the married priests im England are knaves, and their wives are very whores.'[8]

During the time of transition from one footing to another there must have been many, especially among the clergy, who found themselves betwixt and between. Even in 1570 a Northampton-shire vicar was presented by his churchwardens for using 'Latin

* By the public spirit and scholarly taste of Mr. Norman Colville of Penheale.

services of our Lady with Ave Maria, which annoyeth the hearers.'[9] His explanation was that 'he sayeth not such service in the church nor in the hearing of others, but secretly to himself. And he saith that he thinketh himself bound thereto by his order, even of conscience.' When his colleague, the vicar of Lois Weedon, died in the same year his will is in accordance with the old Catholic formula: 'I bequeath my soul to Almighty God, to our Lady St. Mary, and to all the company of Heaven, and my body to be buried in the parish church of Weedon, in the place where St. Margaret's altar stood' – where he had ministered in pre-Reformation days.[10] It is the same spirit as led a priest of the house of Lyme in Cheshire in 1527 to will himself to be buried in front of the altar of the Trinity chapel there, so that the priest should 'always at the time of consecration stand ever over and upon my heart.'[11] Now, in Protestant days, just over the threshold of the century, a Devon vicar asks to be buried 'in the little window of Satterleigh church.'[12] In that request he reveals his heart. But has there not been some impoverishment of the spirit – or, perhaps, of the imagination – in the course of the transition?

On the other hand, we notice by then considerable improvement in conditions, on a somewhat different basis, in a changed spirit. The parish is very ready to criticise its minister now for this or that. By 1572, at Sheldwich, the wardens report that the parish has not received communion since Easter, because 'our vicar is thought to have some infection in his head or body, by reason of the strong breath and savour which proceedeth from him.'[13] For the same reason the parish was not sending children or servants to be catechised; 'because it is against our mind and stomach to receive and communicate with our vicar,' the parish pleaded for a curate to help out, or that they might be suffered 'to go to other parish churches adjoining, for God's love.' For his part, the vicar presented the late churchwardens for keeping copes and vestments and not providing a communion cup. Three years later a couple of minstrels are presented for playing and dancing on the sabbath; one of the dancers wished 'the pox on them that find fault with them that dance on the sabbath-days.' But this was the way things were going: now there was trouble on the Puritan front. At Faversham in 1591 a godmother at the christening of a child 'would not suffer the minister to sign it with the sign of the cross. When the minister offered twice to sign it, she stepped back and would not suffer him; and when the minister did uncover the child's face, she pulled the kercher over it again twice. Then the minister was constrained to take the child from her before he could do it, and then she went into a seat and would not take the child again. Whereupon the minister was constrained to deliver the child to the clerk.'[14] She was evidently a woman of strong convictions. Enough of these fooleries – though they are the stuff of which history is made.

Once the issue was settled at the centre and the Reformation impulse resumed, in the Devon countryside – always excepting Exeter and Plymouth – things moved at a slower pace.* We can observe the parish life, centred upon the churches, exhibiting its essential continuity, with some consolidation and a little expansion. At Broadhempston parish affairs were run by the Sixmen, who audited the accounts of the churchwardens and the parish stores.[15] These were chosen from the leading farmers, not the gentry, though gentlemen could be churchwardens. Similarly in Woodland parish the Fourmen transacted the parish business; there was a rota among the twenty-four farm-places for the election of wardens.[16] This seems to have been the usual form elsewhere: the yeoman-farmers dealt with parish business, provided accoutrements and harness for the soldiers the parish contributed to her Majesty's service, raised funds for parish purposes, including bastards and the poor; larger affairs, of public order, repression of crime etc. were dealt with by the J.P.s, who were always, in the country, from the gentry. A variety of other matters were dealt with by other wardens, ale-wardens and way-wardens; while order was maintained, under the J.P.s, by headboroughs and constables, from down amongst the people. We see that it was a lithe, springy society, not without an element of 'democratic' responsibility, if we may use that much-abused word: all the more responsible for being less democratic.

Parish funds for general purposes were chiefly raised from the church-ales, or feasts; in addition many parishes owned bits of property, from which they derived rents, and stores or stocks which they let out for cash. By 1500 Bovey Tracy owned a green, a cider-orchard, a kitchen and a pound yard.[17] The kitchen was for cooking the parish feast and brewing the ale. By 1588–95 Braunton, above the sands of the Taw estuary, possessed 2 chittles (large boiling kettles), 2 pans, 2 spits, 1 brass crock, 1 brandiron, 3 kieves (brewing tubs), 18 pewter dishes, 10 standards furnished

---

* We can see that village life hardly changed in essence up to the war of 1914–18 in a work of close observation, Henry Williamson's *Life in a Devon Village*; or, in all the fulness of its folklore, in Cecil Torr's *Small Talk at Wreyland*.

(upright frames), 2 steans (stone jars), 2 pottle pots, 5 quarts, 25 cups, 2 dozen trenchers, 2 board cloths, 1 salt of tin. Evidently it was the two dozen or so yeoman-farmers who feasted at the two tables of the parish feast; no doubt the rest of the parish provided for themselves.

The affair raised most of the money the parish had to dispose of for the year; the ale was sold, and more cash was raised by lending out the big kettle for others' brewing. Braunton ale was famous. The baking and brewing went on in the church-house, like a parish-hall today, except for the brewing. Nearly every parish in Devon had a church-house – there are still over sixty of them left – and many parishes had a church-inn; parishes were large, it could be a long way to come to church, and people were obliged to attend. In the church-house wafers and holy bread were baked. At Braunton in 1556 a priest was paid 'to come and say masses when our cattle were plagued' – one sees how naturally the rites of the Church had been interwoven in folklore.[18] But by 1573 the holy-water bucket had been melted down for a third bell; as Armada days approached there were payments for spears and bows and repainting the butts. Then, in 1588, 17s. 4d. was expended 'for building the beacon.'

Chagford had four waywardens to manage the roads, one for each quarter of the parish; their first return was in 1567, they continued right up to the Highway Act of 1862.[19] These men saw to the bridges in that moorland parish, full of streams; three bridges over the Teign were repaired during the years 1560–92. Receipts from the church-ale covered the expenses of the Whitsun Feast. In 1599 the young men's wardens reported 58s. profit from the sale of ale during the year. The parish lent its brewing equipment out to private persons for a consideration. At Islington, a parish on the eastern slopes of Dartmoor, the painted figures on the rood-screen remained right up to 1855; a big parish, the church-house was larger than usual, now 'restored' and made into cottages. This is the parish in which John Ford, the dramatist, was born in 1586, the church in which he was christened – the little family group wending its way along eastward, from the old house on the steep lower slopes of Bag Tor, above the gorge of the river Loman. There are the remains of the original hall-house, lost among ruined walls and granite farm-buildings with unnumbered holes for pigeons: a starveling place.

In the parish of Woodland, near Ashburton, the routine was much the same as elsewhere. William Culling provided the

chamber to store the parish ale in.[20] There were fourteen generations of that yeoman family with the name of William. One
observes a much longer continuance of these farming stocks than
in cities or towns, or even in Midland villages with their greater
exposure to change. The names here – Culling, Gould, Prowse,
Goswell, Soper, Dyer, Bowden, Tucker, Pinsent – go on for centuries. These were the sturdy yeomen who dealt with the accidents
of parish life, those that fell by the wayside, like the burial one day
of 'the poor beggar boy that died by a hedge.'

Parish life was not in essence different far away in the North-
East, in the North Riding or Durham, except for greater rawness
of climate and condition. At Ingleby Arncliffe at the base of the
Cleveland Hills, in winter-time the roof of the church was packed
tight inside with moss to prevent snow driving under the slates.
Only the choir was paved with sepulchral slabs, the rest of the
church had merely an earthen floor.[21] – But I am old enough to
remember when, before 1914, a couple of cottages in my native
village of Tregonissey in Cornwall still had earthen floors.

The enormous parish of Houghton-le-Spring, which was the
most valuable benefice in England, stretched from Bishop Wear-
mouth in north east Durham to the outskirts of the city in the
south west. It had eighteen constables for the numerous hamlets
within it; four churchwardens were chosen each year, four surveyors for highways rising to five in 1600, four sidesmen to help
the churchwardens, and four overseers of the poor.[22] Parish
affairs here, as in other Durham parishes, were regulated by the
'gentlemen', in this parish 'the four and twenty' chosen each year.
In 1604 the rector, gentlemen and twenty-four agreed that all
disputes were to be arbitrated by four of the gentlemen or four of
the twenty-four, equally chosen by the parties, with the rector
always as umpire. One notices again the clear distinction drawn
between the gentlemen and the yeomen of the parish. Class was
naturally reflected in the seating arrangements in church. At
Great Brington church in Northamptonshire, with its splendid
array of Spencer tombs, Lord Spencer sat up in the chancel with
his servants. The uppermost pews in the south aisle were for
Robert Washington and his wife; the benches next to his pew for
his men-servants. (He was great-great-great-grandfather of the
President.)[23] Men sat on one side, women on the other. In well-
ordered parishes the names of communicants were taken down –
to keep an eye on defaulters and recusants. At Halesworth in
Suffolk on Christmas Day 1594 the weather was so cold that the

rector could not thaw his ink to write down the names of communicants.[24]

The parish offered the most convenient unit for the operation of much social legislation. To encourage the woollen industry a statute of 1570 insisted on ordinary menfolk wearing woollen caps on Sundays and holy days – exempt from the regulation were ladies of title, gentlewomen, maidens, also nobles, knights, gentlemen, and such as had borne office of worship. That the statute was operated we may see from such parish registers as that of Cratfield in Suffolk, with its amerciaments for not wearing caps. This went on into the 1590's.[25] Sometimes, as at Burnley, women who were had up for non-attendance at church give as their reason that they had no clothes to wear.[26] One can believe it, for the same registers speak on occasion of 'a poor woman found dead in Horelaw', or 'a poor man found dead in Habergham Eaves.' Life was hard for the very poor, especially for the lonely ones who had no family or connections to protect them. In a subsistence-society social liens were a basic necessity of life.

The best contemporary account of parish social activities is that of Richard Carew in his *Survey of Cornwall*, where, he tells us, 'their feasts are commonly harvest dinners, church-ales, and the solemnising of their parish church's dedication, which they term their Saint's feast.'[27] The harvest dinner might be held any time after Michaelmas and might coincide with Christmas cheer; for the goodman, or 'good liver', would invite neighbours and kindred for jollities that went on for two or three days. Church-ales were run by the young men, two of them as wardens collecting the money: 'this they employ in brewing, baking, and other acates against Whitsuntide.' 'Of late times [i.e. towards 1600] many ministers have by their earnest invectives both condemned these Saints' feasts as superstitious, and suppressed the church-ales as licentious.' Everything shows the growing strength of Puritanism, which had a deplorable (and abortive) victory with the Civil War. Carew inserts a formal disputation on the pro's and con's of church-ales, himself coming down in the end against them – rather surprisingly; but then, he was ethically high-minded and religious, and as a deputy-Lieutenant all in favour of order.

'Pastimes to delight the mind, the Cornish have guary miracles [plays] and three-men songs; and for exercise of the body, hunting, hawking, shooting, wrestling, hurling, and such other games.' Hurling and wrestling were the leading popular sports in Cornwall, as in Cumberland (was there some Celtic inheritance here?) as

again in Brittany. He has an interesting account of hurling: in
East Cornwall 'to goals', and in West Cornwall 'to the country'.
The former was a more organised affair with two teams up to
thirty a side, matched by pairs, each man watching the other
throughout the game; two bushes pitched eight foot or so in the
ground, and two ten or twelve score feet away, were the goals.
'These hurling matches are mostly used at weddings, where commonly the guests undertake to encounter all comers.' Hurling to
the country was an indiscriminate scrimmage, one parish against
another, or several parishes against another quarter; the goals
either two gentlemen's houses, or a town or village three or four
miles apart. This game went on up till our time at St. Columb
Major, a mass hue-and-cry after a silver ball. 'A play both rude
and rough, and yet not destitute of policies in some sort resembling
the feats of war'; for there were forward parties, wings and rere-
ward, with horsemen in ambush. Carew hardly knew whether to
approve the game for its hardihood and masculine training for
war, or to deplore it for the bruises and bones broken. At the end
the field looked more like a battlefield.

That men were sometimes killed at hurling we know from an
unpublished document from 1585. In Maytime that year there
was hurling in the parish of Egloshayle, by the Camel estuary; at
Lower Treworder two labourers tackled each other and fell, one
of them breaking his neck: the poor fellow lived 'from five o'clock
that afternoon [it was Sunday, 9 May] until nine in the evening.'[28]
The other fetched up in Launceston gaol: thus we know. There
were similar accidents at games and sports. On 9 June 1567 there
was shooting at the butts in the churchyard of St. Philleigh.
Thomas Vyvyan shot an arrow beyond the butts, not knowing that
there was anyone there, and mortally wounded James Galty.[29]
Carew tells us of a famous archer, a gentleman, 'one Master Robert
Arundell, whom I well knew, who could shoot twelve score
[arrows], with his right hand, with his left, and from behind his
head.'[30] One Mayday in 1583 Thomas Merick was walking in the
mow-acre at Padstow, when he met a sailor, John Triplett of
Tintagel, carrying a caliver. Merick chaffed him as to what he
could do with the blunderbuss; Triplett said 'I would shoot at thee
if thou were a rebel,' and pointed the gun at him. It went off,
giving Merick a leg-wound of which he died.[31]

Wrestling was the most popular sport with the Cornish, on
which they most prided themselves, 'nor can their once countrymen and still neighbours, the Bretons, bereave them of this laurel.'[32]

There was hardly any gathering of boys in Devon or Cornwall 'who will not as readily give you a muster of this exercise as you are prone to require it.' The champion Cornish wrestler of the time was John Goit, one of her Majesty's guard: a very clean-made, agile fellow who was an equally good seaman, able to take charge of a ship as either master or captain. And was a good fellow besides.

Sports varied with the nature of the country and climate; but also in accordance with class. Deer-hunting was for the upper classes; hunting foxes, badgers, otters, polecats, squirrels – which were all classed as 'vermin' – was for everybody. Hawking, the expertise of falconry, was an aristocratic or 'gentle' exercise; killing birds in general, anyhow, was a popular sport. Fishing and angling were open to everybody, though gentlemen had their private fishponds and waters. Coursing the hare was a popular sport, so too with archery, when organised; bowling was more select, middle and upper class, though inns had their bowling alleys, not always permitted. Horse-racing was just beginning to be organised; fencing and duelling – those Italianate delights – were coming in from abroad. Both these were for the socially superior.

Elizabethan England had a much greater extent of forests, though they were shrinking; so there were still wild, red deer in places improbable to us, in the Forest of Dean, the Isle of Purbeck, a few even in Epping Forest. They roamed wild in such areas as Cumberland and Westmoreland, Wales, Exmoor and Dartmoor, crossing the Tamar sometimes into Cornwall. A far larger population of fallow deer were preserved in gentlemen's parks in every county. When Elizabeth went hunting in Epping Forest in 1589 she shot from a stand at Chingford lodge: it was more in the nature of a deer-drive.[33] The deer would have been fallow deer, since we hear of a 'buck' being given to the freeholders of Leighton – it would have been a 'hart' if it were red deer. A buck found dead in Waltham Forest, 'shot with a gun', in this year 1589, is one of the earliest of such references. Another stag found hurt was divided, half to Lord Rich, half to the poor – somebody must have had a sense of humour.

James I had a perfect mania for hunting, but even Elizabeth did her duty by the sport and must have derived some pleasure at least from its accompaniments. In September 1600, when she was an elderly woman, we hear that she is 'excellently disposed to hunting, for every second day she is on horseback and continues the sport long.'[34] John Selwyn was the keeper of her park at Oatlands in Surrey: a small man but very active, he once leaped from his horse on to the back of a deer, in front of the Queen, and killed it with his sword at her feet. We see him still on his brass in the church of Walton-on-Thames, in ruff and beefeater's hat, hunting horn slung over his shoulder, plunging his sword into the stag's neck.

It was a very gentlemanly thing to hunt: in fact one could hardly be considered a gentleman if one didn't. *The Institution of a Gentleman* tells us, 'there is a saying among hunters that he cannot be a gentleman which loveth not hawking and hunting . . . A like saying is that he cannot be a gentleman which loveth not a dog.'[35] Even Burghley once and again killed his buck; but Robert Cecil, for all his disability and his immense burden of work, was a keen sportsman – an agile little hunchback in more ways than one. In 1600 he was stocking his park at Theobalds with deer, and was in a hurry to enjoy the sport without waiting for them to breed there. So he got his friends to contribute. Lord Willoughby sent a number in his own ship from Boston to London, and thence up the Ware. 'In my conceit you take the right course, for to have but a little time of sport as you have and to be long a-making of it, the long expectance doth deprive the pleasure of it. I shall give you but deer you have inheritance of, for they have fed themselves often in your father's wood [i.e. in Lincolnshire], and it is no more than reason they should do the son some service.'[36] However, they did not live to do so: all the deer died from bruising themselves two by two in being shifted in carts.

The Earl of Lincoln was deeply in debt to Cecil, who was able to lend money on a large scale, with the profits of office. The Earl sent on some twenty deer in a little bark, but half of them died in removing; he himself had not been able to see to their disembarking, his coach having broken with the weight of Cecil's £1000.[37] Others made their contributions: Gilbert, Earl of Shrewsbury sent twenty-three hind calves, ten from young Rutland, ten from Ampthill, three from Sir Edward Denny, one from Mr. Felton. Next, Cecil is taking more land into his park and having 'a coursing place' made there, and paddocks. He is setting up a stud, and Willoughby offers him 'a young jennet, rightly bred both by sire and dam.'[38] He would have sent a mare, but at that time they were great with foal and too far off. From Henry VIII's reign, when there had been a statute on the subject, an effort was building up to improve the breed of horses.

The leading book on hunting was that ascribed to George Turberville, of an old Dorset family (commemorated by Hardy in his novel), for which George Gascoigne wrote prefatory verses in 1575, enforcing the view that it is

> A sport for noble peers, a sport for gentle bloods,
> The pain I leave for servants such as beat the bushy woods.

This view is reinforced by the title, *The Noble Art of Venery or Hunting*. Just as the ritual of hunting and the terms of art came originally from France, so much of the book is collected from French authorities: most early hunting books go back to the medieval classic, *Le Livre de Chasse* by Gaston de Foix. To this Turberville has added from his own experience, particularly on the treatment of diseases in hounds and dogs. The book was regarded as authoritative and had several editions; my own copy of the 1611 edition is profusely and appreciatively annotated by a seventeenth-century owner. The woodcuts are derisorily primitive, the horns of the stag so inaccurate as to be hardly recognisable – but then the English were backward in book-production.

In 1591 Sir Thomas Cockaine, of Ashbourne in Derbyshire, produced a charming little book, *A Short Treatise of Hunting*.[39] Its value is that it is original, based on his own experience and has therefore a living personal touch. It is dedicated to the Earl of Shrewsbury, in whose grandfather's house Cockaine had served in his youth and where he garnered his experience. He recalls hearing Ambrose, Earl of Warwick, say that 'amongst all the sorts of men that he had conversed withal in his life, he never found any better or more honest companions than hunters and falconers.' Ambrose was an easy-going sportsman himself, always popular, to whom Turberville dedicated his book on falconry – a very different proposition from his grand brother, Leicester. Cockaine's direct approach (not unlike Mrs. Beeton's) is pleasant: 'You must breed fourteen or fifteen couple of small ribble hounds, low and swift and two couple of terriers, which you may enter in one year by this rule following . . .' Not even personal experience prevented him from subscribing to the folklore that the roe did not sweat when hunted as other deer do, for 'he hath a little hole in his foreleg, whereat . . . issueth out all his moisture.' Though Cockaine claimed that he was 'no scollerd', the good old man helped to found the well-known grammar-school at Ashbourne.[40]

Shakespeare's plays, especially the earlier ones, are full of references to deer-hunting and always with the free and easy flow of terms of art that betokens an adept. His terms are almost always those that apply to fallow-deer; that would be right, for Warwickshire was full of deer-parks, but had no red deer. He writes, too, with affection for the music of the hounds; for in Elizabethan hunting the toot of a cowhorn was rather feeble, restricted to high and low, while the hounds were noisy and bred for a variety of voices, making a peal or chorus:

> matched in mouth like bells,
> Each under each. A cry more tunable
> Was never holla'd to, nor cheered with horn.

But the most tell-tale couplet always seems to me:

> What, hast not thou full often struck a doe,
> And borne her cleanly by the keeper's nose?

No Elizabethan could resist deer-poaching; the records and documents, a diary like Throckmorton's, are full of it, the local courts constantly dealing with offenders. At Staffordshire Quarter Sessions Francis and Everard Digby, though clerics, are both up before the J.P.s in the late 1580's and early 1590's for breaking into people's parks and hunting their deer, with two or three friends and their hounds.[41] Simon Forman was a servitor at Oxford for a bit, to two clerics, Thornborough and Pinckney: they would go hunting on Shotover 'from morning to night, and they never studied nor gave themselves to their books, but to go to schools of defence [fencing], to the dancing schools, to steal deer and conies, and to wooing of wenches.'[42] Nevertheless, Thornborough did well enough: he lived to become a bishop. These two were Magdalen and St. Mary Hall men, but we hear even of scholars of Balliol unable to resist the appeal of poaching deer on Shotover.[43] This would have been about the time when Milton's grandfather was keeper there, buried outside the western end of the little church at Forest Hill he would not attend. Turberville's book on falconry came out in the same year as that on hunting, but under his own name and with his own verses as prologue and epilogue:

> In my conceit no pleasure like to hawks . . .
> It sets the senses all to work, there may none idle be,
> The tongue it lures, the legs they leap, the eye
> > beholds the glee,
> The ears are busied eke to hear the calling spaniel's
> > quest . . .

And this is contrasted, in proper sportsman's spirit, with trifling the time away at indoor games:

> To check at chess, to heave at maw, at mack to pass
> the time,
> At coses or at sant to sit, or set their rest at prime[44] . . .

Turberville's book is even more encyclopaedic, more thorough and detailed than the others, and it is almost wholly extracted out of the Italian and French authorities. After all, falconry was oriental in origin, and the foreign provenance of the sport is stamped on every page of the book, with its treatment of vultures, Barbary falcons and Tunisian hawks. We are given a complete natural history of these birds, based on Aristotle and Pliny, brought up to date by Sforzino, Giorgio, and various French writers – another example, from a perhaps unexpected field, of English adaptation of Renaissance knowledge. It was not until 1615 and 1619 that original English works appeared on the subject. In any case it is no part of our purpose to go into the techniques of these sports, but to extract the social element, see how they illustrate the society.

In his *Britannia* Camden has an eloquent passage on the amazing flights of birds over the island, and this in itself brings home a general theme. Outside the one great city, and the few towns of any size (and even partially within them), all Nature lay at the doors of the island's inhabitants. The skies teemed with birds, the rivers, streams, coasts with fish for the taking. And in various parts the cliffs bred the country's commonest and favourite hunting bird, the peregrine falcon, though the Barbary falcon soared higher and was therefore sought after by grandees. Hear Drayton, in *Polyolbion*, that encyclopaedia of the country in verse:

> That those proud eyries bred wheras the scorching sky
> Doth singe the sandy wilds of spiceful Barbary . . .
> Outbrave not this our kind in mettle, nor exceed
> The falcon which sometimes the British cliffs do breed.

The popularity of the sport, with its new-found sophistication, with the gentry is caricatured by Ben Jonson in *Every Man in his Humour*, where a simple country squire says, 'I have bought me a book and a hood and bells and all . . . Why, you know an a man have not the skill in the hawking and hunting language nowadays, I'll not give a rush for him.' The most popular form of the sport was 'flying at the brook', where the master's dog flushes the quarry from the ground while the hawk waits overhead to make its deadly stoop. Drayton has an enthusiastic description in his Song XX *à propos* of the marsh-lands in Suffolk, while we find Arthur Throckmorton enjoying an occasional day's flying at the brook in Northamptonshire.[45]

What store a country gentleman set by his hawks and hounds may be seen from Sir Piers Legh's bequest to Derby's son and heir, Ferdinando, Lord Strange in 1587: 'all my hawks of what kind and sort soever they be, and all my hounds of such and every sort: a small gift wherein in times past I have had singular good liking.'[46] However politely he depreciates his gift, he hoped it would help to procure the continuance of the office of Captain of the Isle of Man for his son. When Ralegh's Indian falcon was sick of the buckworm, he wrote to ask Robert Cecil, 'if you will be so bountiful to give another falcon, I will provide you a running gelding.'[47] Thus for comparative values. Ralegh was ranger of the forest of Gillingham and keeper of the park there, on the northern edge of Dorset – remains of ancient Selwood. Everybody wishing to please the powerful Secretary knew that to present him with a falcon was a way to recommend oneself, he was so keen on the sport – a very different inflexion from his father, who was more like a cleric or a don. In 1598 Sir Henry Lee sends Cecil a haggard, though nothing so good as he could wish her, but he has had a right good lanneret [female of the species] given him and will try her out for Cecil.[48] The year before Lee wrote from charming Ditchley in Oxfordshire, in some discontent with his rustication from the delights of Court: 'in my idle fits in this barren place, where seldom is anything good, my chance hath been to light upon a reasonable doe, such a one as hard Cotswold may yield.'[49]

Sir George Carew from Ireland sent Cecil Irish hawks and hounds; Cecil responded with tobacco and Venice glasses – equal rarities. A sick falcon of Cecil's was confided to Sir George Savile to be nursed: 'her feathers were all broken, but a fair falcon she is likely to prove this next year, when I shall desire she may deserve your honour's good liking again.'[50] Cecil kept hawks at Collyweston, near his ancestral Stamford. In July 1598 Sir Edward Stafford is writing, 'I met yesterday at Collyweston with my friend Flint, your man and your hawks, which I assure you are very well, and I see by Flint your tassell [male goshawk] shall fly where one must have very good eyes to see her. He hopes at my return back to have them lured and ready to fly, but he dare not be too busy with them this hot weather.'[51] Gilbert Shrewsbury turns a pretty compliment to the great man: 'I told you of a goshawk that my Lady of Ormonde had sent you out of Ireland. I perceive there is a falcon sent you also from her. For the falcon, she soars too high for my compass, and therefore God speed you well with her; but for the goshawk that flies near the earth more humbly, like my nature and fortune, I have her in my custody, with meaning that you shall never see her.'

We hear at this time of some-one in the Fleet for taking liberties with Cecil's game.[52] His correspondence is full of his sporting interests – no wonder James called him his 'Little Beagle', a tribute to his infallible nose in affairs of state. How the invalidish Secretary had time for it all passes comprehension: he must have had exceptional nervous vitality. But, then, he died worn out before fifty.

For a rare voice in opposition to the sport we may cite Carew, who thought the fad for hawks mere folly: 'both Cornish and Devonshire men employ so much travail in seeking, watching taking, manning, nursling, curing, bathing, carrying, and mewing them, as it must needs proceed from a greater folly that they cannot discern their folly herein.'[53]

Organised horse-racing goes back to Elizabeth's reign, but in a sense its origin is to be traced back to her father, as with so many things, for it was he who took steps to improve the breed of horses, statutorily, and introduced the Italian art of training them in the manage. He also was the patron of the new Italian school of fencing. Henry's patronage of masculine sports, of Renaissance art and architecture, his passion for music and gifts as a musician, in addition to ship-building, the creation of a Royal Navy, his interest in military engineering and gunnery, gives a more complete picture of the man than the usual disproportionate concentration on Divorce and Dissolution, and helps to account for, what might not otherwise be so easy to understand, the undoubted popularity of the old tyrant.* Elizabeth but carried on her father's work, more humanely and in ladylike fashion; he was the originator.

In horsemanship all Europe learned from the Neapolitan school, and Henry brought to his Court as riding-master one who, at a second remove, had learned the methods of the famous Pignatelli, and was a pupil of Grisone. Three sons of his continued to teach in England:

* There is hardly anything of this in the biographies of him by A. F. Pollard and J. J. Scarisbrick.

Who brought the proudest coursers to his beck
And with his hand, spur, voice and wand did tame
The stately steeds that never brooked the check.[54]

In addition to insisting upon controlling the breeding of horses,
gelding the little nags and ponies that ran free with the mares on
the moors, finer breeds were imported from Spain, Italy, Germany,
Turkey, Barbary. We remember Richard II's Roan Barbary,
which Shakespeare writes with such feeling about that a perceptive observer thinks he may have owned one.[55] Then, too, there
were the young bloods among the English nobility who learned
a more sophisticated horsemanship, along with other things, on
their foreign travels. Philip Sidney, for example, became the
patron of two Italian riding-masters at work in England.

His uncle, Leicester, as Master of the Horse was in control of
the Queen's stud – as Sir Ralph Sadler was of her hawks and used
to train them on the Wiltshire downs.[56] Leicester had an Italian
riding-master in his service, Claudio Corte, who wrote *Il
Cavallerizzo* (with *Il Cortegiano* in mind). One can still see Leicester's copy of this book at Belvoir Castle, his initials and crest –
R.D. with the bear and ragged staff – stamped on the binding.
Thomas Blundeville dedicated to Leicester what became the
standard book on horsemanship in England, *The Four Chiefest
Offices belonging to Horsemanship . . . The Office of the Breeder, of the
Rider, of the Keeper, and of the Farrier*, 1565–6, which went through
several editions. In fact, it was a translation of the authoritative
Italian book on the subject, by Grisone. Leicester, we see, bore
his own part in domesticating Renaissance influences; he knew
Italian, encouraged Italians, and wrote a beautiful Italian hand.
A list of the horses in the Queen's stable in October 1598 tells us
what she and her ladies rode.[57] She rode Grey Pool or Black
Wilford; young Lady Southampton, when she was but Mistress
Vernon, a bay; Roan Howard for Mistress Elizabeth Russell,
Grey Fitton for Mistress Fitton, until she disgraced herself. There
were many more.

With the general improvement in the breed, the way was open
for horse-racing. It was not an exclusive preserve of the gentry, for
we find the corporations of some towns promoting it. In Cumberland Langanby was the famous old course, rivalling Garterly in
Yorkshire. On 13 April 1585 Richard Dudley writes from Yanwath
– still there, not much changed – that he cannot meet the commissioners coming from Yorkshire on 26 April, for he has a horse
to run at Langanby.[58] Kingmoor was for the burghers of Carlisle,

and the corporation supported the races. This is reflected in the unique relics the corporation still possesses in two inscribed silver gilt bells – silver bells were the prizes in Elizabethan races. The larger says:

> The sweftes horse thes bel to tak
> for mi Lade Dakar [Dacre's] sake.

The smaller has: '1599. H.B.M.C.', which stands for Henry Baines, Mayor of Carlisle in that year.

Doncaster races were early in starting: a plan of 1595 shows two race-courses on the Town Moor, and from 1600 the Corporation was managing the races.[59] In that year one Wyrrall caused a stop to be set on the Moor at the west end of the course; the mayor and two gentlemen cut it down. By 1614 the first racing official to be known by name was appointed – Anthony Hogg. It is said that Chester races were even earlier, but Ormerod gives no details. By 1603 Blandford races were in full swing, under the management of the town; for the town steward received during racing-week £82. 16. 3 for dinners and suppers, and for the play for six nights, £11. 7. 0.[60] At Nottingham the annual races on Coddington Moor began about 1620, under the patronage of the Corporation of Newark, with a gold bell and a silver bell for prizes.[61] But already we find the races at Brackley in Northamptonshire well-established in 1610–11: in Throckmorton's Diary we find his son-in-law, Wotton, going over from Paulerspury to run a horse-race with Wenman from Oxfordshire, or a party of menfolk going to Baynard's Green to see Wotton's horse race Babington's for the bell, and a wager of £50.[62] All was in train for the great expansion of racing in the coming centuries. The foundations were laid in the Elizabethan age, as in so many other things.

Coursing the hare with hounds was more popular: cheaper and more available. Naturally it depended upon the area being good hare-country – as to that we still have some indication in the frequency of the inn-sign, 'Hare and Hounds'. The Elizabethan regulations drawn up by the Duke of Norfolk still form the basis o all coursing meetings, though one or two terms of art have fallen into desuetude: the fellow who looses the greyhounds is now called the slipper, where the Elizabethans called him the fewterer, a word of French, and ultimately Celtic, derivation. The rule was supposed to be that a hare was not to be coursed by more than a brace of greyhounds, and should be given a start of twelve yards.

Heath-country, bare downs and stubbles being best for hares, coursing was much to the fore in the Midlands and eastern counties. Shakespeare is full of references to coursing, which must have been a favourite sport with him in his youth. Whatever else he was, he was a countryman born and bred: most sports are constantly being illustrated in his writings. Not all, however: he had predilections among them, all the more convincing. The Cotswolds, convenient to Stratford, were good coursing country. At the beginning of *The Merry Wives of Windsor*, Slender asks: 'How does your fallow greyhound, sir? I heard say he was outrun on Cotsall,' (i.e. Cotswold). Northamptonshire was equally good country. Kelmarsh hares were said to equal those of the Chilterns in swiftness.[63] Drayton has a description of a coursing there, in which the hare ultimately foils the hounds.[64] Not so in Shakespeare's far livelier description of coursing in *Venus and Adonis*: in that Poor Wat is run to the death.

Fowling was to the fore wherever there were stretches of water, not only along the coasts, in estuaries and marshes, but over inland waters, especially where there were ponds and lakes. We hear, for example, of the regular setting of decoys on the forest lakes of Nottinghamshire, though naturally the paradise of fowlers were the Fens, the marshy areas of eastern counties like Suffolk, Essex and Lincolnshire – the wolds of which were no less noted for coursing. A section of *Polyolbion*, Song XXV, is devoted to the 'Pleasures of the Fens', in which every kind of fish receives its due. Before the marshes of Yorkshire were drained there was an abundance of snipe – 'snites' Elizabethans called them: we have seen what a regular item of diet they and all game-birds were in big houses.[65] Smaller birds were available to all and sundry, whether hunted, snared, netted, limed, caught by 'bush-beating' at night, or increasingly by 1600 shot by guns. Such sports were still active in the country neighbourhood of my youth. Young Barnfield, who was a Staffordshire gentleman, was familiar with them; Daphnis hopes to tempt his Ganymede with country sports:

> Or if thou wilt go shoot at little birds,
> With bow and bolt, the throstle-cock and sparrow,
> Such as our country hedges can afford's –
> I have a fine bow, and an ivory arrow . . .

But

> To catch the long-billed woodcock and the snipe,
> The partridge, pheasant, or the greedy gripe

he suggests 'springs in a frosty night'.

A noticeable exception to Shakespeare's general interest in country sports is that of fishing and angling – too slow for that busy, hasty man. Everywhere there was plenty of fish, from what we learn, in rivers large and small. Many more rivers were salmon rivers then – the Trent, for example, famous for its salmon. It was the custom at Nottingham for the mayor to entertain the corporation at the annual fishing.[66] The fishery was farmed and brought in a good revenue to the town; regulations were made to preserve spawn, and against salmon and trout being taken out of season. In Dorset the salmon fishery on the Frome was leased from 1561; both Frome and Piddle were salmon rivers then.[67] In Cornwall these fish did not much come up the rivers west of the Fowey or along the north coast, but they came up all the Welsh and North Country rivers in great numbers. In Worcestershire the Teme, with its pools, was as perfect as a Welsh stream for angling.[68] The Severn had no pollution then and was full of fisheries, while even the Thames was a first-class salmon river. In inland Northamptonshire every small stream had its trout – it was a county of small streams; while Nene and Welland had plenty of pike, roach, tench, eels.[69] The abundance of fish – not to speak of the sea-fishing around the coasts – is testified to by all the diets that survive in household accounts.

The best account of fishing, fisheries and angling is again Carew's, for he was an enthusiastic angler, an Elizabethan Isaac Walton. He has a long account of sea-fishing – seine-fishing – and curing, as well as of the oyster-fisheries of Cornwall.[70] I cannot refrain from quoting his account of the seal. 'The seal is in making and growth not unlike a pig, ugly-faced, and footed like a moldwarp [mole]. He delighteth in music or any loud noise, and thereby is trained [drawn] to approach near the shore and to show himself almost wholly above water. They also come on land and lie sleeping in holes of the cliff, but are now and then waked with the deadly greeting of a bullet in their sides.' Carew has, besides, a whole section on the construction of his own fishponds and fish-traps at Antony, and their working, complete with verses:

> I wait not at the lawyers' gates,
> Nor shoulder climbers down the stairs;
> I vaunt not manhood by debates,
> I envy not the miser's fears:
>   But mean in state and calm in sprite,
>   My fish-full pond is my delight.[71]

This kindly, slow-paced man was but an ambling poet; but he was so devoted to fish and fishing that at this time, 1598, he published a poem *The Herring's Tayle*, which no-one has been able to make head or tail of.

Cockfighting must have existed from early times, but it received royal recognition from Henry VIII and a marked extension in his daughter's reign. Just about the time of the attack on the monasteries Henry built a regular cockpit at Whitehall, elaborately contrived and useful for other spectacles, or dramatic performances. Cockfighting was an entirely masculine diversion and Elizabeth never patronised it; but gentlemen paid high prices for game cocks, their training and trimming, and large wagers were placed on the birds. The Cockpit became a famous part of the complex of Whitehall – 10 Downing Street is near its site; at the Restoration it was, perhaps no less appropriately, the residence of Lady Castlemaine, Charles II's mistress. London had many cockpits, one of the best known being on the site of Drury Lane Theatre. At Oxford, one section of the Codrington Library at All Souls is still known as the Cockpit, evidently the site of one originally outside the College walls. At the back side of old country houses family tradition can still point out the depression where the cockpit was; I have myself encountered an old Cornish gentleman who confessed, with some apology for it, that he could not conquer his addiction to the sport. It still goes on surreptitiously. (And what about the classic description of it in Los Angeles in Nathaniel West's novel, *The Day of the Locust*?)

At Derby Cockpit Hill, near the site of the old Castle, has borne the name since Tudor times; in 1617 a new cockpit was built in another part of the town, Nuns Green, for the menfolk hitherto deprived.[72] In Cumberland cockfighting was immensely popular – as elsewhere; at Melmerby Sports, which took place at old Midsummer (5–6 July), the wrestling took place in the cockpit.[73] As no doubt elsewhere. We derive a direct impression of the excitement cockfighting provided from a letter from a young St. John to a Legh: 'we are here very busy with our cocks, but they match them slowly. There are as yet but thirteen battles made, whereof there are eight of them played yesterday, and our country [i.e. county] men have got four battles clept [called]. I cannot write by reason of over-eagerness in following the taint [a tilting term] whilst it is hot.'[74] And, for the care they took of their birds, here is a young Legh declining a match, 'for that the weather may be too warm for us to send our cocks so far at the season you specify'; moreover, two of their chiefest cockers, being sheriffs in their respective counties, would be engaged in their duties.

With the vulgar opulence of James's Court wagers increased very much in size. Lady Anne Clifford tells us how, in 1616, her husband the Earl of Dorset won £200 at a cocking match. 'All this time my Lord was in London . . . he went much abroad to cocking, to bowling alleys, to plays and horse races.'[75] In Maytime he went to a meeting at Lewes, with a crew of young sparks including Wat Ralegh, where 'there was much bull-baiting, bowling, cards and dice, with such-like sports to entertain the time.' The serious-minded Russell strain in her disapproved: she stayed at home and grieved. At Court was much cock-fighting, 'where the Lords' cocks did fight against the King's.' This was 'somewhat chargeable' to Dorset, but it procured him James's favour.

Bull-baiting must have been a prehistoric sport, to judge from the evidences of Crete and Lascaux; but one has a tell-tale indication from Derbyshire in that one bull-ring was within the prehistoric circle of Doveholes.[76] Bull-baiting lasted there, as elsewhere, into the 19th century, but it went back beyond the memory of man. Bear-baiting was a more recent sport, at least it much increased in our period, for numerous bears were imported for the purpose. As an organised sport in London it went together with bull-baiting; in the country at large rather separate activities.

It appears that the considerable amount of writing about Paris Garden as the centre of bear-baiting is mistaken.[77] It did not take place at Paris Garden, which had bowling alleys and was a place for quieter pleasures, such as Simon Forman enjoyed. It took place at the Bear Garden on Bankside about a quarter of a mile from Paris Garden; but since devotees landed by wherry – the Elizabethan equivalent of taxis, for it was easier to go any distance by water up and down the Thames – at the stairs at Paris Garden, the latter name was apt to swamp that of the Bear Garden. The sport began to flourish there in the latter part of Henry's reign, and to be disapproved of by more sensitive puritanical spirits, like Crowley. John Bradford, one of Mary's many martyrs, noticed God's judgment upon certain gentlemen going to the bear-baiting there on a Sunday: their wherry overturned and they were drowned. Machyn in his Diary noted when a serving man was killed by a big blind bear that broke loose. And every Elizabethan knew about the disaster on a Sunday in January 1583 when the scaffold there broke down under the press of people and eight of them were killed.

In 1590 there were kept at the Bear Garden three bulls, five big bears and four others, over a hundred dogs, a horse and the ape that provided regular amusement by riding horseback to round off the entertainment. Visitors from abroad found this very funny to see the ape clinging to the pony, shrieking and grimacing at the dogs yelping at them. Perhaps it was. Some of the bears were well-known characters to their *aficionados*, Harry Hunks, Great Ned, above all, Sackerson. John Davies describes with disapprobation the idle young gentleman of the inns of court who spent his time going to see plays or bear-baitings:

> Stinking of dogs and muted all with hawks,
> And rightly too on him this filth doth fall
> Which for such filthy sport his books forsakes,
> Leaving old Plowden, Dyer and Brooke alone
> To see old Harry Hunks and Sackerson.

And when Dekker writes that 'a company of creatures that had the shapes of men and faces of Christians took the office of beadles upon them, and whipped Monsieur Hunks till the blood ran down his old shoulders', one's sympathies are all with the Puritans. There is the barbarism of the age – our own has been worse; for such is *l'homme moyen sensuel*.

Nevertheless, these spectacles were considered proper entertainments for visiting notabilities. At the beginning of her reign the Queen provided one such for the French ambassador, and next day he crossed the Thames to the Bear Garden for another. At the end of her reign, in Maytime 1600, we hear from Court: 'her Majesty is very well. This day she appoints to see a Frenchman do feats upon a rope in the Conduit Court. Tomorrow she hath commanded the bears, the bull, and the ape, to be baited in the Tiltyard. Upon Wednesday she will have solemn dancing.'[78] These state entertainments must have been somewhat comparable to gala bull-fights in Spain today. As for bear-baiting about the country, at fair-time and feasts, or upon no particular occasion at all, references in town-records are so frequent as not to be worth specifying. Sometimes a name carries on the old interest – Bearward Lane below the Castle at Nottingham, or Bearcroft at Barthomley in Cheshire.

For nearly all of these sports a dog was indispensable. And we are fortunate to have a treatise on British dogs from the pen of Dr. Caius (Key or Keyes), the second founder of Gonville and Caius college at Cambridge. He wrote it for his friend Conrad

Gesner's History of Animals, and it therefore follows a categorical academic form: concise and scientific, it could have been made more interesting if it were more personal. It was in Latin – Caius was opposed to writing in English – and was translated by Abraham Fleming in 1576.[79] In due form we are given the different types of dogs in being, defined in accordance with the purposes they served. Harriers were for hunting the hare, fox, badger, otter, etc. though usually trained specially for one of these. Terriers were for going into earths and holes after rabbits, foxes, badgers. Bloodhounds were in special use on the Borders for tracking down cattle-stealers. With no conception of evolution, Caius may not have realised that they were descended from dogs that had lapped man's blood.

But we can learn from him that the favourite greyhound is not so called after the colour grey. Where dictionaries tell us that the derivation is doubtful, Caius informs us that the word comes from *gradus*, or degree, since they held prime favour, 'being simply and absolutely the best of the gentle [i.e. gentlemanly] kind of hounds.'[80] That English greyhounds were already prized abroad towards 1600 we see from a letter from Marshal Biron to Essex asking for 'levriers et dogues de votre pays' for boar-hunting.[81] A new kind of white and black spaniel, with mingled colour inclined to a marble blue, was coming in from France, since the English were 'greedy gaping gluttons after novelties.'[82] And then there were lapdogs, which Caius could not abide; though no Protestant – he was in fact a crypto-Catholic – he turns quite moralistic on the subject. 'These puppies, the smaller they be the more pleasure they provoke, as more meet play-fellows for mincing mistresses to bear in their bosoms, to keep company withal in their chambers, to succour with sleep in bed, to lay in their laps, and lick their lips as they ride in their wagons.' (We notice how much addicted to alliteration the poet Fleming was.) Their only use was 'to succour and strengthen quailing and quamning stomachs, to bewray [discover] bawdry, and filthy abominable lewdness' – and Caius cites a classical instance.

Caius goes on to the English shepherd dog, and teases us with an endearing personal reminiscence, when he once reined in his horse and stood quite still to watch a shepherd dog obeying his master's whistle and rounding up the flock. He informs us that in England the shepherd followed the sheep, unlike everywhere else, where the shepherd led his flock. We have another pleasant touch with the account of the tinker's cur carrying his master's satchel of tools. Then there are dancing dogs, watch-dogs and house-dogs that will rake the coals out of harm's way from the fire at night. For, however scientific an Elizabethan may be, there is always a vein of credulity. In the year 1564 a hare, 'a wild and skippish beast', astonished people by playing upon a tabouret and dancing in measure. There is also some confusion as to species and *genera*. Caius did not know whether to call beaver dog or fish, or whether a seal was not a dog; he thought that a bear could cross with a mastiff. We learn that woolly Icelandic dogs were being imported, and that some people kept tame foxes. Harrison says that some gentlemen were already preserving foxes for sport where the people would have destroyed them. Lastly, we hear of the great English mastiffs, which 'are said to have their generation of the violent lion.'[83] Three of them were matched against a bear, four against a lion – one hears of occasions when these splendid creatures were ripped open by a tormented beast, and thinks of William Faulkner's famous story, 'The Bear'.

How much these dogs were prized we can see from a letter of Leicester – and at the same time glimpse something of his undoubted charm. He writes to thank Sir Piers Legh: 'I perceive you will not forget me, and assure yourself that, as occasion shall serve, I will not be unmindful of your continual remembrance of me . . . From the Court, the XIXth of November 1584. Your loving friend, R. Leicester,'[84] Not content with that, the great man took up pen once more to write, 'I thank you very heartily, Sir Piers, for your hound and will requite you the loss of him with as good a thing.' The Lyme mastiffs were a famous breed, of immense size and pale lemon colour, large heads like bloodhounds, black ears and muzzles, and soft brown eyes. In 1604 James sent a pair to Philip III: we recognise their descendant still with the children in Velazquez' 'Las Meniñas.'

We appreciate the variety of sports open to one, the exercises that make a full man, in Ascham's summary: 'to ride comely, to run fair at the tilt or ring, to play at all weapons, to shoot fair in bow, or surely in gun; to vault lustily, to run, to leap, to wrestle, to swim; to dance comely, to sing, and play of instruments cunningly; to hawk, to hunt, to play at tennis, and all pastimes generally which be joined with labour, used in open place, and on the day light, containing either some fit exercise for war, or some pleasant pastime for peace.'[85] This is, of course, an upper-class view, the ideal of the all-round gentleman: not many peasant farmers or labourers would have time, energy or inclination for many of them. As with Clemenceau's view of the Ten Commandments, 'only three or four need be attempted.' On the other hand, the slow pace of agricultural labour, the ebb and flow of seasons and weather, the numerous saints' days and holidays – including Sunday, which was pre-eminently the day for sports (hence the fuss made by the Puritans) – gave far more opportunity for games and sports to the people at large than we might suppose.

Sunday was the day for football, a game much more like hurling, in which the ball was carried, a mass game with two sides pitted against each other, and a rough game as we have seen. This provides a Puritan like Stubbes with the gravamen of his case. 'Any exercise which withdraweth us from godliness, either upon the sabbath or any other day, is wicked and to be forbidden . . . As concerning football-playing, I protest unto you it may rather be called a friendly kind of fight than a play or recreation, a bloody and murdering practice than a fellowly sport or pastime. For doth not everyone lie in wait for his adversary, seeking to overthrow him and to pitch him on his nose, though it be upon hard stones, in ditch or dale, in valley or hill, or what place soever it be, he careth not, so he have him down. And he that can serve the most of this fashion, he is counted the only fellow and who but he?'[86] And so on. But we do not need to set much store by the moral indignation of a Stubbes, a merchant in that *genre*; as for his humanity, we remember his recommendation that poor prostitutes should be branded with a hot iron. We are more interested in the facts.

In Derbyshire a mob game of football was played generally on Shrove Tuesday.[87] At Ashbourne there was a contest between the parishes of St. Peter and All Saints. The ball was tossed up in the market-place at noon; a general scrimmage ensued. In winter there was stark naked footracing over the ice, with hundreds of spectators – nor was Derbyshire the only county; it must have been a North Country sport, where there was ice in winter. Derbyshire was also 'much given to dance after the bagpipes; almost every town hath a bagpiper in it.' Then there was tilting at the quintain, a sport used particularly at weddings – we see why: the quintain was a post on the village green; the Master of the quintain came to the bridegroom with a white spear in hand all decked with flowers, which the bridegroom broke at his first tilt. We hardly need to call in Freud to explain that piece of folk-ritual.

In many parishes all over the country Whitsun week had a couple of days devoted to games. Shakespeare has a phrase,

> Methinks I play as I have seen them do
> In Whitsun pastorals . . .

and, unlike Philip Stubbes, he bids us 'apprehend nothing but jollity.' In the Cotswolds Robert Dover, a country lawyer of Barton-on-the-Heath, deliberately organised the 'Cotswold Games' and ran them for forty years against Puritan prejudice. 'They consisted of cudgel-playing, wrestling, the quintain, leaping, pitching the bar and hammer, handling the pike, playing at balloon or handball, leaping over each other, walking on the hands, a country dance of virgins, men hunting the hare (which, by Dover's orders, was not to be killed), and horse-racing on a course some miles along.'[88] That good Warwickshire man, Drayton, paid him the tribute:

> We'll have thy statue in some rock cut out,
> With brave inscriptions garnishèd about,
> And under written, 'Lo! this is the man
> Dover, that first these noble sports began.'

More sophisticated games, as with horsemanship and falconry, came in from abroad, in particular tennis, introduced from France. Perhaps even football, in its organised form, reached us from a higher culture. 'Giovanni de' Bardi's *Discorso* (1580) shows strategic and tactical football played in Florence at a time when in England it was chiefly pursued by the rabble in the streets.'[89] Tennis was the game of 'real', or royal, tennis. The reverberating quarrel between Sir Philip Sidney and the Earl of Oxford, that was the beginning of the latter's fall from favour, took place on the tennis court. It led to a challenge, though the Queen forbade a duel and Sidney withdrew to the country. And while Southampton's recently wedded wife was giving birth to a child, the father was losing large sums at tennis-play in Paris.[90] It was obviously a very grand game, only for grandees. Stephen Gosson was as much down on bowling, for this reason, as Stubbes was down on everything. 'Common bowling alleys are privy moths that eat up the credit of many idle citizens, whose gains at home are not able to weigh down their losses abroad; whose shops are so far from maintaining their play that their wives and children cry out for bread.'[91] The amount of gambling that accompanied sport even then was a legitimate source of grievance. But the tolerant Stow's objection to bowling was more that it injured archery, and archery was not only a sport but a form of national service.

There was a good deal of legislation about it, including Henry VIII's making archery-practice compulsory, and this was continued under his daughter. The longbow had been the English 'secret weapon' at Crécy and Poitiers, responsible for a long run of medieval victories against the French with far greater numbers. We still have a memento of those far-off days in the not infrequent ancient yew-trees in parish churchyards, for the longbow was made chiefly of yew. As a weapon it was having to yield ground to modern fire-arms, though patriotic conservatives regretted the necessity or even, like Sir John Smith who wrote a discourse on the subject, refused to face the fact. Archery achieved an English classic with Roger Ascham's *Toxophilus*, which was written to please Henry VIII – and did. It is not without significance that this admirable example of Tudor prose should have been accomplished by the second Greek scholar of his day. We do not need to analyse the book here: it is a work rather of national policy, though, in addition to its Renaissance parade of classical knowledge, it goes in masterly detail into the technique of the art. According to Camden, Ascham was so much addicted to cockfighting and archery, that they kept him poor – if so, rather endearing of so high-minded a scholar.

We should note, however, the expert's disapprobation of English amateurishness, which was to be characteristic of our attitude to sport. 'Learning to shoot is little regarded in England, for this consideration: because men be so apt by nature they have a great ready forwardness and will to use it, although no man teach them, although no man bid them. And so of their own courage they run headlong on it, and shoot they ill, shoot they well, great heed they take not.'[92] The 'playing-fields of Eton' – not without some relevance here – were in those days the 'shooting-fields'. One such young archer at the butts at Stratford gives us an autobiographical reminiscence:

> In my schooldays, when I had lost one shaft,
> I shot his fellow of the self-same flight
> The self-same way with more advisèd watch,
> To find the other forth and, by adventuring both,
> I oft found both.

The development of the art of fencing in itself illustrates concisely several of the themes of this book. There was the backwardness of the sixteenth-century English as against the Continent: they remained wedded to their old sword-and-buckler style of combat, in which they gave a good account of themselves to the end. They put up a strong opposition to the new ideas of sword-play coming out of Italy. There the Italians had made the decisive discovery of the superiority of the sword, in itself combining the advantages of offence and defence, and the rediscovery of the Roman practice of the thrust, the conclusiveness of the point, which had brought such signal results in the ancient world.[93] In England the masters of arms were men of the people, roughs and toughs, a discreditable profession strongly disapproved of by the City fathers in London and all *bons bourgeois*. Meanwhile the Italians were developing the elegant, controlled art of fencing, with its rules and terms, its finish like any other art. Along with it developed the rapier, a narrower and lighter weapon than the old broadsword, but with a long range, and in place of buckler a parrying dagger in the left hand. These Renaissance weapons dominated personal combat for a century, in themselves expressing the individualising spirit of the time. With this came the rise of the duel, as against medieval wagers of battle.

In Italy the masters of fencing were gentlemen, on some equality with their clients; in England they were rather unsavoury plebeians. It was something of a social solecism that in order to meet what was an aristocratic punctilio, a point of honour, a gallant had to resort to a low-class fencing master. Henry VIII came to the rescue once more, or at any rate imposed rules and regulations by granting a recognised status to the London Masters of Defence in 1540.[94] This made a beginning, though conservatism in the profession, reflecting rooted English prejudices, remained strong to the end of the century. Sword-and-buckler play was a national game; had not the champion John Peeke of Tavistock defeated three Spaniards with rapier-and-dagger in the presence of the Duke of Medina Sidonia at Xeres? Why forsake old tried weapons, which had answered so well, for foreign innovations? By 1598, however, Porter was writing, in *The Two Angry Women of Abingdon*, 'sword-and-buckler fight begins to grow out of use. I am sorry for it. I shall never see good manhood again. If it be once gone, this poking fight with rapier and dagger will come up. Then the tall man will be spitted like a cat or a rabbit.' It was with a rapier that John Day, the playright, killed his fellow dramatist, Harry Porter, the author of that piece.

'The rapier was decidedly a foreigner; yet it suited the

Elizabethan age, for it was decorative as well as practical. Its play was picturesque, fantastic – almost euphuistic, one might say . . . Its phraseology had a quaint, rich, southern smack, which connoted outlandish experience and gave those conversant with its intricate distinctions that marvellous character, which was so highly appreciated by the cavalier youth of the time. The rapier in its heyday was an admirable weapon to look at, a delicious one to wield. And besides, in proper hands, it was undoubtedly one that was most conclusive. It was, in short, as elegant and deadly as its predecessors were sturdy and brutal.'[95] English aristocrats travelling abroad took up the new weapons and learned fencing from foreign masters. Gentlemen at Court adopted the rapier and the new style; thence they spread outward and downward. Italians were brought in as fencing-masters, and the last three decades saw a succession of experts, Rocco, Jeronimo and Saviolo, who taught gentlemen for considerable fees. Stow tells us that the monopoly of old English sword-and-buckler came to an end about the time of the decisive crisis of the reign, 1569–72.

Rocco had his school of fencing in Blackfriars, where he must have added one more to the nuisances which gave such displeasure to the dowager Lady Russell. He had leased his premises from John Lyly, the dramatist – and dramatics displeased her even more. Rocco had aristocratic patrons, however, as good as she, Lord Willoughby, Lord North, and Sir Walter Ralegh. When Rocco gave up, the premises were taken over by Thomas Bruskett, about whom, our authority says, 'we know nothing.'[96] But he must have been another Italian – it is the English form of the name Bruschetti. Jeronimo was probably Rocco's son; in 1590 he joined partnership with a newcomer, Vincentio Saviolo, and together they 'taught rapier-fight at the Court for the space of seven or eight years.' An unfortunate accident polished off Jeronimo. He was out in his coach with a wench he loved well, when he was challenged to fight by one Cheese, who had no knowledge of the new rapier-play at all, but was a good man with a sword. With two thrusts of it he killed the Italian master in front of his woman. Cheese was 'a very tall man, in his fight natural English.'[97] This event must have given pleasure to patriots.

Saviolo, however, remained the head of his profession and received plaudits to his character besides. Essex was his patron, as Southampton was Florio's; and Florio naturally gives us a favourable portrait of 'that Italian that looks like Mars himself', while describing the native sword-and-buckler as 'a clownish and dastardly weapon, and none for a gentleman.'[98] This group was responsible for the domestication of Italian works on the art of fencing. A translation of Grassi's book, originally published in 1570, appeared in 1594, the *True Art of Defence*: some indication of the time-lapse in the widening cultural ripples from Italy. Next year came out Saviolo's own book on the Use of Rapier and Dagger, with a second part on Points of Honour and honourable Quarrels. It is worth noting that Saviolo specifically followed Castiglione in method and treatment. The book was answered by a counterblast from the old English school, George Silver's *Paradoxes of Defence*, 1599. Silver was a Hampshire gentleman and his tribute to Saviolo was generous: 'this was one of the valiantest fencers that came from beyond the seas, a far better man in his life than in his profession he was, for he professed arms; but in his life a better Christian.' The future was with the rapier. Progress was registered in the art of killing.

Consistently with this the development of the duel also expressed the changed manners and tone of the time. It is significant that in 1571 one of the last judicial combats before law Judges as umpires was arranged, but did not take place. Here was the medieval form, a public combat to decide a legal right or wrong. It was like the spirit of the age that the duel now vindicated, not loyalty or the law, but 'personal honour, pride, or vanity.'[99] And it is an Elizabethan of Italian descent, Ludovic Bryskett (Bruschetti), Philip Sidney's friend, who describes the code of honour (so called), in which 'giving the lie' was the final provocation, which could be met only by fighting a duel. In his *Discourse of Civil Life* he says, 'it is reputed so great a shame to be accounted a liar that any other injury is cancelled by giving the lie. And he that receiveth it standeth so charged in his honour and reputation that he cannot disburden himself of that imputation but by striking of him that hath so given it, or by challenging him the combat.'[100] To decline it was regarded as running away and losing one's honour. This kind of barbaric childishness among men – women were more sensible – was rampant and encouraged in Germany in our time up to the last war. In seventeenth-century France it was not merely the fashion, but a mania: not all the authority of Richelieu could put a stop to it.

In England both Elizabeth and James I tried valiantly to discourage the nuisance, and in this country it never quite reached the dimensions of a social disease. We have seen the disapprobation of William Thomas, who appreciated so much of Renaissance

Italy, for this aspect of it. It is given vivid expression in *Romeo and Juliet* with the characters of the quick-tempered Mercutio and the murderous swordsman, Tybalt. A famous character of a somewhat different type, a professional bravado, cowardly underneath, is Jonson's Captain Bobadill, from whom Shakespeare got the hint for Parolles. Here are the latter's words saying farewell to the young men going to the wars: 'noble heroes, my sword and yours are kin. Good sparks and lustrous – a word, good metals. You shall find in the regiment of the Spinii one Captain Spurio with his cicatrice, an emblem of war, here on his sinister cheek: it was this very sword that entrenched it. Say to him I live.' What asses such men were! The wise and sceptical Montaigne, as translated by Florio, says the last word on the subject: 'the reputation and worth of a man consisteth in his heart and will; therein consists true honour.'[101]

That there were braggadoccios of the kind lurching about London we know well enough, and there were constant flare-ups, affrays, duels about the country. Within a few months of the year 1599 we find the following. On a June day two West Country gentlemen, Nicholas Slanning and John Fitz with their consorts, met on the moor between Plymouth and Tavistock, where Fitz killed Slanning and divers others were hurt. Slanning left two young sons, the elder about twelve. 'His living is here esteemed to be so good as any gentleman's in these parts. Mr. Fitz is fled.'[102] We know about the feud between Cavendishes and Stanhopes in Derbyshire. In July 'Sir Charles Cavendish, accompanied with three of his servants, was lately set upon in his own ground near his house by Mr. Stanhope. Sir Charles and one of his men were hurt in three or four places, and Mr. Stanhope left three of his people behind him.' That was an affray, not a duel; but, in the next sentence, 'Harry Macwilliam is slain by J. Compton, who is likewise hurt in divers places, but now past danger of death.' At the end of the year Cecil laid Sir Calisthenes Brooke by the heel over a challenge to a peer (challenge and calumniate are cognate words). Brooke pleads from the Fleet, 'I have been here as many more days as the lord, though he were the commandment-breaker, as appeareth by his challenge. It is imputed a fault in me that I presented not myself to punishment as he did – a course against nature.'

Duelling was a gentlemanly sport, We look into the minds of its practitioners in the challenges with which the disagreable Lord Grey, pursued Southampton – not the manliest of men, in the pejorative sense of the word. Grey writes to him, 'as the chief impediment why you refused France you alleged the Deputy's speedy departure: he is gone, you here, and yet I hear not of you. But to conclude all wordy disputations – worthy rather of women than men of war – I now call you by my third letter, and expect the performance of your first, that you going not presently into Ireland, we may into France.'[103] And so on. In the end, to save 'honour', Southampton went over to the Netherlands where he might meet his opponent. Thereupon the Queen imposed her direct prohibition upon their fighting, 'as noblemen of valour who are fit to reserve yourselves for her Majesty's service, and not to hazard them upon private quarrels.'[104]

What fools she must have thought men were!

CHAPTER VIII

CUSTOM

How full the year was for Elizabethans, filled and tricked out by custom! One has the same sense of surprise as one has in reading Hardy's novels at how occupied simple people's lives were with the diurnal routine of labour, markets and fairs, feast days and holy days, sport and gatherings, fasts and rejoicings; observations of this and that, days when one mustn't do one thing and must do another; wassailing, maying, dancing; Shrovetide games, Whitsun ales and plays, Christmas disguisings; customary obligations and beliefs, ghosts, fairies, witches, spirits, souls of the departed; the events of family life, birth, marriage, death. In Hardy's novels the round and ritual of an agrarian society, in all their fulness, are for the last time completely expressed in our literature; and not only the traffic but many of the beliefs, as they had remained unchanged since the Elizabethan age, such a recognisably familiar one as that expressed in 'The Christmas Oxen':

> Christmas Eve, and twelve of the clock,
> 'Now they are all on their knees,'
> An elder said as we sat in a flock
> By the embers in hearthside ease.

All was geared to the seasons and the necessities of agriculture, as were again the festivals of the Church. There were all the observances of the Church, in addition to those of folk custom; or, rather, the two were intimately intertwined. Today, if we have a perceptive eye, we can still recognise the relics of these observances, the fossils of their beliefs, far more active and potent once; for Elizabethans were actors in their world, not passive participants in a worthless culture. Such conditions were immensely more propitious to the life of the imagination, as we can see in their literature and their speech. In justice we must admit that there is a certain creativeness in folk custom and belief, even under the eroding (and corroding) circumstances of modern society. And also we shall see operating, as the result of the Reformation, a kind of rationalising campaign on the part of Reformers and Puritans against the proliferations of the unconscious, the super-fluities and elaborations of belief – they called them 'superstitions', unaware that their own were no less so: an instinctive campaign against the instinctual, often absurd enough on both sides. No doubt it meant some progress in rationalisation; at the same time it involved a certain impoverishment of the life of the unconscious, deliberate restrictions upon its free movement, in part direction in accordance with the (not wholly) rational will. Nevertheless no absolute contraction in the life of the spirit occurred – as in our dominantly secular, scientific society, with the consequent drying up of inspiration for the arts. For the blissful interval between the Elizabethan Settlement and the Civil War an optimum balance seems to have been struck: hence its astonishing cultural achieve-ment. *Fortunatos nimium, sua si bona norint*, as Clarendon remarked of the years before the catastrophe.

The customary life of the people was given a framework and chronology by the calendar; it was particularly active and viva-cious at the major festivals and lesser feasts of the Church, as it still is, if less significantly and with somewhat different emphases, in the country today. We are all familiar with Christmas obser-vances: they were not essentially different then, though the inflexion varied. Tusser adjured his readers:

> Get ivy and hull [holly], woman, deck up thy house,
> And take this same brawn for to seethe and to souse.
> Provide us good cheer, for thou knowest the old guise
> [way]:
> Old customs that good be let no man despise.
>
> At Christmas be merry and thank God of all,
> And feast thy poor neighbours, the great with the
> small . . .

When we turn to an Elizabethan gentleman's diary, Throck-morton's for example, this is what he regularly did at his new-built house at Paulerspury near Towcester. Every Christmas he distributed pieces of beef and groats to a score of poor neighbours, on the next days he dined the village people, two townships at a time. 26 December he usually entertained Plumpton end and Church end, on the 27th Pury end and Heathencote; on a third occasion Whittlebury men.[1] But there were already people who looked with no favourable eye on Christmas entertainments. Tusser observed of them,

> Take custom from feasting, what cometh then last:
> Where one hath a dinner a hundred shall fast.
>
> To dog in the manger some liken I could
> That hay will eat none, nor let other that would;
> Some scarce in a year give a dinner or two,
> Nor well can abide any other to do.

When the Puritans triumphed in the Civil War, they abolished Christmas; but the popular instinct eventually beat them.

The Christmas season was accompanied by customs of which Puritans, and some of which even normal Protestants, could not approve. Up to the Reformation there was a practice in some cathedrals and colleges of appointing a boy-bishop who bore rule in choir, with his attendant deacons and acolytes, from St. Nicholas day to Holy Innocents, 6 December to 26th. It is comparable with the Lord of Misrule at the Inns of Court or in the halls of great houses; or again the Elizabethan custom, particularly in the North Country, of 'barring out' the school-master, from whom the scholars extracted concessions before letting him in. It is not difficult to understand the rationale of these customs. It is well known that sixteenth-century school-masters were harsh in the treatment of their boys, but it is less well known that there was an instinctive belief that beating drove knowledge into the boys – really a case of sympathetic magic. These customs of 'barring out', of a period of misrule, or boy-bishoping, provided a psychological let-up from a too strict discipline. Many other customs have a comparable rationale, if not justification. Actually the emollient régime of Henry VIII abolished the boy-bishop in 1542. When Bishop Bonner restored it under Mary, it was popular: people said, 'St. Nicholas yet goeth about the City.'[2] With the victory of the Protestants at Elizabeth's accession, it fell into disuse – to be revived occasionally as an archaeological antiquity in our time.

Then there was bringing in the Yule log, in some areas an ash fagot – ash, holly and mistletoe have a significance going back to pre-Christian times. Wassailing the trees at this season was fairly general where there were apple orchards as in the West Country: people sprinkled the branches or roots with cider to make them bear, drank the remainder and danced round the trees. Shakespeare refers to the 'wassail candle', which may be the same as the

Yule candle. Ringing in Christmas often began on St. Thomas's Day, 21 December, on which day poor women had free licence to beg, who would not do it at other times, and went 'a-gooding' – it was good for the soul to give. There was much bell-ringing – to which Puritans objected: with more reason than we appreciate, for bells were thought to keep spirits and storms away, apart from exciting people as they did (and still can do). The old custom had been to ring the church bells all night on All Hallows' eve: it benefited souls in purgatory. Suppressed by Henry VIII, it was revived under Mary; under Elizabeth there was an Injunction against over-much bell-ringing, but the custom continued, to fall only gradually into disuse. In its way, a nice epitome of the course things took.

One custom at this time, still more prevalent at New Year, is more difficult to explain: the care that was taken to see that a dark-haired man was 'first foot' into the house. In a lesser number of districts it was a fair-haired man who brought luck to the house. The distribution should be plotted, for it might have some racial significance.[3] Folklore and folk-custom are richer, fuller and more tenacious in the Highland Zone of Britain, i.e. roughly north and west of a line from Newcastle to Exeter, as against the Anglo-Saxon South, East and Midlands. It may well be that in North and West the dark man entering the house is a friend, and not an enemy. Folklore and custom continued more vigorously in such an area as Cornwall – one reason for turning to it more frequently for illustration, as again Carew has the best Elizabethan observations upon such matters.

Guise-dancing and mumming were kept up during the Christmas period, which lasted from Christmas eve to Twelfth night. This continued at St. Ives in Cornwall into the second half of the nineteenth century, by which time it had become an uproarious pantomine. Father Christmas was a new introduction, since folk-custom is self-proliferating, but St. George of the Mummers' play was traditional. My father remembered it being performed in his youth in the courtyard of the 'Seven Stars' inn at St. Austell. It was then, at the same time as the St. Ives disguising, on its last legs; but the latter was started up again in the 1930's.

Barnaby Googe tells us that in Elizabethan days Shrove-tide occupied the four days before Ash Wednesday: a last flare-up before the austerities and pinched fare of Lent.[4] The Pancake bell was rung from the church-tower: John Taylor, the Water Poet,

says that this alerted and excited people, who began to cast care
to the winds and think of their pancakes and little else. Curiously
enough, ringing the Pancake bell survived more widely and up to
a later date than most other special ringings, while tossing the
pancake has survived unbroken, not only at Westminster School –
that playground of tradition – but in many parishes. In earlier
times there was cock-fighting and 'barley break' was played, which
we remember from the catches and dance-tunes that went with
it. Elizabethans, characteristically, engaged in a horrid sport at
this time: tying cocks by a length of cord to a stake, pelting them
with sticks, and appreciating the agility with which the poor
creatures learned to evade the missiles, if they survived.[5] Such was
the barbarism of the people; such are humans. In this context one
can understand better the torture, executions, burnings, hangings
and quarterings of the time (not that the Germans have been any
better in ours). Even so, after the dreadful inhumanity of Henry
VIII and Mary, Elizabeth's reign provided a notable example of
lenity, until the crisis of the war with Spain.

We have already seen that Elizabeth I maintained the elaborate
Catholic ceremonies of Maundy Thursday at Court – and indeed
Elizabeth II attends them, in an attenuated form, in Westminster
Abbey still. This was the washing of the feet of poor women to the
number of the Queen's age – thirty-nine in the year of St. Bartholomew. There was a service, as there still is, in commemoration
of Christ's washing the feet of his disciples, and a lavish distribution of gifts, now reduced to tokens.

All this was preliminary to the high point of the Church's year,
Easter-tide. It was ushered in by the tolling of bells on Good
Friday, solemnly as for a death or burial; at Ayot St. Peter the
custom prevailed into the twentieth century of tolling the bell at
3 p.m., the hour of Christ's death, thirty-three times for the years
of his age.[1] Hot cross buns are still baked, but we have forgotten
their purpose: they had curative properties, and all over the
country, from Sussex to Durham, they were preserved as remedies
for sickness in cattle or men, for luck, as a preservative against
shipwreck etc., nor did they ever become mouldy. Cramp rings
were hallowed, made from the handles or rings of coffins – one sees
sympathetic magic at work; this was one of the sacred capacities
of the monarch, which was exercised up to that very sacred person,
Charles II. They were good for curing fits, as the touch of the
sovereign could cure the King's Evil – Dr. Johnson was touched
for it, as a boy, by Queen Anne. It does not seem to have done him

any good. Those common-sense persons, the Hanoverians, did not
chance their arm or risk their aura so far. Good Friday was a
favourite day for witches' conferences or 'sabbaths'. Miners would
not go down the mines on Good Friday or Christmas Day; this
occasioned some surprise in Jeffersonian America, when Cornish
miners carried their old customs over there.

On Good Friday the Easter Sepulchre had formerly been set
up, and there was watching and praying by it day and night till
Easter morn. With the Reformation this fell into desuetude; now
it is all back again in many Anglican churches. A number of stone
Easter Sepulchres remain *in situ*; the Paschal candle, often of
considerable size and expense, was discontinued in Elizabeth's
reign: also now back again. Easter, like Whitsun, was a time for
mystery plays and church-ales, while in some places feasting in the
churches went on up to Laud's time. Many people got up at dawn
to see the sun dance for joy at our Saviour's birth – quite unaware,
of course, that they were taking part in something far more ancient
and, unbeknownst to themselves, in sun-worship. In the next
century Suckling could still write of a pretty girl:

> And, O, she dances such a way,
> No sun upon an Easter day
> Were half so fine a sight.

The observance of 1 April as All Fools' day, which was so
appropriately regular in the Cornwall of my youth, does not seem
to go back to the Elizabethan age. On St. George's day, 23 April,
it was proper to wear blue, St. George's colour;[7] though we are
now instructed on the highest authority that he never existed,
that is no bar to popular observances in his honour. Upon Low
Sunday, the first after Easter, then more usually called Little
Easter Sunday, there was an interesting ceremony at Lostwithiel.
'Upon Little Easter Sunday the freeholders of the town and manor
. . . did there assemble: amongst whom one, as it fell to his lot by
turn, bravely apparelled, gallantly mounted, with a crown on his
head, a sceptre in his hand, a sword borne before him and dutifully
attended by all the rest also on horseback, rode through the
principal street to the church. There the curate in his best beseen
[apparel] solemnly received him at the churchyard stile and
conducted him to hear divine service. After which he repaired
with the same pomp to a house fore-provided . . . made a feast to
his attendants, kept the table's end himself [i.e. alone] and was
served with kneeling, assay [tasting] and all other rites due to the

estate of a prince.'[8] Carew says that the ceremony went back time out of mind; to us it is of interest as showing how deep a hold the idea of kingship had in earlier societies. In other counties, Gloucester for instance, this was the day for electing a mock-mayor with suitable ceremonies.

A fortnight after Easter came Hock-tide, the origin of which is obscure; it was a time for collecting money for repairs to the church, the universal symbol of the unity of the communal life. There were sports and wrestling – the Elizabethan phrases, 'a Cornish hug', 'a Cornish fall', show how much wrestling was associated with Cornishmen in the popular mind. Laneham tells us that Coventry performed an annual play on Hock Tuesday. Ascension day, or in some places Whitsun, was the time for beating the parish bounds. This was important, not only for customary but also for legal reasons, for delimitation of property, manorial rights, tithes; and we see again the earlier idea of beating into the heads of the younger generation the knowledge of boundaries to be handed on to the next. The custom was quite general, and has survived in some places. It still continues at St. Mary's in the centre of Oxford, where the parish boundaries run through All Souls college. Still on Ascension day the vicar, curates, church-wardens, parishioners and choirboys proceed through the quadrangles, the elders with wands in hand, though no-one is beaten. Instead, there is scrabbling for pennies on the lawn, and a large breakfast in Hall.

Ascension-tide at Oxford was marked by strife in 1598 and the ill-feeling between Town and Gown which was always easy to arouse and, in the Middle Ages, had often led to bloodshed. We hear first the University's account of the matter, sent up by the Vice-Chancellor and Heads of Houses, to Essex and Buckhurst. 'The inhabitants assembled on the two Sundays before Ascension day, and on that day, with drum and shot and other weapons and men attired in women's apparel, brought into the town a woman bedecked with garlands and flowers, named by them the Queen of May. They also had morris dances and other disordered and unseemly sports, and intended the next Sunday to continue the same abuses.'[9] The University authorities attempted to interfere with the good citizens and arrest some of them. They were met with some volleys of shot and others of bad language; the Vice-Chancellor protested to the mayor and got 'a frivolous and dilatory answer.' When we reflect that among the signatories were such elect spirits as Henry Robinson, John Case, and the

Puritanical John Reynolds, we can appreciate their ire. The town
authorities had a different account of the affair – which goes to
show how difficult it is to establish exact truth as between humans.[10]
But Mayday ceremonies still continue at Oxford, with carols
saluting the dawn on the top of Magdalen tower and morris-
dancing in the streets – and who remembers John Reynolds? The
sour Long Parliament officially abolished Mayday rejoicings in
1644, but it can never have extinguished them; and Charles II
came back in Maytime 1660.

Mayday and the eve of Mayday was a time of rejoicing and
excitement everywhere, as innumerable evidences remind us. At
Minehead the hobby-horse ceremony continued up to the
threshold of this century.[11] It still goes on at Padstow, in greater
force than ever, and in unbroken continuity. So too with Helston
Furry day on 8 May, with dancing in the streets and in and out oi
people's houses decorated for the occasion with greenery. Many
of the May-time songs have come down to us, some of them
conveying the old usages. 'It's dabbling in the dew makes the
milkmaids fair' refers to the custom of girls going out early on May
morning to wash their faces in the dew – but that rite of Spring
meant more than they knew.

Whitsun, as we have seen, was the principal time for church-
ales, plays and pastorals; in some places – Chester for example –
where the plays had been performed at the feast of Corpus Christi,
at its ending with the abolition of transubstantiation, they were
transferred to Whitsun. The proceeds, with offerings like traditional smoke-farthings, i.e. from houses with a chimney, went to
church or parish purposes. At Minchinhampton a hostile memory
recorded, in 1575: 'expended at the bishop's visitation to the
sumner for Peter-pence or smoke-farthings, sometime due to the
Anti-Christ of Rome, 10d.'[12] (So much for what St. Pius V
achieved by excommunicating and 'deposing' the Queen five
years before.) At Mere, where smoke-farthings were also rendered,
we read in the church-wardens' accounts for 1568: 'John Watts,
the son of Thomas Watts, is appointed to be Cuckoo King this
next year, because he was Prince last year; and Thomas Barnard
the younger is elected Prince for this next year.' In these societies
very much under rule, there is felt the necessity to parody their
serious, grand events, and provision is made for it: a kind of
safety-valve.

Midsummer eve saw the lighting of fires all over the country:
bonfires, or bone-fires, since they originally consumed bones.

These relics of fire-worship are, of course, immensely older than Christianity and continued in fullest force in Celtic areas like Ireland, where women still leap the fire, or in Cornwall where the fires are at least still lit. In many parts it was the custom to watch all night in the church-porch, where the spirits of the neighbours were seen to enter at midnight: those who came out again would marry in the year, those who remained within would die. Divination was practised at several proper seasons – Easter, among others – for maids to discover, by the curdling of egg-yolk in water etc., whom they would marry or at least their lovers. At Midsummer the proper means of divination was by the sowing of hempseed. I still remember the charm used in Cornwall:

> Hempseed I sow,
> Hempseed I mow:
> Let him that is my true love
> Come after me and hoe.

One recognises the sexual invitation.

On St. Peter's day shortly after, 28 June, at Polperro and Mevagissey there was a procession down to the harbour, for St. Peter was a patron of fishermen. At Mevagissey in my time this still continued – but there was no folk-memory that in earlier days the image of the patron-saint was carried down to the sea to bless the waters and increase the fish. And so to harvest, the conclusion of which was celebrated with similar customs all over the country, under different names: Harvest Home, Harvest Queen or Corn Baby, Hockey Cart or Crying the Neck, as it was usually known in all the West of England. Thence to Michaelmas with its Michaelmas goose that had fattened on the stubbles, feasting the neighbours and paying rents and dues. For these last purposes we still retain Michaelmas and Ladyday: nothing more conservative than calendar customs. Lastly, again, to the remembrance of the departed with All Saints and All Souls, 1 November and 2 November. For this, in addition to all the bell-ringing and tolling, special soul-cakes were baked – no doubt originally for the dead. In Lancashire and Cheshire where the custom of 'souling' still lingers on, the cakes are given to the children who come round singing; in Cheshire the traditional Soul-caking Play has been revived.

In addition to all this, there were the Saints' days with their particular parish feasts, fun and games. Trinity Sunday was Feast Sunday in my parish at St. Austell, and the subsequent days were given up to the fair, sports and so on. No doubt Trinity was chosen by the Church in the Middle Ages to be near to the feast of the original Celtic saint, unrecognised in the Roman calendar, so as to disturb as little as possible the age-long custom. The medieval Church was much kinder to folklore and popular custom, the life of the unconscious and of the imagination. The Protestant Reformation tried to restrict and direct it, but was only partially successful: it is likely to survive Protestantism.

We see what a sufficient framework for customary life the calendar provided; in addition there was the far-ranging equipment of folklore in general and its particular contexts and applications. We can only illustrate its richness selectively; and, first, for the essential events of the family, birth, marriage, death. Naturally an immense amount of traditional lore coagulated around these. It was the regular thing to baptize infants within a few days of birth; this was rationalised as necessary to prevent the infant soul from going to Hell. Even such an intelligent man as Archbishop Whitgift thought that this nonsense was probably true.[13] But the real explanation lies in folk-belief: 'a baby before baptism and a mother before churching were in constant peril from evil spirits, witches and fairies, and every precaution had to be taken to protect them, both at the time, and before and afterwards.'[14] It is extraordinary to think that the churching of women, i.e. their purification after child-birth – as if having children, which may well be regarded as an inconvenience, were in itself sinful – still continues in various parts and has a service provided for it in the Book of Common Prayer. But human idiocy is endless and irremediable – the real original sin.

The omens were carefully watched for future prospects of good and evil; for exact prognostications the science of astrology needed to know the precise hour and minute of birth. Then a useful forecast could be made. It was foretold of William Herbert, third Earl of Pembroke, that he would die at fifty: he died two days after his fiftieth birthday.[15] In many parts it is still the proper thing to carry the baby upstairs before the mother comes down, for mother and child to come downstairs first on a Sunday, and for the mother to be churched on that day, her first time of going abroad. Around the coasts it was thought that birth took place as the tide came in, and life ebbed with the tide – one sees the sympathetic magic in it, the power of analogy in primitive minds, the inability to think straight, except, of course, in relation to work or tools, handicraft or technique (to which most people's 'thinking' is confined). In the

Severn country until recently the belief lingered on that the father
suffered birth-pangs as well as the mother; in a Yorkshire village
when the father of an illegitimate child could not be traced, they
searched the village for a man ill in bed: he was the father.[16] One
might be in darkest Africa. A child born with a caul cannot be
drowned; so for centuries, up to the last war but one, sailors have
been willing to pay good money for cauls. The seventh child of a
seventh child has second sight, and other gifts. As recently as the
1950's a farming couple at Wadebridge in Cornwall, not noticeably
below average intelligence, were cosened of hundreds of pounds
by a gipsy claiming to be a seventh child of a seventh child, who
'placed the money on the planets' on their behalf.

Courtship, copulation and marriage were similarly embedded
in magical beliefs and rites, many of which remain in force – or in
inverted commas, in the realm of 'as if'. There were many forms of
divination for a girl to discover her future husband, or at least
lover: from Cornwall I recall

> I cross my shoes in the letter of T
> Hoping my true love to see . . .

A charm to ensure love was to obtain some of the beloved object's
hair to wear in ring or bracelet. One appreciates how persuasive
and convincing Simon Forman's arts were in this context, the
noble Howard women who sought to procure the loves of Southampton and Somerset. A girl should not stride over a broom-
handle before marriage, though she might leap over it after the
ceremony – if not with impunity, at least with legitimate consequences. Once having caught her man, a woman should never put
off her wedding-ring – one remembers that the medieval Church
blessed the ring at the ceremony. Even after the Reformation the
Church continued to impose close seasons for marriage, though I
do not know the anthropological significance of this. Carrying the
bride over the threshold was a relic of marriage by capture; tying
an old shoe to the carriage perhaps perpetuates the notion of
marriage by purchase; the throwing of rice, or of cake at the
bride's return from church in earlier days in Yorkshire, is a
fertility charm. There was a belief that a man was not liable for
his woman's debts if he married her in nothing but her smock or
shift.

Evidences of some of these usages remain in the church registers.
At Much Wenlock, 4 August 1547, 'here was wedded early in the
morning Thomas Munslow, smith, and Alice Nycols, which wed-

ded to him in her smock and bareheaded.'[17] At Cottenham in Cambridgeshire the parson in 1572 reminded himself of the prohibited seasons thus:

> Conjugium Adventus prohibet, Hilarius relaxat,
> Septuagena vetat, sed Paschae octava remittit,
> Rogamen vetitat, concedit Trina potestas.[18]

At St. Martin's, Leicester, in 1576 the marriage of a deaf-and-dumb man necessitated the approbation of the bishop and his commissary for a special ceremony. The mayor and his brethren attended and the whole parish witnessed that 'the said Thomas [Tilsey], for the expressing of his mind instead of words, of his own accord used these signs. First, he embraced her [Ursula Russell] with his arms and took her by the hand, put a ring upon her finger, laid his hand upon his heart and then upon her heart, and held up his hands towards heaven. And to show his continuance to dwell with her to his life's end, he did it by closing of his eyes with his hands and digging out of the earth with his foot, and pulling as though he would ring a bell, with divers other signs.'[19]

Evidences remain from every county as to the prevalence of child-marriage, not infrequently of infants carried in arms to be married for property considerations, to assure one or other a livelihood. The custom was that, if later the marriage was consummated, it held good; if not consummated and the children grew up to refuse each other, then divorce was possible on ground of nullity. It is through these cases that we derive an intimate insight into the matter. Let us turn to the diocese of Chester, for which a selection of such cases has been published. Humphrey Winstanley was the ward of the Catholic Sir Thomas Gerard, who forced the boy, when under twelve, to marry Alice Worsley, a girl of seventeen.[20] They were married in 1558–9 at a chapel of Sir Thomas's called the Brynn in Winwick, by a chantry priest; but the boy would never give his consent by word or deed, or live with the girl. John Southworth, the later recusant, had married the boy's aunt, and after her death took him for bedfellow when he returned from school. William Pole was married at eleven to Elizabeth Tilston aged eight, by special licence 'in a morning about cock's crowing, with torchlight and candle-light, in the parish church of Marbury' with only one witness beside the curate. John Bridge, aged eleven, was married to Elizabeth Ramsbotham aged thirteen, as the result of a bargain between his grandfather and her father, who paid over a sum of money to buy them a piece of land. After the marriage the boy 'would eat no meat at supper; and when it was bedtime the said John did weep to go home with his father . . . Yet nevertheless, by his father's entreatment and by the persuasion of the priest, the said John did come to bed far in the night; and there lay still till in the morning, in such sort as the deponent [his wife] might take unkindness with him; for he lay with his back toward her all night. And neither then nor any time else had carnal dole with her, nor never after came in her company, more than he had never known her.'

In a chamber of Widford Hall a base daughter of the owner, Mr. Dampart (Davenport?), then a child under eight, was married to John Andrew, aged ten, whose father wanted to unite his half of a holding on the estate with the other half that the squire was leaving to his daughter. A good idea – but 'at the time of the marriage they knew not what they did, or else this respondent [the bridegroom] would never have had her . . . The first night they were married they lay both in one bed, but two of her sisters lay between him and her.'[21] Neither of them could fancy each other, then or after. John Somerford, aged three, and Jane Brereton, aged two, were carried to their wedding in their friends' arms, who spoke the words for them; one witness, a gentleman, said it was the youngest marriage that ever he was at; the bride could hardly yet speak. We find several of these marriages, for property reasons, among the Lancashire gentry, Southworths, Duttons, Osbaldistons. James Ballard, aged about ten, was married to Anne, who was a little older, in the parish church of Colne one Christmas night, 'about ten of the clock, without the consent of any of his friends, by one Sir Roger Blakey, then curate of Colne. The morning after, the boy told his uncle that Anne 'had enticed him with two apples to go with her to Colne and to marry her'; that same morning, 'he repented the said marriage when he perceived what he had done; and ever sithence hath dissented from the same and never remained in her company for any space.' The curate was punished by the Archbishop of York for his unseemly conduct, but we see what Archbishops had to put up with.

Death and burial had their rites and customs, some of which have survived, though it was in this region that the Reformation dealt its heaviest blow to the customary life. By the end of the medieval period a vast non-productive expenditure had been built up on hundreds of chantries and thousands of masses for the souls of the dead, trentals and quintals and hundreds of masses for such a soul as Henry VIII – all sheer waste. The Dissolution of the Chantries was an effective step in the more economic re-deployment of so much wealth, and the increased energies of the Elizabethan age testified to the benefits. But it was more difficult to extirpate the natural human concern for the departed. The Protestant denial of the doctrine of purgatory was a blow to the age-long, primitive belief that departed spirits, wherever they were, could be helped or profited. The folklore belief could not be entirely eliminated, and in remoter parts of the country, especially in the North Country, prayers for the dead long continued. In North Wales, too, at Beaumaris in 1570 similar rites accompanied Lewis Roberts' interment, 'out of mere ignorance and in compliance with a foolish custom', as the bishop of Bangor explained to the Council: the parties had all been made to do penance.[22]

All kinds of omens accompanied death, and many families retain their occult knowledge of them. Country people in my youth still adhered to the custom of touching a corpse, as I remember from experience: the notion was that it was a discourtesy, and unlucky, to omit to do so. Funerals were for all classes, except the poor, an occasion for ceremony, as we can see from Machyn's Diary, and among the nobility for immense extravagance. Even for the middle and yeoman classes the funeral feasts, or 'baked meats' as we still have the phrase, were a considerable item. So, too, were the payments for tolling and knelling. In the Elizabethan age the bell was tolled at a person's passing, the 'passing bell'; there was also the funeral knell. Altogether, an Elizabethan city was clamorous with the ringing of bells of all kinds – one may get some idea of it still from living in the centre of Oxford in term-time. Shakespeare has frequent references to bells – understandably, since they were a constant accompaniment of contemporary life. He several times speaks of the passing bell as 'sullen': it was usually the heaviest tenor-bell that was thus rung:

> No longer mourn for me when I am dead
> Than you shall hear the surly sullen bell
> Give warning to the world that I am fled
> From this vile world with vilest worms to dwell.

Shakespeare's youngest brother, Edmund, the actor, was buried in St. Saviour's, Southwark, on the last day of icy December 1607, 'with a forenoon knell of the great bell.'[23]

There were regular and long-standing customs in the ringing, a kind of language, to tell people who were passing. We know the custom in a good many Huntingdonshire parishes. At Abbotsleigh for an hour after death on the tenor for a man, on the fourth for a woman, the first for a child; prior to this the bells were rung downwards three times for a man, twice for a woman, once for a child.[24] Almost every parish followed its own custom in the matter. Other counties, other customs: often nine strokes for a man, six for a woman, followed by the number of the dead person's age. But no-one realises that the original purpose of the death-knell was to protect the passing soul from the assault of demons. How full those lives were, with one thing and another! There were also bells for waking up the parish in the morning and sending it to bed at night, to send the harvesters out into the fields and bring them home in the evening. In many parishes the Gleaning Bell, usually the lightest, was rung during harvest at seven in the morning and six in the evening. The Pancake Bell was rung on Shrove Tuesday, usually at noon. In Huntingdonshire Priest Bells remained at a number of places, that at Brampton still known in the Victorian age as 'the old Roman Catholic priest's bell.'[25] Presumably these were sanctus bells, rung at the Elevation in the Mass; one such still remained in its cote, unused, into the nineteenth century at Great Staughton. For the most part the little sanctus bells were sold: we can see their empty bell-cotes on many churches. All parish accounts show that care of the bells, ringing, replacing, adding to them were among the heaviest charges upon their communities, which became increasingly proud of them with the development of change-ringing, the lovely peals of bells that became a unique characteristic of the Church of England – now becoming stilled over the country.

The turning point in the art of bell-ringing came around 1600 with the invention of the whole wheel, which enabled the bells to be swung right round and yield their maximum sound.[26] Medieval bells were taller and heavier, but far fewer, and must have jangled like continental bells. Great Tom at Christ Church, Oxford, is a famous specimen: it came from Osney abbey and was already well known in the Elizabethan age. When the Protestant Jewel was engaged in his slanging match with the Catholic Harding (they had been at school at Barnstaple together), Jewel reminded Harding that in the Edwardian time 'ye wished your voice had been equal with the great bell of Osney, that ye might ring, as ye then said, in the dull ears of the deaf Papists.'[27]

There was in consequence much activity in bell-founding, a

considerable enlargement of the industry. There were large foundries in London, Nottingham, Leicester, Worcester, to take only that stretch across the country; many smaller founders working elsewhere. In Warwickshire the Elizabethan bells came chiefly from Leicester, where the Newcombe family was at work from 1562 to 1616, along with the Wattses who were active from 1587 to 1615.[28] Several members of these families became mayors of Leicester. A smaller foundry was operating at Buckingham under the Appowells, 1550–78; and some Warwickshire bells came from Gloucestershire. The well-known dynasty of Purdues at Bristol began at Penselwood in 1584. It is pleasant to come upon the tracks of people we know from the Throckmorton Diary in the bells they gave to their churches. In the autumn of 1593 Arthur Throckmorton stayed with his Underhill cousins at pretty Ettington, on the road into Stratford-upon-Avon from the south. Two years later George and Humphrey Underhill gave each a bell, from the Leicester foundry, to their church.[29] In 1591 Edward Newcombe and Francis Watts cast the bell for the Gild Chapel at Stratford, which Shakespeare heard so often from just across the road at New Place, after he purchased it from another of the Underhills in 1597.

Henry Topsel was a small individual bell-founder, who started at Beccles in Suffolk and moved to West Tarring in Sussex, nearer the supply of Wealden iron, where his son carried on for another thirty years.[30] Topsel made a bell for Hedenham in Norfolk in 1585; we have all the expenses about the bell he made for Cratfield in Suffolk, for its hanging, making a baldrick (or collar) for it, a bell-stock, irons, rope and for 'bringing the bell home.' This last was the occasion for a feast in many a parish. The new voice of the age is expressed in the inscriptions on the bells. Medieval bells have invocations of the Virgin and the Saints – touching in their faith – or, no less revealing, such inscriptions as 'Voce mea viva depello cuncta nociva', in the belief that the voice of the bell would expel evil spirits. Elizabethan inscriptions are sententious and admonitory, 'Come, come and pray', or 'Praise God only', or 'Fear God and Obey the Queen'; sometimes purely secular, from 1595, 'Embrace Trew Museck'.[31]

Folk-beliefs regarding wells and waters go back to a still more ancient antiquity. The Reformation dealt a blow at the use of holy water, though its purpose is recalled in the phrase 'to hate as the devil hates holy water'.[32] The church accounts show the holy water buckets being sold for more useful objects, the stone stoups falling into disuse – to be revived in a good many places in this century. Similarly with holy wells: Cornwall, like Brittany, had many more than most places and in our time they are being restored – on an antiquarian basis, though people still cast their wishes into them. Carew remembered when some wells were wellknown for their healing properties: St. Nun's at Altarnun, for example. 'In our forefathers' days, when devotion as much exceeded knowledge as knowledge now cometh short of devotion, there were many bowsening places for curing of madmen.'[33] He describes the treatment, which was to knock the person backward into the pool, toss him up and down in the water, then take him to church for exorcism. 'Upon which handling, if his right wits returned St. Nun had the thanks. But if there appeared small amendment, he was bowsened again and again, while there remained in him any hope of life, for recovery.'

Wells did not altogether lose their healing properties at the Reformation. In 1600 a new-found well in Delamere Forest in Cheshire became suddenly famous for its cures.[34] Many people visited it, some to drink the water, some to wash in it. It cured ague – of which John Greenway and his three sons were all rid – sore eyes, blindness, rupture, gout, 'aches and griefs in the joints', lameness, wild-fire (erysipelas) and deafness. On 2 August 1600 William Johnson came to the spring on crutches and walked home unaided, leaving his crutches on the holly-tree – note that it was a holly-tree – as a thank-offering for his cure. Many others also benefited: no need to go to Lourdes. Perhaps the spring had some useful brine in it, like the spring at Nantwich. This last was blessed on Ascension day, 'the Old Biot was decorated with flowers, ribbons and green boughs', while the gathered people sang hymns of thanksgiving.

Healing properties attached to the prehistoric stones which are a feature of the more primitive parts of the country. In Cornwall rickety children were passed through the hole of the Men-an-tol (stone of the hole). But passing a sick child through a split-ash tree was quite widespread, and still obtained into the twentieth century.[35] It may be with the idea of curing the woman that the cucking-stool was so widely used in Elizabethan times for scolds or shrews or scandal-mongers. Many parishes, but particularly towns, provided themselves with one, usually with wheels to cart the woman about. At Oxford the cucking-stool was heavily repaired in 1556, but in 1560 a new one was made.[36] In 1579 another was necessary: the Council ordered that it 'be made upon wheels that it may be drawn from place to place, to punish such women as shall undecently abuse any person of this city by words.' In Scotland the 'brank' had been for some time in use, by which such women were clamped and gagged; it might be a useful trophy in the bitchy literary life of London today.

All the world danced, at Court, in town and country. They always had: the intensity of medieval life is, *pace* Huizinga, its prime characteristic. But there was an increase in its conscious cult, with many new dances coming in from abroad, and even dancing schools opened in London, which much annoyed the Puritans. 'The horrible vice of pestiferous dancing,' said Stubbes, 'is an introduction to whoredom, a preparative to wantonness, a provocative to uncleanness and an introit to all kinds of lewdness.'[37] Calvin considered dancing 'the chief mischief of all mischiefs . . . there be such unchaste gestures in it as are nothing else but enticements to whoredom.' *Verb. sap.* Stubbes's paragraph headings will be sufficient to indicate his attitude. 'Clipping, kissing, groping, etc., hurts the body and lames the mind . . . The Israelites' dancing: not men with women . . . Our cheek-by-cheek dancing is beastly to behold . . . It sprang from the teats of the Devil's breast . . . Each sex should dance by itself.' No notion that this might lead to worse, from his point of view: would he prefer sailors dancing together, or exclusive men's bars on Third Avenue? In justice we must put both sides to the Elizabethan debate on such matters.

The dances of the time fall into two categories, though there was some interchange between them: Court and folk dances. Of the latter the best known is morris dancing, presumably of a Spanish-Moorish origin, which never completely died out in the Cotswolds and has had a widespread revival from there in our time. In *2 Henry VI* York describes Jack Cade as capering

> upright like a wild Morisco,
> Shaking the bloody darts as he his bells.

On the title page of Will Kemp's *Nine Days Wonder*, when he danced his way from London to Norwich in 1599, we see him capering in a morris dance, the bells jangling on his legs, his man playing tabor and drum beside him. This was a famous exploit in its time, receiving the kind of popular *reclame* that the newspapers accord to comparable exhibitions today. But Kemp was a gifted actor, who played the comic parts in Shakespeare's middle comedies, and himself invented jigs and dance-entertainments. Parish accounts show plenty of morris dancing about the country.

We have already noticed the special dancing that went with the Hobby Horse at Minehead and Padstow, the Furry Dance at Helston. At Abbots Bromley in Staffordshire a very ancient ritual dance has survived.[38] It was performed on Wakes Monday in September and seems to enact the killing of the reindeer. The reindeer horns, with sixteenth-century carving on them, are stored in the church-tower, but they are the property of the community not of the vicar. Early in the morning the dancers receive the priest's blessing and tour the outlying farms; afternoon and evening they dance for the village, a dance grave and impersonal, a dedicated ritual. They are twelve, going out from the church, six with antlers, a man dressed as a woman, Maid Marian, a hobby horse, a jester, two boys – one with bow and arrow, another with triangle beating time. First they dance in a circle, then turn inwards in a loop as for the kill. In the second figure they face each other in sets of three raising the antlers, appearing to lock, meeting and retiring as in fight. In the Victorian age only the village wheelwright could play the traditional tune; in our time it was said of the oldest dancer in this ancient rite, 'he worships the Horn Dance, if he worships nothing else.'

The simplest forms of country dances were 'rounds', the dancers forming a circle; we still dance such as Sellinger's, i.e. St. Leger's, Round. Many more dances were coming in from abroad: hays, from their name, must have a French origin; the 'branle', or brawl, was similarly French. The galliard, pavan, coranto and volta came from Italy. In *Twelfth Night* Sir Toby Belch asks Sir Andrew Aguecheek, 'Why, dost not thou go to church in a galliard, and come home in a coranto?' In *A Midsummer Night's Dream* we hear of a Bergamask dance: its name bespeaks its origin. The dump was a slow and mournful dance, with a tapping of the foot, and a sliding step: it must have been obsessive. Beautiful music was written for all these dances by the composers: we still listen to the Earl of Salisbury's or the Lady Monteagle's Pavan, the Earl of Essex's or Captain Piper's Galliard, the Earl of Oxford's March, Monsieur's (i.e. the Duke of Anjou's) Alman, or the Gipsies' Round. Weelkes and Morley wrote songs based on morris dances.

Dancing inspired not only music but also literature; the ballad was closely wedded to the dance, broadsides were sung, and Sir

John Davies wrote a fine philosophical poem on dancing, *Orchestra*. He dedicated it to Richard Martin, whom he had cudgelled over the head in Middle Temple hall years before when they were both young:

> To whom shall I this dancing poem send,
> This sudden, rash, half-capriole of my wit?
> To you, first mover and sole cause of it,
> Mine own self's better half, my dearest friend.

The capriole – the word caper is a shortened form of it – refers to its leaping movement like a goat, with two feet together, and evidently came like so many good things from Italy. Davies describes the different dances of the time, but his approach is philosophical.

> Dancing, bright Lady, then began to be
> When the first seeds whereof the world did spring,
> The fire, air, earth and water, did agree
> By Love's persuasion – Nature's mighty king –
> To leave their first disordered combating,
>   And in a dance such measure to observe
>   As all the world their motion should preserve.
>
> Since when they still are carried in a round
> And, changing, come one in another's place;
> Yet do they neither mingle nor confound
> But everyone doth keep the bounded space
> Wherein the dance doth bid it turn or trace:
>   This wondrous miracle did Love devise,
>   For dancing is love's proper exercise.

In this we see that Davies the poet is at one with Stubbes and Calvin, that 'enemy of the human race', as he has been shortly called.[39]

Many of our ballads, and some even of our nursery rhymes go back to that time.[40] In *Bartholomew Fair* Squire Cokes recalls 'the ballads over the nursery chimney at home of my own pasting up.' Earliest of all that survive are children's counting-out formulas, unrhymed but rhythmical, along with some of the riddles. Counting out scores – eena, meena, mina, mo – are connected with the Celtic numerals: shepherds in the mountains of Cumberland counted their sheep thus up into the nineteenth century. (A friend reminds me that the youth of the parish of Barton in the Lake

District were the last to shoot with cross-bows – up to 1914.)
Children, by nature conservative, catch the memories of the
oldest members of their families: I remember the passionate
interest I had as a child to hear about the 'old days' in the village,
the memories of my grandparents' generation, nothing that my
parents had to say held such an intense interest. In *The Merry
Wives of Windsor* Master Slender lends Alice Shortcake a book of
riddles – almost certainly that mentioned by Laneham in the
Kenilworth entertainment of 1575: of these riddles seven are still
known to the children. Of infant amusements, the game of
Handy Dandy, in which a small object is juggled from hand to
hand, is referred to by Skelton, Shakespeare, Florio, Robert
Browne; and Chapman quotes in 1598, 'handy, dandy, prickly
pandy: which hand will you have?' Many of these games and
rhymes have their equivalents all over Europe, and plenty survive
in Britain, sometimes in full, sometimes in fossil form.

'Hush-a-bye, baby, on the tree top', probably goes back to the
sixteenth century – Elizabethans said 'babby'. Our nursery
rhyme, 'The frog he would a-wooing go', goes back at least to a
ballad of 1580, 'A most strange wedding of the frog and the
mouse.' *Deuteromelia* of 1609 has 'Three Blind Mice'; and out of
Ravenscroft's collections of songs, we see the beginnings of six still
enjoyed by children of our century. It is often thought that 'Ride
a cock horse' may refer to Queen Elizabeth, with 'rings on her
fingers and bells on her toes', and the white horse could be the
white horse she rode at Tilbury at Armada-time, which made an
undying impression on the popular imagination. We have an
indication of that still in the number of beds she is supposed to
have slept in all over the country. 'Who killed Cock Robin?' goes
back earlier, into the Middle Ages. While the significance of 'Old
King Cole', who meant something special to Elizabethan dramatists, is lost. Can it have been some racial memory of the epony-
mous founder of Colchester, oldest of Roman cities in Britain?

Characters like Mother Hubbard, Tom Thumb, Jack Sprat,
and little Tommy Tucker who sings for his supper, were already
well known – but it is interesting to watch transmutations into art.
In 1580 the organist of Winchester cathedral, John Lant, collected

Jack boy, ho boy news,
The cat is in the well:
Let us ring now for her knell,
Ding-dong, ding-dong bell.

This became a canon later published in *Pammelia*; but the traditional burden appears as the burden of songs in *The Tempest* and
The Merchant of Venice:

> Thirty days hath September,
> April, June and November –

our way of remembering it is the same as Shakespeare's: it is cited
by several Elizabethan writers. Little Tommy Muffet was indeed
the worthy Dr. Thomas Muffet, the Elizabethan entomologist
whom we shall come to in time: he wrote the first English book on
spiders. Little Jack Horner certainly picked out a plum when at
the Dissolution he picked out one of the best manors of Glastonbury abbey in Mells: his descendants still live there, now Catholics
again.

'Love I sit, Love I stand' – we still have examples of the type
of riddle beloved in the sixteenth century, the simple entertainments of their winter firesides without TV. 'Ladybird, ladybird' –
to kill one is still considered unlucky. The Man in the Moon had a
lantern and a bush of thorns, as in *A Midsummer Night's Dream*: he
had been banished for strewing the church path with thorns to
prevent people from coming to church. In the Cornish version of
'See-saw, Margery Daw' a pisky came and carried her away. This
is one of the very few instances of the fairies being mentioned in a
nursery rhyme; it was dangerous: they were always liable to come
and carry children away.

The belief that the piskies – pixies – lead men astray, make
them lose themselves, still exists in Cornwall: the phrase is to be
'pisky-led'. A whole lore of its own belonged to mining: the mines
were inhabited by tommy knockers, who gave useful warnings of
calamities, and had to be propitiated or at least regarded. That
the unconscious is still creatively at work in our mechanical world
may be seen from the lore about 'gremlins' in the R.A.F. Carew
cites cases of mineral veins discovered as the result of dreams –
obviously the unconscious at work; and then adds sagely, 'but I will
not bind any man's credit, though that of the authors' have herein
swayed mine. And yet he that will afford his ear to astrologers and
natural philosophers shall have it filled with many discourses of
the constellation of the heavens, and the constitution of men's
bodies, fitting to this purpose.'[41] A considerable lore grew up
about names and the taboos upon them. Carew tells us that when
fishing boats put out, see that 'you talk not of hares or such uncouth
things, for that proves as ominous to the fisherman as the beginning

a voyage on the day when Childermas [Innocents' day] fell doth to the mariner.' But, then, there was another lore about the hare, most ominous of animals. Witches turned themselves into hares; it was very unlucky for a pregnant woman to catch sight of a hare: hence hare-lip in her child.

Belief in fairies was much more widespread then than now; ghosts, and even witches, seem to possess stronger survival value. The essential thing about fairies is that they were the Little People, who lived in the mounds to be seen in many parts, and danced within the fairy rings we see marked in the fields. They were thought to be not malevolent, unless provoked or improperly treated; they could be beneficent if propitiated; for the rest, apt to be petulant, childish, a-moral, not burdened with human responsibilities. Here once more is the mirror-world of wish-fulfilment, a necessary safety-valve for restrictive societies. Fairies were undependable, revengeful if slighted, liable to steal children away, and so it was as well to prevent them from entering the house by nailing an iron horse-shoe to the door, as the Pennsylvanian Dutch farmers today mark their great barns with *hexen-symbolen* to keep witches out.

A Midsummer Night's Dream provides a perfect handbook to Elizabethan fairy-lore: it is the stuff out of which the play is made – the first work to create the long tradition in this *genre* in our literature, up to *Puck of Pook's Hill* and beyond. With Shakespeare the subject-matter is indigenous: as a countryman he drew it direct from the life of the countryside, not from books, as did the classically-minded Lyly. Puck is a traditional figure in country lore:

> you are that shrewd knavish sprite
> Called Robin Goodfellow. Are not you he
> That frights the maidens of the villagery,
> Skim milk, and sometimes labour in the quern,
> And bootless make the breathless housewife churn,
> And sometimes make the drink to bear no barm,
> Mislead night-wanderers, laughing at their harm?
> Those that Hobgoblin call you, and sweet Puck,
> You do their work, and they shall have good luck.

The whole play is full of fairy-lore; it looks as if Shakespeare had some of it left over unused, to put somewhat improbably into the mouth of Mercutio in *Romeo and Juliet*. This is the long description of Queen Mab, full of poetic imagination, that ends up with a return to country beliefs:

> This is that very Mab
> That plats the manes of horses in the night,
> And bakes the elf-locks in foul sluttish hairs
> Which, once untangled, much misfortune bodes.

The fairy-lore of the age was given perfect expression, when it was all over, in an enchanting poem, Drayton's *Nimphidia* – not the less affecting for its echoes from those two plays by his fellow-Warwickshireman.[42] Drayton's starting point is the liking people have for fairy-stories:

> Another sort there be that will
> Be talking of the fairies still,
> Nor never can they have their fill,
>   As they were wedded to them:
> No tales of them their thirst can slake
> So much delight therein they take,
> And some strange thing they fain would make,
>   Knew they the way to do them.

As with Shakespeare, the poem is a delicate fusion of the poet's imagination with familiar country lore:

> Hence shadows, seeming idle shapes
> Of little frisking elves and apes,
> To earth do make their wanton scapes
>   As hope of pastime hastes them:
> Which maids think on the hearth they see,
> When fires well near consumèd be,
> Their dancing hays by two and three,
>   Just as their fancy casts them.

> These make our girls their sluttery rue
> By pinching them both black and blue,
> And put a penny in their shoe
>   The house for cleanly sweeping;
> And in their courses make that round
> In meadows and in marshes found
> Of them so called the fairy ground,
>   Of which they have the keeping.

Hamlet is no less sufficient a guide to Elizabethan lore about ghosts, though the ghost of Caesar in *Julius Caesar* adds further point to our conception, and there are other references to illuminate the dark subject. When ghosts appear the lights turn blue. Ghosts haunt churchyards, perhaps particularly where there is a charnel-house – there was a charnel-house in the churchyard at

Stratford. I have always been charmed by the little page in *Romeo and Juliet*:

> I am almost afraid to stand alone
> Here in the churchyard; yet I will adventure.

Ghosts appear at midnight and must away before cockcrow. They walk the earth, until they are appeased – some, like Hamlet's father, by revenge. Others, unappeased, have to be 'laid' or exorcised; in the North Country it was held that only a Catholic priest could exorcise a ghost – there was a rationale in that. In our time Anglican clergymen have taken to doing it. A favourite method of exorcism is to drive the ghost into some receptacle and seal it up there. A wicked eighteenth-century vicar of Luxulyan, who 'walked', was driven, in the form of a black cock, into a cloam (earthenware) oven.

Did Shakespeare believe in his ghosts? The question has been often debated in regard to *Hamlet*. It is probable that, as a man of his time, he did; we may be certain that his audience did. And they were, naturally enough, of particular interest to Simon Forman.

Hardly anyone disbelieved in the existence of witches, perhaps not even the unfortunate creatures themselves: to do so was in itself atheistical, according to Sir Thomas Browne. The signs and characters of witches were generally agreed upon by society. They were usually, though not always, female and they fell into two main classes. There were white witches, whose works were thought to be beneficent and to whom people resorted for cures or help of various kinds, such as to find lost objects. Then there were those that trafficked with the powers of evil, dealt in ill-wishing people, bringing misfortune upon them or their cattle, caused people to fall ill or die, tormented them by sticking pins into the wax images of those they had a grudge against, or by various acts caused them to waste away. They could control winds and raise storms on land or at sea. Harrison tells us that in the Isle of Man witches 'oftentimes sell winds to the mariners, enclosed under certain knots of thread'; from Hakluyt we learn that Lapland sorcerers could do the same.[43] Caliban's mother was a witch so powerful that she could control the moon – but she was merely a creature of the imagination. People recognised that the familiars of a witch were a cat, sometimes a hare or a toad: all creatures with their own mysterious night-life. Witches flew by night, could transport themselves on a broomstick (the Freudian symbol is obvious), and could change themselves into another shape.

Custom

It is evident that both classes, along with conjurers like Doctor Pinch in *The Comedy of Errors*, or Doctor Dee, Edward Kelley or Simon Forman in real life, were practitioners of magic, dabblers in the marginal life of the conscious shading off into the unconscious. Occult science is not here my subject, merely customary beliefs; but in the twentieth century we can at least recognise an area of experience of which the phenomena are not wholly explicable rationally. There was a much wider use, and even knowledge, of herbs in those days – sometimes one can recognise where a vanished homestead has been by the herbs, or elderberry trees growing near – and no doubt white witches have always used herbal lore to effect cures for cattle and people. We may reasonably go further and allow that a certain instinctual expertise often enabled them to help neurasthenics or paralytics – much as healers of various sorts can sometimes produce results today.

In any case the addiction to all kinds of these practices and their practitioners remains alive. Not only in remote parts of the country but in towns and suburbs cases continue to crop up of people sticking pins hopefully into the images of their enemies; the trade in fortune-telling and love charms is with us still, if psychiatrists and psychologists have tended to oust confessors and witches from favour. To us the correlation between social misfits or the socially disapproved and witchery or sorcery is clear. Anything that does not fit into the conventional categories of society is suspect; by the same token, those who are suspect can see things about human beings that they themselves cannot, and the misfits can both help and injure them. To medievals sodomy was sorcery: in primitive societies it is dangerous to be different. Then, to look at the other side of the medal, those who are different are apt to have their own grudge against society. Those of us who have known the intimate crevices of village life will recall the type of old crone given to 'ill-wishing' neighbours. Among Elizabethan witches there were those who would do others harm if they could: it would be merely an enlargement, to an abnormal extent, of a normal human propensity. Witches were certainly abnormal: so they were feared, made use of, and persecuted. What added to the fear was, as usual, uncertainty: people could not always tell who was a witch and who not.

The barbarous cruelty of the age in tormenting and killing such self-deluded crones is not my subject here. The fact that they often were driven to confess themselves to being witches brings them very close to the phenomena of treason trials in our own

225

enlightened age. A Calvinist Scot on the throne, whose terror of witches was even greater than his dislike of women, lent corroboration to the growing witch-mania which it never received from the civilised and sceptical Queen. The mania reached its disgraceful peak with the deplorable Commonwealth. Its development leads us properly into a consideration of the mentality of the society and time.

CHAPTER IX

MENTALITY AND BELIEF:
WITCHCRAFT AND ASTROLOGY

PERHAPS we may use the word 'mentality' to indicate those mental phenomena verging from the unconscious to the conscious, the mixture of belief, ritual and magic, superstition and conviction, inclination and aptitude, emerging from the rich dark recesses of experience towards the light of day, into the sphere of the rational. We will reserve the more strictly intellectual – even though hardly ever so purely intellectual as it fancies itself to be – till later, and watch it, as we should, being shaped from this mass (or mess) of mingled nonsense into sense.* For of such is the mental life of most people, and such the mentality of a society.

In the sixteenth century everybody believed in the supernatural; everybody believed, more or less, in magic, or the possibilities of magic; everybody believed, to a greater or lesser extent, in the stars. Popular phraseology still bears evidence of how widespread these beliefs were, how they dominated the mind. We still speak of our 'lucky stars', to be 'born under a lucky star'; we still describe people's temperaments in terms that derive from the planets, martial or mercurial, venereal or saturnine. Or we speak of 'raising Cain', 'raising the Devil', or 'raising Hell'. Quite apart from the fact that large sections of the population, even in supposedly advanced countries, believe in astrology, magic, spirits, ghosts, the supernatural: we do not need to look to darkest Africa for witchcraft.

Nor need we go so far with a contemporary anthropologist as to regard magic as 'the most powerful influence on conduct the world has ever seen.'[1] We may reserve that rôle for religion. On the other hand, religion is closely associated with magic, in its origins arises out of magic rituals; the word 'religion' expresses the fact that it is society's deliberate organisation of all that, an essential ligament in holding societies together. Lecky tells us in his book on

* This will be dealt with in the succeeding volume.

the Rise of Rationalism that, where supernatural phenomena are concerned, men will believe in the teeth of the evidence, or disbelieve in spite of the evidence, but never because of the evidence. Perhaps we should, in justice, amend this to 'hardly ever'; but it is not surprising, for in regard to mental phenomena (though not so much in regard to physical or material) most people have no conception what evidence means.

This is one of the most contemptible of human characteristics – for the specific consideration that it goes directly against the highest of human potentialities, man's reason. (One has only to think, in our own particular field, of the lunacy – note the planetary reference of the word – of Baconians, Oxfordians, Marlovians.) However, we must not be too moralistic in regard to this field of phenomena, however rigorously we submit them in the end to the judgment of the rational.

The fundamental aim of all magic is 'to impose the human will on nature, on man, or on the supersensual world in order to master them . . . whereas pure science and art are concerned with the disinterested contemplation or investigation of life.'[2] They come later in the process – thus we shall deal with them later. 'Astrology is applied astronomy, based on observation of the heavens and on mathematical calculations. Alchemy is experimental chemistry. Both were founded on the belief in one principle underlying the universe. Astrology aimed at controlling and guiding the destinies of man by means of fore-knowledge.' Alchemy sought to secure power by reducing the plurality of physical phenomena to oneness, thus to transmute metals to gold, find the philosopher's stone. The third branch of the subject, ritual magic, 'aimed principally at control of the spirit world', by means of ritual, prayer, incantations, spells, charms – ultimately, the magic of words.

It seems fairly clear that the whole of man's mental life has evolved out of this dark world: all the more honour then to those superior minds to whom alone we owe our emergence into light.

Quite primitive societies observe, worship and reflect on the stars. The Indians of Virginia were fascinated by what Hariot could show them through his perspective glass. A more advanced civilisation such as the Aztecs of Mexico had a complex system of astronomy, partly for the religious and astrological purposes that went with it. We must keep always in mind the two-fold aspects of the indigenous astral beliefs in a society, and the more sophisticated astrological systems in part worked up from them, in part imposed upon them.

Astrology as a system – we must not call it a science – achieved sophisticated form, and was debated as such, primarily by the Italians of the Renaissance. They come first in every field: other Continental, and then English, writers depend upon their formal treatises for arguments for and against. In the end, the English but recapitulate the discussion, though giving it their own character, at once less esoteric and more popular, overwhelmingly in the vernacular.[3] We may take this as one more indication, where there are so many – notably the drama – of the greater integration of Elizabethan society. Miss E. M. Butler adds to this: 'it is an extraordinary experience to follow the dark trail of ritual magic from the Continent (and notably from Germany) to England, and to find oneself escaping from puerility and squalor into poetry, fairy tales, and romance.'[4] She specifically contrasts the 'pothouse odour' of the German Faust with spirits like Ariel and Puck. But this is by no means the whole story.

Dr. Dee, the learned mathematician – in popular parlance this was often equivalent to magician – defined astrology as 'an art mathematical, which demonstrateth reasonably the operations and effects of the natural beams of light and secret influence of the stars and planets' in accordance with assigned positions. To the Elizabethan mind it was unreasonable to suppose that there were no planetary or celestial influences upon men, since so much of the vegetable growth on the earth visibly depended on the sun, while the moon's influence was no less visible in the tides. It was sometimes debated whether astrology should be banned from a well-ordered community – More had banned it from Utopia – as it was before the Queen on 23 September 1592; but this was an academic disputation, and in fact no-one could do without it in some shape or form.

Certainly not the Queen. The horoscope for the most propitious day for her coronation had been cast by Dr. Dee – and nobody could say that that had not been successful. Her attitude is expressed in a personal letter of reproach to Mary Stuart in 1568 for her changeableness (Elizabeth thought of herself as constant, *semper eadem*): 'if it were not that I consider that by nature we are composed of earthly elements and governed by heavenly, and that I am not ignorant that our dispositions are caused in part by supernatural signs, which change every day, I could not believe that in so short a time such a change could take place.'[5]

The Queen always treated Dr. Dee with favour, was familiar with him and generous to him. Besides being an eminent scholar, the first mathematician of the first half of the reign, he was of old Welsh family: a cousin of Blanche Parry, of Mistress Scudamore, another maid-of-honour, and of the Aubreys – a Welsh border cousinage. In October 1578 Dee was at Richmond conferring with her and her doctor about her sickness.[6] On 11 February 1583, passing by Dee's house she called him out, and he notes in Greek characters, 'Her majesty asked me obscurely of Monsieur's estate.' This refers to the Duke of Anjou, who was ill: the negotiations for a marriage with him were long over, but Elizabeth always had a curious *tendresse* for him. Dee told her that he would be a suicide. (Anjou died the next year.) In 1588 Dee gave to his medium, Edward Kelly, the convex mirror 'so highly and long esteemed of our Queen and the Emperor Rudolph II' – this was when they were abroad in Bohemia. On Dee's return from his notorious sojourn, he was again well received by her. Passing by his door – she sometimes came within doors to speak with him – she put down her mask to promise him 100 angels (coins not spirits) to keep Christmas withal. She sent him a personal message giving him warrant 'to do what I would in philosophy and alchemy, and none should check, control, or molest me.' On 3 May 1594, 'the Queen sent for me to her in the Privy Garden at Greenwich,' where, walking alone with her in the evening – with only Lady Warwick and Lady Cecil in the garden – 'I delivered in writing the heavenly admonition, and her Majesty took it thankfully.' She rewarded his services with the Wardenship of Manchester College.

People then had so much more need of the stars, when they depended upon them to indicate the time by night, as the sun by day. Here is Shakespeare's carrier in the inn-yard at Rochester: 'Heigh-ho! an it be not four by the day, I'll be hanged: Charles' wain [i.e. the Great Bear] is over the new chimney, and yet our horse not packed.' Astrology was held necessary in medicine, when the humours were affected by particular planets, especially in surgery where different parts of the body were under different influences. So too in agriculture; good old Tusser bids us:

> Sow peason and beans in the wane of the moon,
>   Who soweth them sooner, he soweth too soon;
> That they with the planet may rest and arise
>   And flourish with bearing most plentiful wise.[7]

A house at Burnley had this inscription: 'Sun, Moon, Mars, Mercury, Jupiter, Venus, Saturn, Trine, Sextile, Dragon's Head, Dragon's Tail: I charge you all to guard this house from all spirits whatever, and guard it from all disorders, and from anything being taken wrongly, and give this family good health and wealth.'[8] Many people would know what these references meant that are esoteric to us. Trine and sextile refer to favourable aspects of the planets, when one-third or one-sixth of the zodiac is distant from each other; that is, four signs or two signs out of the twelve. The Dragon's Head refers to the intersecting point of the ascending moon's orbit with the sun's, while the Dragon's Tail refers to its intersection when descending.

In *King Lear*, Edmund, Gloucester's bastard, says: 'my father compounded with my mother under the Dragon's Tail, and my nativity was under Ursa Major, so that it follows I am rough and lecherous.' But he goes on to add, for he is a cynic and no believer: 'Fut, I should have been that I am had the maidenliest star in the firmament twinkled on my bastardising.' When his father elaborated on the theme, 'these late eclipses in the sun and moon portend no good to us,' Edmund comments: 'This is the excellent foppery of the world – that, when we are sick in fortune, often the surfeits of our own behaviour, we make guilty of our disasters the sun, the moon, and stars. As if we were villains on necessity; fools by heavenly compulsion; knaves, thieves, and treachers [traitors] by spherical predominance; drunkards, liars, and adulterers, by an enforced obedience of planetary influence; and all that we are evil in, by a divine thrusting on – an admirable evasion of whoremaster man, to lay his goatish disposition on the charge of a star!'

Edmund says that in his own character: we are not to accept it as necessarily Shakespeare's view. As so often, he expressed every point of view on a subject, as becomes the dramatist. All the same we can observe him expressing the regular opinions of the time, normal, moderate, representative. He frequently states the view, which he would hold in common with his audience, that a man's disposition is affected by the star he is born under: Autolycus under Mercury, so that he is thievish and up to tricks; the braggart soldier, Parolles, not 'under a charitable star', but under Mars; Antony's star is dimmed by that of Augustus; no good can come to Richard III, at whose birth good stars were in opposition. Shakespeare expressed the common view that comets were portents of exceptional events, the deaths of princes, and the like. The moon coming nearer the earth than usual in its orbit, 'makes men mad' (or, perhaps we should emend, madder than usual). He occasionally uses these beliefs, like everything else, to raise a laugh; but that is no evidence that he, and the audience, did not believe them. When Prince Hal sees Falstaff and Doll Tearsheet together, he exclaims: 'Saturn and Venus this year in conjunction! What says the almanac to that?' Poins carries on the joke by describing Bardolph as 'the fiery Trigon's man . . . lisping to his master's old fables, his notebook, his counsel-keeper.' The 'fiery Trigon' is Falstaff: a combination of three signs of the zodiac, Aries, Leo and Sagittarius, triply hot, dry and thirsty. The Elizabethan audience would be familiar with the term, and its significance lost on us.

Shakespeare's attitude was the common-sense of the day, swinging to and fro between the earlier expression in *Love's Labour's Lost*:

> These earthly godfathers of heaven's lights,
> That give a name to every fixèd star,
> Have no more profit of their shining nights
> Than those that walk and wot not what they are . . .

and Kent's fatalistic acceptance in *King Lear*:

> It is the stars,
> The stars above us, govern our conditions.

Perhaps it comes to rest on the polarity of the position,

> The fault, dear Brutus, is not in our stars,
> But in ourselves, that we are underlings.

This is to say, not that Shakespeare was a sceptic on the matter, but his was as usual the moderate, almost normative, one of the day. This was not that the stars had no influence, nor that they were all-powerful and human will nothing, but that they had an inclining influence, corroborating and strengthening one's disposition in its direction.

Two schools of thought with regard to the uses of astrology, i.e. judicial astrology, are represented by Melancthon and Calvin.[9] Melancthon's attitude was favourable, and he defended it as at least a probable science. Calvin was hostile, not on any enlightened grounds, but in the interests of a greater obscurantism. He disapproved of any art by which man tried to learn what God did not wish him to know: it revealed a lack of trust in God, i.e. Calvin writ large. Would that man who thought himself bound by the necessity of his horoscope ever call upon God, or would he impute adversity to his own sins? Astrology enabled men to blame their stars, instead of their sins: it was a detraction from man's free will. Predestination was in order theologically, but not astrologically: Calvin was a theologian, not an astrologer. Q.E.D.

These attitudes were reflected in imitative England: on the whole, moderate Anglicans took Melancthon's view, Puritans of course took Calvin's. The first full-scale attack was that of a subsequent Puritan, William Fulke; a compiler of prognostics himself, he disapproved of the judicial use of astrology, i.e. to foretell the future. 'Those things that are above us pertain nothing unto us; and those things which are above our reach are not to be sought for with much curiosity.'[10] It is precisely Calvin's position: the obscurantism of Puritanism. We may take leave to observe that, at the moment of writing man has reached the moon by following the opposite path, the exploration of knowledge – though, significantly, a fundamentalist South American Indian killed himself at once in protest at this infringement of God's ordinance.

Naturally the popular Stubbes agreed with Calvin: the stars do not cause men's dispositions but merely incline the soul. 'Indeed I confess they have effects and operations, but yet are they not the efficient causes of anything good or bad. Otherwise than thus, it pleaseth the majesty of God to work by them as by his instruments . . . and not after any other sort.'[11] The loud-mouthed Perkins, who administered spiritual consolation to so many tender consciences in both Old and New England, was of the same opinion. He strenuously repeated the familiar platitudinous arguments: how can twins have the same horoscopes? Or when Jacob and Esau were born so close together that one held the other by the foot, and yet had such different lots in life? This was considered a very strong proof against astral prediction. To wish to know the future is to distrust God (i.e. Perkins' counsel), and of course eclipses of sun and moon and their effects cannot be foretold. John Chamber, a very Protestant canon of Windsor, considered the case of the Countess of Holland who had 365 children 'all hatched at once': could they all have the same fortune? Or Siamese twins? Obviously not. Stubbes took to mind, rather than heart, the sad case of Sodom and Gomorrah: were all those abandoned persons born under the same planet, to share the same fate? Or all those drowned in the Flood? Surely not.

The argument proceeded in nonsense-terms on both sides, the

arguments against astrology being as puerile as those for it. Astrologers worked on the basis of too few stars, not all those visible, let alone those invisible. Moreover, not enough time had elapsed from the creation of the world for the records of nativities to warrant a system: astrologers claimed that the Chaldeans kept a record of 407,000 years, whereas it was not yet 6000 years from the beginning of the world, nor 4000 from the division of tongues. – So much for ordinary mortals' reasoning: one sympathises with Shakespeare. Or with Samuel Butler, who reflected that, since so many people believed in astrology, there must be as much pleasure for fools in being cheated as in cheating. The sad and humane observer notices, however, that these very people who were opposed to astrology, Perkins especially, were very strong on the necessity of putting witches to death. John Chamber added his complaint against a system that allowed astrologers to go free, though witches were punished.

An attack on astrology on a higher intellectual plane was that of the ambivalent, and therefore intelligent, Lord Henry Howard. A Catholic, his book *A Defensative against the Poison of Supposed Prophecies* (1583) has a good deal more in it than astrology, though it is learned in the subject. Under the cover of orthodoxy, flattery of the Queen (whom he had offended) and a dedication to Walsingham (as against Burghley, who had brought Howard's brother to the scaffold), Lord Henry managed to insinuate a defence of his family's questionable record and assert his brother's innocence of treason. His book originated, he tells us, in 'the mortal malice' he had felt all his life against the fond prophecies that had led his father, Surrey, to the scaffold for presuming upon hopes of the throne.[12] He takes malicious pleasure in pointing out that the admirable Cardinal Pole had disclaimed astrological predictions of his rise to eminence, while the Protestant Sir John Cheke would do nothing, not so much as a short journey, without first consulting the stars. A great aristocrat, who hated Elizabeth's new deal, Howard expresses constant contempt for the people and their liability to panic, their belief that the stars will fall, that doomsday is at hand, that the world will be consumed by fire or 'of late' by a second flood. Then suddenly, in a digression, he lets us into the private tradition of the Howard family, which owed its dukedom and everything to Richard III, as to Richard's 'heinous fault': there was no doubt about that.*

* When writing my book, *Bosworth Field*, I was not aware of this corroboration of Richard III's guilt.

The Catholic Howard was at one with Calvin, since both were religious men, in holding it irreligious to attempt to search into God's secrets. But Lord Henry was at least free from popular delusions, and able to distinguish between coincidence and cause. Because it happens sometimes to thunder about the season when swans hatch their young, many simple people believed that 'a swan cannot hatch without a crack of thunder.'[13] He gives other examples of such credulity, not only among the idiot people: a lady of his acquaintance was 'tormented with a grievous fit and passion of the mother' – i.e. a choking fit, a symptom of hysteria – at the sight of an eclipse and thought it directly caused by the eclipse. Lord Henry put it down rather to the cold she caught. He took pleasure in pointing out that the blazing star (the Nova of 1572) – from which some had prognosticated an earthquake, others that 'our bodies should be parched and burned up with heat' – had been followed by nothing worse than a cold summer, 'never less inclination to war, no prince deceased in that time.' The Queen's courage in confronting the late comet gave him an opportunity for flattery. 'I can affirm thus much, as a present witness by mine own experience, that when divers went about to dissuade her Majesty (lying then at Richmond) from looking on the comet which appeared last – with a courage answerable to the greatness of her state, she caused the window to be set open, and cast out this word, "*Jacta est alia*", the dice are thrown.' (She was no more taken in by him than she was by the comet.)

Howard allows that the planets had some influence upon changes and alterations on earth, but that they worked along with secondary causes, to make 'things either ripe or rotten, frail or durable, by an universal force, according to their proper kinds and qualities.'[14] This was in keeping with the best opinion, as exemplified by Father Parsons and the Anglican bishop Carleton: they agreed that the stars affected the humours, and through them the body, and thus indirectly the mind. Howard disallowed alchemy, necromancy, geomancy and the black arts as unlawful, but he believed naturally and easily in spirits and familiars. He had been present at Court when the Italian Scotto had performed conjuring tricks before the Queen: everyone present had been beguiled by them. Then how much more may the sight be deceived by familiars? Thus it is that spirits give us intelligence of the state of absent friends – in other words the phenomena we recognise today as telepathy. With regard to the political use of fond prophecies – from which his family had suffered, and against which Parliament legislated in 1562–3, making their dissemination a misdemeanour – Howard concludes sensibly: 'the knowledge and experience which the wiser sort hath had of counsels, forces, persons, times, and practices may minister more certain guesses in this case than all the stars or planets in the firmament.'

Nevertheless the 'wiser sort' did not always exemplify it, and in our own day Hitler had his astrologer, as some operators on the stock-markets of the world are said to have theirs; while universities in enlightened new India sport lectures in the subject.

At the time of the blazing star, or Nova, of 1572 which created such consternation, one of the wisest sort in the country, Burghley himself, thought it well to consult a leading scientist, Thomas Digges. He reported: 'I have waded as far as ancient grounds of astrology and authors' precepts of approved credit will bear me, to sift out the unknown influence of this new star or comet, which is like to be no less vehement than rare.'[15] Digges appended the results of his investigations as to the quarter from which calamity was to be expected, what regions menaced, what kind of creature likely to be affected, with 'the efficient infernal cause . . . like to play the chiefest part in this fatal tragedy.' More he could not say 'without conference of this situation of the heavens with private nativities.'

Now Digges was a scientist, not a charlatan, one of the first to accept the new Copernican astronomy; this offers a fascinating glimpse into his mind, and shows that there was no difference between him and the professional astrologers on the subject. Lord Keynes was naively excited – as no historian would be – by his realisation of the magus element in Isaac Newton;[16] but astronomy separated itself out of astrology, as chemistry out of alchemy, in the course of development. We see something of the effect upon an intelligent mind, in Howard, when the experience of the Nova was followed by none of the portended effects.

At the turn of the century there was a controversy on the subject which throws interesting lights on the mentality of the age, not only in regard to astrology, but psychology and even anthropology. John Chamber's *Treatise against Judicial Astrology* (1601) was dedicated to Lord Keeper Egerton, with a tribute to his wisdom in choosing able and fit persons for preferment, and his diligence in repelling the unfit.[17] (This was true of Egerton, a weighty and responsible person, plumb in the middle of the state.) Chamber exhorted the Lord Keeper to hold on his course in an ill age, when all men's eyes were on him, all men's faces turned towards him – especially, we may add, for preferment. (Elizabethans engaged in a feverish, ulcerated struggle for preferment: it was an acute struggle for survival, and devil-take-the-hindmost.) Chamber survived as prebendary of Windsor and Fellow of Eton: he deserved it.

Chamber observes that judicial astrology is becoming increasingly questioned, and he gives a long catalogue of reasons why. We need not go into them all, most of them are the routine objections, from authority or the uncertainties of the subject: there are divine proofs against astrology, difficulties in the art from the number of the stars, the uncertainty of not knowing whether to choose the hour of conception or birth for prediction, the diversity of fortune of twins, the objection that God has reserved the knowledge of the future to himself. More interestingly, Chamber urges that the true use of the stars is to advance the knowledge of astronomy, and approves the lately reformed almanacs confining themselves properly to changes of the moon, eclipses, etc. He is very interesting on the Nova in Cassiopaeia of 1572, though he dates it wrongly, which had electrified observers, for the heavens were supposed to be fixed and unchanging, according to Holy Writ and Aristotle. 'By the judgment of all the best observers it was out of the reach of meteors [which were thought to be exhalations from the earth], as being as high as the sun from the earth at least. In this case we must grant, either that this star was bred and corrupted in heaven – which, being granted, it will follow that the like may and doth happen in others also – or that there be more planets than seven, whose courses are unknown to us; or lastly that the fixed stars do not keep their eighth orb, but have their several circuits and motions.'[18] So the doubt that had troubled Hipparchus (over the changes in position of the fixed stars in periods of time) recurred when a new star was observed: whether it might not happen again, and whether the fixed stars were not movable.

Chamber's astronomical knowledge was not inconsiderable. Twenty-seven years before he had read the Astronomy lecture at Oxford, with an exposition of Ptolemy's Almagest, and appends to his book an *Astronomiae Encomium*, a scholarly survey of its history. In the course of his attack on astrology, Chamber gives us some information about contemporary astronomy. Mathematicians calculated that there were over seventy million stars: the astrologers' star-catalogue contained 1028 – not enough to go by. It was agreed that Saturn was 91 times the size of the earth, Jupiter 95 times, Mars 1½, the Sun 167, the Moon 1–39th. Chamber cited Sextus Empiricus' account of the Chaldean reckoning of time and dividing the zodiac, from the *Contra Astrologos*. It was rare for an Elizabethan to know the sceptical work of Sextus Empiricus – the fact that a translation passed for long as a work of Ralegh's, *The Sceptic*, was but another indication of the dangerous tendencies of that mind. In any case the trend of Chamber's remarks shows the ancient astronomy being questioned, ready to be transformed by the genius of Kepler and Galileo.

Some 'figure-flingers' – Chamber's rude word for astrologers – answer the difficulty regarding twins by arguing that they have diverse conceptions. But as to this no-one can say. Some physicians hold that there is a preparation required of the seed in the mother before there can be any conception: the time of this cannot be known to the astrologer, thus prediction is impossible. Chamber had often been asked by women how the mandrake helps conception in women, when it both makes and mars men? He considered this – really a piece of sympathetic magic – 'a doting opinion'. His answer was that 'if their husbands could not make them conceive, there was small hope in the mandrake apple.'[19] There is a herb, androclon, resembling the form of a man, which some take to be mandrake. 'Where we may well note the wonderful force of folly and superstition, there being in this herb not so much as the smallest resemblance of a man, not so much as in the root . . . yet we see how generally it is holden that it is very like a man for shape. If in these things which are so familiar, which we may daily handle and make trial of . . . superstition hath so prevailed, how much sooner may it prevail in matters of religion, which we cannot make any such trial of, as not being subject to sense?' Well, exactly.

Chamber was not without a sense of humour, rare in these discussions. The year 1588 had been predicted to turn out a wonderful year, which in a way it did. But instead of listening to astrological predictions, the Spaniards might have fared better 'if they had been provided of a pilot such as was Henry Nicholas in Chaucer' – evidently Chamber had been reading the new 1598 edition of the poet, as Elizabeth was at just this time.[20] He tells us a well-known story of a Cornish chough. 'One missing a silver spoon, which was hidden by a Cornish chough which he had in his house, and going to the figure-flinger to know what was become of his spoon, the figure-flinger answered the party which had it had long legs, went in a black coat with a pair of red stockings, he had a beak nose and was born westward from that place; he might seem to be a gentleman from his high birth, but he thought no Englishman from his strange tongue. Now the chough indeed had long legs, red shanks, black feathers, a beak, was born westward and high, and instead of speech chattereth. With this blind description many were called into suspicion, but the poor chough in the end was found to have hid the spoon.' This was the kind of thing that amused Elizabethans, and country people for long after.

Here are examples of Chamber's anthropological curiosity. 'Among the Indians and Bactrians there be many thousands of those whom we call Brachmanni, [Brahmins], who, what for tradition by fathers, what for laws, neither worship images nor eat any live thing, neither ever drink wine or ale, but refraining from all evil tend only upon the service of God.'[21] 'By the laws in Persia men might marry their daughters and mothers; neither did they this in Persia only, but when they change their country and climate they retain and use these abominations.' The Amazons have no husbands, so in spring they go to neighbour countries and lie with the men; then they kill all male children, bringing up only the female – but these lucky ones had not all been born under the same constellation. Chamber concludes: 'to be short, daily men are born everywhere, and everywhere we see them observe their own laws and fashions' – the stars do not change their habits fixed by custom. Countries differ not according to the stars, but according to education, feeding, institutions, conditions, in which climate is to be included.

We are reminded at this point what an extraordinary encyclopedia of anthropological knowledge Hakluyt's *Principal Navigations* opened out to the Elizabethans: a whole new province for their minds to take possession of and expand into.

Sir Christopher Heydon's reply to Chamber, *A Defence of Judicial Astrology* (1603) is a less lively, ponderous work, actually more interesting for its knowledge of astronomy. Sir Christopher addresses himself loftily to the learned only: his appeal is not to those 'ignorant either in divinity, philosophy, or in the mathematics; it is a sufficient reason for me to account the vulgar no competent judges in our controversy.' He traverses Chamber's book laboriously chapter by chapter, answering his commonplaces with similar commonplaces, such as that it is recognised by divines themselves that superior bodies govern inferior, therefore the celestial the terrestrial. He tells us that 'astronomy and astrology – both are indifferently taken and used by the learned for one and the selfsame art.'[22] This is intellectually inferior to the distinction implied in the churchman's work, yet Heydon was well up in the latest astronomy, had read Copernicus, Regiomontanus and Tycho Brahe, and was obliged to the mathematician, Edward Wright, for further instruction. He himself had observed the ascensions and declinations of the stars by means of a large armillary; he possessed a plumb watch, with works of brass, less subject to alterations of weather. Astrologers have more exact instruments than Chamber allows: precision is possible (i.e. precision for nonsense purposes). He cites William Gilbert for an argument from the influence of the magnet on iron, a thing void of sense: *a fortiori* for the sensitive body of an infant drawing to it influences from the heavens. In the same breath he looks forward to the publication of Tycho's Progymnasmata for greater exactitude in forecasts, and believes the ancient and modern auguries foretelling deaths. We observe that it is the one with the scientific knowledge who applies it to the support of nonsense, the theologian who argues for sense – such is the duplicity of men's thinking. Heydon cites the astrologer's indubitable help to the physician in tracking the course of disease, otherwise a phlegmatic man might fall into choleric sickness: Hippocrates and Galen are against Chamber. Chamber need not doubt of Arthur's burial at Glastonbury, as Camden reports from Giraldus Cambrensis, 'that was an eyewitness thereof'![23] We must observe how uncertain is the Elizabethan's sense of evidence in this realm.

Astrologers need not care whether the world is one continued orb as Tycho would have it, or the sun the centre of the universe as Copernicus saw it – variety of opinion was no impeachment to the art. No, indeed. Heydon affirmed with Ptolemy that the force of the sun and the quality of the heavens make negroes black, their manners choleric, their bodies hot and dry. Whereas 'of my own knowledge I am able to affirm that the second descendant of a Moor here in England is scantly so much coloured as that the children can be discerned from those that are naturally English.'[24] Heydon is not interested in racial speculation – that had been settled, after all, by the Bible: this is taken merely to prove that our constitutions depend on the quality of the heavens.

Heydon was answered in two more works. *Astronotomania: the*

Madness of Astrologers was written by George Carleton, who was made
a bishop for his pains, 'a bitter enemy to the papists, and a secure
Calvinist.'[25] It is an ill-tempered work, a complete dismissal of
astrology, advancing no new argument, except the consideration
that some astrological predictions that turn out true do so not by
learning 'but by some instinct'.[26] (This may well apply to the
telepathic experiences, the psychopathic insights, of such as Dee,
Kelly, and Forman.) However, the means of knowing events
beforehand are not natural, but diabolical, and the kings' majesty
had pronounced sentence against judicial astrology in his *Demonology*. Evidently Carleton qualified for his bishopric.

A light-hearted attack, with a concrete personal inflexion,
came from John Melton, in *Astrologaster or the Figure-Caster* (1620).
He inquires why the professional astrologers always inhabit the
back-alleys of the city: the Cunning Man on the Bankside, Mother
Broughton in Chick Lane, Master Olive in Turnbull Street, the
shag-haired Wizard in Pepper Alley, Dr. Forman at Lambeth.
The answer was, of course, to keep out of the way of the City
authorities, and out of their jurisdiction if possible. Melton
sensibly pointed out that people's desire for a thrill was an element
in their seeking out astrologers, with their promises of thunder and
lightning, and more lurid excitements: 'when there are no such
inflammations seen, except men go to the "Fortune" in Golding
Lane to see the tragedies of Dr. Faustus: there indeed a man may
behold shag-haired devils run roaring over the stage with squibs
in their mouths, while drummers make thunder in the tiring-
house, and the twelve-penny hirelings make artificial lightning in
their heavens.'[27] Here we see something of the unbroken fascina-
tion of Marlowe's *Dr. Faustus* for the Elizabethans – and see how
natural was Dr. Forman's addiction to the theatre.

Even the forward-looking Bacon, who thought horoscopes an
idle invention, belief in nativities and the hour of birth silly, was
more favourable to astrology than might have been expected and
thought that there was a future for it. He agreed with Ptolemy that
astral influence was general rather than particular, and that the
heavenly bodies did not affect all kinds of bodies, 'but only the
more tender, such as humours, air, and spirit. Here, however, the
operations of the heat of the sun and heavenly bodies must be
expected, which doubtless penetrates both to metals and to a great
number of subterraneous bodies.' He also considered that these
influences operated over large spaces of time, not small pinpoints.
He concluded that 'the celestial bodies have in them certain other

influences besides heat and light: which very influences however act by those rules laid down above and not otherwise. But these lie concealed in the depths of physics.'[28] Bacon therefore envisaged a reformed astrology, which might lead to more reliable predictions, and not only of natural phenomena – floods, droughts, earthquakes – but also of revolutions, wars, civil commotions, migrations of peoples (as of birds). All this sprang from Bacon's immense optimism as to the future extension of knowledge. We may perhaps conclude that, with the best minds of the age, 'the influence of the planets was at one with that of fate and fortune.'

The actual practice of astrologers, however, was based on casting horoscopes for particular persons and purposes. Thus it is that Dr. Dee carefully noted the day and hour of birth of various persons in the margins of his almanacs and calendars, his *Ephemerides Novae* (Cologne, 1570), with calculations of the planets, or his *Ephemerides Coelestium Motuum* (Venice, 1582), with the movements of the planets for 1581-1620.[29] There is thus no mystery about the birth of Dee's famous medium or scryer, Edward Kelly: he was born at Worcester at 4 p.m., 1 August 1555, according to a note left by his father.[30] A small volume beginning with an astrological treatise in an early sixteenth-century hand has various figures cast by Dee to find someone's lost ring, a sack of corn missing, a horse or cow, a goblet or cup.[31] This was the small change upon which Dee or Forman's livelihood was based. On 31 October Lord Herbert came to him for a *toga amissa*, a missing cloak, and again on 2 November. It was found: 'Mr. Belling had it in his coffer, full west very near.' On 19 November, Lady Blount came concerning her gold ring. On 29 August, 'Mr. Fettiplace pro accipitre', for his hawk; next day Dr. Kenall came on behalf of Fettiplace. Kenall was the ecclesiastical lawyer who became archdeacon of Oxford, in whom, Carew said, the principal knowledge of the Cornish language lived and died. There follow inquiries from a Culpepper and a Hastings: Dee's was an upper-class *clientèle*, where Forman's was of all classes.

We have an example of the dangers attaching to political prognostication in the examination of Nathaniel Torporley, Hariot's amanuensis, after Gunpowder Plot in 1605. The Earl of Northumberland was inculpated; Torporley had cast his dead son's nativity. More important, he had cast the King's nativity for Hariot. About the beginning of the Parliament, Hariot had told Torporley that the hour of James's birth might be known more certainly 'because there was a cannon shot off at Edinburgh presently [i.e. immediately] after his birth.'[32] Hariot put up the figure in his study at Essex House: he was merely desirous to see how it agreed with James's 'happy fortune in coming to the Crown.' Hariot had not had an Ephemerides, 'but Magini's, which contained not the journal of the planets and, being loth himself to take the pains to work by Tabulae Prutenicae [the Prutenic Tables for astronomical calculations], willed me to bring that, which I did, by Stadius.' He did not know what use Hariot made of the horoscope, himself made no judgment upon it. No doubt this was deemed harmless enough. Shortly after, Shakespeare was writing *Macbeth*, with the witches' enticement by prophecy to Macbeth to take the crown.

We are reminded by the facts of Dee's career that this was all part of the mental life of the whole of Europe at the time: people of all classes were more fearful of the unknown, more apprehensive and excitable, more credulous and imaginative, easily roused to cruelty. The most famous 'prophecies' were those of Nostradamus, a French Jew, who was the favourite astrologer of Catherine de Medici and her son Charles IX – the brilliant Valois Court was feverish with astrological and other excitements, sexual and murderous. The prophecies of Nostradamus still circulate today: he had very ominous predictions in store for the year 1999, while one of his quatrains has been taken to refer to the death of George V and the abdication of Edward VIII:

> Le jeune nay au regne Britannique
> Qu' aura le père mourant recommande,
> Iceluy mort Londre donra topique,
> Et a son fils le Regne demande.[33]

We may justly say that Elizabeth's Court was much less *émotionné* about this kind of thing than the Valois', and that the English mentality on the whole was less explosive than the Continental.

The English, however, had their excitements. In spite of the disappointing effects of the Nova of 1572 (in England, for the events of that year were all too exciting in France), people began to be worked up about the approaching conjunction of Saturn and Jupiter in 1583. This was further stimulated by Richard Harvey's prognostication for the year, on top of a translation of Geverin's *Of the End of this World and the Second Coming of Christ*. Holinshed tells us that, as the dire event approached, 'the common sort of people, yea and no small multitude of such as think scorn to be called fools [there is little distinction] . . . whilst they were in expectation of this conjunction, were in no small imaginations, supposing that no less would have been effectuated than by the said discourse [Harvey's] was prophesied.'[34] When the time drew near, noon on Sunday 28 April 1583, many were scanning the sky for a sign, 'some strange apparition or vision in the air.' With the book on the Second Coming, 'some conversing and conferring looked for no less than was prophesied and, talking very religiously, seemed as though they would become sanctified people.' Many of us have known such idiots in our own time. 'Howbeit, the day of conjunction being past, with a certain countercheck and the said astrological discourse in some parts defective, and no such events palpably perceived as were prognosticated, people fell to their former security and condemned the discourser of extreme madness and folly.' After this exposure of his nakedness, when 'the whole university hissed at him', Harvey entered the church where, not being successful, he leaned to the Puritan side. The unbelieving Marlowe thought him 'an ass, good for nothing but to preach of the Iron Age' – there was something asinine about the Harveys. Even so, Harvey was not wholly nude: there were people to cover him with the excuse that perhaps the calculations had gone wrong; they did not wish to think that the *whole* thing was nonsense.

It should suffice to cite Harvey's *Discourse* briefly as one example for all of the kind. Harvey was a naïve young man, more learned than most prognosticators, very much under the wing of his exhibitionist brother, Gabriel, who had encouraged the work 'for what general good I can do my country thereby or what special fruit I can reap thereof unto myself' – a characteristic Harvey note.[35] The tract was dedicated, hopefully, to the bishop of London, if not for its own then for Cambridge's sake (were they not all Cambridge men?). Young Harvey cited Cardan's tribute to Edward VI, blissfully unconscious of the howler the famous mathematician had made: he had forecast long life and prosperity for the boy-king, who died at sixteen. Credulity is proof against anything.

However, Harvey was able to assure his expectant readers that the conjunction of Saturn and Jupiter would be marked by fierce and boisterous winds, and divers persecutions threatened unto sundry ecclesiastical persons. There would be much hatred, discord, factions and contention, with impious behaviour on the part of the wicked. Great rains, hail, thunder, lightning would be followed by excessive heat. The earthquake of April Fools' day,

1580, was cited – upon which brother Gabriel had pronounced a severe discourse to a jolly company that had gathered simply to make merry. Babylon would be brought down: 'screechowls and ostriches shall walk in her houses, apes and satyrs shall dance in her beautiful buildings' – one sees the effect of too much Bible-reading. The tract ends with a compendious table of Phlebotomy for use, with the best times for bloodletting and appropriate diet. This was in accordance with the usual practice of prognostications.

By 1600 the annual almanac 'had taken a fixed shape, which continued with very slight variations during the next two centuries.'[36] It contained the ecclesiastical calendar, with saints' days, and days of proper observance; juxtaposed were the conjunctions and oppositions of sun and moon, with the rules for movable feasts. Then there were those for bloodletting, bathing, and purging, with a figure of man's anatomy, the signs of the zodiac on the body for guidance. There followed the prognostication, which foretold the weather and what to expect in the way of events, how to hold oneself in regard to them, with useful warnings, directions in regard to sowing, harvest, etc. In short, these works were indispensable, as the mechanicals in *A Midsummer Night's Dream* show:

> *Snug, the joiner:* Doth the moon shine that night we
> play our play?
> *Bottom, the weaver:* A calendar! a calendar! Look
> in the almanac; find out moonshine, find
> out moonshine!
> *Quince, the carpenter:* Yes, it doth shine that night.

Since almanacs were so indispensable, and many of them were issued earlier in the reign with unsettling predictions of disaster, the government brought them under control. In 1571, a time of some crisis, the printers Watkins and Roberts were given a monopoly of issuing annual almanacs and prognostications; this continued until 1603, when the patent was taken over by the Stationers' Company.[37]

From being the leading mathematician of the first half of the reign Dr. Dee progressed to becoming the great Magus of the latter half. His association with Edward Kelly, the medium upon whom he depended and with whom he conducted his *séances*, at Cracow, Prague and Trebona (Triban), 1583–88, achieved European notoriety. It has been usual to treat Dee and Kelly as charlatans, viewing them anachronistically from the perspective of a later rationalism. The superior mind of Miss E. M. Butler saw that this is mistaken, and indeed a proper understanding of the age brings home how much more complex the matter is. Dee and Kelly undoubtedly believed in the reality of the phenomena they were investigating – crystal-gazing, the calling of spirits and angels, the interchanges with them and the instructions received from them; the search for the philosophers' stone, the transmutation of metals into silver and gold. Dr. Dee has left an immense mass of materials, mainly in manuscript, from which it is possible to portray him more fully than almost any Elizabethan – here we can only give it brief attention. But where nearly all Elizabethan diaries are extrovert, confined to external events, Dee's takes us into the interior of his mind and heart.

Edward Kelly is a more questionable character. It was said that he spent some time at Gloucester Hall at Oxford – if so, probably as a servitor, like Forman at Magdalen and with similar consequences: a desire for knowledge and prestige and, without qualification or security, inferiority-complex and anxiety amounting to persecution-mania. Gloucester Hall was the haunt of crypto-Catholics, among them Thomas Allen, Leicester's favourite astrologer whom he used for casting nativities. 'In those dark times astrologer, mathematician, and conjurer were accounted the same things, and the vulgar did verily believe him to be a conjurer. He had a great many mathematical instruments and glasses in his chamber, which did confirm the ignorant in their opinion, and his servitor would tell them that sometimes he should meet the spirits coming up his stairs like bees.'[38] At some time Kelly served as an apothecary and acquired some knowledge in chemistry. He came to possess a manuscript of St. Dunstan on the philosophers' stone – for St. Dunstan was a Magus – and people believed that it was the original from Glastonbury. We must remember that certain books had magic properties. And Kelly had had dealings with graves: he had been apprehended and pilloried in Lancashire for digging up a grave and using the newly buried corpse for necromancy. After that he took to a wandering life in Wales, where he may have picked up some mineral lore.[39]

Before Kelly came to Dr. Dee he had had assistants who were less satisfactory at the work. Roger Cook had been with him for fourteen years, and then grew jealous of the Doctor's private dealing with a Dutch seeker. Cook was 'of a melancholic nature, picking and devising occasions of just cause to depart on the sudden.'[40] Dr. Dee made him good offers of money and 'some pretty alchemical experiments whereupon he might honestly live.' Apparently Dee revealed to him, 'his great secret of the elixir . . . of the salt of metals' – perhaps a Paracelsan prescription; in vain, for Cook left him. Barnabas Saul helped with the spirits, to whom he was susceptible. When lying in Westminster Hall, over some law matter, he was 'strangely troubled by a spiritual creature about midnight.' A few months later Saul 'confessed that he neither heard nor saw any spiritual creature any more.' In the same spring of 1582 Robert Gardiner, a Shropshireman, imparted to Dee information about the material of a stone divinely revealed to him and a philosophical secret of a spiritual creature, solemnly declared along with common prayer. For Dee was a devout Christian, much addicted to the uses of prayer. If it were Kelly who came to Dee under the name of Talbot, then he helped to oust Saul and take his place. The psychological atmosphere around the good Doctor, himself a reverend old gentleman, was full of backbiting and treachery, insecurity and persecution-mania, tension and the insatiable passion to know about the unknown and unknowable.

Once Dee had recruited Kelly to his service the famous partnership held. Kelly became indispensable to him in his searches and experiments; though Dee had already begun crystal gazing – '25 May 1581, I had sight *in crystallo* offered me, and I saw' – as an intellectual he had difficulty in communicating with the spirits.[41] Their relations began symptomatically with a quarrel and a reconciliation. Kelly was unmarried, but he was bidden by the spirits to take a wife, 'which thing to do I have no natural inclination, neither with a safe conscience may I do it.'[42] But the spirit swore him on his sword to do it, and Kelly took a young girl to wife. He could not abide it, he treated her badly, there were quarrels; Kelly was impulsive, neurotic, very queer. Then Mrs. Dee took against him, and with difficulty the Doctor pacifiedher; for he had an overriding need of Kelly. Dee was filled with an insatiable passion for knowledge beyond the possible; it was he who drove Kelly forward to long *séances*, hours of waiting and prayer and nervous tension. What suggests Kelly's sincerity is that at time he could not bear it; he was always reluctant; he sometimes protested that the spirits were evil, not good: 'my heart standeth against them.'[43] Once he burst out, 'I ever told you I do not believe them, nor can believe them, nor will desire to believe them.' Dee drove him relentlessly on, beseeching, coaxing, supporting him, promising him good things, revelations of deep secrets for them both. Sometimes in the tension of the *séances* Dee swooned; sometimes Kelly was exhausted, and refused to take part, or threatened violence. Still it went on, for years, driven by Dee's maniacal desire for knowledge. Dee was really the English Faust.

We must remind ourselves that he was a gentleman, as also that he was Welsh, living in good society, acquainted with and well thought of by the Queen and leading people at Court – Burghley and Walsingham, Leicester and the Sidneys: he cast young Philip Sidney's horoscope. It was in the Presence Chamber at Westminster that he met the leading intellectual of France, Jean Bodin, and in Leicester's apartment at Greenwich that he became acquainted with the Polish Count Laski. A person of importance in Poland, Laski was anxious to recruit Dee and Kelly's powers to advance his political ambitions. In the autumn of 1583 Laski took them, their wives, families and servants across Europe to Cracow; subsequently they were joined by Kelly's brother, Thomas, and his family. Their *séances* were able to promise Laski decisive alterations of state in Germany and Poland. Rumours of their powers and performances incited the Emperor Rudolph II to invite them to Prague, his capital. With the ambivalent talents of the homosexual, Rudolph himself was a mathematician, much interested in astrology and experience both sensory and extrasensory. At this time he had the astronomer Tycho Brahe in residence there, and a number of English enjoyed the delights of the capital he built, including a youth known as Anton von Rumpf. Young Arthur Throckmorton had passed the winter of 1580–1 there, so we miss the information we should have had from his invaluable Diary if it had been only two or three years later.[44]

It was here in Prague that the partnership between Dee and Kelly reached its most intense phase. They put in hours at crystal-gazing – and concentration upon this can lead to very odd states of mind. We hear of Kelly's megrims, his sensitiveness to thunderstorms, his outbursts of temper, evidently projections of his inner conflict and antagonism towards Dee. For Dee is insatiable: he wants to know what angels are in power over what kingdoms, what are the causes of disease, and so on, endlessly. Disappointed of preferment at home, Dee hoped to become the Emperor's *philosophus* and *mathematicus*, he began by transmitting an angelic message that if only Rudolph would leave off his sins, he would qualify for power over all the world.[45] Dee got the Spanish ambassador, who claimed to be descended from the medieval Magus, Raymond Lull, to present his book of hermetic philosophy,

Monas Hieroglyphica. This procured Dee an audience, but Rudolph was more interested in the promise of the philosopher's stone that in the reform of his life. In Dee's hermetic view spiritual transmutation was necessary to effect transmutation of the elements: hence the necessity for all the spiritistic *séances* – here was the link – the straining towards a good life, the prayer and fasting.

The alchemical search was no less ardent. We know something about their equipment and possessions. The Old Ashmolean at Oxford has Dee's cabbalistic table-top of marble, which was portable. They had minerals and metals, from which they extracted the essences; they had glass and bone, and probably mercury. Kelly had a supply of powder from the mines, which had the effect of transforming the appearances of metals; he had 'the very book of Dunstan', books of the black art, and himself set up as a writer of tracts and verse – he was literate. One day Dee notes 'Mr. Edward Kelly's lamp overthrow: the spirit of wine long spent too near, and the glass being not stayed with books about it, as it was wont to be, and the same glass so flitting on one side the spirit was spilled out and burned all that was on the table where it stood, linen and written books.'[46] No doubt, mewed up and keeping close in their study with its spirit-lamp, *tot vapores, quot apparitiones.*

Based as they were on Prague, 1584 to 1586, they travelled about. Dee had been in Central Europe before, in Hungary in 1563, where he had seen Rudolph's father, Maximilian, to whom he had dedicated the *Monas*, enthroned at Pressburg. The hermetic philosopher had the cosmopolitan acquaintance of an international *savant*. In April, May and June 1585 he had three audiences of the famed Stephen Bathory, king of Poland.[47] But, back in Prague, their activities aroused the hostility of the Church. In Lent 1586, while Kelly was fasting, hoping to confess his sins to a Jesuit and receive Catholic communion (he had confessed and been absolved the year before in Cracow), the Papal Nuncio demanded to see Dee. Polite diplomatic converse on the sad state of divided Christendom did not mitigate the Nuncio's demand for the surrender of their books. To which Dee replied, they 'are our private documents and our introductory lessons in a celestial school. We talk about them most unwillingly and only when we receive a divine command or permission to do so.' Kelly gave way to one of his paroxysms of anger when they realised that one Pucci, whom they had admitted to their *séances*, was really set by the Jesuits to spy on them. To the Church, Dee and Kelly were necromancers raising evil spirits, while 'in a state of ecstasy and rapture'; and in May Sixtus V issued a brief requiring their extradition. The Emperor conformed with it in appearance, and Dee and Kelly travelled about in Germany, until Rudolph gave them licence to return and take up residence at Trebona, with his friend Count Rosenberg, where Dee remained for the next two years. Here the *séances* and experiments continued with greater ardour and concentration than ever.

Such closeness to the discovery of the great secret necessitated a closer spiritual compact. It was revealed to Kelly, whose wife remained barren, that Dee and he were to share in all things and have their wives in common. Dee: 'Hereupon we were in great amazement and grief of mind that so hard and – as it yet seemed unto me – so unpure a doctrine was propounded and enjoined unto us of them whom I always, from the beginning hitherto, did judge and esteem undoubtedly to be good angels. And had unto E. K. *offered my soul as a pawn* to discharge E. K. his crediting of them as the good and faithful ministers of Almighty God.'⁴⁸ Kelly thought this a proper excuse for not dealing with them any more, 'as his prayer to God of a long time hath been.' Not so the good Doctor, who, grieved to the heart as he and his wife were, thought that the spiritual admonishment must be obeyed. He told his wife, 'Jane, I see that there is no other remedy; but as hath been said of our cross-matching, so it must needs be done.' Jane took a good deal of pacifying, weeping and trembling for a quarter of an hour; but at length 'she showed herself prettily resolved to be content for God's sake and his secret purposes to obey the admonishment.' A solemn covenant was entered into and signed by all four. For Dee it did not matter if the women apprehended but imperfectly: 'if it offend not God, it offended not me, and I pray God it did not offend him.'⁴⁹ Dee was very devout, but perhaps by this conduit the key to all knowledge was to be gained.

Dee became convinced that at last Kelly had discovered the secret. In May 1588, 'Omne quod vivit laudet Deum! Haec est dies quam fecit Dominus! E. K. did open the great secret to me, God be thanked.'⁵⁰ Sir Edward Dyer, an early client of Dee's was in Prague at the time and told the Archbishop of Canterbury later: 'I do assure your grace that that I shall tell you is truth: I am an eye witness thereof and, if I had not seen it, I should not have believed it. I saw Master Kelly put of the base metal into the crucible, and after it was set a little upon the fire and a very small quantity of the medicine put in and stirred . . . it came forth in great proportion perfect gold to the touch, to the hammer, to the test.'[51] Thus the well-known courtier. Young Arthur Dee, who as a boy succeeded Kelly as his father's scryer after they had parted, was convinced that he had seen projection effected and the transmutation of pewter dishes and flagons into silver, which the Prague goldsmiths bought.[52] (Arthur – observe the Celtic name his father gave him – remained always faithful to the hermetic nonsense he was brought up in, and had an interesting career as doctor to the Tsar in Russia.) Kelly was now in the highest honour with the Emperor, who made him a knight of the Holy Roman Empire – henceforth he is always referred to by Dee, and by Burghley, as Sir Edward Kelly.

For this was now the year 1588, *annus mirabilis* portended by the astrologers; the English government, well apprised of these marvels, was anxious to get Dee and Kelly back for the good of their country. The Russian Tsar also made a handsome bid for their services. Sir Edward Dyer had been sent out to get Kelly back by any means available. Burghley instructed Dyer again and again to get him 'to return to his native country, to honour her Majesty, as a loyal natural subject, with the fruits of such great knowledge as God hath given him.'[53] At the crisis of the Armada Burghley is writing, 'if I might have my wish, next to his own coming home, I wish he would, in some secret box, send to her Majesty for a token some such portion as might be to her a sum reasonable to defer her charges for this summer for her Navy, which we are now preparing to the sea, to withstand the strong navy of Spain, discovered upon the coasts between Brittany and Cornwall within these two days.' Then to Kelly himself: 'Good knight, let me end my letter conjuring you in God's holy name not to keep God's gift from your natural country, but rather help make her Majesty a glorious and victorious power against the malice of hers and God's enemies . . . Let no other country bereave us of this felicity, that only – yea only by you, I say – is to be expected.'[54]

Dee answered the summons and came home. But the Emperor was not allowing the treasure of Kelly out of his clutches: he took him into protective custody and kept him in the castle of Pürglitz for the next two years. It was like Stalin's treatment of Kapitza before the war. For, observe, it was not that Rudolph thought Kelly a charlatan, it was precisely because he believed that the Englishman could transmute metal into gold, if only he would: he was holding back. Nor need we consider Kelly a charlatan: no doubt he too was a believer, but the powder was running out and success eluded him. Thus the Emperor played a cat-and-mouse game, to get the secret out of him. When Dee returned to Mortlake, he remained in touch with Sir Edward, had letters from him, and hopes of his return. In March 1593 Dee dreamed two nights together of Kelly, 'as if he were in my house familiar with his wife and brother' – immediately thereupon came a letter from the brother.[55] Sir Edward was back in favour, and promised a privy councillorship. In March 1595 a visitor returned from Prague brought Dee information of Kelly. Then, on 25 November: 'the news that Sir Edward Kelly was slain.' He had been imprisoned again and, attempting to escape, he fell from a window – according to the custom of Czechoslovakia – broke his legs and died of his injuries.

Eleven years earlier the spirits had warned he would come by a violent end.

We have seen enough of the mentality of the time now to view the question of witchcraft in proper proportion, and not to be misled by an excited rhetoric into false estimates and poor historical judgment. (Rhetoric in an historian leads to bad history.) Everybody in that age believed in the supernatural, everybody believed in spirits; the phenomena of bewitching – the survival of the word in common use should be an index of the two-sidedness of the subject – and being bewitched were indigenous and ubiquitous. Every parish had its 'cunning women', its 'white witches', good as well as bad; it is fairly certain that the good immensely outnumbered the evil ones. When the communion cloth was lost from the village church of Thatcham in Berkshire, the churchwardens went to 'the cunning woman' of Burfield to find it for them.[56] Gifford in his *Dialogue* mentions that 'a wise man' recovered a stolen communion cup in his Essex neighbourhood – just as we have seen people resort to Dee and Forman for help. We find a gaol-keeper at Canterbury letting a convicted witch have her freedom to go in and out, telling everybody that she did more good by her physic than two local preachers of God's Word.[57] Many such old crones were mid-wives and in the absence of doctors (apt to be more lethal) effected cures with herbs.

We are here concerned with people's attitude of mind on the subject, rather than any narrative of witch-hunting as such. And to keep a sense of proportion in these matters we must remember that, if a witch could be condemned to death for procuring the death of another person, that was equivalent to murder in the mind of the age; an immensely greater number of people were condemned to death for stealing a sheep, cutting a purse, or such offences. We are told that in the Home Counties altogether some thirty persons were hanged for witchcraft in the first twenty-four years of the reign.[58] But in the single year 1596 some forty persons were hanged in the single county of Somerset for various felonies; in Devon alone in 1598 seventy-four persons were sentenced to be hanged.[59] This was the usual thing all over the country: it serves to put the barbarity of persecuting witches into the proper perspective. The fact is that the exaggerated figures on the subject are ludicrous, and the historical picture drawn from them quite out of focus. H. C. Lea, whose collections form the basis for a recent excited view of the subject, thought that some 90,000 persons had been executed as witches in England over the whole period while the statutes were in force; a reliable modern estimate is something less than one thousand in the course of two centuries. Evidently Lea had no critical sense whatever, cannot have known what a figure meant; and those who accept contemporary Continental figures for the burnings of witches abroad are no less naive – one should know that in history earlier statistics are almost always unreliable.*

A sounder authority tells us that 'those who believe that in Britain the evils of witchcraft swept the country like an epidemic would be grievously disappointed in searching the records of our Courts of Justice. Thousands of indictments may be turned over without a single accusation of sorcery coming to light; and as for a verdict of a coroner's jury pointing to the belief that death was due to the practice of any form of magic, I have heard of no more than one.'[60] 'Witchcraft trials were sufficiently unusual events to excite the interest of the reading public,' and so our evidence of them comes mainly from tracts and news-sheets. The truth is that such outbreaks were sporadic and marginal to English society; a subtler understanding of it should indicate that outbursts were local, depending on chance conjunctions of people given to hysteria, usually young females or children, taking against old

* H. R. Trevor-Roper, in 'The European Witch-Craze of the 16th and 17th Centuries', *Religion, the Reformation and Social Change*, 162, after telling us on p. 99 that Lea's 'History of Witchcraft', 'had it been written, would no doubt have stood as firm' – as his work on the Inquisition ('it is inconceivable that this work on the Inquisition, as an objective narrative of fact, will ever be replaced') on p. 162 tells us that 'C. L. Ewen's careful study of the records of the Home Circuit has discredited all such wild guesses.' Precisely; but Professor Trevor-Roper does not seem to have noticed the contradiction. I suspect that his naive acceptance of contemporary Continental figures is equally mistaken.

crones in their neighbourhood, with persons disposed to religious excitement and inclined to be persecutors.* Thus it is that several of the more notorious outbreaks occur in the one area of Essex. There are whole areas of the country where one never hears of an outbreak, however intimately one may be acquainted with its local history during the period. One sees the harm that is done to history by theorising about it – history is not a theoretical subject; thus one gets this matter as much out of focus as that of the Rise of the Gentry, when the proper method to investigate its incidence is more modest, concrete and local.

So there was no unilateral increase of witch-hunting in England marching forward to a culmination under the Commonwealth. Kittredge tells us 'the plain and simple truth is this: during the twenty-two years of James's reign there was no more excitement on the subject of witchcraft, and there were no more executions, than under the last twenty-two of Elizabeth. James's accession was not in any sense the signal for an outburst of prosecution. The first bad year was 1612, when he had been on the throne for almost a decade.'† In that year there were two bursts of witch-hunting, one in Lancashire, the other in Northamptonshire: if we could know all the facts, we should find they were owing to special circumstances in each case. It was because these two events were so exceptional that they drew so much attention. Kittredge tells us categorically that there is not a particle of evidence that James brought forward the new statute of 1604, and that it was hardly more severe than the Elizabethan statute of 1563, which it mostly followed word for word. James had written a book on *Demonology* earlier in Scotland, where interest in the subject was naturally more intense owing to the religious enticement; but he merely

* This is the common-sense answer to Professor Trevor-Roper's rhetorical question, 'Why did one man, like Matthew Hopkins, appear in 1645 rather than in 1635?' The simple answer is that Charles I and Laud would never have allowed Matthew Hopkins his head in 1635 – he was there all right – but ten years later the Puritans, victorious in the Civil War, did. It is no answer to theorise doubtfully, 'when we compare England with the Continent, we see that the rhythm of English persecution follows very closely that of the Continental craze of which it is a pale reflection.'

† 288–9. Similarly Kittredge refutes, 251–3, the charge which Trevor-Roper uncritically repeats that Bishop Jewel imported the witchcraze into England from the Continent. Kittredge had already gone into the question and shown that Jewel was mainly referring to the lapse into superstitions under Mary, while his reference to witches was an aside, relating to ordinary indigenous beliefs in the matter. 'It shows no trace of Continental influence; it conveys no suggestion of the Witches' Sabbath and its enormities . . . and these are the only utterances of the kind that have been discovered in all Jewel's published works, which extend to thousands of pages.' What one expects in an historian is a sense of proportion and judgment, not preconceived ideas backed up by rhetoric.

expressed what was the dominant opinion among people at large, as did the statutes of the English Parliament.

People suspected of being evil-doing witches were almost always those who deviated from expected social norms: rebarbative old women with secondary male characteristics, people with unusual birth marks upon them, solitary and poverty-stricken persons with a psychosis and a scunner against society. Many such people at any time would like to get their own back for what they suffer, would do harm to others if they could; the difference is that more primitive societies believe that they can do it, and they often believed it themselves. The Elizabethans had no systematic knowledge of the workings of the unconscious; the motive of revenge has been very much underestimated in all this. To this we must add the even greater motive of power over others, sometimes the desire to extract money or love, sometimes envy or simple hatred.

Witches were almost always poor, lower-class people, sometimes desperate with poverty or bitter dependence. The theory of witchcraft had been built up by educated persons, usually theologians or at least clerics. In an age which was saturated by the supernatural, with a mesmerised fixation on a personal God, a personal Devil was no less real to them. The belief was that the Devil could not actually destroy a man unless he had renounced God.[61] The theory was that witches made a compact with the Devil, and that they had sexual relations with him in the form of an Incubus – one sees the element of sexual hysteria in this. Sometimes they had relations with their familiars in animal form; but again we must remember that bestiality exists at all times and in all human societies. The intensity of the belief in their relations with the Devil, acting as his agent to destroy or harm other human beings, is only another form of belief in the supernatural.

On the other side, there was little understanding of the causes of disease, especially of mental disease, melancholia, the manic-depressive temperament, neurosis, psychosis – though intelligent Elizabethans were beginning to appreciate hysteria for what it was. Similarly with tuberculosis, or internal ulcers, or cancer. When people 'pined away', without visible cause, it was often put down to being bewitched or ill-wished. When the young Earl of Derby was dying in 1594 – better known as Ferdinando, Lord Strange, patron of the players – he was convinced he was bewitched. A wax image was found in his bedroom; a homely old woman was 'mumbling in a corner of his honour's chamber, but what God knoweth' (probably praying for him); the Earl had strange dreams and saw a ghastly apparition.[62] It is not improbable that he was dying of venereal disease, for he had had a gay, dissolute life. The doctors thought he was ill of a surfeit followed by over-exertion; but it was bad enough to think anything, to be dying at thirty-four, just after succeeding to the earldom.

The subject has to be seen against the whole background of the age: persecution and obsession with the subject were more barbarous and severe in some areas of the Continent – though contemporary figures of witch-burnings are not to be relied on. Differences are observable: in England witches convicted of the death of a person might be hanged, as with a murderer, but this was by due process of law, not by the fiat of German princelings or the systematic and relentless pursuit of inquisitors, who burned them in scores. Moreover, witches' sabbaths, the gatherings of hundreds of such ghouls for their infernal purposes, which were so widely believed in on the Continent, simply did not exist in England, much more moderate in this as in regard also to torture. Ewen tells us that, from the records of the courts, 'in the Home Circuit the chance of a witch suffering the death penalty, when arraigned before the regular justices, was small, eighty-one out of every hundred escaping the rope.'[63] He goes on to say that the proportion increased severely during the decade 1598–1607; but again one must remember that there were many cases of convicted witches being reprieved, while a sentence to imprisonment for any offence was dangerous enough, the conditions of prisons being so unhealthy and mortality so high in them. Common sense – as against thetoric – tells us that witch-hunting to the death was exceptional and largely a matter of chance, like the chance that brought the odious Matthew Hopkins, 'Witch-finder general', to the fore under the Commonwealth: that one man procured more deaths than anyone. It was an ill-chance that raised him up, but a chance – like the chance that brought out McCarthy in America, or Oswald: nothing more; no conspiracy – the product of erratic historical judgment.

We can now, perhaps, see the subject in better perspective.

It is a suspicious circumstance that Essex should have been the scene of four noteworthy persecutions, in 1566, 1579, 1582, 1589. There may well have been some special reason making it so; for we find a local J.P., Brian Darcy, taking the lead in several of these cases, using 'detestable methods' in bullying, beguiling or trapping these poor people into confessing their guilt.[64] He was evidently a persecutor: we need no further theorising to discover why Essex was specially troubled by witches. (We know a great deal more about the procuring of confessions, from Nazi Germany and Soviet Russia, nowadays.) We can see how this worked from the notorious case of the Throckmorton children of Warboys in Huntingdonshire, supposedly bewitched by Mother Samuel, a poor old woman utterly dependent upon this family, already prone to credulity. The trial made a sensation because of the prominence of the families involved and, throwing light on the usual phenomena, may serve for all.

Robert Throckmorton's girls took to having fits – it was a way of drawing attention to themselves – and they took against a poor ill-favoured neighbour, Mother Samuel, who came to the house to work. They insisted that they were bewitched by her, and could not bear the sight of her; when she kept away they had fits again and demanded that they must see her. The poor woman put their behaviour down to pure 'wantonness'; but so many good people, Cambridge dons, clergymen and uncles, took such an interest in their condition that they were encouraged to carry on. 'Such were the heavenly and divine speeches of the children in their fits to this old woman . . . as that, if a man had heard it, he would not have thought himself better edified at ten sermons.'[65] These young creatures were evidently spoiled, and would have been better for a sound thrashing. The poor woman was compelled to live in the house, victim of this ill behaviour; she was harried to and fro, experimented upon, tormented to confess, grew ill and sleepless, until she began to believe that she was to blame. 'O, sir, I have been the cause of all this trouble to your children.' That was enough – but fortunately nothing worse happened to the little miscreants. They were the centre of attention and received much sympathy. Visited by their uncle, Henry Pickering, from Christ's (a Puritanical college at Cambridge, home of the vociferous Perkins), who brought several scholars to view them, he told the much-persecuted woman that 'there was no way to prevent the judgments of God but by her confession and repentance: which, if she did not in time, he hoped one day to see her burned at a stake; he himself would bring fire and wood, and the children should blow the coals.'[66] This kindly man became a parson in Northamptonshire, and grandfather of Dryden.

What settled Mother Samuel's fate was that Lady Cromwell crossed her path. This was the second wife of Oliver Cromwell's grandfather, a neurotic invalid who took much interest in the condition of the Throckmorton girls and, reproaching Mother Samuel one day, received ill words from her. Returning home, Lady Cromwell worsened, began to have dreams of the witch and her cat – and when, after a year, her ladyship died, Mother Samuel was at last brought to book. Harried by the Justices and the rector – several of these were the girls' uncles – scratched by the women and children to make the blood come out of her, driven from pillar to post, she at length was convinced that she was responsible for Lady Cromwell's death. This, of course, was equivalent to murder; she was arraigned, with husband and daughter for complicity. The daughter was made to repeat, 'as I am a witch and consenting to the death of Lady Cromwell, I charge thee, Come out of her.' The devil came out, and the children recovered from their fits. Everybody was convinced, including the poor husband; in April 1593 all three were hanged, mother, father and daughter. Such was the celebrated Warboys affair.

At Chelmsford in 1566 three women were arraigned. One of them was hanged; a second woman continued her career of witchcraft, and was hanged along with two more, at Chelmsford in 1579.[67] At St. Osyth's in 1582 a clutch of some thirteen or fourteen persons were indicted; nearly all the secondary books on the subject say that as many were hanged. Common sense should suggest that this is incredible; and, in fact, the legal records confirm that two were hanged, the rest reprieved, acquitted or discharged. Once more the persecuting J.P., Brian Darcy, was to the fore in hounding these creatures; but only in the case of two women, Ursula Kemp and Elizabeth Bennet, was the death penalty exacted.[68] Again there was a drive in Essex against witches in 1589, when ten women and one man were tried; three were declared not guilty, one bailed, two were guilty but reprieved (one being pregnant), three were hanged that year, a fourth the year after.[69] Why was Essex more given to this sort of thing than any other area? – fifty years later it was the scene of the atrocious activities of Matthew Hopkins, son of the godly minister of Wenham. It was simply owing to having produced two nasty persecutors in a dominantly Puritan area. That is all: it is quite enough.

With this background witchcraft was a subject of intellectual discussion, though with much less excitement than on the Continent. In the 1570's the books of Lavater and Daneau on spectres and witches were translated; in 1587 George Gifford, minister of God's word at Maldon in benighted Essex, produced his *Discourse of the Subtle Practices of Devils by Witches and Sorcerers*. Interested in the subject, in such an area, he produced a second work in 1593, *A Dialogue concerning Witches and Witchcrafts*.[70] For a Puritan, he was moderate and comparatively tolerant. He had no doubt that as the result of 'raising up suspicions and rumours of sundry innocent persons, many guiltless are upon men's oaths condemned to death and much innocent blood is shed.' On the other hand, 'the word of God doth plainly show that there be witches', and, since the word of God said so, proved witches must be put to death. To doubt this was atheism. There were people who actually believed that there were no witches, but this was disproved by the confessions of the witches themselves. These were infallible arguments; the witch-hunters held these trump-cards so long as people believed the nonsense of the literal interpretation of scripture, and had not the sense to see through the confessions. But the gist of Gifford's argument was that these things were the works of the Devil, whom 'God hath given leave to do evil.' Gifford was contemptuous of the ignorant people who thought that witches could do what they did of themselves – i.e. raise tempests, destroy corn and fruits, lame cattle, kill men, women and children: these were the works of the Devil through their means, but always by God's leave. No idea, of course, that the one position was as much nonsense as the other.

In 1584 there appeared a work intellectually far superior to anything else on the subject in the whole discreditable course it ran: Reginald Scott's *The Discovery of Witchcraft*.[71] Among the prose works of the age it may be rated as a great book: I cannot think that those who mention it in passing can have read it – it is a long book – or they would have perceived Scott's passionate indignation at the barbarous cruelty unleashed by this obsession, his compassion for the poor creatures that suffered, his complete understanding of their hysteria, the delusions they had in common with their persecutors, the emptiness of the confessions extorted by torture, mental or physical, the care with which he had devoted himself to the subject, reading all the books on it, and the trouble he took to investigate personally the cases that came under his view. 'If you read the executions done upon witches, you shall see such impossibilities confessed as none, having his right wits, will believe. Among other like false confessions, we read that there was a witch confessed at the time of her death or execution, that she had raised all the tempests and procured all the frosts and hard weather that happened in the winter 1565 – and that many grave and wise men believed her.' Considering that he wrote his book thus early, in 1584, it is not an anachronism to condemn those people for the fools they were, when a humane and intelligent contemporary was able to see already that the whole thing was nonsense.

Though Scott had to doff his cap at the biblical warrant for the existence of witches – and was a religious man himself, a moderate Anglican – he obviously believed that they did not exist. He begins warily, in such an atmosphere, by questioning the physical impossibilities and miracles attributed to witches, showing up the absurdities imputed to them by papists – a shrewd tactical move – as by poets, and finally witchmongers. He then exposes the cruelties practised by these last and the inquisitors. He is obviously shocked by the filthy stories, the obscenities of witches' copulation with devils, the sucking their teats, etc., which appeared in the classic attack, Krämer and Sprenger's *Malleus Maleficarum* (1486) – product of a diseased German imagination, exactly paralleled by Streicher's anti-Semitic obscenities in our day. But it is not long before Scott's anger and contempt break through. 'All must be true that is written against witches: if a witch deprive one of his privities [as many believed they could] it is done only by prestigious means, so as the senses are but illuded. Marry, by the Devil it is really taken away, and in like sort restored. These are no jests, for *they be written by them that were and are judges upon the lives and deaths of those persons*.'[72] As for the beliefs of the idiot people, taken in by every sort of knavery, imposture and delusion – 'And know you this, by the way, that heretofore Robin Goodfellow and Hobgoblin were as terrible, and also as credible, to the people as hags and witches be now.' And Scott was clear that 'in time to come, a witch will be as much derided and contemned, and as plainly perceived, as the illusion and knavery of Robin Goodfellow'. Nevertheless, humans being what they are, it took two centuries before this consummation was achieved – when John Wesley complained that it was infidels that had 'hooted witchcraft out of the world.' But, then, credulity was his vocation.

Scott was probably inspired to write his book by the appearance of Bodin's *Démonomanie* in 1580, the most influential book of the age on this subject, by the leading French political and economic writer.* It was the most powerful target to select – and also the

* It is proper to describe him as such, without calling him 'the Aristotle, the Montesquieu of the sixteenth century' – mere rhetorical exaggeration again (Trevor-Roper, 122). A more judicious estimate of Bodin is to be found in R. Trevor Davies, *Four Centuries of Witch Beliefs*, a reliable account of the subject. For a perceptive

most disgraceful, for the barbarity as well as the credulity of Bodin passes belief. He accepted all the marvels of witchcraft, the flying through the air to attend witches' sabbaths, the worship of Beelzebub, sometimes as at Poitiers in 1564 presided over by 'a huge black goat, around whom they danced, after each of them bearing a candle had . . . kissed him under the tail . . . At the end of the proceedings the Devil dismissed them saying, Revenge yourselves or die.'[73] Here is the revenge-motive, on the part of starving and desperate people, which undoubtedly led many of them into wishing harm to others.

Bodin's fantastic stories are based on the confessions of witches – but the confessions were extracted by torture. Scott, a decent English gentleman, was shocked by Bodin's cruel procedures. 'Bodin's own practice [as a judge] was to torture children and delicate persons, but not the old and hardened' – less could be gained from them.[74] 'The judge who does not send a convicted witch to the stake should himself be put to death. A person accused of witchcraft should never be acquitted, unless the falsity of the accusation has been more obvious than the sun.' Rumour in itself should suffice to condemn a witch. Bodin loaded the dice against the victims: no loophole was to be allowed. Scott's is a complete and damning exposure of the French 'Aristotle' showing up the self-contradictions, the 'subtle and devilish device' Bodin proposed to torture these poor souls, the rubbish he believed as evidence, the total absence of any justice of mind in the judge.[75] But it was Bodin who had the influence, not Scott – a lurid imputation on the mentality of the age. Bodin's performance was such that it has been suggested that he had a secret motivation – perhaps, since he had heterodox and too tolerant views on religious subjects, he unconsciously wished to make his orthodoxy more emphatic where he could.[76] His performance is more understandable against the

diagnosis of Bodin, cf. the contemporary Samuel Harsnet. 'There is no great wit without a mixture of madness. John Bodin the Frenchman is a perfect idea of both these, who, being in his younger years of a most piercing, quick, speculative wit, which grew of a light stirring and discursive melancholy in him, fell in the middle of his age to be a pure sot . . . This man . . . his wit being deeply woaded with that melancholy black dye, had his brain *veram sedem daemonum*, the theatre and sporting house for devils to dance in. For he hath in his brain such strange speculations, phantasms and theorems for devils as a man may see a great deal of madness mixed with his great wit. For he holds that devils may transform themselves into any shape of beasts or similitude of men, and may have the act of generation with women as they please . . . that a witch by ointments and charms may transform herself into the shape of any beast, bird, or fish, that she may fly in the air, that she may deprive men of their generative power, and may cause hail, thunder and wind at her pleasure, etc.' Samuel Harsnet, *A Declaration of egregious Popish Impostures* (1603), 131–2.

disgraceful events of the religious wars in France, the mutual massacres, smoking people out of caves, the frequent murders and assassinations.

The interesting thing about Bodin intellectually is that his position rested upon a natural scepticism: since we know so little of natural and physical laws, it is absurd to refuse 'to believe the facts of sorcery because we cannot explain them.'[77] It is like Newman's sceptical mind using the epistemological difficulties in establishing any certain knowledge to suggest – why then not angels? No-one has realised that the whole of Scott's Book XIII is really an answer to this – that the real magic lies in the wonderful works of Nature and nature's secret workings. This was the direction Bacon was to enforce, which led to the astonishing developments of scientific knowledge, once the fires of religious exaltation and conflict had been banked down.

Scott's scepticism was simple and straightforward: he recognised nonsense when he saw it. He took the trouble to investigate cases himself, and exposed at least one of hearing strange voices as ventriloquism.[78] He regarded the confessions obtained by threats and torture as valueless, the beliefs of the old crones themselves as the product of hysteria or delusion – he might have added, the mental climate of the time. He regarded much of what we have been investigating as jiggery-pokery, imposture, astrology and alchemy as 'juggling, conjuring arts.' As for the people – 'the common people have been so assotted and bewitched with whatsoever poets have feigned of witchcraft, either in earnest, in jest, or else in derision, and whatsoever loud liars and coseners herein have invented, and with whatsoever tales they have heard from old doting women . . . and finally with whatsoever they have swallowed up through tract of time, or through their own timorous nature of ignorant conceit [supposition] concerning these matters of hags and witches, that they think it heresy to doubt in any part of the matter, specially because they find this word witchcraft expressed in the Scriptures.'[79]

No wonder so rational, so forward-looking, so modern-minded a book was not paid attention to at the time: it blew much of the credulity of the age sky-high. Nevertheless, it had its influence: a number of believers in witchcraft, especially theologians like Perkins, had Scott in mind in their replies, though incapable of comprehending the completeness of his destruction of their position. A number of people read him, including, it seems, Shakespeare, to whom his sceptical, humane and compassionate nature would be sympathetic. Scott's indirect influence in creating a more civilised attitude may be more important – such as came about with Charles I and Laud, to the anger of the Puritans. His attitude of mind appealed in Holland, a civilised and comparatively tolerant country: in 1609 his book was translated into Dutch, at the request of the law and history faculties at Leyden. A second edition was called for in 1637. It was thus one of the few English books thought worthy of translation into a foreign language. With the French attitude of cultural superiority, the most effective answer to Bodin was given no currency in that tongue.

Naturally more influential than so emancipated a mind as Scott was the ever-popular Perkins: he represented what ordinary fools thought. After his death his course of sermons on the subject was published as *A Discourse of the Damned Art of Witchcraft*, by an Essex Puritan, one of the Pickerings involved in the Warboys affair, and printed by the Cambridge University printer. The book is dedicated to Chief Justice Coke, 'always favourable to the House of Levi', appealing to his equity and moderation. What his moderation was we know from his bullying of Ralegh and others at their trials. As for equity, Perkins holds to the position that the convicted witch must be punished with death 'by the law of Moses, the equity whereof is perpetual' – which means that the taboo in force with a lot of savage Old Testament Jews are to be enforced two thousand years later, indeed in perpetuity. (One sees with sympathy what Whitgift, Bancroft and Laud had to put up with from these people.) Perkins went one better: of the two, good witches and bad, 'the more horrible and detestable is the good witch . . . it were a thousand times better for the land if all witches, but specially the blessing witch, might suffer death.'[80] It was fortunate that the country did not act on the advice of this Cambridge divine so profuse with his moral counsels, for the immensely more numerous 'wise women' did useful work with their midwifery and herbal cures, while the bad witch at least sought to do harm. To what do we owe this complete inversion of sense? To Perkins' religious beliefs, of course: both kinds of witch have made a compact with Satan. At no point does Perkins meet Scott, whom he has in mind, with a rational argument, simply with an insinuation and an assertion of nonsense: 'the *patrons of witches* be learned men, yet they are greatly deceived in fathering the practices of sorcery upon a melancholic humour' (i.e. hysteria.)

Satan, Perkins informs us, 'is as it were God's ape.'[81] Exactly: their crazy fixation on the one superfluous concept produced its reflex in the other. Pickering in his Preface embroiders on Perkins' theme: as God made a covenant with his Church (which? one might ask), so Satan makes covenant with his instruments; as God has sacraments, so Satan his charms and figures; as God revealed his will to his prophets, so Satan to his soothsayers and sybils; as God has his ministers, so Satan has his in witches, both men and women. Thus we perceive that the beliefs and propositions of one system are as nonsensical as those of the other upon which they depend, and that all the human suffering inflicted and endured, indefensible on any rational grounds, was defended only by the nonsense propositions they believed in.

Belief makes fools of all.

That this was so was brought home less tragically, more ludicrously, at the end of the century by the excellent Samuel Harsnet's exposures of claims to exorcise evil spirits on both sides, Puritan and Catholic. Set on by the highly intelligent Bancroft, Harsnet laid about him with a will: his books are spirited and amusing, with a sense of humour that recommended them to Shakespeare. (But a sense of humour, with those people, was irreligious: as Montherlant says, 'Mais comme il est très difficile de persuader les gens qu'ils sont idiots.')

Harsnet's first book was an exposure of the pretences and frauds of a group of Puritans at Nottingham; but he began, tactically, with an onslaught on the Pope's claims to work miracles. 'None but he and his priests can dispatch a miracle as easily as a squirrel can crack a nut: a miracle in the bread, a miracle in the wine, a miracle in holy water, a miracle in holy oil, a miracle in our Lady's milk, a miracle in the ass's tail, a miracle in lamps, candles, beads, breeches, rags, bones, stones, *omnia stultorum et miraculorum plena.*'[82] Already 'the least bone of a canonised saint, traitor St. Campion forsooth,' was working miracles. (In fact a drop of the martyr's blood falling upon Henry Walpole at Campion's execution converted him into becoming a Jesuit, and ultimately a martyr himself. An interesting example of an Elizabethan mentality.)

An issue emerges here. The Catholics claimed that their priests alone had the power to exorcise devils. Protestants agreed that the age of miracles had ended in the first Christian centuries. What could they put up against Catholic claims which, under the impulse of the Jesuits and seminaries, were bringing in converts in the 1580's? – Evidently, the answer was to show that Protestant

ministers could exorcise spirits too. A Puritan, John Darrel, took
to displaying his gifts in this direction. 'Open the curtain and see
their puppets play', says Harsnet, who was clearly fond of players
and play-acting. Quite young, Darrel had cast one devil out of a
Derbyshire girl and then, on her repossession, eight more. For ten
years he rested, like God on the seventh day, 'out of work', until
in 1596 he cast a devil out of a Burton boy – a triumph which was
written up by a minister, while holy Mr. Hildersham, a leading
Puritan, gave it his *imprimatur*. Upon this Darrel was sent for into
Lancashire to exercise his powers, by a credulous Starkie: Darrel
did not disappoint, he dispossessed seven persons in that house
'at one clap' – though one of the women subsequently fell into the
hands of the seminary priests and was taken round by them to
Catholic houses 'to display her counterfeit fits and cures.'

Darrel's greatest triumph was at Nottingham, where his
exploits made a big stir, and raised up factions in both church and
town. His exorcism of devils from a youth called Somers brought
him such success that 'they made choice of me for their preacher
and not only so but flocked to the house of God, made haste and
were swift to hear the Word.'[83] Those present at the scene of
dispossession were struck with such fear that 'they quaked and
trembled and wept most bitterly.' Somers was a young singer,
whose talents for mimicry Darrel had noticed in an alehouse at
Ashby; the youth had an artistic, perhaps a neurotic, temperament, for he later ascribed his depression to 'singing filthy and
wanton songs.' Darrel set to work on him and taught him how to
simulate fits, the usual symptoms of hysteria, hearing voices, the
devils at work in him. Darrel's object was a righteous one: it was
'to confound all atheists who think there are no devils', and to
convince 'the papists, who hold that our ministers cannot dispossess any.'[84]

And it worked like mad. Soon people took sides, the town
'became extraordinarily divided, one railing at another at their
meeting in the streets . . . The pulpits also rang of nothing but
devils and witches: wherewith men, women and children were so
affrighted as many of them durst not stir in the night, nor so much
as a servant almost go into his master's cellar without company.
Few grew to be sick or evil at ease but straightway they were
deemed to be possessed.'[85] People crowded into the chamber to
look upon the possessed lad's sufferings, till delivered by the ministrations of Darrel, supported by his fellow-ministers. But people
were taking sides, some holding that 'the Devil himself, envying

the happy estate of Nottingham by means of Mr. Darrel's preaching there, did raise up that slander of possession to hinder it.' Evidently there were unbelievers about; the faithful complained of their want of faith – like Aimée Semple Macpherson at the walking on the waters at Long Beach.

Darrel refused to perform his act at the church of St. Mary's, for fear that it might be imputed to the holiness of the place, not himself. The performance took place in a low dark room. Darrel planned a new fast to take place after Assizes 1598, to dispossess Somers anew. He had put it across people that the youth was unaware of what he was doing in his fits, dancing on his bed with lewd gestures, falling backwards into the fire, pretending to extra strength, guessing how much money was in the gaoler's purse (when he had already heard the gaoler whisper how much). Several heard something say within the youth, 'Ego sum Rex, Ego sum Deus', with his tongue turned into his throat and his lips shut. Another had seen something run up Somer's legs, into his belly, making a swelling in his cheek. After Somers's exposure, Vicar Aldridge admitted that he wanted to believe and, having heard that witches had spirits in the form of kitlings, they came to his mind when the coverlet moved: a man's senses may be deceived when 'put into a great fear.'[86]

This kind of thing went on for months, up and down. The 'wiser sort laughed to scorn', but there were not many of those; and when it threatened to die down, Darrel put Somers up to detecting witches. Somers pointed out thirteen in Nottingham, mostly old widows, one of them blind. Darrel asked the Mayor to start a witch-hunt, but nothing could be found against the women – except two, who were detained. This roused some people against Somers, who, tiring of his tricks, took refuge in St. John's poorhouse, where he confessed everything. Somers's motive was quite simple: he wanted to be bought out of his apprenticeship to a musician. Darrel had done this for him and found a place for him 'to keep silver-haired conies', but then wanted him nearer at hand to advance the good work. Darrel wrote his instructions in a school text-book, *Sententiae pueriles* – hence the Latin tags; he coached him in his tricks, making muscular movements under the coverlet and twitching his toes. Foaming at the mouth, Somers had expounded the Apostles' Creed in one of his fits, 'a glorious interpretation which much edified the simple people.'[87] The foaming was procured by a piece of black lead in Somers's mouth: when discovered, Darrel said it was the practice of the Devil to put black lead into a possessed person's mouth. Wise Mrs. Aldridge, the vicar's wife: 'The Devil would not show anything to them that did not believe.'

Darrel was hard put to it at the exposure of all this, but proceeded to foist the blame for Somers's dissembling on a supposed conjurer, one Ayer; then Somers was induced to say that the Devil, in the form of a black dog, had persuaded him to dissemble. And Darrel had his faithful supporters: a fellow Puritan minister, Brinsley, had seen the dog 'at the chamber door and did think the dog's eyes did glow like fire.' (The dog was a spurrier's black spaniel.) Darrel's companions did not fear to come forward in his defence in the press. His fellow 'minister and preacher of the Word of God', George More, from his lodging in the Clink came out with an uncompromising justification of their doings in Lancashire.* The seminary priests also in the Clink told More to his face that their doings there had all been 'conjuring and knavery'; but 'this was no marvel, for if the Church of England had the power to cast out devils, then the Church of Rome was a false church.'

There was the serious point at issue: conflicting claims to exist, the basic fight for power.

Harsnet exposed Catholic doings of the sort in a second book, *A Declaration of egregious Popish Impostures* (1603). The events brought to light went back to the exciting years 1585–6, the years of the Babington Plot when the Jesuit campaign was at its height, and involved far more important and interesting people. It is a fascinating story – as Harsnet says, 'let the comedy begin.' 'This play of sundry miracles' took place at various Catholic houses, Lord Vaux' at Hackney, the Earl of Lincoln's in Canon Row, at Barnes's at Fulmer, but above all at Sir George Peckham's at Denham. Edmund Peckham was 'the chief procurer in the comedy', an intemperate person who had ruined his estate and had wife, concubine and family to maintain. A dozen priests – some venerated among the English Martyrs – maintained the house as a place for exorcism, to which Protestants inclining that way could be brought to be converted by the miracles they

---

* George More, *A True Discourse concerning the certain Possession and Dispossession of seven Persons in one Family, which also may serve as part of an Answer to a feigned and false Discovery, which speaketh very much evil of this as of the rest of those great and mighty works of God which be of the like nature.* (1600). Observe the unquenchable Puritan spirit. Harsnet was answered by a second rude tract in that year, *A Detection of that Sinful Shameful Lying and Ridiculous Discourse of Samuel Harsnet,* which showed not only the unlikelihood but the 'flat impossibility' of Somers' counterfeiting. These people were unteachable.

witnessed. The priests impressed upon them the view that many Protestants were possessed – some said all Protestants were – and there was great resort there of the doubtful: in six months a hundred were reconciled. They made a mistake, however, in inviting one Buckinghamshire neighbour, who said roundly, 'I marvel that the house sinketh not for such wickedness committed in it.' This was John Hampden's father, whose wife was the aunt of Oliver Cromwell.

The subjects on whom the priests practised were three men and three women. Richard Mainy was Peckham's brother-in-law; educated overseas, he was a melancholic with a touch of *hysterica passio*, on account of which he had had to leave the order of Bonshommes in France, and had no other means of subsistence. Father Dibdale and the sainted Father Cornelius took him up and gradually convinced him that he was possessed and could not be healed until he returned to the Catholic faith he had abjured.[88] Thus he became thoroughly entangled. Francis Marwood would tremble all over at the touch of the Blessed Edmund Campion's girdle, which had come from Jerusalem and which he wore at Tyburn. They had other relics of Campion for application: Father Weston, the well-known Jesuit Provincial held that 'certain pieces of Father Campion's body did wonderfully burn the Devil.'[89] They had a thumb of his, and a bone from Father Bryan which worked wonders. The third man was Sir George Peckham's man, Trayford. Sara, Alice and Frances Williams's father was also Peckham's servant – they thought Sara, their chief exhibit, 'a meet person to keep their counsel however they should deal or practise with her.'

There was a great resort of priests to this laboratory of spiritual experiment: Father Weston alias Edmunds, the chief Jesuit, Dibdale next, with Cornelius, Ballard, Tyrrell, Sherwood and others. There also came Babington, Chideock Tichborne and others of those engaged in the Babington Plot. Father Weston wrote a book putting forward the achievements of Exorcism, which procured them great reputation, 'allured to those strange attempts by Mr. Ballard. Both Mr. Babington and divers of his company were often at the exorcisings. It prevailed greatly with them when they saw we had great commandment over devils' – it prepared Catholic minds and hearts for the attempt.[90] The older priests, Heywood, Dolman, Redman, and the graver sort in prison at Wisbech disapproved of these doings: they knew of them beyond seas but did not want them brought into England.

Life at Denham was full of excitements. On the morning of the burial of a zealous Protestant there was a howling storm: Mainy convinced the company that it was the Devil welcoming him, many people wept, and his widow became a Catholic for life. The house was crawling with spirits; written on the walls under the hangings were strange names, which the priests said were their names, Hobberdidance, Flibbertigibbet, Modo, Mahu, which they put the girls up to call on in their fits. (Shakespeare made use of these names, which Edgar cites in his madness, in *King Lear*, along with other evidences that he had read Harsnet). Not all their doings were funny; they exorcised Elizabeth Calthrop until she was found dead at the bottom of the stairs. Sara Williams *was* afraid to go into the corn chamber, because there had been conjuring for money there. Mainy threw fits every Friday, and thought that he would die on Good Friday. One night there was a scraping in a chamber like a rat, and some ran out saying it was an evil spirit. 'And Master Cornelius being in the next chamber came presently [immediately] forth in his gown, with his book of exorcisms in his hand, and went into the corner where the noise was. There he began to charge the devil upon pain of many torments that he should depart. He flung holy water upon the walls and used such earnest speeches as this examinate [Sara Williams] was very much afeared. Howbeit she well observed that for all his speakings and sprinkling of holy water, the noise did not cease till he had knocked with something upon the ceiling. Whereby she since hath verily thought it was either a rat or some such thing that made the noise, and not the Devil.'[91]

But this was some time after she had been brought to her senses. As Somers had been supported by Darrel, so Sara was supported by the priests: for nearly four years she was carried about from place to place by them helping to advance the faith. Before this she had never had any visions; during this period the priests made her tell them her dreams and turned them into visions; when they gave her the holy potion to drink or held her head over burning brimstone she often did not know what she said. (Like Aldous Huxley with mescuel or L.S.D.) She now stoutly denied any possession by spirits, said that her visions as well as Mainy's trances at Mass were all false, and much resented the treatment she received. Here comes in the strong element of sex-hysteria in this highly celibate atmosphere. The priests would put Campion's thumb into her mouth. Mainy feigned to be very saintly, but in fact he pursued Mistress Plater 'very wickedly bent'. At one time of menstrual trouble the priests applied 'a relic to the secret place and so with a maid at Lord Vaux' – now she loathed to think of it.[92] The priest (subsequent martyr) Sherwood would pinch her blue all over and say it was the Devil. At Lord Vaux' house, 'a little before she was exorcised in the chair, the priests caused a woman to squirt something by her privy parts into her body, which made her very sick. She was so used once or twice more at Hackney and once at Denham . . . to her hurt.' The priests gave out that the devil departed by 'her priviest part'. When she married, they told her husband she would never bring him any children, 'the Devil had torn those parts in such sort': she had since had five children. That not all was unenjoyable in all this we learn from the sidelight that 'in Christmas time there was gaming and mumming at Lord Vaux' house . . . she saw the mummers dressed with their vizards, whereby she learned to talk of such things.' Here is the play-acting element that we saw in the Puritan Darrel's *protégé*, Somers.

If the priest Dibdale had lived longer she would have been sent beyond seas for a nun – he had laid aside £40 for it. She used to receive presents of silver and gold, which she would hand over to Dibdale; after his execution she delivered it to Father Alexander. When had up before the J.P.s at Oxford for recusancy, she would confess nothing: she was instructed by the priests, who maintained her in prison, never to take any oath, then she might say anything, 'though it were untrue, to excuse herself.' Here was the Catholic doctrine of equivocation, which made such a bad impression for the Jesuit Provincial, Garnet, at the time of Gunpowder Plot.

Her sister Frances had had similar experiences. Before Denham she used to go to church; then the priests got hold of her and persuaded her she was possessed. She was rebaptised with proper rites, as all three girls were: salt in mouth, spittle on mouth and eyes, oil on lips and nose. She would be bound in a chair, given the holy potion, her nose held over the pan of burning brimstone, when Sherwood would thrust a pin into her shoulders and legs: it was the Devil who cried out. She too had had Campion's thumb, or relics of the Blessed Margaret Clitheroe, stuffed into her mouth. She told a story of a cat-whipping session at Denham, when several priests had flogged a cat round a room until it escaped. In the Marshalsea she had been married to Harrington by a priest – at any rate certain Latin words had been said over them after Mass. When she became pregnant Father Blackman advised her to say that the father of her child had gone overseas. This opened her eyes and she had submitted and been examined before the Privy Council, where she divulged what she knew of the spy, Stoughton, who carried over girls and boys to become nuns and priests. She then went back to live with her father, where Harrington joined her and they lived as man and wife, he allowing her twenty marks a year. When she was pregnant he put £100 into her father's hand, in case she had a child. When Harrington was apprehended as a priest, she was allowed to visit him: he wept at having abused her, but denied that he had married her. He was condemned and executed – or, in other words, martyred – in February 1594, when she married Ralph Dallidown, who received her £100. But the priests – Sherwood, Gerard, Blackman, Greene – persecuted her for conforming, and said it was the Devil's work. They had a point when her husband committed manslaughter: they said it was due to her relapse and the Devil had made her husband kill a man. But the man was a servant to Master Roper the recusant who lay in Southampton House – a known resort of Catholics: this man had threatened to shoot her with a pistol for revealing her sister's whereabouts for examination.

Anne Smith was another hysteric: when she had a fit at Denham she was exorcised by Father Cornelius in alb and stole, who made an exhortation to her bound in a chair, reciting exorcisms at which she shivered and quaked. The (afterwards) Blessed John Cornelius, with four other priests, had exorcised her from morning to night. Among the visitors to salutary Denham she recalled Salusbury – executed as a Babington plotter – Father Gerard and Mr. George Peckham. Anthony Tyrrell, who had betrayed Babington, turns up again years afterward, with a written deposition. He recalled how Father Martin Aray had told him, turning into Paul's churchyard, the good news that Philip of Spain was ready to invade and 'we must advance the Catholic cause all we can.'[93] This was the background to the excitements at Denham: the government was quite right to break up the nest and scatter the birds. Tyrrell had known all along that the exorcisings in themselves were folly. After he lapsed and confessed all to the Lord Treasurer, he veered back to his Catholic bias, when the priests urged him to deny his confession. 'For the general conceit among all the priests of that Order [the Jesuits] is that they may deny anything which, being confessed, doth turn to the dishonour of the Catholic Church of Rome.' They argue that the magistrates are not valid judges, the Queen herself being excommunicate, neither are the examinations or judgments.

One appreciates that this was war to the knife: the government was dealing with an unscrupulous Fifth Column. When people enter – somewhat uselessly, always with their *parti-pris* – upon theoretical discussions on these matters, here is the reality: the reality of life. There are plenty of people today who exhibit similar characteristics, comparable credulities, and whose mental life proceeds on the same level. So we need not doubt the attainability of historical knowledge: it is – as Elgar said of music – all round us.

If it is a reflection on that age that Perkins was both more representative and more influential, it is a commendation that it could produce in Scott and Harsnet persons so rational, so sceptical and humane.

In the sequel we shall study the attempts at more rational formulations, the shaping of their intellectual positions, along with the achievement in the arts and sciences.

NOTES

Chapter I

1. J. Burckhardt, *The Civilisation of the Renaissance in Italy*, trans. S. G. C. Middlemore, 308.
2. W. K. Ferguson, *The Renaissance in Historical Thought*, 1
3. *Ibid.*, 4.
4. Burckhardt, 313.
5. Sir Kenneth Clark, 'The Young Michelangelo', *The Horizon Book of the Renaissance*, 106.
6. Ferguson, 61.
7. Cf. J. A. Symonds, *Renaissance in Italy. Italian Literature*, Parts I & II (ed. 1909), 11.
8. Cf. J. Pope-Hennessy, *The Portrait in the Renaissance*.
9. G. Mattingly, *Renaissance Diplomacy*, 55, 60.
10. L. Bradner, 'From Petrarch to Shakespeare', *The Renaissance: Six Essays*, ed. W. K. Ferguson, 102.
11. Cf. Symonds, *op. cit.*, Part II, 264-5.
12. L. Einstein, *The Italian Renaissance in England*, 344.
13. Clark, 107.
14. Baldassare Castiglione, *The Book of the Courtier*, trans. Sir Thomas Hoby, Everyman edn., 68.
15. *Ibid.*, 290.
16. Cf. Mattingly, 217.
17. D. Hay, 'Italy and Barbarian Europe', *Italian Renaissance Studies*, ed. E. F. Jacob, 63.
18. Ferguson, 268-9, 276.
19. Cf. R. Weiss, 'Italian Humanism in Western Europe, 1460–1520', in Jacob, 69 foll.
20. Cf. D. S. Chambers, *Cardinal Bainbridge in the Court of Rome*, 1509 to 1514; J. Wegg, *Richard Pace: A Tudor Diplomatist*.
21. Cf. J. K. McConica, *English Humanists and Reformation Politics under Henry VIII and Edward VI*; L. B. Smith, *Tudor Prelates and Politics, 1536–1558*.
22. R. B. Merriman, *Life and Letters of Thomas Cromwell*, I. 9–10.
23. *Ibid.*, 86.
24. At least since F. Seebohm's classic, *The Oxford Reformers*.
25. Sir George Clark, *A History of the Royal College of Physicians of London*, I. 41.
26. C. D. O'Malley, 'Tudor Medicine and Biology', *Huntington Library Quarterly*, Nov. 1968.
27. J. Cartwright, *The Perfect Courtier. Baldassare Castiglione*, I. 180, foll.
28. Cf. E. Auerbach, *Tudor Artists*.
29. L. Einstein, *The Italian Renaissance in England*, 76.
30. L. R. Shelby, *John Rogers, Tudor Military Engineer*, 135.
31. *Ibid.*, 129.
32. *Ibid.*, 132.
33. *Ibid.*, 148.
34. Sir John Summerson, *Architecture in Britain, 1530–1830*, I.
35. E. K. Waterhouse, *Painting in Britain, 1530–1790*, 10.
36. Cf. *Dict. Nat. Biog.*, under Parker, Henry.
37. Cf. J. Buxton, *A Tradition of Poetry*, 26-7.
38. Summerson, 10.
39. *Ibid.*, 18.
40. John Shute, *The First and Chief Grounds of Architecture*. Facsimile ed., Introduction by L. Weaver. Dedication, A ii.
41. A. M. Hind, *Engraving in England in the 16th and 17th Centuries*, 60–61.
42. Cf. A. Blunt, *Philibert de l'Orme*.

43. Cf. the modern abridged edition ed. by G. B. Parks.
44. Cf. E. R. Adair, 'William Thomas', in *Tudor Studies*, ed. R. W. Seton-Watson, 133 foll.
45. Einstein, 118.
46. Thomas, ed. Parks, 50.
47. *Ibid.*, 21, 37.
48. q. Adair, *loc. cit.*
49. ed. by J. A. Froude in 1861.
50. Thomas, *History of Italy*, Dedication.
51. Thomas, *Principal Rules of the Italian Grammar*, 1550, Dedicatory Epistle. (The copy in All Souls College Library was presented by Dudley Digges, formerly Fellow, who also gave the Venice 1537 ed. of Ariosto.)
52. q. Adair, *loc. cit.*
53. Thomas, *ed. cit.*, ix.
54. Cf. my essay, 'Bisham and the Hobys,' in *Times, Persons, Places*, 188 foll.
55. *Dict. Nat. Biog.*, under Sir Thomas Hoby.
56. *The Travels and Life of Sir Thomas Hoby*, ed. E. Powell. *Camden Soc. Misc.* X. 4.
57. *Ibid.*, 8, 24, 25.
58. *Ibid.*, 45.
59. *Ibid.*, 19.
60. *Ibid.*, 54.
61. *Ibid.*, 61.
62. *Ibid.*, 116–17.
63. For the following account I ami ndebted to Mr. John Buxton's admirable *Sir Philip Sidney and the English Renaissance*, ch. 3, whence the quotations come.
64. *Dict. Nat. Biog.* under Thomas Wilson.
65. Thomas, ed. Parks, xvi.
66. Cf. my *Ralegh and the Throckmortons*, 89 foll.

Chapter II

1. Cf. Frances Howard from Court to the Earl of Hertford in January 1585: 'Many persuasions she used against marriage . . . and how little you would care for me . . . how well I was here and how much she cared for me. But, in the end, she said she would not be against my desire. Trust me, sweet lord, the worst is past, and I warrant she will not speak one angry word to you.' *H.M.C.*, *Bath Mss.*, IV. 158. Frances Howard became Hertford's second wife, and they lived unhappily together for thirteen years.
2. Cf. R. C. Strong, 'The Popular Celebration of the Accession Day of Queen Elizabeth I,' *Journal of the Warburg and Courtauld Institutes*, XXI. 86 foll.
3. F. A. Yates, 'Queen Elizabeth as Astraea', *Ibid.*, X. 65.
4. q. E. Armstrong, *Ronsard and the Age of Gold*, 42–3.
5. F. A. Yates, 'Elizabethan Chivalry: the Romance of the Accession Day Tilts', *Journal of the Warburg and Courtauld Institutes*, XX. 4.
6. Cf. for his biography, E. K. Chambers, *Sir Henry Lee*, though with the usual impercipience of this massive scholar, he misses the significance of Lee's one claim to fame. Miss Yates comments justly, 'Chambers has given us a useful book on the life of Lee, but we need to study also Lee's imagination, Lee as the expert on humanist chivalry, Lee as one of the builders of the Elizabethan mythology.' Her article supplies the defect.
7. q. E. K. Chambers, *William Shakespeare*, II. 153.
8. q. Yates, 17.
9. *Corr. J. van Oldenbarnevelt*, ed. A. J. Veenendaal, III. 572 foll. I am grateful to Sir George Clark for drawing my attention to this and translating it from the Dutch for me.

10. *H.M.C., De L'Isle Mss.* II. 187.
11. *H.M.C., Salisbury Mss.*, VII. 41, 55.
12. *Ibid.*, 385, 425.
13. *Ibid.*, 294.
14. *H.M.C., De L'Isle Mss.*, II. 254.
15. *Ibid.*, 178.
16. *Ibid.*, 196, 267, 274, 281, 283, 294-5.
17. *Ibid.*, 217.
18. *H.M.C., Salisbury Mss.*, VIII. 541.
19. *Ibid.*, 271.
20. *Ibid.*, X. 308.
21. *Ibid.*, 313, 330.
22. E. Lodge, *Illustrations* (2nd ed., 1838), II. 17–18.
23. *H.M.C., De L'Isle Mss.*, II. 328–30.
24. Lodge, II. 98.
25. *H.M.C., Bath Mss.*, IV. 158.
26. *H.M.C. Salisbury Mss.*, X. 172–3.
27. *Egerton Ms.*, 2806. I am grateful to Sir John Neale for drawing my attention to this, a Book of Warrants to the Great Wardrobe. Mrs C. C. Stopes printed some extracts from it in an article reprinted in her *Shakespeare's Environment*, 269 foll.
28. *Elizabethan England* (by W. Harrison), ed. L. Withington, 110.
29. Cf. my *Ralegh and the Throckmortons*, 104.
30. *H.M.C., Salisbury Mss.*, X. 58.
31. *Letters and Memorials of State*, ed. A. Collins, II. 203.
32. Sir John Harington, *Nugae Antiquae*, (ed. 1779), II. 139–40.
33. *H.M.C., De L'Isle Mss.*, II. 390.
34. *Ibid.*, 265, 322.
35. *Letters of Philip Gawdy*, ed. I. H. Jeayes, 137.
36. *Gossip from a Muniment Room*, ed. Lady Newdigate-Newdegate, 1, 5, 9.
37. *Ibid.*, 11.
38. *Ibid.*, 13–15.
39. *Ibid.*, 19–20, 27, 29.
40. *Ibid.*, 36.
41. *Cal. Carew Mss., 1601–3*, 20.
42. *H.M.C., Salisbury Mss.*, XI. 202.
43. *Cal. Carew Mss., 1601–3*, 13; Newdigate, 38.
44. *H.M.C., Salisbury Mss.*, XI. 340, 361, 561.
45. q. *D.N.B.*, under William Herbert, 3rd Earl of Pembroke.
46. Newdigate, 42, 45, 46.
47. *Ibid.*, 76.
48. *Ibid.*, 79, 80, 82–3.
49. *Ibid.*, 118, 153–4. Mary died in 1647 and was buried at Gawsworth.
50. *H.M.C., De L'Isle Mss.*, II. 384.
51. *Letters of Philip Gawdy*, 103.
52. J. Cartwright, *The Perfect Courtier. Baldassare Castiglione*, v, vi.
53. Castiglione, *The Book of the Courtier* (Everyman ed.), 3, 5.
54. *Ibid.*, 42.
55. Castiglione, 96, 108, 109.
56. *Ibid.*, 261.
57. *Cal. S.P. Dom., 1601-3*, 154–5.
58. Harington, *ed. cit.*, II. 263–4.

Chapter III

1. *The Agrarian History of England and Wales*, vol. IV, 1500–1640, ed. J. Thirsk, xxx. I am chiefly indebted to her Introduction and chap. 1 in the above paragraphs.

2. *The Agrarian History of England and Wales*, vol. IV, 1500–1640, ed J. Thirsk, 3.
3. *Ibid.*, xxxi.
4. W. G. Hoskins, *Provincial England*, 86.
5. *Ibid.*, 88.
6. *Ibid.*, 90.
7. G. Scott Thomson, *Lords Lieutenants in the Sixteenth Century*, 49–50.
8. *Musters, Beacons, Subsidies, Etc.*, ed. J. Wake, *Northamptonshire Record Soc.*, liii.
9. *Ibid.*, 123.
10. Hoskins, 101.
11. C. Cross, *The Puritan Earl*, 137 foll.
12. *Ibid.*, 246, 258.
13. J. Hurstfield, in *V. C. H. Wiltshire*, V. 106.
14. *Ibid.*, 81.
15. q. S. T. Bindoff, 'Parliamentary History, 1529–1688', *ibid.*, 124.
16. Cf. *ibid.*, 111 foll., on which the above paragraphs are based.
17. This analysis is based on the returns in *Members of Parliament*, Part I (1878), 403 foll.
18. J. J. Alexander, 'Exeter M.P.s, Part III: 1537 to 1688', *Trans. Devon. Assoc. 1929*, 193 foll.
19. T. Atkinson, *Elizabethan Winchester*, 38, 95.
20. D. Drake, 'M.P.s for Barnstaple, 1492–1688', *Trans. Devon. Assoc. 1940*, 251 foll.
21. q. D. Slatter, in *V.C.H. Leicester*, IV. 67.
22. J. W. Walker, *Wakefield: Its History and People*, 319.
23. *Ibid.*, 495 foll.
24. Cf. *Devon Monastic Lands: Cal. of Particulars for Grants, 1536–1558*, ed. J. Youings.
25. *Ibid.*, xxviii.
26. *V.C.H. Wiltshire*, VII. 31.
27. Sir Anthony Wagner, *Heralds of England*, 205.
28. Published in the Camden Soc., 1st Series.
29. C. S. Davies, *A History of Macclesfield*, 307.
30. Romans, 208.
31. W. Camden, *History* (ed. 1675), 617.
32. q. M. Prestwich, *Cranfield*, 180.
33. W. G. Hoskins, *Provincial England*, 75, 76.
34. *Ibid.*, 75.
35. Cf. J. W. Gough, *Sir Hugh Myddelton*, and A. H. Dodd, 'Mr Myddelton the Merchant of Tower Street', in *Elizabethan Government and Society*, ed. S. T. Bindoff, J. Hurstfield, C. H. Williams, 249 foll.
36. Dodd, 280.
37. By W. K. Jordan in a series of authoritative volumes from 1959 onwards, upon which my account is based and which are cited in place.
38. W. K. Jordan, *The Charities of London, 1480–1660. The Aspirations and the Achievements of the Urban Society*, 20.
39. W. K. Jordan, *The Charities of Rural England, 1480–1660. The Aspirations and the Achievements of the Rural Society*, 215.
40. *Ibid.*, 221.
41. Jordan, *The Charities of London, 1480–1660*, 60, 60.
42. Jordan, *The Charities of Rural England, 1480–1660*, 20.
43. Jordan, *The Charities of London, 1480–1660*, 153.
44. *D. N. B.*, under Thomas Sutton.
45. *D. N. B.*, under Sir William Craven.
46. J. Stow, *A Survey of London*, ed. C. L. Kingsford, I. 174, 181.
47. Jordan, *The Forming of the Charitable Institutions of the West of England*, (*American Philosophical Society*), 3.
48. Not 'Lady Mary Ramsay': scholars should get these titles right, for they are apt to indicate different persons.

Notes

49. *Ibid.*, 29.
50. *Ibid.*, 47.
51. *Ibid.*, 77.
52. Jordan, *The Charities of London, 1480–1660*, 313.
53. Cf. Jordan, *Social Institutions in Kent, 1480–1660*, (Archaeologia Cantiana).
54. Cf. Jordan, *The Social Institutions of Lancashire, 1480–1660*.
55. Cf. the will of George Trafford, a Catholic, in 1572. *Ibid.*, 14.
56. *pace* Jordan, *ibid.*, 48.
57. *The Oldest Register Book of Hawkshead, 1568–1704* ,ed. H. S. Cowper, xxxv; F. S. Cheetham, *Lancashire*, 152.
58. W. G. Hoskins, *Provincial England*.

Chapter IV

1. E. K. Chambers, 'The Court', *Shakespeare's England*, I. 95.
2. J. Nichols, ed., *The Progresses . . . of Queen Elizabeth*, I. 'The Queen's Progress, 1566', 3, 4.
3. *Ibid.*, 'The Queen's Progress, 1572', 27.
4. *Ibid.*, 30.
5. *Ibid.*, 'The Queen's Progress, 1573', 36.
6. *Ibid.*, 46–7.
7. *Ibid.*, 49, 52.
8. Cf. *The Expansion of Elizabethan England*, 174–7.
9. Nichols, I. 'The Queen's Entertainment at Wilton', 19.
10. Printed in Nichols.
11. Nichols, II. 'The Queen's progress, 1578', 9–10.
12. Now among the archives at Hatfield.
13. Nichols, II. 'The Receiving of the Queen's Majesty into her City of Norwich', 12 foll.
14. Cf. F. Peck, *Desiderata Curiosa*, I. 22–6.
15. Henry Percy, *Advice to His Son*, ed. G. B. Harrison, 80–1.
16. *Ibid.*, 81–2.
17. *Ibid.*, 77, 84.
18. Now at Chatsworth.
19. For example, she purchased all Edward Savage's lands in Stainsby and Heath for £2050; Thomas Shakerley's manor of little Longstone and all his lands in the Peak, for £2450; Roulston in Nottinghamshire for over £1000 from Mr. Lodge, giving him £50 at the same time to make the bargain. And so on.
20. Henry Peacham, *The Complete Gentleman*, ed. 1634, 2.
21. H.M.C., *Salisbury Mss*. XIV. 150.
22. M. A. Tierney, *The History and Antiquities of Arundel*, II. 356.
23. F. R. Raines, ed., *The Derby Household Books* (Chetham Soc.), 23, 88.
24. Lady Newton, *The House of Lyme*, 37–8, 46.
25. *Salisbury Mss.*, VII. 296–8.
26. E. Lodge, *Illustrations of British History*, 2nd ed., I. xxxi.
27. *Salisbury Mss.*, VII. 270.
28. *The Gentleman's Magazine*, LV (1785), 32.
29. From a paper kindly lent me by Miss Sylvia Thrupp.
30. John Smyth, *Lives of the Berkeleys*, ed. Sir J. Maclean, II. 221–2.
31. Ian Grimble, *The Harington Family*, 90 foll.
32. G. Holles, *Memorials of the Holles Family, 1493–1656* (Camden Soc.), 8–9.
33. *Ibid.*, 39, 41.
34. *Ibid.*, 41–2.
35. *Ibid.*, 125–7.

36. W. G. Hoskins, *Provincial England*, 137–8.
37. Alan Simpson, *The Wealth of the Gentry, 1540–1660*, 161, 166.
38. *Ibid.*, 27.
39. q. *ibid.*, 57.
40. Hoskins, 131.
41. *Ibid.*, 132, and v. in detail, W. G. Hoskins, *Devon, passim.*
42. *Ibid.*, 134.
43. H. Forrester, *The Timber-Framed Houses of Essex*, 13.
44. Hoskins, 135–6.
45. C. M. L. Bouch and G. P. Jones, *The Lake Counties, 1500–1830*, 84–7.
46. It appears that in over a hundred larger Essex houses this feature still remains; cf. A. C. Edwards, *A History of Essex.*
47. W. Harrison, *Elizabethan England*, ed. L. Withington, 9.
48. D. Portman, *Exeter Houses, 1400–1700*, 36.
49. q. M. Campbell, *The English Yeoman*, 58, 62.
50. H. J. Carpenter, 'Furse of Moreshead', *Trans. Devon. Assocn., 1894*, 179.
51. Harrison, 13–4.
52. *The Derby Household Books*, ed. F. R. Raines, 9, 95.
53. Hoskins, 146.
54. *Ibid.*, 147–8.
55. U. M. Cowgill, 'The People of York, 1538–1812', *Scientific American*, Jan. 1970, 104 foll.

Chapter V

1. Harrison, *ed. cit.*, 84, 88–9.
2. *Ibid.*, 91–2.
3. *Ibid.*, 94.
4. J. C. Drummond and A. Wilbraham, *The Englishman's Food*, 75, 84.
5. By Stat. 5 Eliz. c. 5, see R. H. Tawney and E. Power, *Tudor Economic Documents*, II. 110 foll.
6. Drummond and Wilbraham, 63–4.
7. Harrison, 96.
8. Drummond and Wilbraham, 66.
9. Harrison, 93–4, 98 foll.
10. E. K. Chambers, *William Shakespeare*, II. 99–101.
11. H.M.C., *Various Collections*, II. 67 foll.
12. *Ibid.*, 76–8.
13. *Ibid.*, 78–9.
14. *Ibid.*, 73–5.
15. For the prices and amounts I cite the schedule: 'Pepper, 30 lb at 2½ the lb, £3; cloves, 1½ lb at 11s the lb, 16s 6d; mace, 1½ lb at 15s the lb, 22s 6d; sugar, 8 loaves weighing 10 lb a piece, at 18d the lb, £6; cinnamon, 2 lb, 15s; ginger, 2½ lb at 2s 8d a lb, 6s 8d; nutmegs, 1 lb, 8s; currants, 54 lb at 4d a lb, 18s; great raisins, 32 lb at 3d a lb, 8s; prunes, 53 lb, 9s 8d; almonds, 10 lb, 12s 2d; dates, 3 lb, 2s 6d; liquorice, 20 lb, 5s 10d; anniseed, 20 lb, 20s; almonds, more 4 lb, 4s 8d; biscuits and carroways, 4 lb, 6s 8d; isinglass, 1½ lb, 5s; saunders (sandal-wood?) 2 lb, 3s 4d. Total for one year in spice, £17. 4. 6d'. *Ibid.*, 86.
16. *Derby Household Books*, 5.
17. J. Nichols, *Progresses*, I. 'Expense of Queen Elizabeth's Table', from Harleian Mss., 609.
18. H. Hall, *Society in the Elizabethan Age*, 212 foll.
19. Cf. my *Ralegh and the Throckmortons*, C. VI.
20. *Ibid.*, 276–7.
21. Sir John Harington, *The Metamorphosis of Ajax*, ed. P. Warlock and J. Lindsay, 48.

22. *Ibid.*, 93–4.
23. *Ibid.*, 100.
24. *Ibid.*, 88.
25. I. Grimble, *The Harington Family*. 124–5.
26. Harington, 78.
27. cf. my edition of *Shakespeare's Sonnets*, 280–3.
28. Mark Eccles, *Shakespeare in Warwickshire*, 24.
29. W. G. Hoskins, *Two Thousand Years in Exeter*, 61.
30. Portman, 50–1.
31. John Stow, *Survey of London*, ed. C. L. Kingsford, I. 175, 303; II. 69.
32. *Minutes and Accounts . . . of Stratford-upon-Avon* (Dugdale Soc.), II. 106, IV. 143.
33. *Ibid.*, IV. 122.
34. *Ibid.*, IV. 74–5.
35. *Records of the City of Oxford, 1509–1583*, ed. W. H. Turner, 162, 398, 422–5.
36. *Records of the Borough of Leicester, 1509–1603*, ed. M. Bateson, III. 86, 177, 191.
37. Stow, I. 18.
38. Cf. J. W. Gough, *Sir Hugh Myddelton*, CC. II–IV.
39. *Cal. of Plymouth Municipal Records*, ed. R. N. Worth, 128, 129, 130, 137.
40. Stow, II. 54–5.

Chapter VI

1. q. J. E. Neale, *Elizabeth I and her Parliaments*, 1559–1581, 49.
2. Cf. Elizabeth Jenkins, *Elizabeth the Great*, 17. I should like to pay tribute to this perceptive portrayal of her personality from a woman's point of view – from which historians have something to learn.
3. Cf. Anthony Hamilton, *Memoirs of Count Grammont*, ed. Sir Walter Scott, 263 foll.
4. *Correspondence of Matthew Parker*, ed. J. Bruce and T. T. Perowne, (Parker Society), 156–7.
5. q. E. K. Chambers, *The Elizabethan Stage*, I. 107.
6. Cf. for a medical view, I. Aird, 'The Death of Amy Robsart', *E.H.R.*, 1956, 69 foll.
7. C. Read, 'A Letter from Robert, Earl of Leicester, to a Lady', *Huntington Library Bulletin*, no. 9 (April 1936), 15–26.
8. Ms. Ashmole 226, Bodleian Library.
9. *Ibid.*, 195.
10. John Aubrey, *Brief Lives*, ed. A. Clark, II. 216–17.
11. Ms. Ashmole, 236.
12. E. Hasted, *History . . . of the County of Kent* (ed. 1782), II. 764.
13. *Ibid.*, II. 770.
14. Ms. Ashmole, 236.
15. Cf. *The Life and Letters of Sir Henry Wotton*, I. 34–6, by L. Pearsall Smith, who, however, knew nothing about these consultations.
16. This is quite correct: the see of Salisbury had been vacant since October 1596, with the death of John Coldwell, who was Whitgift's man; cf. *D.N.B.*, under Coldwell.
17. Ms. Ashmole, 195.
18. *Ibid.*, 236.
19. G. Hennessy, *Novum Repertorium Ecclesiasticum Parochiale Londinense*, 44, 45.
20. A. Collins, *Letters and Memorials of State*, I. 361.
21. Ms. Ashmole, 226.
22. *Ibid.*, 206.
23. Cf. *D.N.B.*, under Dove.
24. This adds a few details to his biography in *D.N.B.*
25. Ms. Ashmole, 219.

26. Ms. Ashmole, 206.
27. *Ibid.*, 236.
28. *Henslowe's Diary*, ed. W. W. Greg, 113.
29. Ms. Ashmole, 226.
30. Cf. *The Complete Peerage*, by G. E. C. (Revised ed.), VI. 584.
31. *H.M.C., Bath Mss.*, IV. 161–2.
32. Sir L. Dibdin and Sir C. E. H. Chadwyck Healey, *English Church Law and Divorce*, 27–8.
33. q. *ibid.*, 147–9.
34. q. *ibid.*, 152.
35. *Corr. of Matthew Parker, ed. cit.*, 406.
36. q. C. I. A. Ritchie, *The Ecclesiastical Courts of York*, 174.
37. Cf. J. Collinson, *The History . . . of Somerset* (ed. 1791), III. 250–3; in the account of the family Mary Portman's existence is ignored.
38. One evidence of these transactions is that the manor of Stawell was held of Sir Edward Dyer in 1605, presumably in trust. Collinson, III. 431.
39. *Staffordshire Quarter Sessions Rolls* (William Salt Archaeological Society), IV. 388–9.
40. *Ibid.*, IV. 393.
41. *Ibid.*, IV. 359.
42. *Ibid.*, I. 338.
43. *Child-Marriages, Divorces, and Ratifications*, ed. F. J. Furnivall, (*E.E.T.S.*), 97.
44. *Staffordshire Quarter Sessions Rolls*, III. 10–12.
45. U. M. Cowgill, 'The People of York, 1538–1812', *Scientific American*, Jan. 1970, 104 foll.
46. Sir F. Pollock and F. W. Maitland, *History of English Law*, II. 556–7.
47. *Statutes of the Realm* (ed. 1817), III. 441, a° 25 Henry VIII, cap. 6.
48. *The Statutes at Large*, ed. D. Pickering, VI. 208–9, a° 5 Eliz., cap. 17.
49. David Knowles, *The Religious Orders in England*, III. 296–7.
60. S.P. 12/151, 45. This is omitted in B. M. Ward's too laudatory account, *The Seventeenth Earl of Oxford, 1550–1604*, C. V.
51. *Ibid.*, 46.
52. Cf. *ibid.*, 49.
53. *The Voyages and Colonising Enterprises of Sir Humphrey Gilbert*, ed. D. B. Quinn (Hakluyt Soc.), I. 102.
54. S.P. 70/146, 41, 45.
55. S.P. 12/86, 14.
56. Cf. G. Marañon, *Antonio Pérez*.
57. John Aubrey, *Brief Lives, ed. cit.*, I. 71.
58. T. Birch, *Memoirs of the Reign of Queen Elizabeth*, I. 143.
59. 'Extracts from Sir Simonds D'Ewes Journal', in J. Nichols, *Bibliotheca Topographica Britannica*, VI. 26–7.
60. *Salisbury Mss.*, XI. 94.
61. Cf. in full, P. H. Kocher, *Christopher Marlowe*, 34–6.
62. Barnfield's *Affectionate Shepherd*, ed. J. O. Halliwell (Percy Soc. XX), 4 foll.
63. Cf. Eric Partridge, *Shakespeare's Bawdy, passim*, which is very instructive on the subject, and quite right.

Chapter VII

1. W. K. Jordan, *The Charities of Rural England, 1480–1660*, 26.
2. P. de Sandwich, 'Some East Kent Parish History', *Home Counties Magazine*, IV. 208.
3. *Ibid.*, V. 208.
4. q. *ibid.*, X. 181.
5. q. *ibid.*, V. 254.

6. q. *ibid.*, V. 140.
7. *Ibid.*, V. 217, 286.
8. *Ibid.*, V. 114.
9. q. G. Anstruther, *Vaux of Harrowden*, 76.
10. q. *ibid.*, 75.
11. Lady Newton, *The House of Lyme*, 16.
12. q. J. H. B. Andrews, 'The Parish of Satterleigh and Warkleigh,' *Trans. Devon. Assoc.*, 1960, 36 foll.
13. *Home Counties Mag.*, X. 29.
14. *Ibid.*, VI. 318–19.
15. H. R. Evans, 'Broadhempston', *Trans. Devon. Assn.*, 1958, 62 foll.
16. H. R. Evans, 'Woodland', *ibid.*, 1960, 159 foll.
17. G. W. Copeland, 'Devonshire Church Houses', *ibid.*, 250 foll.
18. A. H. Slee, 'Braunton and its Manors', *ibid.*, 1941, 195 foll.
19. G. W. Ormerod, 'Historical Sketch of the Parish of Chagford', *ibid.*, 1876, 62 foll.
20. H. R. Evans, 'Woodland', *ibid.*, 159 foll.
21. W. Brown, *Ingleby Arncliffe and its Owners*, 10.
22. R. W. Ramsey, 'Records of Houghton-le-Spring', *E.H.R.*, 1905, 673 foll.
23. G. Baker, *The Hist. and Antiquities of the County of Northampton*, I. 513–14.
24. *Cratfield Parish Papers*, ed. J. J. Raven, 121.
25. *Ibid.*, 102.
26. W. Bennett, *History of Burnley*, 73–4.
27. R. Carew, *The Survey of Cornwall* (ed. 1769), 68 foll.
28. Chancery Miscellanea, Bundle 52, File 3, no. 111.
29. *Ibid.*, no. 103.
30. Carew, 73.
31. Chanc. Misc., Bdle 52, File 3, no. 115.
32. Carew, 75–6.
33. *V.C.H.*, *Essex*, II. 581, 618.
34. q. P. Chalmers, *The History of Hunting*, 287.
35. q. *ibid.*, 273.
36. *Salisbury Mss.* X. 46.
37. *Ibid.*, 117, 322, 323.
38. *Ibid.*, 148.
39. Reproduced as Shakespeare Association Facsimile, No. 5 (1932).
40. *V.C.H.*, *Derbyshire*, II. 255.
41. *Staffordshire Quarter Sessions Rolls*, I. 207; II. 12, 27, 62. This Everard Digby must be the interesting anti-Puritan philosopher, who wrote (in Latin) the first English book on swimming, and was in the habit of disturbing the puritanical devotions in chapel at St. John's College, Cambridge, by blowing his horn and hallooing in the court. His thought will be dealt with in the following volume.
42. Ms. Ashmole, 208.
43. *Salisbury Mss.*, VII. 174.
44. For these indoor games, and the meanings of the words, *v.* A. F. Sieveking, 'Games', *Shakespeare's England*, II. 468 foll.
45. Cf. my *Ralegh and the Throckmortons*, 278, 279, 287.
46. Lady Newton, *The House of Lyme*, 46.
47. E. Edwards, *Sir Walter Ralegh*, II. 85.
48. *Salisbury Mss.*, VIII, 425.
49. *Ibid.*, VII. 517.
50. *Ibid.*, VII. 171.
51. *Ibid.*, VIII, 283, 297.
52. *Ibid.*, 286.
53. Carew, *ed. cit.*, 25.
54. q. from Nicholas Morgan's *Perfection of Horsemanship*, A. F. Sieveking, 'Horsemanship, with Farriery', *Shakespeare's England*, II. 412.

55. q. from Nicholas Morgan's *Perfection of Horsemanship*, A. F. Sieveking, 'Horsemanship, with Farriery', *Shakespeare's England*, II. 412.
56. *V.C.H., Gloucestershire*, II. 299.
57. *Salisbury Mss.*, VIII. 417.
58. *V.C.H., Cumberland*, II. 440–1.
59. *V.C.H., Yorkshire*, II. 505.
60. *V.C.H., Dorset*, II. 316.
61. *V.C.H., Nottinghamshire*, II. 388.
62. Cf. my *Ralegh and the Throckmortons*, 284, 288–9.
63. *V.C.H., Northamptonshire*, II. 376.
64. Drayton, *Polyolbion*, Song XXIII.
65. *V.C.H., Yorkshire*, II. 525.
66. *V.C.H., Nottinghamshire*, II. 402.
67. *V.C.H., Dorset*, II. 320.
68. *V.C.H., Gloucestershire*, II. 318.
69. *V.C.H., Northamptonshire*, II. 377.
70. *Carew, ed. cit.*, 28 foll.
71. *Ibid.*, 104 foll.
72. *V.C.H., Derbyshire*, II. 304.
73. *V.C.H., Cumberland*, II. 482.
74. Lady Newton, *The House of Lyme*, 66–7.
75. *The Diary of the Lady Anne Clifford*, with Introductory Note by V. Sackville-West, 28, 30, 52.
76. *V.C.H., Derbyshire, loc. cit.*
77. All this confusion has been cleared up in a definitive article by C. L. Kingsford, 'Paris Garden and the Bear-Baiting', *Archaeologia*, vol. 70, 155 foll.
78. A. Collins, ed. *Sidney Papers*, II. 194.
79. Reprinted at the end of *The Works of John Caius*, ed. E. S. Roberts.
80. *Ibid.*, 38.
81. *Salisbury Mss.*, VIII. 321.
82. Caius, ed. Roberts, 13, 18, 40.
83. *Ibid.*, 23.
84. Lady Newton, *op. cit.*, 41–2.
85. q. A. F. Sieveking, 'Games', *Shakespeare's England*, II. 451.
86. Philip Stubbes, *Anatomy of the Abuses in England*, ed. F. J. Furnivall (*New Shakespeare Society*), 183–4.
87. *V.C.H., Derbyshire*, II. 304.
88. *D.N.B.*, under Robert Dover.
89. A. F. Sieveking, *loc. cit.*, II. 454.
90. Cf. my *Shakespeare's Southampton*, 127.
91. q. Sieveking, *loc. cit.*, II. 465.
92. *The Whole Works of Roger Ascham*, ed. J. A. Giles, III. 86.
93. Cf. the excellent article on Fencing, in *Encyclopædia Britannica*, 11th ed.
94. J. D. Aylward, *The English Master of Arms*, 18, 26.
95. *Encyclopædia Britannica, loc. cit.*
96. Aylward, 48, 51.
97. q. *ibid.*, 53–4.
98. q. *ibid.*, 54–5, 60.
99. Sieveking, *loc. cit.*, II. 404.
100. *Ibid.*, II. 402.
101. q. *ibid.*, II. 406.
102. *Salisbury Mss.*, IX. 193, 246, 421.
103. *Ibid.*, XIV. 147.
104. *Ibid.*, X. 262.

Notes

Chapter VIII

1. Cf. my *Ralegh and the Throckmortons*, 279.
2. A. R. Wright, *British Calendar Customs* (ed. T. E. Lones), III. 196.
3. Cf. C. Hole, *English Folklore*, 127.
4. Wright, ed. Lones, I. 1, 8–9.
5. W. G. W. Watson, *Calendar of Customs . . . Connected with the County of Somerset*, 62.
6. Wright, ed. Lones, I. 69.
7. Watson, 141.
8. R. Carew, *Survey of Cornwall, ed. cit.*, 137b.
9. *Salisbury Mss.*, VIII. 201.
10. *Ibid.*, VIII. 203.
11. Watson, 164 foll.
12. Wright, ed. Lones, I. 150. 152.
13. J. F. H. New, *Anglican and Puritan*, 65.
14. C. Hole, *op. cit.*, 3.
15. *D.N.B.*, under William Herbert; John Aubrey, *Brief Lives*, ed. A. Clark, I. 317–18.
16. C. Hole, 5.
17. J. C. Cox, *The Parish Registers of England*, 86.
18. *Ibid.*, 79.
19. *Ibid.*, 84.
20. *Child-Marriages, Divorces, and Ratifications, etc.*, ed. F. J. Furnivall (*Early English Text Soc.*), 2 foll.
21. *Ibid.*, 15 foll.
22. *Cal. S.P. Dom., 1547–80*, 377.
23. Cf. my *William Shakespeare*, 339.
24. T. M. N. Owen, *The Church Bells of Huntingdonshire*, 61.
25. *Ibid.*, 55, 66, 103.
26. T. Ingram, *Bells in England*, 8.
27. q. J. E. Booty, *John Jewel as Apologist of the Church of England*, 71.
28. H. T. Tilley and H. B. Walters, *The Church Bells of Warwickshire*, 2, 28 foll., 38 foll., 45, 47.
29. *Ibid.*, 32, 38.
30. *Cratfield Parish Papers*, ed. J. J. Raven, 110.
31. q. Ingram, 20.
32. C. S. Burne, *The Handbook of Folklore*, 143.
33. Carew, 123.
34. C. Hole, *Traditions and Customs of Cheshire*, 65–6, 69.
35. Burne, *op. cit.*, 155.
36. *Records of the City of Oxford*, ed. W. A. Turner, 258, 284, 403, 410.
37. Stubbes, *ed. cit.*, 154 foll.
38. M. A. Rice, *Abbots Bromley*, 66 foll.
39. C. M. Bowra, *Memories*, 83.
40. In this section I am much indebted to I. and P. Opie, *Oxford Dictionary of Nursery Rhymes*, 6 foll.
41. Carew, 9, 32.
42. I should like to pay tribute to the admirable Introduction by John Buxton to his *Poems of Michael Drayton* (The Muses' Library).
43. q. H. Littledale, 'Folklore and Superstitions'; *Shakespeare's England*, I. 543.

Chapter IX

1. Lord Raglan, q. in E. M. Butler, *The Myth of the Magus*, 1–2.
2. E. M. Butler, *Ritual Magic*, 3.

3. D. C. Allen, *The Star-Crossed Renaissance*, 143.
4. E. M. Butler, *Ritual Magic*, 251.
5. *Salisbury Mss.*, XIII. 87. I have translated the passage from the original, idiosyncratic French.
6. *The Private Diary of Dr. John Dee*, ed. J. O. Halliwell, *Camden Soc.*, 5, 19, 29, 32, 37, 49.
7. T. Tusser, *Five Hundred Points of Good Husbandry*, ed. W. Payne and S. J. Herrtage, *English Dialect Society*, 88.
8. W. Bennett, *History of Burnley*, 158.
9. f C. D. C. Allen, *The Star-Crossed Renaissance*, 57, 71.
10. q. *ibid.*, 108.
11. q. C. Camden, 'Astrology in Shakespeare's Day', *Isis*, vol. 19, 26 foll.
12. H. Howard, *A Defensative against the Poison of Supposed Prophecies*, ed. of 1620, 105b, 11b, 120b, 124b.
13. *Ibid.*, 71b, 72b, 76, 77.
14. *Ibid.*, 78, 84, 115b.
15. SP 12/90, 12.
16. J. M. Keynes, 'Newton, the Man', in *Newton Tercentenary Celebrations, The Royal Society*, 1947.
17. The copy in the Huntington Library is Egerton's, probably the presentation copy.
18. Chamber, *Treatise*, 18.
19. *Ibid.*, 30, 108.
20. *Ibid.*, 38, 39.
21. *Ibid.*, 69. 70, 127.
22. Heydon, *Defence*, 2.
23. *Ibid.*, 226.
24. *Ibid.*, 529.
25. Anthony Wood, q. D. C. Allen, *The Star-Crossed Renaissance*, 139.
26. Carleton, *Astronotomania*, 4.
27. q. Allen, 138.
28. q. *ibid.*, 151.
29. Mss. Ashmole, 487, 488, Bodleian.
30. Dee, *Private Diary, ed. cit.*, 1.
31. Mss. Ashmole, 337.
32. SP 14/216, 122.
33. H. C. Roberts, *The Complete Prophecies of Nostradamus*, 325.
34. q. S. Dodson, 'Holinshed's Sources for the Prognostications about the years 1583 and 1588', *Isis*, vol. 38, 60 foll.
35. R. Harvey, *An Astrological Discourse . . . With a brief declaration of the effects which the late eclipse of the sun, 1582, is yet hereafter to work.* Preface.
36. T. Buckmaster, *An Almanack and Prognostication for the Year 1598*, Shakespeare Association Facsimile, No. 8, Intro. v.
37. *Ibid.*, vi.
38. John Aubrey, *Brief Lives*, ed. A. Clark, I. 27.
39. [A. E. Waite, ed.], *The Alchemical Writings of Edward Kelly*, xv foll.
40. Dee, *Private Diary*, 12–15.
41. *Ibid.*, 11.
42. q. C. F. Smith, *John Dee (1527–1608)*, 79.
43. q. E. M. Butler, *Ritual Magic*, 261, 263.
44. Cf. my *Ralegh and the Throckmortons*, 85–9.
45. C. H. Josten, 'A Translation of John Dee's *Monas Hieroglyphica*', *Ambix*, XII. 89 foll.
46. Dee, *op. cit.*, 25.
47. C. H. Josten, 'An Unknown Chapter in the Life of John Dee', *Journ. Warburg and Courtauld Inst.* XXVIII. 233 foll.
48. *A True and Faithful Relation . . .*, ed. M. Casaubon, ed. 1659. Actio Tertia, 12–13.

Notes

49. q. Smith, 188.
50. Dee, *Private Diary*, 27.
51. R. M. Sargent, *At the Court of Queen Elizabeth. The Life and Lyrics of Sir Edward Dyer*, 103.
52. *Elias Ashmole, 1617–1692, Autobiographical and Historical Notes . . .*, ed. C. H. Josten, IV. 1372.
53. *Ibid.*, 114, 115.
54. q. Smith, 207.
55. Dee, *Private Diary*, 44, 48, 51–2, 54.
56. G. L. Kittredge, *Witchcraft in Old and New England*, 197–8.
57. C. L. Ewen, *Witch Hunting and Witch Trials*, 37.
58. C. L. Ewen, *Witchcraft and Demonianism*, 46.
59. A. H. A. Hamilton, *Quarter Sessions from Queen Elizabeth to Queen Anne*, 31.
60. C. L. Ewen, *Witchcraft and Demonianism*, 7.
61. T. A. Spalding, *Elizabethan Demonology*, 80.
62. C. L. Ewen, *Witchcraft and Demonianism*, 175.
63. C. L. Ewen, *Witch Hunting and Witch Trials*, 31.
64. W. Notestein, *A History of Witchcraft in England from 1558 to 1718*, 44. For Brian Darcy's activity, *v.* Ewen, *Witchcraft and Demonianism*, 46, 156–63.
65. *Ibid.*, 47–51.
66. q. Kittredge, 304.
67. Ewen, *Witchcraft and Demonianism*, 144–6, 152.
68. *Ibid.*, 155.
69. *Ibid.*, 166.
70. *Republished as Shakespeare Association Facsimile*, No. 1.
71. Republished in 1930, with Intro. by Montague Summers. The title page of this book spells him Scot, but he was one of the well-known Kent family of Scotts of Scott Hall.
72. *Ibid.*, 45, 74.
73. R. Trevor Davies, 25–6.
74. *Ibid.*, 27.
75. Scott, 12.
76. Cf. article on Bodin, *Biographie Universelle*.
77. R. Trevor Davies, 26.
78. The case of Mildred Norrington of Westwell in Kent, Scott, 72 foll.
79. *Ibid.*, 274.
80. Perkins, *ed. cit.*, 174, 194.
81. *Ibid.*, 123.
82. Samuel Harsnet, *A Discovery of the Fraudulent Practices of John Darrel* (1599). Preface.
83. *Ibid.*, 126.
84. *Ibid.*, 17.
85. *Ibid.*, 8.
86. *Ibid.*, 206.
87. *Ibid.*, 219.
88. For Father John Cornelius, *v.* my *Tudor Cornwall*, 356–9, 364–7. Harsnet adds a further dimension to his saintliness.
89. Harsnet, 120.
90. *Ibid.*, 207, 250.
91. *Ibid.*, 195.
92. *Ibid.*, 189, 202, 203.
93. *Ibid.*, 246 foll.

INDEX

Abbot, William, serjeant of Henry VIII's cellar, 73
Abbots Bromley, Staffordshire, 218
Abortion, 154
Accession Day celebrations, 33, 90; — — Tilts, 33, 37–40
Albert, Cardinal Archduke, 40, 43
Alchemy, 228, 236, 246–7
Aldus, publisher, 10–11
Allen, Thomas, astrologer, 246; —, William, Cardinal, 88
Almanacs, 245
Almshouses, 81, 83–4, 85, 86, 102–3
Amalfi, duke and duchess of, 25
Amazons, the, 239
America, 205, 228
Anjou, François, duke of, 135, 146, 230
Appowell family, bell-founders, 215
Archdell, Sara, 150–1
Archery, 194
Ariosto, 5, 35, 37, 133
Aristotle, 237
Armada, the Spanish, 65–6, 251
Arundel, Charles, Catholic exile, 160
Arundell family, of Lanherne and War-dour, 73, 74; —, Robert, gentleman archer, 175
Ascension Day celebrations, 206, 216
Ascham, Roger, 191–2, 194
Ashbourne, 178, 192
Ashford, 169
Astrology, 228–52
Audley End, 95
Aylesbury, 38
Ayot St. Peter, 204

Babington conspirators, the, 267, 268, 271
Bacon family, 76, 109, 116–17; —, Francis, 42, 69, 76, 82, 161–2, 241–2; —, Sir Nicholas, 26, 116
Bacton, Herefordshire, 41
Ballard, John, priest, 268
Bancroft, Richard, archbishop, 263, 264
Bandello, Matteo, novelist, 5
Barnfield, Richard, poet, 163–4, 185
Barnstaple, 64, 70, 214
Basing House, Hants, 92
Basingstoke, 83
Bastardy, 106, 114, 156–8
Bate, John, farthingale maker, 47
Bath, 85; — abbey, 111; —, William Bourchier, earl of, 70
Bathory, Stephen, king of Poland, 249
Bear-baiting, 188–9
Beaumont, Francis, of Bedworth, 54
Beer, 127–8

Bell-founding, 214; — -ringing, 213–14
Bellot, Thomas, benefactor, 85
Belvoir Castle, 183
Berkshire, 252
Bess of Hardwick, countess of Shrewsbury, 44, 81, 100–5
Bettes, John, painter, 14
Bindloss family, 119
Birmingham, 123
Biron, Charles de, Marshal, 190
Bisham abbey, 23, 26–7
Blague, Thomas, dean, 145, 147–9; Alice, wife of, 147–50
Bland, Adam, Queen Elizabeth's skinner, 47
Blandford races, 184
Boccaccio, Giovanni, 5
Bodin, Jean, 248, 260–2
Bondmen, 122
Bonner, Edmund, bishop, 9–10, 202
Bovey Tracy, 171
Bowes, Sir Martin, 82–3
Bowling, 193–4
Boxley, Holy Rood of, 168
Brackley races, 184
Bradford, John, Protestant martyr, 188
Brahmins, 239
Braithwaite family, 119
Braunton, 171–2
Bridges, Elizabeth, maid of honour, 50–1
Bridgnorth, 64
Brinsley, Puritan minister, 267
Bristol, 63, 84–5, 91, 94, 215
Brittany, 175
Broadhempston, Devon, 171
Brooke, Sir Calisthenes, 146, 198
Brothels, 140–1
Bryskett, Ludovic, 27, 197
Bucer, Martin, Reformer, 23
Buckingham, 215; —shire, 38
Buckland abbey, Devon, 73
Bull-baiting, 188
Burbage, Richard, 38
Burckhardt, Jakob, 3, 4
Burnley, 174, 231
Bury St. Edmunds abbey, 76, 109
Butler, Samuel, 234
Byrd, William, 8

Caius, Dr. John, 189–91
Calvin, Jean, 217, 219, 232–3
Cambridge university, 8, 13, 83, 86, 92, 95, 244, 257, 263; — colleges, Caius, 86, 189; Christ's, 257; King's, 13; St. John's, 97; —shire, 211
Camden, William, 180, 194, 240

286

Index

Campion, Edmund, Jesuit, 264, 268, 269
Canterbury, 91, 94, 252
Cardan, Jerome, 244
Carew, Lady, 37, 48; —, Richard, 174–5, 182, 186–7, 203, 205–6, 216, 221–2; —, Sir Peter, 22
Carleton, George, bishop, 241
Carlisle, 183–4
Caron, Noel de, Dutch envoy, 39–40
Carr, Robert, earl of Somerset, 152, 162
Cartmel, 88
Castiglione, Baldassare, 6–7, 9, 11, 23, 26, 55–8
Catherine de Medici, 35, 243
Cavendish family, 100–5; —, Henry, 104; —, Sir Charles, 198; —, William, earl of Devonshire, 101–5; and see Bess of Hardwick
Cecil family, 75–6, 109; —, Sir Robert, earl of Salisbury, 41, 43, 56, 59–60, 98, 198; — — on Queen Elizabeth I, 59–60; — — and sport, 177, 181–2; —, Sir William, 1st Lord Burghley, 23, 26, 31, 32, 41–2, 45, 48, 58, 60, 66, 91, 92, 109, 234, 236, 251; — —, his buildings, 95; — —, his household, 96–8; — —, his wife, Mildred, 45, 97; —, Thomas, 2nd Lord Burghley, 59
Chagford, 172
Chamber, Dr. John, on astrology, 233–4, 236–8
Chandos, dowager Lady, 51, 52, 53
Chapman, George, 220
Charities, 79–88
Charlecote, 92
Charles I, 7, 263; — II, 204; — V, emperor, 24
Charms, 210
Charterhouse, 82
Chatham, 86
Chatsworth, 100, 102, 104
Chaucer, Geoffrey, 7, 16, 238
Cheese, a swordsman, 196
Cheke, Sir John, 26, 29, 234
Chelmsford, 258
Chelsea, 13, 102, 103
Chenell, Dr., physician, 133
Cheshire, 51, 66, 67, 170, 208, 216; —, races in, 184
Chester diocese, 211–12; — plays, 207
Christmas, 96, 104; — celebrations, 201–3, 270
Church, the Elizabethan, 167–71, 200–1, 204, 210–15; and see Bancroft, Reformation, Whitgift
Churchyard, Thomas, 94, 96
Cinque Ports, 42

Cinthio, Giovanni B. G., novelist, 5
Civil War, the, 77, 80, 81, 88, 92, 133, 174, 202
Clarendon park, 94
Class, social, 30, 71–89, 106–10, 119–22, 124
Clitheroe, Margaret, 270
Cobham, 86; —, William, 7th Lord, 86
Cockaine, Sir Thomas, 178
Cockfighting, 187–8
Coke, Sir Edward, Lord Chief Justice, 263
Colchester, 220
Colet, John, dean of St. Paul's, 10
Collyweston, 181
Cooke, Sir Anthony, 26, 108
Cooper, Thomas, bishop, 134
Copernicus, Nicholas, 236, 240
Corn supply, 66
Cornelius, John, Jesuit, 268, 271
Cornwall, 63, 66, 69–70, 72, 112, 114, 115, 117, 174–5, 186, 203, 205–6, 207, 208–9, 210, 216, 221–2; —, duchy of, 66, 122
Cornwallis, Lady, 44; —, Sir Thomas, 116, 120; —, Sir William, 96
Corte, Claudio, riding-master, 183
Cotswolds, the, 185, 193, 217
Coughton, Warwicks, 81
Coursing, the hare, 184–5
Court, the, 7, 11, 12, 30–60, 65, 90–4, 95, 243
Courtenay, Edward, earl of Devon, 14, 22, 29
Coventry plays, the, 94–5, 206
Cox, Richard, bishop, 31
Cracow, 248, 249
Cranfield, Lionel, earl of Middlesex, 76
Cranmer, Thomas, archbishop, 9, 153
Cratfield, Suffolk, 174, 215
Craven, Sir William, 83
Cromwell, Thomas, 9–10, 14; —, Lady, bewitched, 257–8
Croydon, 81, 93, 95
Cumberland, 119, 183–4, 187–8, 219–20; —, George Clifford, 3rd earl of, 39, 78, 113; —, his wife, Margaret, 113

Dancing, Court, 12, 49–50, 218; Folk-, 206, 207, 217–19
Danvers, Sir Henry, 162
Darcy, Brian, persecuting J.P., 256–7, 258
Darrel, John, Puritan exorcist, 264–7
Darrell, William ('Wild'), 132
Davies, John, poet, 189; —, Sir John, poet, 35–6, 219

Day, John, playwright, 195
Dee, Arthur, 251; —, Dr. John, 229, 230, 242, 245–62
Dekker, Thomas, 189
Delamere forest, Cheshire, 216
De l'Orme, Philibert, architect, 17
Denbigh, 77–8
Denham, exorcism at, 267–72
Denmark, 107
Dennis family, 72
Denny, Lady, 49
De Reaulx, M., French envoy, 43
Derby, 64, 102–3, 187; —, Edward, 3rd earl of, 130; —, Henry, 4th earl of, 66, 67, 71, 107, 130; *and see* Strange
Devon, 63, 64, 72–3, 76, 117, 158, 170, 171–3, 253; *and see* Courtenay
Digges, Thomas, scientist, 236
Dissolution of chantries, 213; — of monasteries, 61–2, 64, 67–8, 72–3, 80, 84, 88, 159
Divorce, 153–6
Dogs, English, 11, 181–91; Icelandic —, 191
Doncaster races, 184
Dorset, 152, 181, 186; —, Richard Sackville, 3rd earl of, 188; *and see* Sackville
Dove, Dr. John, theologian, 149
Dover, 65, 93, 94; —, Robert, 193
Drake family, of Ashe, 73; —, Sir Francis, 69, 73, 139
Drayton, Michael, 180, 181, 185, 193, 223
Dudley family, 144; —, Dud, 106; —, Richard, 183; —, Sir Robert, 44, 106, 144; *and see* Leicester
Duelling, 56, 197–9
Durham, county, 66, 87, 173
Dutch, the, 40, 43
Dwarfs, Queen Elizabeth's, 48
Dyer, Sir Edward, 38, 154, 155, 250–1

East Anglia, 62, 77, 85–6, 95–6, 115, 116–17, 185
Easter celebrations, 205–6
Edinburgh, 242–3
Edmonds, Captain Piers, 162
Edward VI, 15–16, 17, 21–2, 244
Egerton, Thomas, 1st Lord Ellesmere, 236–7; —, Lady, countess of Bridgewater, 54
Egloshayle, 175
Eliot family, 72
Elizabeth I, 66, 107, 149, 168, 182, 199, 220, 226, 229, 238, 271–2; — and her Court, 31–50, 103, 111, 133, 135–6, 189, 230, 235, 248; — and her dresses, 46–8, 104; — and her dwarfs, 48–9; —, excommunication and deposition of, 263, 271–2; — and household provision, 126, 130–2; — and hunting, 176–7; — and marriage, 31–2, 45, 142–4; — as Princess, 14, 22–3, 31, 111; — and progresses, 65, 90–6; — at work, 41–4
Elmstone, Kent, 167–8
Elvetham, 96
Engineering, military, 12
English architecture, 13; — art, 7, 8, 14; — language, 7, 14, 20–1
Epping forest, 176
Erasmus, 4, 7, 14, 15
Escorial, the, 95
Essex, 62–3, 66, 73, 118, 149, 252, 254; —, witchcraft in, 256–7, 258–9; —, Robert Devereux, 2nd earl of, 32, 36, 39–40, 41, 44, 50, 57, 109, 114, 162
Eton, 92, 237
Exeter, 63, 64, 67, 70, 76, 120–1, 123, 137; —, Henry Courtenay, marquis of, 67
Exorcism, Catholic, 264, 267–72; —, Puritan, 264–7

Fairfax, Edward, translator, 106, 129; —, Sir William, 128–9
Fairies, 222–3
Family pride, 74, 75–6, 108–10
Faversham, 170–1
Fencing, 195–7
Fens, the, 62, 185
Ferdinand I, emperor, 48
Ferrara, 19
Field, Richard, printer, 136
Fish, Walter, Queen Elizabeth's tailor, 46
Fishdays, 126–7, 129; fishing, 186–7
Fisher, Thomas, 93
Fitton, Mary, 49–54, 59, 183; —, Sir Edward, 51, 52, 53
Fitz, John, 198
Fletcher, Richard, bishop, 31
Florence, 18, 25, 29
Florio, John, 196–7, 198
Flud, Edward, 146; —, amorous wife of, 146–7
Flushing, 42–3
Fontainebleau, 11
Football, 192–3
Ford, John, dramatist, 172
Forests, 176, 216
Forman, Simon, astrologer, 46, 144–52, 179, 241, 242
Fortification, 12
Framlingham, 13

Index

France, 4–5, 6–7, 11, 17, 22, 92, 190, 197, 199, 261
Francis I, as duc d'Angoulême, 7
Fulke, William, 233
Funerals, 75, 213–14
Furness abbey, 88
Furse, John, 121; —, Robert, 121

Galen, 10–11
Gardiner, Robert, spiritualist, 247
Garnet, Henry, Jesuit provincial, 270
Garter, Order of the, celebrations, 11, 39, 91
Gascoigne, George, 38, 95, 178
Gates, Sir Thomas, 146
Gawsworth, Cheshire, 51
Gentleman, idea of the, 110
Gentry, the, 30, 67, 68–70, 71–6, 88, 115–17
Gerard, John, Jesuit, 271; —, Sir Thomas, 211
Germany, 40, 229, 257, 260
Ghosts, 223–4
Gifford, George, Puritan minister, on witches, 252, 258–9
Gilbert, Dr. William, 240; —, Sir Humphrey, 160–1
Gilling castle, 128–30
Glastonbury, 80, 240, 246
Gloucester, 64; —shire, 206, 215
Goderick, Francis Bacon's catamite, 162
Goit, John, champion wrestler, 176
Goldsmiths, 105
Googe, Barnaby, 203
Gorhambury, 116
Great Brington, Northants., 173
Greek language, the, 10, 26
Greenwich, 86, 91, 230, 248
Gresham family, 83–4, 86; — College, 83; Gresham's School, 83
Grey, Arthur, 14th Lord, 36; —, Thomas, 15th Lord, 198–9
Grimsby, 113–14
Guildford, 81

Hakluyt, Richard, 239
Halesworth, Suffolk, 173–4
Hampden, William, 268
Hampshire, 68, 117
Hampton Court, 9, 11, 13, 41, 91
Hardwick Hall, Derbyshire, 100–5
Hardy, Thomas, 200
Harington, Sir John, the elder, 111–12; — —, the younger, wit and poet, 50, 111, 133–6
Hariot, Thomas, 228, 242–3

Harrington, William, priest, Catholic martyr, 270–1
Harrison, William, 65, 119, 120, 121–2, 124–6, 128
Harsnet, Samuel, 261, 264–72
Hartland abbey, Devon, 73
Harvey, Anthony, 73; —, Gabriel, 95, 244; —, Richard, 243–5
Hatton, Sir Christopher, 32, 36, 66, 105
Hawking, 176, 179–82
Hawkins, Sir John, 86
Helston Furry Dance, 207
Henri III, 31; — IV, 31, 40
Henry VII, 7, 10, 11, 49; — VIII, 7, 9, 11, 12, 13, 14, 15, 20, 32, 67–8, 94, 140, 158, 182, 187, 194, 195
Herbert family, 19, 68, 73, 94; —, Sir William, 109–10; and see Pembroke
Hereford, see of, 146; —shire, 41
Herne, Henry, hosier, 47
Hertford, 66, 92; —, Edward Seymour, 2nd earl of, 74, 96, 152; —shire, 66, 92
Heydon, Sir Christopher, on astrology, 239–40
Hicks, Michael, Cecil's secretary, 42, 70
Hilliard, Nicholas, 39, 57
Historiography, 4
Hoby, Sir Philip, 26; —, Sir Thomas, 23–7, 55
Holbein, Hans, 32–3
Holdenby, Northants, 91, 95
Holland, 263
Holles family, 112–14; —, Sir John, 108–9
Homosexuality, 117, 158–65
Hooker, John, 121
Hopkins, Matthew, witch-persecutor, 254, 256
Horner, Little Jack, 221
Horse-racing, 182–4; —riding, 56
Houghton-le-Spring, Durham, 173
Housing, 114–21
Howard family, 234; —, Charles, Lord Admiral, 36, 39; Frances, duchess of Lennox, 151, 152; —, Lady Catherine, 50; —, Lady Mary, 50; —, Lord Henry, earl of Northampton, 81, 86, 160, 234–6; —, Thomas, 2nd Lord, of Bindon, 153
Humanism, 3–4
Humours, theory of, 127
Humphreys, Dr. Laurence, 92
Hunks, Harry, famous bear, 189
Hunsdon, Henry Carey, 1st Lord, 37, 39, 41, 58–9, 66
Hunting, 56, 176–7, 178–9

Huntingdon, Henry Hastings, 3rd earl of, 55, 66, 67, 71, 99–100; —, wife of, 43; —shire, 66, 214, 257–8
Hurling, 174–5

Ilsington, 172
Ingleby Arncliffe, 173
Inns, 132, 151, 230
Ireland, 54, 78, 147, 148, 161, 162, 181, 182, 199, 208
Italy, 3–8, 9–12, 16–17, 18–20, 23–9, 124, 160, 195, 229; Italian architecture, 4, 12–13, 16–17; — language, 14, 20, 27, 29; Italians in England, 8, 11–12, 48–9, 94, 182–3, 196–7, 235

James I, 57, 82, 107, 162, 165, 176, 182, 188, 191, 226, 242–3, 254–5
Jeronimo, fencing-master, 196
Jesuits, 268, 271–2
Jewel, John, bishop, 214, 254
Johnson, Dr. Samuel, 204; —, President L. B., 136
Johnston, Garrett, Queen Elizabeth's shoemaker, 47
Jones, Inigo, 13
Jonson, Ben, 55, 180; his *Bartholomew Fair*, 219
Julius II, 9
Justices of the Peace, 53, 68, 71, 156–7, 159, 171

Kelly, Edward, medium, 230, 242, 245–52
Kemp, Will, actor, 217–18
Kenall, Dr. John, 242
Kenilworth, 38, 92–3, 94–5, 220
Kent, 63, 64, 66, 86–7, 93; —, condition of churches in, 167–71; —, sexual activities in, 146–7
Killigrew, Dorothy, 145; —, Sir Henry, 24, 26, 145
Knole, 93
Knollys, Sir William, Comptroller of the Household, 51–3

Lambarde, William, 86, 93–4, 168
Lambe, William, benefactor, 86
Lambeth, 144, 145, 151, 241
Lancashire, 62, 66, 67, 71, 80, 86, 87–8, 115, 118, 122, 208, 211–12, 246, 254, 265, 267
Lancaster, Sir James, benefactor, 83
Languet, Hubert, Huguenot scholar, 27, 28
Lanhydrock, Cornwall, 72
Lant, Thomas, herald and painter, 39
Laski, Count Albert, 248
Latin language, the, 11, 20–1

Laud, William, archbishop, 263
Launceston, 169, 175
Lawyers, 72–3
Laycock abbey, 16
Lee, Robert, 38; —, Sir Henry, 38–9, 122, 181
Legh, Sir Piers, 107, 191
Leicester, 64, 67, 71, 76–7, 103, 139, 211, 215; —, Robert Dudley, earl of, 27, 32, 36, 44, 57, 66, 78, 92, 94, 131, 133, 135, 142–4, 155, 183, 191, 246, 248; —, Lettice Knollys, wife of, 32, 45, 144; —, Amy Robsart, wife of, 143, 144; —shire, 62, 66, 67, 122
Leyden, 263
Linacre, Thomas, 10–11
Lincoln, 64; —, Henry Clinton, 2nd earl of, 66, 177, 267; —shire, 64, 66, 104, 115, 177
Littlecote, Wilts., 132
Lois Weedon, Northants., 170
London, 22–3, 61, 63, 64–5, 70–1, 76–8, 120, 127, 135, 138, 139, 140, 165, 187, 188, 195, 217, 241; Blackfriars, 136, 196; — charities, 79–88; Inns of Court, 116, 219; — prisons: Clink, 267; Fleet, 53; Marshalsea, 270–1; —, Tower of, 22, 39
Long family, Wilts., 74
Longleat, 16
Lords Lieutenants, 65–6
Loseley Place, Surrey, 16
Lostwithiel, 205–6
Lyly, John, 95
Lyme, Cheshire, 170, 191

Macclesfield, 75
Machiavelli, Niccolo, 6, 10, 14, 20, 24
Machyn, Henry, 75
Madrigals, 6
Magic, 225, 227–8
Maiano, Giovanni da, painter, 11
Maids of honour, Queen Elizabeth's, 32, 41, 47, 48, 49–55
Maidstone, 64, 86
Mainy, Richard, hysterical subject, 268–70
Malmesbury, 69
Malte, John, Henry VIII's tailor, 111
Manchester, 64, 230
Manners, George, 104; *and see* Rutland
Mantua, 25
Marlowe, Christopher, 90, 160, 162–3, 241, 244
Marriage, 123; — ceremonies, 49; child-—, 210–12; clerical —, 143, 169
Marston, John, 164–5

Mary I, 16, 17, 22–3, 26, 204; — as Princess, 14; *and see* Scots

Martyrs, Catholic, 267–72; —, Protestant, 9, 22, 153, 188

Maundy ceremony, 91

Maximilian II, emperor, 249

Maying, 90, 206–7

Meakins, Richard, town whipper at Stratford, 138

Medici, Lorenzo dei, 6

Medley, William, 161

Melancthon, Philip, 232–3

Melton, John, on astrologers, 241

Merchants, 70, 72–3, 75, 76–8, 79–88, 105, 125–6

Mere, Wilts., custom of Cuckoo King at, 207

Messina, 25

Mevagissey, 208

Mexico, 161, 228

Michelangelo, 4, 6, 10, 12, 25

Middle Ages, the, 4–5, 7, 8–9, 75, 87, 140, 209

Middlesex, 71

Midlands, 63, 119, 185; *and see* separate counties

Midsummer celebrations, 207–8

Milan, 18, 19

Mildmay, Sir Walter, 20

Milton, Richard (John Milton's grandfather), 179

Minchinhampton, 207

Mining, 63, 80, 101, 221

Miracles, 264

Monarcho, Queen Elizabeth's Italian jester, 49

Montaigne, Michel de, 198

Montherlant, Henri de, 264

Monmouthshire, 118

Mor, Antony, painter, 38

More, George, Puritan minister, 267; —, Sir Thomas, 13, 73, 229

Morgan, Sir Matthew, soldier, 43

Morley, Henry Parker, 8th Lord, translator, 14

Mother Margaret, sweeper at Stratford, 138

Much Wenlock, 210–11

Muffet, Dr. Thomas, 221

Music, 6, 218

Myddelton family, the, 77–8; —, Sir Hugh, 78, 140; —, William, 78

Nantwich, 216

Naples, 18, 25

Nashe, Thomas, 95

Netherlands, the, 11, 15, 63, 146, 147, 199

New Romney, Kent, 169

Newcombe family, bell-founders, 215

Newdigate, Anne, Lady, 52, 54

Newton, Sir Isaac, 236

Nicholas da Modena, painter, 11

Nonsuch palace, 15–16, 91

Norfolk, 86, 95–6, 215; —, Thomas Howard, 4th duke of, 82, 97, 107, 184

Northamptonshire, 62, 63, 92, 115, 169–170, 181, 185, 186, 254, 257; *and for* Northampton, *see* Howard, Parr

Northumberland, John Dudley, duke of, 16–17; —, Henry Percy, the 'Wizard Earl' of, 98–9, 153

Norwich, 63, 85, 95–6, 116, 217

Nostradamus, 243

Nottingham, 64, 66, 105, 186, 189; — races, 184; —shire, 111, 112, 185

Nova of 1572, the, 235, 236, 237

Orange, Philip William, prince of, 40

Ormonde, Thomas Butler, 10th earl of, 36

Osney abbey, 214

Owen George, physician to Henry VIII, 84; —, Hugh, traitor, 78

Oxford, 117, 133, 138–9, 216–17, 270; —, Edward de Vere, 17th earl of, 36, 45, 76, 93, 97, 99, 100, 160, 163; —shire, 181; — university, 8, 83, 92, 206–7, 214, 237, 246; — colleges: All Souls, 129, 187, 206; Balliol, 179; Christ Church, 13, 214; Corpus Christi, 167; Magdalen, 179; St. Mary Hall, 179; Old Ashmolean museum, the, 249

Packington, Sir John ('Lusty'), 56

Padstow, 72, 175, 207

Padua, 9, 24, 26, 29

Paris, 169, 193; — Garden, 188

Parker, Bess, Forman's maidservant, 151; —, Matthew, archbishop, 93–4, 143, 154–5

Parliament, 68–70, 140, 156, 158–9, 254–5

Parr, Catherine, queen, 14; —, William, marquis of Northampton, 22, 26

Parry, Blanche, Queen Elizabeth's maid of honour, 32, 41, 47

Paul III, 18–19, 25

Paulerspury, Northants., 201

Peacham, Henry, 106, 110

Peckham, Edmund, 267–8; —, Sir George, 267

Peele, George, 35

Peerage, 30, 106–9

Pembroke, Henry Herbert, 2nd earl of, 66, 68; — —, Mary Sidney, wife of, 37, 48; —, William, 1st earl, 68; —, William, 3rd earl, 52–3, 59, 209; *and see* Herbert

Perez, Antonio, 161

Perkins, William, on astrology and witch-craft, 233, 234, 257, 263–4, 272

Petrarch, 5, 9, 14, 15

Petre, Sir William, 73, 92

Philip II, 95, 271

Physicians, Royal College of, 10

Pickering, Henry, Cambridge don, 257, 263, 264

Pignatelli, riding-master, 182–3

Pius V, 207

Plague, the, 76

Plat, Sir Hugh, inventor, 127

Plays, 94–5, 151, 174, 206; *and see* Dekker, Jonson, Marlowe, Shakespeare

Plymouth, 70, 77, 86, 122, 123, 139, 140

Poitiers, 194, 261

Pole, Reginald, Cardinal, 9,23,29,67,234

Polwhele, Captain William, 54

Polydore Vergil, 4, 7–8

Poor-relief, 79, 80, 81, 83, 84–7

Popham, Sir John, 85

Population 63–4, 85, 86, 118, 122–3

Porter, Henry, playwright, 195

Portman, Mary (Lady Stawell), 153–5

Portrait-painting, 5, 6

Poussin, Nicolas, quoted, 5

Prague, 284–50, 251–2

Prayers for the dead, 80

Preston, 67; —, George, 88

Prideaux family of Padstow, 72

Prognostications, 234–6, 242–5

Progresses, royal, 65, 90–6

Prostitutes, 140–1

Ptolemy, astronomer, 237, 240

Purdue family, bell-founders, 215

Purging, 133, 148

Puritans, 67, 88, 133, 174, 192, 201, 203, 217, 233, 264

Rabelais, François, 134

Ralegh, Sir Walter, 32, 34, 36, 41, 49, 58, 66, 69, 76, 181, 237, 263; — —, Elizabeth Throckmorton, wife of, 49, 52

Ramsay, Lady, benefactress, 84

Raphael, 11

Ratcliffe, 132, 145; —, Margaret, maid of honour, 54–5; —, Sir Alexander, 54–5

Reading, 64

Recusants, Catholic, 44, 67, 71, 271

Redgrave, Suffolk, 116, 117

Reformation, the, 8, 16, 65, 68, 72–5, 78, 80–1, 84, 87, 119, 153, 158–9, 166, 167, 169, 201, 209, 212–13, 215–216

Renaissance, idea of the, 3–8, 10

Reynolds, Dr. John, 206–7

Rich, Richard, 1st Lord, 73

Richard III, 232, 234

Richmond palace, 55, 91, 235

Ridley, Nicholas, bishop, Protestant martyr, 22

Ripon, 83

Roberts, Richard, 72

Robsart, Amy, Leicester's first wife, 143, 144

Rochester, 147, 148, 149

Rocco, fencing-master, 196

Rolle family, 72

Rome, 4, 5, 9, 18–19, 25, 26, 27, 28, 29, 271

Ronsard, Pierre, 35

Roscarrock, Cornwall, 117

Rowe, Sir Thomas, benefactor, 83

Rudolph II, emperor, 230, 248–52

Russell, Anne, 49; —, dowager Lady, 107–8, 134, 136, 196; —, Elizabeth, 50, 183; —, John, 1st Lord, 65, 67

Russia, 251

Rutland, Edward Manners, 3rd earl of, 128–9; —, Roger —, 5th earl, 177; —shire, 66, 74

Sackville, Thomas, 1st earl of Dorset, 29, 36, 93; *and see* Dorset

Saffron Walden, 13

St. Albans abbey, 116

St. Anthony in Roseland, 72

St. Aubyn family, 72

St. Austell, 203, 207–8

St. Bartholomew, Massacre of, 27

St. Cadix, Cornwall, 72

St. Dunstan, as Magus, 246

St. Germans, 72

St. Ives, Cornwall, 203

St. Loe, Sir William, 100

St. Michael's Mount, 72

St. Osyth, Essex, 258

St. Paul's cathedral, 16; — school, 10

St. Philleigh, Cornwall, 175

Salisbury, 63, 68, 74, 94; —, see of, 147, 148

Samuel, Mother, reputed witch, 257–8

Sandys, Edwin, archbishop, 88

Satterleigh, Devon, 170

Saul, Barnabas, medium, 247

Savage, Sir John, 75; —, Thomas, archbishop, 74

Savile, George, 71; —, Sir Henry, 29

Index

Saviolo, Vincentio, fencing-master, 196–7

Scavengers, 138–9

Schools, 90, 202, 204; —, founding of, 67, 81, 82, 83, 84, 86, 178

Scory, Sylvanus, sex-life of, 145–6

Scotland, 8, 217, 254

Scots, Mary, Queen of, 45, 48, 229

Scott, Reginald, on witchcraft, 259–63

Selwyn, John, park-keeper at Oatland, 177

Severn, river, 186

Sex, 124, 140–1, 142–65, 255

Sextus Empiricus, 238

Shakespeare, Edmund, actor, 213; —, John, 137; —, William, 4, 5, 42, 49, 58, 61, 65, 74, 90, 121, 128, 136, 138, 140–1, 162, 193, 202, 213, 215, 221, 230, 262–3; — and sport, 38, 178–9, 183, 186, 194, 198; — on the stars, 231–2

   Plays: *All's Well*, 198; *As You Like It*, 136–7; *Hamlet*, 223; *1 Henry IV*, 151; *2 Henry VI*, 217; *Julius Caesar*, 223; *King Lear*, 231, 232, 269; *Love's Labours Lost*, 49, 232; *Macbeth*, 243; *Merry Wives*, 91, 185, 220; *Midsummer Night's Dream*, 218, 221, 222, 245; *Pericles*, 141; *Romeo and Juliet*, 198, 221–2; *Troilus and Cressida*, 140–1, 162; *Twelfth Night*, 218

   Poems: *Sonnets*, 164, 165; *Venus and Adonis*, 185

Sheffield, Lady Douglas, 44, 144

Sheldwich, Kent, 170

Shenton, William, Queen Elizabeth's jester, 49

Shooting, 175

Shoreditch, 146

Shotover, Oxfordshire, 179

Shrewsbury, George Talbot, 6th earl of, 66, 100–4; *and see* Bess of Hardwick, Talbot

Shropshire, 64, 86

Shute, John, architect, 16–17

Sidney, Sir Philip, 5, 27–8, 37, 39, 75, 183, 248; his *Arcadia*, 5, 39; —, Sir Robert, 42–3

Siena, 25

Silver, George, 197

Sixtus V, 250

Slanning, Nicholas, 198

Smythe, Alice, benefactress, 84

Sodomy, 19, 158–60, 162

Somers, impostor, 265–7

Somerset, 63, 64, 84, 85, 111, 253; —, Edward Seymour, duke of, 16, 159

Southampton, 68; —, Henry Wriothesley, 3rd earl of, 97, 152, 153, 162, 165, 198–9

Southwark, 138

Southworth, John, 211

Spain, 40, 91, 94

Spenser, Edmund, 6, 33–5, 36–7

Staffordshire, 66, 91, 156–8, 218

Stamford, 64, 71, 137, 138

Standen, Sir Anthony, Catholic informer, 29

Stanhope family, 108, 198; —, Sir John, 41, 43, 70

Stawell, Sir John, matrimonial difficulties of, 153–6

Stone, Nicholas, 82

Stow, John, 83, 193–4, 196

Strange, Ferdinando, Lord, 5th earl of Derby, 255–6

Strasbourg, 23, 24

Stratford-upon-Avon, 64, 71, 136, 137, 138, 215, 223–4

Stretes, Guillim, painter, 15

Stuart, Lady Arabella, 100, 103, 104

Stubbes, Philip, 192, 193, 217, 233

Sturm, Johann, educationist, 23, 27

Suffolk, 95, 116–17, 118, 122, 173, 174, 181, 215

Surrey, 15–16; —, Henry Howard, earl of, 14–15

Sutton Place, Guildford, 13

Symonds, J. A., 8, 29

Talbot family, 100–5; —, Gilbert, 7th earl of Shrewsbury, 44, 45–6, 177, 181–2; *and see* Shrewsbury

Tamworth, John, 20

Tartaglia, Niccolo, military engineer, 12

Tasso, Torquato, 5, 28, 106

Taunton, 64, 65

Taxation, 101

Tennis, royal, 191, 193

Thames, river, 65, 139, 186, 188

Theatres, 150, 151, 241

Theobalds, Lord Burghley's palace, 42, 91, 92, 96, 177

Thomas, William, 17–23, 24, 26, 29

Thornborough, John, bishop, 179

Thorne family, benefactors, 84

Throckmorton, Sir Arthur, 24, 49, 133, 181, 184, 201, 215, 248; —, Sir Nicholas, 29; *and see* Ralegh; —, family of Warboys, witchcraft in, 257–8

Throwley, Kent, 146, 168

Thynne, Sir John, 16

Tichborne, Chideock, Babington conspirator, 268

Tilbury, 220
Titchfield abbey, 68, 73, 92
Tiverton, 123
Tonbridge, 63; — school, 83
Topsel, Henry, bell-founder, 215
Torporley, Nathaniel, mathematician, 242–3
Torringiano, Pietro, 10
Toto, Anthony, painter, 11
Translations, 10–11, 14, 24, 26, 28–9, 55–6, 106, 183, 197
Trebona, 250
Tregonissey, Cornwall, 173
Trent, river, 186
Tresham, Sir Thomas, 95
Trevissick, Cornwall, 117
Trissino, Giangiorgio, poet and critic, 5
Truro, 70
Turberville, George, 178
Tusser, Thomas, 201, 230
Tycho Brahe, 240, 248
Tyneside, 63
Tyrone, Hugh O'Neill, earl of, 40
Tyrrell, Anthony, Jesuit, 268, 271

Underhill family, 215
Urbino, 10, 11, 31

Vasari, Giorgio, painter, 5
Vaux, William, 3rd Lord, 267, 270
Velazquez, Diego, 191
Venice, 8, 9, 10, 18, 19, 22, 24, 25, 27–8
Veronese, Paolo, 28
Virgil, 34
Virginia, 146, 228
Vitruvius, 4, 17, 19
Vittorino da Feltre, 10
Volpe, Vincent, painter, 11, 12

Wadebridge, 210
Wadham, Nicholas, benefactor, 85
Wakefield, 71–2
Wales, 66, 71, 86, 87, 115, 148; North —, 77–8, 213; South —, 24, 63; Welsh Border, 18, 19, 86
Walpole, Henry, Jesuit, 264
Walsingham, Sir Francis, 37; —, Sir Thomas, 146
Warboys, witchcraft affair at, 257–8
Warwick, 92–3; —, Ambrose Dudley, earl of, 92, 144, 178; —, wife of, 32, 43, 93, 108, 143; —shire, 62, 81, 215
Washington, Robert, 173; —, President George, 173
Water-closets, 153–5
Watling Street, 65, 103

Watts family, bell-founders, 215
Wells, 85, 154–5
Wells, cult of, 215–16
Westminster abbey, 10, 152; —, St. Margaret's, 55
Westmorland, 118, 119
Weston, William, Jesuit provincial, 268
White, Thomas, benefactor, 85
Whitehall palace, 13, 37–8, 91, 187
Whitgift, John, archbishop, 32, 148, 149, 209, 263
Whithorne, Peter, 24, 25
Whyte, Roland, 42–3, 149
Wickhambreux, Kent, 169
Williams, Frances, 270–1; —, Sara, 269–71; —, Sir Roger, 43
Willoughby, Peregrine Bertie Lord, 177
Wills, 75, 81, 82–4, 86, 170
Wilmcote, Warwicks., 121
Wilson, Thomas, 28–9
Wilton, 68, 73, 94
Wiltshire, 66, 68–9, 73, 74
Winchester, 70, 220; —, dowager marchioness of, 44; —, see of, 68
Windebank, Thomas, 59–60
Windsor, 91, 92; —, Edward, Lord, 27–8
Wisbech, priests confined at, 268
Witchcraft, 225–6, 252–64
Wollaton Hall, Nottingham, 105
Wolsey, Thomas, Cardinal, 9, 10, 11, 58
Wolverhampton, 54
Wood, Richard, 'Dean', 148–50
Woodland, Devon, 171, 172–3
Woodstock, 95
Worcester, 64, 242; Silvestro Gigli, bishop of, 11; —, see of, 88; —shire, 91, 186
Wotton, Sir Henry, 146, 147; —, Thomas, 2nd Lord, 184
Wrestling, 175–6, 206
Wriothesley, Thomas, 1st earl of Southampton, 68; *and see* Southampton
Wroth, Sir Thomas, 26
Wyatt, Sir Thomas, the elder, poet, 14–15, 38; — —, the younger, 22, 23
Wye, Kent, 168

Yanwath, Cumb., 183
Yeomen, 85, 88, 121–2
York, 63, 80, 91, 158; —shire, 66, 71–2, 73, 80–1, 83, 118, 128–30, 210

Zouche, Edward, Lord, 107